In Common

The architects of our lives are divided. There are those who insist that there is still no alternative to neoliberalism. Despite the many crises it has provoked, they continue to push for competition in every sphere of life, to widen the wealth gap, to ignore climate change and to pursue the steady dispossession of our rights and commonwealth.

Then there are those advocating change, those who seek to persuade us that capitalism can be saved from itself. They conceal capitalism behind a human face. They tell us that environmental disaster can be averted through technological solutions. They say that deeply rooted social injustices can be cured with a little more economic growth. That we'll be safer with more police on our streets.

And yet, we know that capitalism is dying, that its lies have been unmasked, that its grip on our world and our lives is maintained only through expropriations, dependency and commodified desires. In Common is a collection of works that see an end to capitalism without apocalypse. It provides us with techniques for building another world, and it narrates practices of alternatives and theories of hope. It is a glimpse into our shared present, for a future in common.

In Common is published by Zed Books under the creative commons license. You are free to share this material, transform and build upon it for non-commercial purposes.

Series editor: Massimo De Angelis

Titles already published:
Stavros Stavrides, *Common Space: The City as Commons*
Massimo De Angelis, *Omnia Sunt Communia: Principles for the Transition to Postcapitalism*

About the editors

Guido Ruivenkamp is an associate professor of sociology and anthropology at Wageningen University, and extraordinary professor at the University of Humanistic Studies in Utrecht. His previous books include *Reconstructing Biotechnologies: Critical Social Analyses* (co-author, 2008), and *Biotechnology in Development: Experiences from the South* (2008).

Andy Hilton is an EFL instructor and English language editor and proof-reader living and working in Istanbul. He has collaborated with various researchers on a number of articles and research pieces on Turkey and with Guido on the 2014 conference and handbook on knowledge and agricultural commons held in Maringá, Brasil.

Perspectives on Commoning

Autonomist Principles and Practices

Edited by Guido Ruivenkamp and Andy Hilton
in collaboration with a common pool of authors

ZED

Perspectives on Commoning: Autonomist Principles and Practices
was first published in 2017 by Zed Books Ltd, The Foundry, 17 Oval Way,
London SE11 5RR, UK.

www.zedbooks.net

Editorial copyright © Guido Ruivenkamp and Andy Hilton 2017
Copyright in this collection © Zed Books 2017

The rights of Guido Ruivenkamp and Andy Hilton to be identified
as the editors of this work has been asserted by them in accordance
with the Copyright, Designs and Patents Act, 1988

Typeset in Minion by seagulls.net
Index by Guido Ruivenkamp and Andy Hilton
Cover design by Dougal Burgess

A catalogue record for this book is available from the British Library.

ISBN 978-1-78699-179-9 hb
ISBN 978-1-78699-178-2 pb
ISBN 978-1-78699-180-5 epdf
ISBN 978-1-78699-181-2 epub
ISBN 978-1-78699-182-9 mobi

Contents

Glossary

The following is presented as a short listing with explanations of key terms employed in this volume, beyond those generally employed in the commons discourse ('access', 'excludable', etc.). These are, of course, subject to revision and reformulation, as well as variations in interpretation. Listed terms used in the explanations are given in italics.

Autonomism A school of post-Marxian thought that emphasises the role of working-class struggle in shaping capitalist development focusing on the emerging, implicit possibilities of subversion, including everyday resistance to the present form of capitalism (so currently, *cognitive capitalism*) and the creation of new forms of working, living and being in common. As a class-struggle Marxism, it thus stresses workers' autonomy (cf. *workerism*) as the guiding principle of Marxist politics (and distances itself from crisis Marxism, in which the working class figures only as victim).

Biopolitical production Derived from Foucault's notion of biopower as the extension of state power over both the physical and political bodies of a population; extended as biopolitics to the complete control of the individual life (by society as well as government), referring quantitatively to social relations and qualitatively to consciousness, intimacy, etc.; applied to production through biopolitical labour.

Capital Drawing from Marx, the conception of social relations as organised by the circulation of commodities, itself determined by appropriation (of use value, for the satisfaction of desire), leading to the expansion of value (for further desire satisfaction, but increasingly to ensure continuing appropriation of the expanding value); thus unbound, implying the control of society, by building on the extraction of surplus value produced by labour-power (also considered as a commodity, cf. the *mass worker*), requiring establishment and enforcement of the *constituted power*; thence, with labour intrinsically antagonistic, determining the *multitude* as oppositional and impelling *biopolitical production*.

Class composition The technical composition (the ratio of constant to variable capital) of the capitalist organisation of labour in production (where materials, tools and machines for production comprise constant capital and the labour power for this is the variable capital); shaping and shaped by the various forms of class struggle in a dynamic and antagonistic political force against capital; thus, forms of (the organisation of) class struggle as they vary with changes in its composition, according (also) to the specific configurations of capital (e.g. currently, in the period of *cognitive capitalism*).

Cognitariat The (middle class) category of workers who sell their cognitive, informational, communicative and affective capacities (their knowing, creating, imagining, expressing, collaborating, etc.) to capital; a fundamental part, therefore, of *cognitive capitalism.*

Cognitive capitalism The (increasing) focus on *immaterial production*, comprising both immaterial products and material products within which immaterial elements are incorporated, particularly through informationalisation, closely related to elements of communication and affect; thus, a specification of the period of *contemporary capitalism.*

Constituent power (*potenza*) The power of the *multitude* that aims at the realisation of its potential, which is always already there as a space within capitalist structures and relations and through which these are altered.

Constituted power (*potere*) The power of the authorities that appears when formal constitutions are formulated, which comes from above and is imposed upon the *multitude.*

Contemporary capitalism The current period of capitalism; referring especially to *immaterial production* in *cognitive capitalism*, but also crucially dependent on the ability of capital to extract value from the wealth produced by the social cooperation of the commoners.

Effective truths Insights into actual concrete practices for possible societal transformations (from Machiavelli).

General intellect Marx's idea (from the 'Fragment on Machines', a passage in the *Grundrisse*) that the development of capital enabling the creation of wealth through added value increasingly comes to depend on technological expertise ('scientific labour') and organisation ('social combination').

Immanence In itself and generally, a relative opposition to transcendence or that which is beyond or outside; thus immanent theory, which takes there to be no transcendent principle or external cause to the world, meaning that the process of life production is contained in life itself; therefore, the innate life instinct and vitality of humans cannot be standardised from outside but represents an immanent perspective, shaped by the actions of the *multitude*, and as such a human potential (*constituent power*).

Immaterial labour Work that is primarily intellectual and linguistic, generating the informational content of a commodity; closely linked to affective labour, which produces or manipulates the cultural content of the commodity, creating a sense of well-being, satisfaction, excitement or passion; regarded as increasingly hegemonic (in 'advanced' economies).

Immaterial production The generation of (abstract, non-concrete) goods (ideas, images, knowledges, codes, etc.) through related occupations (in the third/service sector) and of affective and social relations; tending to create not only the means of social life but social life itself.

Mass worker The human product of Taylorist production practices and Fordist regulation of industrial production and consumption, wherein workers are converted into components of the assembly line, bereft of skill and individual worth but also able to organise to withhold labour and develop radical mass-workers' movements.

Multitude A population that has not entered into a social contract with a sovereign political body, such that individuals retain the capacity for political self-determination (and thus, a *constituent power*); originally from Machiavelli (*Discorsi*) and developed by Spinoza (*Tractatus Theologico-Politicus*); described by Negri (*The Savage Anomaly*) as a positive collective social subject that founds a non-mystified form of democracy and (with Hardt) as the political composition of a collective subjectivity of mutually interacting individuals and non-human entities exercising agency and seeking opportunities for the construction of a real alternative (particularly as set against the expanding enclosures of *cognitive capitalism*).

Operaismo (see **workerism**)

Perspectivist knowledge An epistemological form, referring generally to knowledge as subjective (experiential, value-based) and politically to an approach to knowledge that aims to uncover the ways in which capital's developments are transformed through class struggle into tools for liberation from capital.

Prefigurative power Forms of actions and organisational structures in which the temporal distinction between the struggle in the present towards a goal in the future is removed and the political goals are oriented to the immediate context of everyday life; thus, practices in which the ends of one's actions are equally expressed in the means applied for their realisation, in which, also, any incongruence between a future ideal and the present reality is problematised.

Social worker The human product of post-Fordism in which capitalist production has been extended beyond the boundaries of the workplace into various realms of social life; leading, in turn, to multitudinous forms of resistance to the commodification and individualisation of life and the creation of alternative modes of working, living and being.

Workerism (*operaismo*) Originally an Italian Marxist movement and school of thought that emphasised the fundamental autonomy of workers as drivers of change (in contradistinction to the more traditional view that gave agency to *capital*); hence, the term 'autonomist Marxism', then '*autonomism*'; more specifically, the view that changes in the mode of production within capital are outcomes of workers' struggles, resulting in *capital*'s attempts to restore discipline, forcing a decomposition of the (mass) working class, which in turn gives rise to new struggles and a new *class composition.*

Preface

It was at the Post-Autonomia Conference in Amsterdam on 19–21 May 2011 that the idea was first developed to prepare a book on commons paying particular attention to concrete practices of living, producing and being in common as responses to the enclosures and policies of dispossession related to the logics and processes of capitalist expansion. This initiative was discussed with participants at the conference, including Mathijs van de Sande and Elise Thorburn, who were immediately enthusiastic and committed to making contributions. Subsequently, we organised a small workshop and invited Sonja Lavaert to present her PhD thesis on 'The perspective of multitude: Agamben, Machiavelli, Negri, Spinoza, Virno', and, after an inspiring debate, she also declared her desire to write a piece for the forthcoming collection.

Further discussions with Joost Jongerden and Pieter Lemmens at the University of Wageningen led to our contacting other authors for an emerging volume that took a generally autonomist-oriented perspective in developing insights into new forms of commoning and exchanging theoretical framings for a transition towards a commonist future. Thus, this work seeks to reflect on and develop new conceptual framings about commons as well as describe concrete practices of commoning that might take this already growing project forward at a societal level. Identifying and contacting contributors and editing the articles has taken a long time, as did our processes of shared decision-making. Now, finally, we are able to publish this book, which in itself may be considered somewhat as the result of a process of commoning, insofar as it emerged through a collaborative procedure that required a lot of patience from all the authors but which, hopefully, has finally led to a result with which we are all happy .

Guido Ruivenkamp & Andy Hilton
Wageningen & Istanbul, 2017

Introduction

Guido Ruivenkamp and Andy Hilton

The conceptual shift of the common: from commons to commoning

There has been a proliferation of work on commons-related issues in recent years, or the 'discourse of the common', as this field of social study may be dubbed. The employment of the original notion of access to land in feudal Britain for a contemporary equation of commons with natural resources shared and jointly managed by a group of people (community) has not only been extended but also deepened. Analysed in various dimensions, such as subtractability and exclusion (Ostrom & Ostrom, 1977), it has been extended through a qualitative expansion of the types of resources considered, to include, for example, information and cultural commons (Benkler, 2000). This is relatively well-known and widely discussed. But it has also been deepened with ideas about interpersonal and human–nature relations and ultimately the nature of society, which is rather less often considered. This is an important development, since it represents a fundamental conceptual shift, from 'commons as resources' to 'commons as relational social frameworks' (Bollier & Helfrich, 2015), marked also by the evolution of the noun form of 'common' into the verb 'commoning' to denote the continuous making and remaking – the (re)production – of the commons through shared practices (Bresnihan, 2016). It is this reading of commons on which we focus in the present volume.

The original contemporary focus on commons as resources was characterised by a debate around the (in)effectiveness of their collective management, stimulated by Hardin's (1968) 'Tragedy of the Commons'. Hardin's doomsday scenario of an inevitable overuse of common pool resources leading to their devastation was criticised in at least three ways: it was erroneously built on the assumption of an open access system without specific principles of excludability (Suga, 2103); it problematically presented a small-scale problem (grazing cattle on common pastureland) as a universal phenomenon applicable also at a large scale (Ostrom, 1990); and it assumed common property to be the core issue (land, in Hardin's model), rather than private property (cattle) and the individualist utility-maximising behaviour (overgrazing for personal gain) (Harvey, 2012). Thus, it (wrongly) concluded that only national or private management could prevent a devastation of resources.

In response, Elinor Ostrom and colleagues set about dismantling the powerful myth of this so-called 'tragedy' by presenting a range of empirical examples in defence of the commons. Essentially, they showed that the management of common property resources (CPRs) such as forests, fisheries and land by a user-group organisation (UGO) could be extremely efficient (Ostrom, 1986, 1990 see Ostrom, Tiebout & Warren, 1961). They also extended the idea of commons-as-resources to commons-as-services, including the local provisioning of water and policing. On the basis of a variety of case studies, they identified certain principles and conditions favourable to the production of institutions of community-based resource management and thus to be incorporated into management policies. This work was successful in challenging the reductive narratives of the 'tragedyists' – yet the community-based management models nevertheless tended to be based on the same, essentially liberal assumptions. Their models, too, referred to the need to channel individualistic behaviour (self-interested rationality) and establish another (albeit alternative) property regime. Indeed, they allowed the same, neo-classical economic paradigms of the tragedyists to return through the back door, ultimately, one might argue, reducing the perspectives and potentialities of the diverse economies (Gibson-Graham, 2006, 2008) and non-capitalist social relations, with their different practices and subjectivities.

As noted, however, a gradual conceptual shift away from this commons-as-resources model and could still be observed, even triggered by the debates among the various theoretical strands within the resources model – e.g. Heller's (1998) 'tragedy of the anticommons' and Lessig's (2001) 'intellectual property rights as commons'. Notwithstanding the differing assessment of the feasibility or otherwise of jointly holding and managing resources, the participants in this debate all departed from the notion that a remedy for the unregulated access to resources could only be realised through social arrangements. Indeed, references were made to a wide variety of social arrangements, such as institutional control of resources, substantive community systems of management, the capacities of self-organisation and self-regulation by the resource users and principles of excludability. Thus, commons-as-resources became intertwined with commons-as-social-arrangements.

This conceptual development of the doing and making of commons has involved a direct and profound engagement with the everyday activities and experiences of the commoners through which commons are composed – that is, with commoning. It indicates a quest for different modes of (re)production. And it sets out with a consideration of the ways in which capitalist enclosures have de-valorised and rendered invisible the myriad, situated relations and practices of reproduction that exist between people and the manifold resources on which they rely (Federici, 2001; De Angelis, 2007; Shiva, 2010). Thus, in the shift towards commons-as-practice, a dual operation can be discerned in the activities of commoners, as focused on resisting the logic of capital accumulation while also (or through) creating new forms of working, living and being in common. In this way, commoning becomes committed to political action and a focal juncture of social struggle.

Thus, the present volume takes the commons as a key domain through which social struggles about societal futures evolve, acknowledging that there is a continuous backward and forward movement of enclosure, commoning and de-commoning. That is, in this struggle the creation of spaces for commoning provokes counter-efforts by the dominant forces of capital to politically decompose the initiatives of the commoners with new processes of enclosures and dispossessions. Commons-based initiatives may, for example, be integrated as subordinate aspects *within* capital, ultimately supplementing rather than challenging it (Dyer-Witheford, 1999; De Peuter & Dyer-Witheford, 2010). Indeed, apparently commons-oriented initiatives such as informal cooperatives regularly morph into business enterprises, while carbon-trading models operate to sustain the hegemonic economy of ownership and competition. Similarly, not all forms of enclosure can be dismissed as bad by definition, even from the perspective of the commons. The idea of community as a user group necessarily involves exclusion (of non-members, while, as David

Harvey (2012) points out, the production and enclosure of non-commodified spaces in a ruthlessly commodifying world is surely a good thing. There is, of course, a constant need for critical reflection to interpret the social relevance of commoning practices.

In line with a post-operaistic approach, we perceive the commons as a conceptual space of social struggle through which alternatives are even now being tested, explored and lived. This feeds into a politics of hope that not only identifies alternative spaces within the overarching logic of capitalist accumulation but also suggests possibilities for a life in common here and now. We consider commoning not only as an alternative economy but also – and rather – as an alternative to economy (Gibson-Graham 2006; Dawney, Kirwan & Brigstocke, 2016). Thus, approaching the commons movement as a social struggle for the creation of new forms of relationship, our objective is not to passively and objectively describe processes of enclosure and commoning but rather to search actively and subjectively in support of practices that can create new futures. And it is thus that we apply a broadly autonomist perspective on the practices of commoning, as a quest for an independence from the ordering temporality of capital(ism).

Finally, by way of a rider here, we should note that this volume is not limited to a narrow reading of the conceptual framework of autonomism. It elaborates on and thus goes beyond this – just as, in fact, the autonomists did themselves in applying an original reading of Marx that went beyond Marx (Negri, 1991), while also investigating contemporary commoning realities and presenting projects for further development. The articles compiled here, therefore, embrace a variety of approaches to commoning and autonomism, moving between abstract analysis and empirical example, with investigations into conceptual frameworks, observations on current practices and proposals for a commonist future.

Five autonomist principles for commoning

Five issues or themes may be identified as shared concerns raised by the contributions gathered here – sometimes overtly and sometimes between the lines – and which we regard, anyhow, as crucial to an autonomist approach to commons. Although not intended as exhaustive, this listing does, we believe, serve to identify five autonomist principles for commoning.

First, the authors generally highlight the broad context of current macro-socioeconomics, with several looking at theories and practices as specified by the contemporary period of cognitive capitalism and immaterial labour (Boutang, 2002; Hardt & Negri, 2004: 109; Gorz, 2010). Although taking different approaches to a variety of topics pitched at different theoretical and concrete levels, each of the authors in some way critiques the operation of capital, explicitly and/or implicitly rejecting (the dominance of) the prevailing paradigm of neoliberal development; they indicate and explicate ideas and initiatives that go beyond the individualistic life-styling of contemporary enclosures and the attendant universalising commodification. Very generally, one might say that the various contributions here all follow an immanent research approach, one in which theories and practices of commoning are explored from within and through the struggles and social relations of the present epoch.

Second, the authors generally avoid the focus on commons as shared resources and rather perceive commons as the creation of new forms of sociality, as new collective practices of living, working, thinking, feeling and imagining that act against the contemporary capitalist forms of producing and consuming (variously enclosing) the common wealth. There is, therefore, a general reluctance here to consider commons as things (goods) in need of regulation and protection by private and/or public governmentalities (governing mechanisms); indeed, the private–public binary of the now classical capitalist–socialist opposition is little employed or even referenced. The commons are rather perceived as societal transformations and even, by association, as levers for these, as opportunities entangled within the cooperative and communicative forms of production of cognitive capitalism; these, in turn, are revealed and/or enabled through ruptures (cracks) (Holloway, 2010) within the actual social relations and realised through the development of alternatives to capitalist production and consumption practices.

Third, this search for societal transformation through practices of commoning also implies a vision and presentation of research in which the theoretical conceptualisations about commoning are formulated not primarily from an objectivist but rather from a perspectivist approach. This is an approach characterised by a search for possibilities and initiatives that actively aim to change the societal context in which the development of knowledge is situated and the political constructed. The idea of a certain commitment to 'going beyond the actual to find the possible' leads the perspectivist knowledge researcher to strive for effective truths (Negri, 1991; Virno, 2004) – that is, to develop insights into actual concrete practices for possible societal transformations. Empirical description, therefore, is directly bound to intent (determined by the subject's perspective) rather than imagined as disconnected (idealised as objective abstraction).

Specifically, the authors here refer to practices of societal transformations and the struggles and practices of commoning from the subjective perspective of the multitude – perceived as a collective subjectivity of mutually interacting individuals (singularities) exercising agency – particularly as set against the enclosures and dispossessions of expanding cognitive capitalism and seeking opportunities for the construction of a real alternative. The concept of the multitude is employed as an autonomist perspectivism, wherein the common develops as an alternative to capital, either external to it or within it. Indeed, we hope that the plurality of ideas presented in this volume may stimulate reflection and elaboration of the possibilities for realising a transition towards commonist practices in our actual, day-to-day living conditions.

Related to this quest for the transformative power of the multitude for a more commonist future, a fourth theme evident in the contributions here is that of a generic quest to understand whether and how the multitude in this present epoch of biopolitical production is able to create alternative living and working situations and maintain its autonomy and resistance to the living and labour forms of cognitive capitalism. Two different and opposing positions can be discerned – although many intermediate positions also emerge – concerning the constituent power of the multitude to realise such a transformation towards a more commonist future.

The first and the more optimistic vision, expressed by Hardt and Negri and referred to by various contributors, is that due to the increased commonality of knowledge production and the immanence of autonomous work, conditions emerge in which immaterial labour and the multitude can break free from their domination by capital. As we enter a new era of automation, information and communication – the foundational basis for biopolitical production – increasingly developed cooperatively in and through networks, formed and managed by the immaterial labourers and within which the labourers themselves have become the bearers of the means of production, then these networks and thus the means of production are no longer provided by capital but rather reside within labour. In this vision, it is the living labour and its attributes that are now the most important forces of development, representing the mass intellectuality of the post-Fordist workers instead of the general intellect of the biopolitical production. This implies that the production of knowledges, ideas and communications actually occurs through forms of cooperation internal to labour and external to capital, intrinsically undermining the attempts of capital to organise enclosures and appropriate the wealth produced by labour. It follows, therefore, that a commonist future is slowly being realised through the very immanence of autonomous work and cooperative forms of labour, one that can no longer be relegated to capital's techniques and strategies of control and which thus also provide the conditions for a liberation of the multitude.

The second vision rejects this assumption of an imminent, liberalising trajectory of cognitive labour that will increasingly work for itself and no longer for and under the domination of capital. Instead of the assumption of a growing autonomy of cognitive labour from capital due to the expanding cooperative, communicative forms of production, this vision observes the opposite, namely a growing control on the part of capital over the life, work and social psyche of cognitive labour, particularly due to new information and communication technologies that control its mind and desires, the 'soul' (Berardi, 2009). Thus, the valorisation of cognitive labour by capital is no longer limited to specific areas of exploitation, as in Fordist production, but slowly covers – informs, directs, colonises – the entirety of our lives. It is the whole human as desire rather than just labour as human capital that has become the object of techno-social domination; and it is precisely this, the social libido itself and all the ways in which it is expressed (intelligence, imagination, sociability, etc.), that has been captured. In this vision, the performative power of capital in respect of cognitive labour through information and communication technologies shaping human desires appears irreversible and prevents the realisation of the optimistic vision of the multitude breaking through the web of the empire's power (only occasional 'victories' are possible now, and these may only operate as safety-valve mechanisms).

Although apparently much bleaker, this second vision need or even should not be interpreted as negating all agency, as denying the autonomy and creative power of human activity. It may rather be represented as an exaggerated plea aiming to elicit an appropriately profound response, so that we may better identify the contexts of desire and thereby distinguish the ways in which this autonomy takes shape within the actual context of heteronomous technospheres (the realms of information, communication and biotechnologies) dominating the multitudinous psychospheres, such as the realms of affect, ideation and imagination. It is a plea at least for a consciousness that may re-innovate resistance and the autonomy of the multitude(s) and the analysis of this. This second vision may thus be understood as a call to seek ways in which the new mass intellectuality can develop anew so as to recreate itself in relation to the general intellect of the high technospheres of the contemporary knowledge economy.

This choice of visions and interpretations and the potential for 'positive' outcomes implies some basic questions. Can multitudes generate *social spaces* in which new commonalities are established? To what extent is cognitive capital able or unable to absorb such initiatives and contain the mass intellectuality within its structures? The overriding sense of the contributions here, we suggest, is of a non-deterministic thesis in which – alongside the immanent empowerment of cognitive labour and yet also the subversion and manipulation of this by and for capital – there arise opportunities for an alternative, non-capital-based development. These, simply, may or may not be taken. In line with the political valorisation of autonomy, in fact, this emphasises choice and possibility, a plurality of futures. The utopics and dystopics envisioned for cognitive labour in the period of supposedly 'late' capitalism may thus offer contemporary and forward-looking extremes as reference points within which we seek to navigate possibilities for commoning.

This links to a fifth theme, a concern with the multitudinous practices of commoning and creation of social spaces as evolving within (the contradictions of cognitive) capital and state (which are thus transmuted) or outside the world of commodities (to be realised in a world of commons) or both (within and without). Referring to these three positions and considering them strategically, in terms of multitudinous practices of commoning, the total effect, we think, is of the emergence of a combined vision of the common – so again, a liberal plurality – wherein the cumulative effect is not just one of complete rupture or escape, but rather an ongoing development, including and incorporating ruptures and expanding free spaces along the way.

This is an evolutionary view that nevertheless makes claim to the revolutionary moment, valorising but without hinging on any particular short-term success. It is progress as process, antagonistic to and incompatible with capital, yet also developing within and so conditioned by it. It indicates commoning as an emergent practice designed in specific contexts and performed by people daily as they move in and out of commons and capitalist/statist contexts (environments, circuits). And it represents, we believe, the range of commoning activities and analyses considered by the articles in this volume.

Contributions

Regarding the internal structure of this volume, rather than divide the contributions into sections – which would arguably frame the discussion in a certain, prescribed way – we have followed a more horizontal, rhizomatic approach. We present the pieces in a loosely linked, narrative-type sequence of which the logic of connection – set, roughly, within a framework of moving from autonomism to commoning – is, inevitably, just one of many that we could have chosen.

The volume starts with a discussion by **Mathijs van de Sande** looking at how the resistance of the commoners can be conceptualised in terms of a prefigurative power of the multitude to create autonomous social spaces, referring to Negri's concept of *potentia* or *constituent power* and Holloway's concept of *power-to*. Van de Sande stresses that Negri's constituent power is always already present in the here and now, composing a space within capitalist structures and relations wherein these relations are changed. Holloway's power-to concept, on the other hand, represents the potential of a radical alternative that reveals itself as a moment of rupture, a crack in the texture of capitalism. Van de Sande explains how these different understandings of actions of resistance have specific implications for terminological usage. The concept of the common (singular) *within* capitalist structures is both a precondition for and product of the multitude's resistance to capitalism (Negri); in the plural, the commons are distinctive, momentous and potentially decisive breaks (Holloway).

Then, **Elise Thorburn** reflects on how the multitude can organise its prefigurative power in relation to the specific configurations of cognitive capitalism in this epoch of biopolitical production. Thorburn's analysis critiques Hardt and Negri in relation to the multitude's inevitable emergence in spontaneous and elementary forms of communism through the cooperative nature of its labour, since any movement with political directionality must be consciously organised; she sees their notion of immateriality as overemphasised, particularly in respect of reproductive work as uncovered by feminist analyses; and she regards them as underestimating the effect of capital's division of workers, even in an era of production that requires greater degrees of cooperation, communication and collective labour. Thus, emphasising the need to actively establish politically reorganised forms of struggle that include but are not limited to work, Thorburn suggests the model of the assembly. Referring to her personal experience of the Greater Toronto Workers Assembly, she argues that the specific class composition of biopolitical production can achieve a radical break from the hold of capital (empire). Thus transformed through a practical politics of the common, it follows, the uncentred, disunited multitude of Hardt and Negri may be realised as an internally differentiated but unseparated heterogeneity.

Next, focusing generally on Negri's oeuvre and particularly on the issue of instituting the common as a project of democratic action, **Sonja Lavaert** offers a conceptual history and overview of the multitude. Lavaert sets out by stressing the important role played by Negri's experiences with *operaismo* and his study of Spinoza for the development of an alternative line of modern thought in which ideas are considered as being politically relevant, as having a potential power (*potentia*), insofar as they are related to human vitality. This involves an imagination or subjectivity that cannot be standardised; it represents an immanent perspective shaped by the actions of the multitude and thus a constituent power antagonistic to the constituted power of state institutions. It was this reinterpretation of democracy as an immanent perspective of the multitude as the condition for a politics in general that led to Negri's empire–multitude pairing. Lavaert ponders the relationship to the multitude and resistance of expression for Negri in love and art and laughter, as well as how the immanent analysis of the multitude concept/practice also brought him to advance the idea of a perspectivist knowledge, related to Machiavelli's call for effective truths. Thence, she reviews Virno's question about how a partial and antagonistic perspective of the multitude can pretend to universality and Agamben's search for a method of knowledge that isolates a particular case in its context, claiming that this method may make a new totality comprehensible. This leads her to the *general intellect* concept introduced by Marx, referring to Virno's remarks that the general intellect has irreversibly changed the labour process and yet offers a route towards emancipation.

It is this search for effective truth that brings **Franco Berardi** to stress that the multitude has to reconquer its autonomy in the actual epoch of what he dubs *semiocapitalism*. Berardi narrates the victorious struggle of the industrial workers' movement against the disciplinary rule of the factory and the response of capital with technological innovations instituting a flexibilisation and deregulation of labour that dissolved the political force of the workers' movement. Thus, labour has been fractalised, divided into units of time and activity that are bought and deployed in now the de-territorialised space of a global, recombinant capital. Then, the screen links (cell phone, tablet, etc.) become the assembly lines of cognitive labour, shaping relations between the fractal worker and recombinant capital in the ever more technologically integrated network, while the flow of information reduces and strips the self-reliant social activity of the cognitive workers, submitting their mental energies to the accelerating rhythms of capitalist production and reversing the social autonomy into a pervasive dependence of emotions and consciousness. The only way to go beyond the psychopathological present in which precariousness, isolation and competition take the place of solidarity, according to Berardi, is thus a self-organisation of cognitive work. This implies a disentanglement of the general intellect from the capitalist gestalt that operates as a psychosocial power governing daily life in which debt has become the general frame of subjugation and autonomy now takes the form of (re)claiming a right to insolvency.

In his contribution, **Pieter Lemmens** reflects on this, stressing that the liberation of the common from capital supposes first of all a liberation of the multitudinous desires from the conditions of today's cognitive and consumer capitalism. Referring to the work of Stiegler and Berardi, Lemmens argues that the Hardt–Negri analysis of multitude fails to adequately take into account the new technical and libidinal conditions of today's general intellect, which precisely frustrate the process of social recomposition necessary for the multitude to become autonomous. Critiquing Hardt/Negri along lines not dissimilar to Thorburn (above), Lemmens further disputes their assumption of desire as an inherently positive force, since the general intellect is strongly conditioned by the technologies of the mind (involving traditional and digital forms of communication), which are systematically annexed by cognitive and consumer capitalism. Emphasis is then placed on the relevance of the flow of libidinal energy crossing three interacting systems – referred to as psychic organs, social organisations and technical organs – wherein it is important to conceive the latter in terms of *pharmaka*, meaning that they are intrinsically ambivalent with respect to their conditioning and can thus act not only to discipline but also for self-construction in processes of de-proletarianisation. The digital information and communication technologies, it follows, also carry the potential to support new processes of psychic and collective individuation and hence may also function as tools of autonomy, resocialisation and freedom.

Driven by an overarching preoccupation to mutate the mainstream modes and generate new modes of production and governance from below, **Massimo De Angelis** discusses various elements for a systems theory of commoning. He argues that today's social revolution is nothing other than a diffusion of commoning in which the circuit of commons – a distinct (autonomous and autopietic, i.e. self-regenerating) social system, just like the capital and state circuits – expands as it struggles to take things into its own hands, self-governs on the basis of different and often clashing, internally generated codes and reproduces itself through a set of interrelated practices and values. De Angelis stresses that the phenomenology of commons is grounded in daily life and its social relations of commoning, where commoning is the activity of commoners in organic relation both to the commons (the pooled resources that need to be sustained and reproduced) and to one another. Thus, it becomes a recursive life activity that regenerates and develops those very social relations that are constitutive of the commons. The strength of a commons system then depends on the balance and density of all the relational circuits and extent to which we subordinate the operation of capital to the commons' values of equity, sharing, solidarity and conviviality. This leads De Angelis to conclude with a discussion of the mutation of societies towards a commons hegemony on the basis of boundary commoning, the commoning that produces a structural coupling between and among different commons systems constructing a new, wider and growing sphere of interdependent commons.

This analysis can be understood as elaborated in the contribution by **Murat Öztürk**, **Joost Jongerden** and **Andy Hilton**, in which concrete practices of commoning are described in the limiting contemporary context of smallholders (rural families, the peasantry) in Turkey. Here, commons as social practices are investigated through the ways in which smallholder families and communities move in and out of capitalistic and commoning structures. First, they resist the logic of capital to commodify (they valorise their land and maintain traditional commons); then they articulate a new dual circuit system, combining these commons with financial inputs, including new, non-commodity exchanges based upon kith-and-kin linkages extended by mobility and migration. Thus transcending the rural–urban division of space, the practices of commoning are viewed as productive of re-spatialisation of the common; new spatial lifestyles involving a variety of residence and migratory patterns have emerged that incorporate both a maintenance and (re)generation of commoning values. Thus, the entry of capital into traditional village life has brought about the development of new forms of social commoning that combine the rural and urban and sense of belonging for extended settlement patterns with dual- and multi-place living structures underlying a novel solidarity-network-based commons.

Femke Kaulingfreks and **Ruud Kaulingfreks** refer to central urban squares and parks as another social space in which a sense of the common is created, in this case one that disputes and sometimes usurps the authority of the central power. The physical assembly of large numbers of people in squares – and other, sufficiently similar spaces (like parks) – has proven to be an effective method to surprise and pressure state powers on the part of the disempowered (multitude) struggling to open up another world. Central to this is a topological analysis of the square as an inherently democratic, egalitarian space that awakens a sense of commoning (even as the governing disciplinary powers aim to control it). The political agency of the mass here is not based on a shared programme or identity, but rather on the coming together itself. The multitude is experienced and expressed as a set of singularities that can act politically because, in its internal diversity, it has a longing for a more just and egalitarian governance, for a life that is fundamentally in common. Square protests should not be judged on their demonstrable long-term outcomes, therefore, let alone with respect to their immediate impact on institutional structures; rather, their value lies in their expression of a prefigurative politics, as a practice movement in which certain political ideals are experimentally actualised in the 'here and now'.

In the article by **Jose Louis Vivero-Pol**, another process of commoning is described related to the common right to have food and be well nurtured. Starting from a review of the failures of the current, globalised, industrial food system – following three historical waves of enclosures and privatisation of common resources – Vivero-Pol introduces the possibility of a paradigm shift from the presently dominant corporate food regime towards one premised on a commoning of food. A transitional framework is identified composed of the growing movements for food sovereignty (mainly in the rural South) and alternative food networks (linked especially to the urban North) as a sort of grand coalition of a counter-hegemonic movement, which Vivero-Pol terms a *food commons regime*. This he envisages as a re-valorisation of the non-commodity dimensions of food and agriculture in the establishment of a tri-centric governance system, involving the state and private sector as well as grassroots movements, with new roles for each. Vivero-Pol proposes that within this system, a partner state takes the role of facilitator, supporting alternative, grassroots initiatives that enable polycentric, bottom-up developments for basic foods in which food provisioning is gradually driven by an ethos that focuses more on social aims and satisfying human needs than on profit.

Staying with agriculture, **Guido Ruivenkamp** discusses the production of seeds for food crops in the context of a societal struggle that can go in the direction of either commoning or commodification. First, Ruivenkamp offers an overview overview of the transformations of seeds as natural commons into commodities. Then he stresses how this has also changed the social relations regarding the seeds, shifting knowledge from peasant communities to public and private research institutions, which also involved a change in the material/immaterial composition of the seeds that enabled the institutions to control the labour of cultivation. Ruivenkamp refers then to the responses of various multitudinous practices of re-commoning seeds. These consist of efforts to challenge the mode of ordering imposed by the commodified seeds, recompose im/material forms so as to revitalise local resources and activate common knowledge production, such as through the development of flexible, non-hierarchical networks that re-valorise peasant knowledge. A commonist food production, it is suggested, will be based on these innovative practices, steered by alliances of peasants, farmers, researchers, consumers and citizens, to rewrite the embodied, politicising content of the seeds for re-territorialisation, re-peasantisation and care-ful agri-cultures.

Finally, broadening this discussion, **Stefan Meretz** looks at how commons may become the elementary social form of a new society, analogous to the commodity for (cognitive) capitalism. Meretz emphasises that capitalism should not be perceived as an external system of power but rather as an internalised and objectified system of how we produce and reproduce our livelihood. Thus, he argues, undoing capitalism requires a new way of producing our livelihood, one that can potentially replace the old form of the commodity and its mediation of the reproduction of individual as well as of social life. This new mode of production is based on peer production, a form of commoning that changes not only the social relations among producers and users but also the purpose, shape and usability of the means of production and the resulting products. From a categorical skeleton of a peer-commonist society based on the logics of inclusion, Meretz looks at the practical issue of its scaling up to the level of a full societal mediation. For this, he introduces the concept of *stigmergy* (from behavioural studies of termites) as a type of self-coordination in large decentralised systems in which subsequent actions reinforce and build upon each other, leading to the spontaneous emergence of coherent, apparently systematic activity. Then, he elaborates a five-step ('germ form') model and compares two concrete cases of business initiatives operating with a peer-commonist practice as examples of a trend he observes as being already underway.

Final remarks

This volume is presented as a selection of readings on the subject at hand rather than an attempt at a full review striving for a 'model' presentation. That said, there are two areas of deficit that perhaps ought to be noted, referring to time and place. For the former, we have to acknowledge that the speed of current events relative to the pace of writing and publication means that some of what was treated to as contemporary at the time of writing has since been passed by. While this may occasionally impinge already, we think it should not overly impact on the analysis that is primarily set in a present seen in terms of decades rather than years. Thus, for example, reference to specific protests and neoliberal measures remains pertinent, we believe, even where the specific political conditions and economic situation mentioned appear already historical. While the hopeful era of Occupy and the street protests of spontaneous mutitudes may have already become a distant memory currently overtaken by a new reality of resurgent nationalisms and the alt/far right, this is itself just another passing phase, we believe, in the longer term unfolding dynamic of emerging common(s).

Regarding place, we would not consider criticism of a Western-centric bias to be misplaced. Indeed, moving from the 'developing country' case study of Turkey, an obvious line of geographical development would be consideration of developments in the Middle East and North Africa, thinking of the local dissenting responses to autocratic regressions post-'Arab Spring' in a region where 'governance, state control, and legitimacy are being contested' (Cambanis, 2017). Nevertheless, we also feel that a concentration on the West is not so inappropriate, since it is in the siting of the 'advanced' economies that autonomist thought has developed and which thus most meets the conditions of its analysis.

Finally, we would like to emphasise that our summaries of the various contributions are the result of our personal reading and interpretation. We are aware that there is in all the pieces gathered here a rich ensemble of ideas, and suggestions for which many other ways of presentation may have been championed, centred more, for example, on autonomy, forms of constituent power or instituting the common. We hope, nonetheless, that this volume will stimulate the reader to continue thinking and acting for a more sharing, egalitarian and person-centred – or commonist – society, 'here and now'.

References

Benkler, Y. (2000). 'From consumers to users: shifting the deeper structures of regulation toward sustainable commons and user access', *Federal Communications Law Journal,* 51(3): 561–579.

Berardi, F. (Bifo) (2009). The Soul at Work: from Aleination to Autonomy. Los Angeles, CA: Semiotext(e).

Bollier D. and Helfrich, S. (Eds.) (2015). *Patterns of Commoning*.The Commons Strategies Group in Cooperation with Off the Commons Books. Amherst, MA/Jena/Chaing Mai:Levellers Press.

Boutang, Y. M. (2002). *L'eta del Capitalism Cognitive. Innovazione, proprieta e Cooperazione delle Moltitudine*. Verona: Ombre Corte.

Bresnihan, P. (2016). 'The more-than-human commons: from commons to commoning', in L. Dawney, S. Kirwan and J. Brigstocke (Eds.). *Space, Power and the Commons. The Struggle for Alternative Futures*. Abingdon, Oxon/New York: Routledge..

Cambanis, T. (2017). 'Introduction to Arab politics beyond the uprisings', in *Experiments in an Era of Resurgent Authoritarianism*. New York: The Century Foundation (Carnegie Corporation). At https://tcf.org/content/report/introduction-arab-politics-beyond-uprisings/

Dawney, L., Kirwan, S. and Brigstocke, J. (Eds.) (2016). *Space, Power and the Commons. The Struggle for Alternative Futures*. Abingdon, Oxon/New York: Routledge.

De Angelis, M. (2007). *The Beginning of History*. London/Ann Arbor, MI: Pluto Press.

De Peuter, G. and Dyer-Witheford, N. (2010). 'Commons and cooperatives. Affinities: a journal of radical theory', *Culture and Action*, 4(1): 30–56.

Dyer-Witheford, N. (1999), *Cyber Marx: Cycles and Circuits of Struggle in High Technology Capitalism*. Champaign, IL: University of Illinois Press.

Federici, S. (2001). 'Women, globalization, and the international women's movement', Canadian Journal of Development Studies, 22: 1025–36.

Gorz, A. (2010). *The Immaterial. Knowledge, Value and Capital*. Calcutta: Seagull Books.

Gibson-Graham, J. K. (2006). *A Postcapitalist Politics*. Minneapolis: University of Minnesota Press.

Gibson-Graham, J. K. (2008). 'Diverse economies: performative practices for "other worlds"', *Progress in Human Geography*, 32(5), 613–632.

Hardin, G. (1968). 'The tragedy of the commons', *Science*, 162: 1243–48.

Hardt, M. and Negri, A. (2004). *Multitude. War and Democracy in the Age of Empire*. New York: Penguin Press.

Harvey, D. (2012). *Rebel Cities. From the Right to the City to the Urban Revolution*. London/Brooklyn, NY: Verso.

Heller, M. A. (1998). 'The tragedy of the anticommons: property in the transition from Marx to markets', *Harvard Law Review*, 111: 621–688.

Holloway, J. (2010). *Crack Capitalism*. London: Pluto Press

Lessig, L. (2001). *The Future of Ideas: The Fate of the Commons in a Connected World*. New York: Vintage Books

Negri, A. (1991). *Marx beyond Marx. Lessons on the Grundrisse*. Brooklyn, NY: Autonomedia/Pluto.

Ostrom, E. (1986). Issues of definition and theory: some conclusions and hypotheses. National Research Council (Ed.), *Proceedings of the Conference on Common Property Resource Management (April 21–26, 1985)*. Washington, DC: National Academy Press.

Ostrom, E. (1990). *Governing the Commons: The Evolution of Institutions for Collective Action*. Cambridge: Cambridge University Press.

Ostrom, V. and Ostrom, E. (1977). 'Public goods and public choices', in E. S. Savas (Ed.), *Alternatives for Delivering Public Services: Toward Improved Performance*. Boulder, CO: Westview Press.

Ostrom, V., Tiebout, C. M. and Warren, R. (1961). 'The organization of government in metropolitan areas: a theoretical inquiry', *American Political Science Review*, 55(4): 831–842.

Shiva, V. (2010). 'Resources', in W. Sachs (Ed.), *The Development Dictionary: A Guide to Knowledge as Power*. London/New York: Zed Books.

Suga, Y. (2013). 'The tragedy of the conceptual expansion of the commons', in T. Murota and K. Takeshita (Eds.), *Local Commons and Democratic Environmental Governance*. Tokyo/New York/Paris: United Nations University Press.

Virno, P. (2004). *A Grammar of the Multitude*. Los Angeles/New York: Semiotext(e).

Chapter 1

The prefigurative power of the common(s)

Mathijs van de Sande

Introduction

If we want to grasp how capitalist structures and relations are resisted from and by 'the common' and/or 'commons', we need to ascribe a certain power to it/them. This power, moreover, must be substantially and essentially different from capitalist forms of power. First and foremost, it needs a conceptualisation 'from below'. The objective of this contribution is to provide such a conceptualisation, for which purpose three central concepts are employed: 'prefiguration', '*potentia*' and 'power-to'.

First, I define and conceptualise the notion of 'prefiguration'. Prefiguration or 'prefigurative politics' is an experimental political practice in which the ends of one's actions are mirrored in the means applied in their realisation. These ends are thereby conceived as inherent in the practice itself and their immediate realisation is aimed at. In other words, from a prefigurative perspective on political practices, the oppositional relations between means and ends and between a 'future ideal' and the 'here and now' are problematised. However, as I will argue, this concept of prefiguration needs further politicisation outside the context of contemporary anarchist theory. What is more, this concept could also be useful to our endeavour of conceptualising a power from below and offers us a valuable perspective on various conceptualisations of resistance as it occurs today.

Second, two closely related yet significantly different concepts of power from below are defined and compared. To begin with, I look at Antonio Negri's notion of '*potentia*' or 'constituent power'. Departing from the Spinozist opposition between *potentia* and *potestas*, Negri's conceptualisation of the former as a historical and non-dialectical understanding of power will be reconstructed. Then this concept is related to his contemporary work on 'the multitude', and finally reconceptualised as a prefigurative form of power. I describe *potentia*/constituent power as an active potential that creates an 'outside', but 'inside' the capitalist relations and structures it seeks to confront.

Next, I turn to John Holloway, another contemporary autonomist thinker, who is often related to and compared with Negri but who departs from a significantly different ontological background. His conceptualisation of power from below, which he terms as 'power-to', is also reconstructed. As opposed to 'power-over', power-to is presented as an alienated capacity, a potential that seeks actualisation but is limited by a power 'from above'. Holloway argues that power-to breaks through this alienated form of itself and thus creates spatial-temporal 'cracks' in the texture of capitalist relations and structures. Power-to is equally termed as a prefigurative power, which constructs a 'beyond' and sheds light on a future to come.

After that, Holloway's concept of power-to and Negri's *potentia* are juxtaposed, along the lines of the conceptualisation of prefiguration. In presenting both as prefigurative understandings of power, I investigate the consequences and implications these divergent conceptions have for our understanding of current forms of resistance against capitalist structures. Finally, these differences are further concretised through a comparison between (Hardt and) Negri's concept of 'the common' and Holloway's reference to 'commons'. This also allows us to grasp the prefigurative characteristics of (the production of) the common and/or commons in its/their antagonist relationship to capitalist structures and relations.

Prefigurative politics: mirroring means and ends

Resistance to capital comes in many forms. Diverse and heterogeneous as they may be – from relatively spontaneous expressions of public space occupation and mass street protest to 'direct action' networks and 'civil society' projects seeking to implement alternative forms of cooperation and production – many of these resistances share, to a greater or lesser extent, a form of political action in which means and ends are not strictly divergent, but strongly reflected in each other. This conception of political action, which is commonly referred to as 'prefiguration', is a useful tool that enables us to make intelligible a broad diversity of contemporary political practices.

Prefiguration as a notion is applied in contemporary anarchist literature both as a descriptive term, by means of which the practices of (predominantly anarchist and/or alter-globalist) activist movements are portrayed, and as a normative concept, on the basis of which an ethico-political agenda is defined. Most commonly, these two applications of the term coexist or converge, even completely. The anarchist anthropologist David Graeber, in an interview on 'Occupy Wall Street', in which he took part, describes this 'prefigurative' movement in the following manner:

It's very similar to the globalization movement. You see the same criticisms in the press. It's a bunch of kids who don't know economics and only know what they're against. But there's a reason for that. It's pre-figurative, so to speak. You're creating a vision of the sort of society you want to have in miniature. And it's a way of juxtaposing yourself against these powerful, undemocratic forces you're protesting. If you make demands, you're saying, in a way, that you're asking the people in power and the existing institutions to do something different. And one reason people have been hesitant to do that is they see these institutions as the problem. (Quoted in Klein, 2011)

Hence, 'prefiguration' first of all addresses a methodological problem. One wishes to alter certain political and/or economic structures, but at the same time one may regard the means most commonly applied for this purpose (e.g. the positions of power and the existing institutions) to be a part, or even the cause, of the very problems themselves. The possibility (or necessity) of changing the world by means of the state and other hierarchical structures has long been debated within radical political movements. Can radical change be realised directly, or should it be enforced by the use of (state) power, a seizure of which would precede this process of transformation? As the moral philosopher Benjamin Franks suggests, the latter view implies an instrumentalist approach to radical strategy, in which the means of emancipatory struggles are subordinated to their objectives. According to this consequentialist view of political practice, Franks argues,

The ultimate end, the seizure of state power or 'revolution', justifies particular types of political behaviour. Actions are judged by whether they assist or hinder the revolutionary goal. Likewise the model for a centralised party structure is also advanced on the same consequentialist grounds. The end … justifies the means, even if the methods are autocratic. (Franks, 2003: 23)

A prefigurative view of political practice leads to a critical reconceptualisation of the relationship between means and ends here. However, as much as it refuses to reduce the former to the latter, a prefigurative perspective equally rejects a one-sidedly means-oriented depiction of political struggle. According to Franks, a deontologist understanding of politics, in which the act is evaluated exclusively on the basis of one's means and intentions, 'maintains this problematic division between means and ends, only this time the emphasis is on the former' (Franks, 2003: 25, 114). In a prefigurative practice, however, political means and ends are considered to be mirrored. The means embody the objectives of a certain political practice, and its ends comply with the processes that lead to their realisation; or the ends comprise a realisation of the means. It is not merely or even primarily the consistency between means and ends that matters, but rather the way in which they mutually reflect each other in political practice. In other words, rather than a mere accordance between means and ends, in a prefigurative account of political action the relation between these two is itself problematised.

This prefigurative view of political struggle in practice has two further consequences. First, it means that both the means and the ends, in their mutual relatedness, are formulated, tested and evaluated throughout the political process. Prefiguration is a process rather than the implementation of a pre-set strategy (Maeckelbergh, 2009: 94). Second, and as a result, this process is inherently experimental and experiential – one continuously and contemporaneously develops and redefines an image of both the objective of one's political actions and the means applied in these actions. This implies that prefigurative practices are characterised by a strong immediacy and sense of urgency. Prefigurative actors seem to experience the urge to live their social and political ideals in the 'here and now'. In his ethnography on 'Direct Action', for instance, Graeber (2009: 210, 527) describes the strategies applied by alter-globalist movements as the creation of a 'micro-utopia', or 'acting as if one is already free'. Similarly, the alter-globalist activist and anthropologist Marianne Maeckelbergh (2009: 67) states that 'practising prefiguration means removing the temporal distinction between the struggle in the present toward a goal in the future'. More than a mere strategy, in other words, prefiguration is most commonly considered as a way to reach beyond the experiential distinction between longer-term revolutionary goals and the urge to free ourselves in the present. Indeed, as Uri Gordon (2008: 39) states:

> Anarchists often explain their actions and modes of organisation as intended not only to help bring about generalised social transformation, but also to liberate themselves to the greatest degree possible. On such a reading, the motivation for anarchists to engage in a prefigurative politics lies simply in their desire to inhabit liberated social relations.

Hence, although in a prefigurative practice one aims at long-distant, idealistic (or, sometimes, even 'utopian') political goals, these are fully oriented to the context of everyday life. Prefiguration, in other words, is the attempt to create the 'other world' we deem possible in the here and now. In that sense (and only in that sense), no distinction can be drawn between a future ideal and its experimental – yet direct – realisation. Of course, prefiguration never fully embodies that which is prefigured, but nevertheless – as will become clear in my reading of Antonio Negri – as an 'active potentiality' it cannot, in fact, be understood outside the context of its practical realisation.

Toward a politicisation of prefiguration

The concept of 'prefiguration' or 'prefigurative politics' was initially derived from studies of the civil rights movements in the 1960s and 1970s (e.g. Breines, 1982; Polletta, 2002). Today, however, it is most predominantly used in anarchist or autonomist theory – often (but not exclusively) in reference to political movements that consciously identify with these theoretical currents. Anti-fascist and squatters' movements in Europe and the USA, the Zapatistas in southern Mexico, the Landless Farmers in Brazil and the alter-globalisation movement (which experienced a partial revival in the form of 'Occupy') have been extensively referred to as the most obvious examples of prefigurative practices (Franks, 2003, 2006; Gordon, 2008; Graeber, 2009; Maeckelbergh, 2009; Day, 2010). The political objectives of these movements – such as democracy, 'horizontalism' or equality – are realised prefiguratively, in the forms of their actions and organisational structures. There is a need, however, to further politicise this concept by extending it from this predominantly anarchist discourse to a broader description of current political movements and practices. Three considerations urge us to develop such a politicisation.

First of all, the recent global waves of political upheavals and revolts – the 'Occupy' movements in the US and Europe, the square occupations by 'Indignados' in Spain and the massive protests in Greece, the 'Arab Spring' (e.g. the occupation of Tahrir Square; see van de Sande, 2013), the various mass occupations and street protests that may be economically grouped as occurring in 'emerging markets' (Brazil, Turkey, Bulgaria) – demand that we rethink our approach to political struggle and resistance in general. As critically engaged theorists, we should put more effort into providing the methodological and normative tools that will enable us to place ourselves in these movements' positions, or rather that allow these movements to speak for themselves in critical political theory.

Second, although we routinely make sense of specific political practices by ascribing certain 'outcomes', 'intentions', 'means' and 'ends' to them, this assumes an abstraction that prevents us from doing justice to these practices from their own viewpoint. Understanding the internal dynamics and rationale of a particular practice of resistance, in other words, cannot take place from a generalising, retrospective point of view. Instead, we are in need of methodological approaches that help us to understand how means, ends, objectives and outcomes correlate and interplay with one another in political practice itself. The concept of 'prefiguration', I claim, gives rise to such an alternative approach, and therefore deserves a broader application. When taken out of its contemporary, predominantly anarchist context, 'prefiguration' may be a suitable tool by which to understand practices of politics and resistance more broadly.

Third, political struggle is necessarily first and foremost a struggle for, about or against power. Intuitively, a prefigurative understanding of power appears rather self-contradictory, as power is most commonly conceptualised precisely in terms of a means–ends distinction. Most of the sources referred to above do, in fact, elaborate on the relationship between power and prefiguration, but only to problematise the internal power relations within a political movement or organisation. Instead, my objective here will be to develop applications of 'prefiguration' in an analysis of political power as such. The central question here is not merely how to deal with power prefiguratively, but rather how to formulate a conception of power that is prefigurative – to conceptualise, in other words, prefiguration as power.[1]

Two concepts of power 'from below' spring to mind here: those of '*potentia*' or 'constituent power' in the thought of (Michael Hardt and) Antonio Negri and of 'power-to' in the recent works of John Holloway. Although these conceptualisations appear rather similar, there is a subtle difference between them, and this has significant consequences for an understanding of prefigurative power. In the following sections, I first define 'constituent power' and 'power-to' in terms of prefiguration and then go on to apply these conceptualisations of prefigurative power in the context of 'the common' or processes of 'commonisation', thereby drawing a distinction between 'commons' and 'the common'. This not only allows us to grasp the development of prefigurative power as a process, but also to differentiate between the perspectives on (the possibility of) resistance offered by power-to and *potentia* as different conceptions of prefigurative power.

Potentia/constituent power

In 1979 and 1980, while imprisoned for his involvement in a (legitimate) oppositional movement, Antonio Negri wrote an extensive study on the political and metaphysical works of the seventeenth century philosopher Baruch de Spinoza. Negri's study of Spinoza, *The Savage Anomaly*, revolves around the distinction between two conceptions of power that can be found in Spinoza's thinking: *potentia* and *potestas*:

> Potentia as the dynamic and constitutive inherence of the single in the multiplicity, of mind in the body, of freedom in necessity – power against Power – where potestas is presented as the subordination of the multiplicity, of the mind, of freedom, and of potentia. (Negri, 1991: 190–91)

In Negri's reading of Spinoza's *Ethics*, this distinction between *potentia* and *potestas* is approached from the perspective of the former, and its constitutive characteristics are shown to form the core of a Spinozist understanding of power, which, as Negri states, 'can be defined in only one way: against Power'.[2] It would lead us too far to elaborate on the ontological differences between these two forms of power, but let us briefly stress one significant contrast between them in Spinoza, following Negri.

Negri's understanding of Spinoza's *potentia/potestas* distinction relies, among other things, on the 34th and 35th propositions from Book I of the *Ethics*, in which God's power (or rather 'Power') is discussed. According to Spinoza (1955: 74 [I.P34]), 'whatever we conceive to be in the power [*potestas*] of God, necessarily exists'. Power in this sense is the active capacity to create, a capacity from which its realisation necessarily follows. Whatever can be understood to be in God's power (*potestas*) is necessarily actualised. This conception of power is rather different from its counterpart, *potentia*. When referred to as '*potentia*', 'God's power', Spinoza (1955: 74 [I.P35]) argues, 'is identical with his essence'. Hence, in this formulation, '*potentia*' expresses the identity between power and its essence: power is not equated with capacity here, but with essence itself; '*potentia*' is not actualised, but an inherent necessity. Thus, as Negri stresses, there is a subtle but nevertheless highly important difference between these conceptualisations of power: whereas in *potestas* that which is potential needs actualisation, in *potentia* the actuality is already enclosed; it is an active potentiality (Negri, 1991: 191–2). In Spinoza's political writings, this active potentiality is identified as the power of the multitude, a power 'from below'. *Potestas*, on the other hand, is the power of authorities, which comes from above and is imposed on this multitude (Negri, 2004).

The distinction between *potentia* and *potestas* is further developed from the perspective of the former and placed in a political-historical context by Negri in his *Insurgencies: Constituent Power and the Modern State*. Employing the terms 'constituent power' (*potentia*) versus 'constituted power' (*potestas*), Negri here depicts their relationship as a non-dialectical, historical antagonism. Again, 'constituent power' is conceptualised as the form of power that is intrinsically linked to democracy, whereas constituted power is its institutionalised counterpart; the repressive, inflexible and dense power that appears as soon as formal constitutions are formulated, when states and other authoritarian structures are formed. Constituent power, the power of the multitude, is the force that thrusts history, offensively aiming at the realisation of its potential. Rather than being dialectically related, constituent power and constituted power are just directly and antagonistically opposed, and cannot be synthesised or reconciled with each other.

Negri repeatedly refers to the unavoidable negativity inherent in constituent power, and defines its 'active elements' in terms of 'resistance and desire'; but it is also productive, since it actively forms the alternative to that which it negates. Moreover, constituent power is the very process in which new relations are formed, Negri stresses, as it does not aim at its own institutionalisation, but, far from this, strives to 'construct more being – ethical being, social being, community' (Negri, 1999: 23). This 'construction of being', as Negri formulates it, is an open process rather than an end-oriented development. Hence, a central element that has been ascribed to a prefigurative conception of political struggle (above) can also be identified in Negri's understanding of political power. The problematic distinction between means and ends that is questioned in a prefigurative practice is implicitly dealt with in Negri's conception of 'constituent power', in which this distinction dissolves. What is left is an open power; the practice of struggle itself.

This is not to say that historical processes are considered to be fully contingent in Negri's anti-dialectical analysis, or, rather, that a historical perspective is completely done away with in his thought. Rather, we see how 'constituent power' is introduced as a prefigurative interpretation of historical continuity. Negri's analysis of political struggle is further developed throughout *Insurgencies*, which introduces an alternative, non-linear view on historical progress. The antagonistic relation between 'constituent' and 'constituted power' manifests itself in the revolutionary event, such as the American and French Revolutions, the 1905 and 1917 revolutions in Russia and the Paris Commune. These are the moments in which constituent power expresses itself in its confrontation with constituted power and liberates time and space to realise its radical alternative – if only for a short while. Once these moments or spaces have been institutionalised, its processes moulded in a dense, systemic form, 'constituent power' has long been pushed back beneath the surface again. In fact, since 'constituent power' manifests itself as this democratic and political moment, in which existing relations of power and production are politicised, the point at which it is blocked (for example through institutionalisation) is where history comes to a standstill; the political is closed again. In fact, however, this blocking may also be seen in a wider context as interruption, a pause until the continuation of history. The process in which constituent power develops, Negri argues, shows two different historical continuities – the first of which is depicted as follows:

> [W]hereas the American Revolution, by introducing an unde-fined constitutional dialectic of the singular and concrete rights of freedom, spreads the process of political emancipation, the French Revolution works this space in terms of equality and from the standpoint of the liberation of labor – thus posing the foundations of the Bolshevik effort to constitute the political arrangement of living labor. Therefore, this process has an initial continuity, that of an increasingly complex, complementary, and progressive plot: the rational expression of a dense project of the emancipation of social freedom and its realization in the political. (Negri, 1999: 304)

Constituent power is a 'plot' that develops over time: little by little, it gains terrain on constituted power, but this expansion is always, at least partly, repressed and forced back by the latter. This is the 'back-and-forth movement' that Hardt and Negri refer to in *Commonwealth*: the realisation of constituent power is a gradual process in struggle with constituted power, without a synthetic conciliation between the two. Constituent power, so to speak, gradually 'accumulates' throughout history. The irruptions that this constituent power brings about, however, are prefigurations of its full potential. Therefore, within this 'first trajectory', Negri (1999: 304) argues, a second historical continuity is implied, which is 'not a process of objective configuration, but of subjective action'. Here, constituent power is a prefigurative tendency, 'continually reopened and redefined as absolute in its reopening' (Negri, 1999: 305).

> The constituent project is explicitly a creative project. Democracy as the 'absolute form' of government, as both Machiavelli and Spinoza define it, becomes an effectual possibility – that is, it transforms theoretical potentiality into a political project. The project is no longer that of making the political coincide with the social, but that of inserting the production of the political into the creation of the social. Democracy is the project of the multitude, a creative force, a living god. This is the second terrain of the historical continuity of the concept of constituent power. (Negri, 1999: 307)

In other words, the radical alternative that is unfolded by constituent power exists as a 'second nature', as a real, existing reversion of the status quo that is actualised in the constituent act. The 'living God' of democracy – the actual potentiality of the radical alternative – is the multitude's expression that realises its potentiality, so to speak, in the shadow of political reality, in order to unfold itself in the 'constitutive praxis' that coincides with the moment of rupture. These 'two terrains of historical continuity' reappear as the 'double temporality' of 'multitude' in Negri's later writings in collaboration with Hardt. Here, the distinction between 'empire' and 'multitude' – again derived from Spinoza's thought – is centred on the basis of a new analysis of the current world order. Leaving behind the classical Marxist conception of class society, 'multitude' is presented as a more comprehensive conception of political subjectivity. Rather than a ruling class that exploits the working class, 'empire' represents a worldwide network that manages and controls global relations of production, power and exchange. 'Multitude', on the other hand, is the inherently productive, heterogeneous and multifaceted counter-structure of empire. Its historical role is the creation of a 'counter-empire', which exists autonomously of empire as 'an alternative political organization of global flows and exchanges' (Hardt & Negri, 2000: xv).

Multitude's objective is both to 'contest and subvert empire', and simultaneously (and in fact, as part of the same practice), to 'construct a real alternative' to it. Multitude therefore exists both as this autonomous alternative structure in opposition to empire and as the potential new order that will topple and replace the old. In other words, it is both history and future. Hence, in reference to the famous syndicalist Industrial Workers of the World, the 'counter-empire' of multitude is frequently referred to as a 'new society within the shell of the old' (Hardt & Negri, 2000: 207; 2009: 8). As Hardt and Negri argue, a distinction could therefore be made between an 'ontological' and a 'political' multitude, the former of which

> is the multitude that, as Spinoza says, through reason and passions, in the complex interplay of historical forces, creates a freedom that he calls absolute: throughout history humans

have refused authority and command, expressed the irreducible difference of singularity, and sought freedom in innumerable revolts and revolutions. (Hardt & Negri, 2004: 221)

It will, however, 'require a political project' to bring this multitude into being, 'on the basis of these emerging conditions'. The former, in other words, is the multitude of the present, which is always 'already-there'; the latter, however, is its future, which is latent as potentiality, existing as a 'not-yet' (Hardt & Negri, 2004: 221–2). These 'two multitudes', however, mutually presuppose each other. After all, whereas the 'political project' of multitude can only be realised provided that this multitude is 'already latent and implicit in our social being', this potentiality fully depends for its existence on its immanent actualisation.

As we saw before in Negri's interpretation of *potentia*, therefore, there is a sense in which we cannot distinguish between potentiality and its actualisation: they have a logical equivalence in that they presuppose each other. Multitude, or – and one could argue that this is the same – the power of multitude, is prefigurative precisely because it cannot exist as a potentiality without actualisation. In other words, since multitude exists precisely as an active potentiality, it already exists simultaneously with the relations and structures it aims to alter, and thus prefigures its full potential in this actual existence. Prefiguration thus could be depicted as the 'unfolding' of a temporality that exists 'next to' the present. The 'here and now' aspect we earlier ascribed to our conception of prefiguration is particularly essential here. As Negri states in his writings on revolutionary times, the 'time of class struggle' cannot simply be defined as a 'negative time' that passes from one stage or status quo (in)to a future: 'It is also *prefigurative power*'. The future is, so to speak, enclosed in the practice of the 'now', in the imminence of *potentia* as a potential that is always actual. 'The time of class struggle', Negri therefore argues, 'in itself contains the future and it continually attempts to shape it' (Negri, 2005: 97; emphasis original).

Alongside this 'contemporaneity of the future and of the present', there is also a spatial element to prefigurative power. As Hardt and Negri repeatedly stress, Empire no longer has an 'outside' – in a territorial sense, as well as economically, politically and juridically. Strictly speaking, Empire has no spatial characteristics at all: it is rather an '*ou-topia*, or really a *non-place*' (Hardt & Negri, 2000: 190). Insofar as it is everywhere, Empire is nowhere, and as it cannot be pinned down to a specific territory or location: the inside–outside dialectic simply no longer works. In their preface to *Empire*, Hardt and Negri (2000: xv) therefore state that 'The struggles to contest and subvert Empire, as well as those to *construct a real alternative*, will thus take place *on the imperial terrain itself* – indeed, such new struggles have already begun to emerge' (emphasis added). Hence, a direct relationship is implied between the construction of an alternative and its foundation within the territory of Empire itself. Since we can neither properly speak of an 'outside' nor, therefore, of an 'inside', this resistance 'from inside', this realisation of a 'real alternative', entails the composition of a space rather than a mere occupation. Thus, in the very formation of opposition, constituent power effectively creates an 'outside' (that nevertheless is 'inside').

As Hardt and Negri (2000: 185) formulate it, the struggle against modern sovereignty and constituted power 'is situated *within* the historical evolution of the forms of power, *an inside that searches for an outside*'. Here, we can once more recognise strongly prefigurative characteristics – again, defined in terms of a 'here and now', but this time with an emphasis on the 'here'. This depiction of a process in which the active potentiality of an 'outside' is unfolded in the 'inside', I suggest, might be a fruitful way to grasp the prefigurative workings of constituent power. The realisation of the radical alternative in struggle, therefore, is not only a '*pre*figuration', in the (temporal) sense that it realises a future order in the reality of the present, since it is also an 'ex-figuration' or 'alter-figuration', the experimental figuration of a 'not-yet' potentiality, a (spatial) externality that comes from (and remains) within.

Hence, we can conclude that what we refer to as 'prefiguration' in the context of (Hardt and) Negri's thought is the historical process of development of *potentia* or constituent power, seen from a perspective in which the 'historical continuities' of this power – or the 'double temporality of multitude' – are understood to be convergent; 'prefiguration' is neither the mere implementation of a potency that exists as a 'not-yet', nor solely the accumulation of power as a 'political project', but the creation of an 'outside' which remains 'inside', in which the potentiality of multitude *exists as* its power. We will return to this conceptualisation of prefigurative power in the context of 'the common'.

John Holloway – another political thinker often associated with autonomist Marxism, but whose work in several respects offers a substantial critique to that of Negri (and Hardt) establishes 'power-to' as an alternative conception to power 'from below', which in fact is more explicitly related to prefiguration. Although there are as many similarities as differences between Holloway's thought and Hardt and Negri's, we will concentrate on the latter here.

Power-to and power-over

Contrary to what might be inferred from the title of John Hollo-way's ([2002] 2010a) *Change the World without Taking Power*, the author does not entirely reject 'power' or its role in the revolutionary process. One of his central arguments, rather, is that a distinction should be made between what he refers to as 'power-to' and 'power-over':

> Power, in the first place, is simply that: can-ness, capacity-to-do, the ability to do things. Doing implies power, power-to-do. In this sense we commonly use 'power' to refer to something good … Whereas power-to is a uniting, a bringing together of my doing with the doing of others, the exercise of power-over is a separation. … Power-over is the breaking of the social flow of doing. Those who exert power over the doing of others deny the subjectivity of those others, deny their part in the flow of doing, exclude them from history. (Holloway, 2010a: 28–9)

Holloway suggests, therefore, that the world can be changed without taking power-over. At first sight, it may be tempting to equate the distinction between power-to and power-over with (Hardt and) Negri's *potentia* vs. *potestas* (or constituent power vs. constituted power). Holloway (2010a: 169) indeed stresses that his position and Negri's bear strong resemblances, in particular with respect to the centrality of oppositional struggle in their thought, and their rejection of state power as a revolutionary means. There are some substantial differences, however. Clearly, *potentia* and power-to are both conceptualised as a power 'from below', formulated in terms of 'doing' rather than a static 'being', and therefore based on, as well as directed to, a political practice of resistance that takes place in reality; it is in relation to the 'other' power, the power 'from above', that the difference between *potentia* and power-to becomes apparent. In Holloway's account, power-to and power-over are more closely related than Negri's terminology suggests. Therefore, Holloway (2010a: 36) states,

> posing the distinctions in … terms [of 'potentia' and 'potestas'] can be seen as pointing merely to a difference whereas what is at issue is an antagonism, or rather, an antagonist metamorphosis. Power-to exists as power-over, but the power-to is subjected to and in rebellion against power-over, and power-over is nothing but, and therefore absolutely dependent upon, the metamorphosis of power-to.

In other words, power-to and power-over are different sides of the same coin, rather than essentially different forms of power. Power-over is the alienated – or, to apply Holloway's terminology, 'fetishised' – form of power-to. As we have seen, Holloway defines power-to in terms of a capacity, an 'ability to-do'. Power-over in capitalist society, Holloway argues, exists as the breaking of this capacity, of the 'flow of doing', and the division between this 'doing' and the 'done'.[3] Hence, the relation between these forms of power, which exists as a breaking or 'metamorphosis', is rather different from the antagonism between *potentia* and *potestas*. Indeed, Holloway (2010a: 41) argues,

> the relation between constituent and constituted power remains an external one. Constitution (the transformation of constituent into constituted power) is seen as a reaction to the democratic constituent power of the multitude … In the face of power-over

(constituted power) it tells us of the ubiquity and force of the absolute struggle of the multitude, but it tells us nothing of the crucial nexus of dependence of power-over (constituted power) upon power-to (constituent power). In this sense, for all the force and brilliance of his account, Negri remains at the level of radical-democratic theory.

Here we come to a central argument, in which Holloway clearly distances himself from what he refers to as the 'autonomist' current. Holloway praises the operaist Mario Tronti, not only for stressing the need to centralise struggle itself in our analysis of capitalist relations of power and production, but also, in Holloway's (2010a: 160) words, for 'seeing working-class struggle as determining capitalist development'. So far, as Tronti argues in his famous article 'Lenin in England',

> [We] have worked with a concept that puts capitalist develop-ment first, and workers second. This is a mistake. And now we have to turn the problem on its head, reverse the polarity, and start again from the beginning: and the beginning is the class struggle of the working class. (Tronti, 1979: 1)

Departing from Tronti's argument, Holloway agrees that later, in its further development, autonomism may have been meritorious in insisting on 'seeing the movement of capitalist rule as being driven by the force of working class struggle'; even so, autonomists like Hardt and Negri only tend to understand capital as a 'function of the working class', rather than as its 'product' (Holloway, 2010a: 165). Hardt and Negri may question the theoretical separation between capital in its development and class struggle as made in 'traditional' Marxism. Nevertheless, Holloway (2010b: 190) argues, in their thought, the 'categories themselves are never understood as conceptualizations of struggle, so that the externality remains'.[4] In other words, capital, in Holloway's view, does not just develop autonomously in an attempt to defend itself against the constant pressure of the extending power of a working class, but fully comes forth from and is therefore (nothing but) an alienated form of this working class itself – rather than a 'function', which nevertheless remains external to it.[5]

A comparable shortcoming appears in Negri's distinction between *potentia* and *potestas*, Holloway argues, with the relation between the two treated as external to the conception of power itself. Negri's *potentia* and *potestas* are essentially different concepts of power and cannot be reduced to each other, while Holloway's power-to and power-over are intimately connected; whereas Negri ascribes a certain autonomy to *potentia* or constituent power, Holloway rejects its inherent 'positivity', and stresses that power-to can only be negatively related to its alienated form of power-over, which is actively resisted by the former. Power-to, therefore, is a frustrated or repressed (one could even say self-repressed) capacity. It is a potentiality that can only be actualised by overcoming its alienated form. Nevertheless, this 'can-ness', the 'unalienated doing', does in fact exist, 'as present antagonism to its denial, as present projection-beyond-its-denial-to-a-different world, as a presently not-yet' (Holloway, 2010a: 35).

Here we come to Holloway's conception of 'prefiguration'. Since power-to is a potentiality that is alienated *as and by* power-over, it can only be realised in a confrontation with the latter. In other words, the confrontation against power-over and the development of potential, which is depicted by Holloway as 'the emancipation of power-to', are one and the same process. This process is what he, in turn, refers to as 'prefigurative':

> The most liberating struggles, however, are surely those in which the two are consciously linked, as in those struggles which are consciously prefigurative, in which the struggle aims, in its form, not to reproduce the structures and practices of that which is struggled against, but rather to create the sort of social relations which are desired. (Holloway, 2010a: 153–4)

In *Crack Capitalism*, Holloway (2010b) concretises this depiction of a prefigurative struggle against capital. As its title suggests, the breaking of capitalism, and therefore the release, so to speak, of a power-to that is repressed behind it, requires a 'method of the crack': the continuous breaking open of already existing cracks in the plastering of capitalist order. The widening of these cracks is an 'opening of a world that presents itself as closed' (Holloway, 2010b: 9), which, in other words, existed already as a potentiality, but needs to be actualised. Throughout Holloway's writings, innumerable examples of these 'cracks' are given: from the more standard means in activist repertoires (squats, social centres, 'Temporary Autonomous Zones', demonstrations or 'reclaim the streets', raves, etc.), and the 'highlights' of historical revolutionary movements (the Paris Commune, liberated regions in Chiapas, the Argentinean revolts of December 2001, etc.) to the everyday (community gardens, alternative consumption patterns, the small acts of refusal in our everyday lives).

Thus, 'the crack' in fact is a spatio-temporal depiction of a prefigurative practice. According to Holloway, it should 'not be seen as a means to an end', since 'there is always an insufficiency about it, an incompleteness, a restlessness'. In other words, the crack is not a means that has its ends external to it but rather something that internalises the end and aims at realising it there and then, if only in a limited time and/or space. 'Prefiguration', or the creation of 'cracks', in Holloway's account, is not the creation of a durable structure so much as a spatio-temporal experiment with its alternative. As Holloway (2010b: 35) argues, a 'crack is not a step on the path of Revolution, but it is an opening outwards'. These momentous disruptions have 'a validity of their own', when, so to speak, looked at from a non-linear perspective, and are 'independent of their long-term consequences'. This validity consists of the durable impression of a 'different world' in its unalienated form, which is unveiled for a moment in the prefigurative practices that fill the 'cracks' in capitalist order:

> Like a flash of lightning, they illuminate a different world, a world created perhaps for a few short hours, but the impression which remains on our brain and in our senses is that of an image of the world we can (and did) create. The world that does not yet exist displays itself as a world that exists not-yet. (Holloway, 2010b: 30–31)

Hence, I conclude, 'prefiguration' in Holloway's account is the construction of a 'beyond'. It is an experimental practice, but one that sets an example, or empowers, and enables one to realise that a different world is possible – before this can-ness falls back into its alienated form as power-over. In the moment of prefiguration, power-to reaches beyond the order it wishes to negate.

Power-to and potentia: a comparison

Let us now compare Negri's conception of *potentia* or constituted power in relation to prefiguration, with the prefigurative account of Holloway's power-to as reconstructed. On Holloway's account, prefiguration is the act that projects 'beyond' itself, and sheds a light of and over the future; for Negri, on the other hand, it is rather the unfolding of this future 'inside' the present. The power that realises the beyond that is prefigured in Holloway's depiction is an alienated potentiality losing its alienated form. The prefiguration of power-to is its actualisation in time and space, its realisation in practice. In the case of *potentia*, on the other hand, we cannot speak in terms of actualisation, since, as we have seen before, in Negri's conceptualisation of *potentia* there is no difference between essence and existence, no theoretical account of power as a 'possibility'. Moreover, unlike power-to, *potentia* is not the unalienated form of its radical counterpart; rather than existing in the 'cracks' of capital, 'constituent power' leads a parallel life with respect to constituted Power' (Casaroni & Negri, 2008: 157). Thus, we can conclude that whereas for Negri prefiguration through *potentia* is the unfolding of an outside in the inside of political time and space, Holloway depicts prefiguration through power-to as an event of actualisation, a moment in which its radical potential is realised.

Both Negri and Holloway refer to the radical alternative as a 'not-yet', but whereas in Holloway's account this 'not-yet' is an alienated and repressed potentiality – the passive potentiality of the 'beyond' – for Negri this 'not-yet' is backed, so to speak, by an *autonomous* 'already-there' potential in a rather active form: the active potentiality of an 'outside' that is 'inside'. We could, therefore, conclude that in Holloway, power exists *in* potentiality, whereas for Negri potentiality *is* power. In the former case, power as power-to becomes prefigurative in its realisation; in the latter, power as *potentia* is prefigurative – and for Negri it is the power as *potentia* that both accumulates and exists as practice in the present, whereas in Holloway's conception of power-to, power may become practice in (or after) its liberation.

Now, what consequences do this – rather theoretical – distinction between Negri's *potentia* and Holloway's power-to have for our conceptualisation of prefiguration in practice? In the following section, we will make one last theoretical step, applying the distinction developed above within the context of production of the common. The aim of this further elaboration will be to show how this theoretical distinction regarding prefigurative power between Negri and Holloway eventually leads to a significant divergence in their understanding of (the possibilities of) resistance against global capitalism.

Commons or the common?

Despite its central position in their more recent work, Hardt and Negri's exact definition of the common remains relatively vague, particularly concerning its relation to the 'commons' (plural). In the introduction to *Multitude*, it is suggested that the difference between the two is historical rather than semantic. Originally 'commons' refers to pre-capitalist, collectively used and/or (cultivated) natural resources, whereas the process of commonisation described by Hardt and Negri (2004: xv) is 'not a return to the past, but a new development' – besides, as they state without much further explanation, '"the common" highlights the philosophical content of the term'. In a later article, however, Hardt further defines this distinction in terms of 'artificiality'. Apart from the natural resources traditionally referred to as 'commons', 'the common' more broadly also encompasses the (immaterial) fruits of biopolitical production:

> On the one hand, the common names the earth and all the resources associated with it: the land, forests, water, air, minerals, and so forth. This is closely related to seventeenth-century English usage of 'the commons' (with an 's'). On the other hand, the common also refers … to the results of human labor and creativity such as ideas, language, affects, and so forth. You might think of the former as the 'natural' common and the latter as the 'artificial' common, but really such divisions between natural and artificial quickly break down. (Hardt, 2010: 350)

Although leaving us empty-handed, Hardt's formulation suggests that a distinction between commons and the common should be drawn on the basis of a paradigmatic difference in form of production. One of the central developments described by Hardt and Negri throughout their work comprehends the 'immaterialisation' of labour, or the 'commonisation' of production processes: ideas, networks, concepts and communication structures have gradually become the products of labour, whose centrality in contemporary economic production has converted the dominant relations of power and property, as well as the role and form of both productive and everyday ('private') life. Indeed, the definition of the common should (at least partly) be formulated in terms of these developments, rather than a natural–artificial distinction:

> This notion of the common does not position humanity separate from nature, as either its exploiter or its custodian, but focuses rather on the practices of interaction, care, and cohabitation in a common world, promoting the beneficial and limiting the detrimental forms of the common. In the era of globalization, issues of the maintenance, production, and distribution of the common in both senses and in both ecological and socioeconomic frameworks becomes increasingly central. (Hardt & Negri, 2009: viii)

The question remains, however, of what would make a suitable criterion for such a distinction. Perhaps commons and the common could be distinguished on the basis of Donald Nonini's (2007: 7) 'natural and social commons' and 'intellectual and cultural commons', where the former are depletable and subtractive, and the latter are 'non-rival goods' that can be 'created and regenerated *only* through social exchange and sociability'. Applying these differences in a distinction between commons and the common leads us to define singular resources as commons, not taking 'artificiality' as a criterion but rather exhaustibility and numerical limitedness. The common, in its turn, comprehends commons as well as those resources that are characterised by the inclusion of production and consumption in a single social process. This implies – and here we finally get to the core of the distinction – that whereas the commons could be defined as a plurality of more or less distinctive recourses, practices and processes, the common is an indivisible whole of social relations, concepts and forms of life. Therefore, the best way to describe the relation between these two concepts is, perhaps, to depict commons as particulars of the common – which is precisely why Hardt and Negri decided not to use the former notion at all.[6]

It is striking that whereas Hardt and Negri refer exclusively to 'the common', Holloway refers to 'commons'. Although this concept does not play a central role in his writings, Holloway does refer to commons as exemplifying cracks in capitalism, which is the point from which our comparison can depart:

> The commons can be seen as the embryonic form of a new society … These common areas, at least to the extent that there is genuine social control and not just state ownership, can be seen as so many cracks in the domination of capital, so many no-go areas where the writ of capital does not run, gashes in the weave of domination. Or rather: if capital is a movement of enclosing, the commons are a disjointed common-ing, a moving in the opposite direction, a refusing of enclosure, at least in particular areas. (Holloway, 2010b: 29–30)

Thus, in his reference to 'commons', Holloway means to describe a broad plurality of practices that develop independently and 'outside' of capitalist structures and relations, to 'cut off an area and put up signs all around it saying, "Capital, keep out!"' (Holloway, 2010b: 28). The commons Holloway refers to are examples of such struggles in which 'the other-doing is very much to the fore' and hence struggles in which the creation of a radical alternative coincides with struggle against capital. In effect, we are back at the definition of prefiguration we started with: Holloway's commons are examples of prefigurative practices in which the distinction between means and ends are dissolved within a 'here and now' practice.

Holloway tends to view resistance as a multitude of everyday-life practices, some of which may not appear very radical at first sight. 'Rebellion', argues Holloway (2010b: 169), 'is always an option, but much more than that, it is an integral part of life'. This argument leads him to an extremely inclusive and simplifying conception of struggle, in which even the decision to read a book in the park (instead of going to work) may easily equal the armed struggle of a guerrilla fighter in the Mexican jungle: as far as Holloway (2010b: 4–5) is concerned, these are both examples of a real, existing resistance. Moreover, even though these examples are presented as forms of struggle that are connected, a strong ahistorical individualism lurks in Holloway's analysis. Of course, one can only appreciate the absence of a 'greater plan' – either historically or politically – in post-totalitarian radical theory. Holloway's prefigurative perspective is indeed valuable in this respect. However, when resistance is depicted as 'doing our own thing, as expressing ourselves' or 'creating small projects', as Holloway (2010b: 248) does, politics becomes limited to an unconnected whole of mere stances and attitudes. The question remains, however, of how these struggles are related to one another. For Holloway, we may find a solution here in the relations of affinity:

It may seem strange to place the car worker who goes to his allotment in the evening next to the young man who goes to the jungle to devote his life to organising armed struggle against capitalism. And yet there is a continuity. What both have in common is that they share in a movement of refusal-and-other-creation: they are rebels, not victims; subjects, not objects. In the case of the car worker, it is individual and just evenings and weekends; in the case of the young man in the jungle, it is a very perilous commitment to a life of rebellion. Very different and yet with a line of affinity that it would be very wrong to overlook. (Holloway, 2010b: 6)

However, apart from this vague appellation to a 'logic of affinity' (Day, 2005), Holloway hardly explains what the 'continuity' consists of. Actually, the relationship between different forms and practices of struggle and resistance only exists on a rather idealistic plane. In practice, as Holloway has argued in the preceding description of 'the commons', these singular, separable practices may relate to each other, or share strong similarities, but they do not converge into a broader whole – indeed, as he formulates it, they are only parts of 'a *disjointed common-ing* … a refusing of enclosure, at least in particular areas' (Holloway, 2010b: 30; emphasis added).

Hardt and Negri struggle with the same problem. As Ernesto Laclau (2005: 241) has argued, what is lacking in their description of the struggle between empire and multitude is any account of political articulation between divergent forms and practices of resistance. Indeed, early on in *Empire*, Hardt and Negri (2004: 54) state that multitude's different struggles have become 'incommunicable'. They thereby not only fail to acknowledge that for the multitude to be politically successful, it needs its many different, globally spread struggles to correlate, but, and on the contrary, indicate that this is not possible, or at least has become so. However, as Andy Knott argues, Hardt and Negri gradually revoke this 'incommunicability thesis' throughout the *Empire* trilogy. Already in the latter part of *Empire*, and certainly in *Multitude*, they suggest that multitude's struggle against empire can only become political once such a communicability between different struggles and practices is constructed. And finally, in

Commonwealth, Knott (2011: 201–5) suggests, Hardt and Negri attempt to deal with this problem by presenting precisely the common as that (in) which these struggles share – and which, therefore, binds them together.

Thus, although both Holloway's and Hardt and Negri's understanding of political struggle depart from a broad diversity of practices and resistances – rather than a single, centralised and homogeneous political or historical project – the conceptualisations of commons and the common as explicated here reveal how their positions diverge in their understanding of resistance to capitalist structures/relations. Let us briefly elaborate on this point, by outlining this essential distinction in more detail.

The 'cracks' in the texture of capitalism that Holloway refers to function primarily to widen, expand and connect practices of resistance to capital's enclosure. These cracks, in other words, are openings within a texture that is not their own – they are disconnected practices of de-alienation on the surface of relations and structures that are antagonistically opposed to them, but which, at the same time, are their own alienated forms. In other words, 'cracks' – and therefore commons (among other forms of resistance) – are the voids in the texture of capital. They cannot be ascribed any positive autonomy, any externality to the very structures they aim to subvert and alter. Moreover, it remains unclear how Holloway understands these different commons to communicate and collaborate with each other – all these separate practices of resistance share is the texture in which they perform as cracks, and not the ways in which this 'cracking' takes place.

In Hardt and Negri, on the other hand, the common *is* the texture – or, better perhaps, the 'matter' – of multitude: the development of multitude and the common are tightly inter-woven. Therefore, rather than a mere whole of distinctive practices, the common is precisely that (in) which these many different practices share, in which they take place. The production of multitude is a process of the common, which is both a means of production and its product, the structure that results from it. In other words, 'the common is both precondition and result of the production of the multitude'; it is the material of an experimental prefigurative project, but simultaneously it is its own model (Hardt & Negri, 2004: 339, 349); and, most importantly, it is therefore autonomous from and external to the capitalist structures and relations which, in their turn, try to intervene, break into and gain control over the processes and practices of commonisation.

Hence, whereas Holloway's commons are the prefigurative moments within the structure of capital that reach 'beyond' it, Hardt and Negri's common forms – and consists of – its 'outside', the already-present future that is an active potentiality. The prefigured and prefigurative common, in other words, is more than the illuminated contours of a future alternative; it is its real existing form in the 'here and now'. The commons, so to speak, are the anticipating and voluntarist forms of a prefigured future, while the common, far from being an anticipation, is the actual condition for revolutionary change, not merely a perspective on the future, but rather this already-existing future itself. Notwithstanding their rejection of dialectics and teleology, Hardt and Negri ascribe a historical role to the common – a role it already fulfils, of course – in its 'growing separation from capitalist exploitation and command'. Again, in reference to the organisation and extension of the common, Hardt and Negri

(2009: 301) invoke the image of 'a new society within the shell of the old'.

Conclusion: the prefigurative power of the common(s)

Four theoretical steps have been made here. First, I distilled a definition of 'prefiguration' from contemporary autonomist theory. 'Prefiguration' was defined as a practice in which 'means and ends' are considered to be mirrored in practice itself, and prefigurative practices were characterised by a strong orientation to the 'here and now', as they question the temporal distinction between a present struggle and the future goals it strives to realise. This concept of prefiguration was then applied to two understandings of power 'from below': first, Negri's concept of *potentia* or constituent power and, second, Holloway's notion of power-to. I reformulated and compared these concepts as divergent prefigurative understandings of power. In power-to, prefiguration is the realisation of a power that pre-existed in an alienated form, and which, in the act, shows its potential through actualisation. In the case of *potentia*, on the other hand, we can perceive a wholly different understanding of prefiguration as process, one in which the active potential is always 'already-there'. Through its development over time, *potentia* increasingly exists as an alternative external to and autonomous from the structures it struggles against. In other words, whereas power-to is prefigurative in the sense that it experimentally shows the possibility of a radical alternative, *potentia* directly and sustainably forms – and therefore prefigures – this alternative in the here and now.

The final step related Hardt/Negri and Holloway's divergence on the issues of power and prefiguration to a conceptual distinction between commons and the common. Holloway conceptualises 'commons' as (just) unconnected – 'disjointed' – cracks in the surface of capitalism, thereby realising spatio-temporal breaks and ruptures in its functioning. Hardt and Negri, on the other hand, involve the common as a means to overcome this 'disjointedness' or 'incommunicability' between different struggles. Hence, the division between 'commons' in Holloway and 'the common' in Hardt and Negri develops along the same lines as that between 'power-to' and *potentia*. Whereas in Holloway, commons are the moments in which power-to actualises itself, in Hardt and Negri, the production of the common and the development of *potentia* are one and the same:

> Accumulation of the common means not so much that we have more ideas, more images, more affects, and so forth but, more important, that our powers and senses increase: our powers to think, to feel, to see, to relate to one another, to love. In terms closer to those of economics, then, this growth involves both an increasing stock of the common accessible in society and also an increased productive capacity based on the common. (Hardt & Negri, 2009: 283)

This leads us to two different conclusions. First, in a political conceptualisation of prefiguration, what we need is a criterion that binds divergent forms of struggle and resistances together. This element is clearly missing both in the anarchist ethico-political formulation in terms of a means-and-ends distinction and in Holloway's perspective on power-to and its actualisation through the cracks in the structures of capitalism. This is just what is provided by Hardt and Negri, expressed as the common that lays the relations between widely different struggles.

But in Hardt and Negri's perspective, a convincing explanation of *how* the already-there is actualised in a political struggle is lacking. It remains unclear, that is, how multitude's struggle against empire finds articulation in practice. Therefore, and this is our second conclusion, such a conceptualisation of the common as a plane of prefigurative processes – as that which binds together struggles and resistances against capitalism and thereby politicises them – demands a more elaborate formulation of the politico-historical role of the common, and a more detailed understanding of how this binding together, this taking part of different struggles in the common, takes place in practice. The concept of 'prefiguration', I argue, could fulfil a key role in this further conceptualisation, as it encompasses a practical approach to struggle and resistance, a conception of power 'from below', and an understanding of the common as that which both creates and simultaneously exists as the alternative to capitalist structures from within.

Notes

1   Maeckelbergh (2009: 115) in fact touches upon this problem in her definition of 'prefigurative power'.

2   In the foreword to his translation of *The Savage Anomaly*, Michael Hardt stresses that the Italian distinction between *potere* (*potestas*) and *potenza* (*potentia*) (in French: *pouvoir* and *puissance*; in German *Macht* and *Vermögen*) cannot be made in English. As a reference to *potestas* he therefore writes 'Power' with a capital 'P', whereas 'power' stands for *potential* (see Hardt, 1991: xi–xii).

3   This division is the transformation from an active doing to a passive, which is labour. For a more elaborate development of this position, see Holloway's (2010b) *Crack Capitalism*.

4   In fact, Negri suggests that this externality gradually follows from class struggle. In response to Holloway's argument that the operaist movement developed a 'functionalist' perspective of the relationship between class struggle and capital, Negri (2010) argues the following: 'With respect to this presumed functionalism, *operaismo* simply turns this picture upside down; the antagonistic pressure of the force of labor (exactly because dialectics was pushed aside) does not avoid but rather deepens the contradictions. This deepening of contradictions has two effects. The first is to accentuate the consistency of the subjects (i.e. labor force, proletariat, class, multitude) and to impress upon this subjective reality a continual process of metamorphosis, a dispositive of ontological transformation. Second, and consequently, there arises the effect of pushing the subject (labor force, proletariat, class, multitude) each time further outside of capital – exodus is precisely the result of this process. It is a process nonetheless, a struggle, not a utopia, an indefinite lineage, not one that has been concluded, real, not dreamed.' Hence, the 'positivity' or externality is never a given, but exactly the relation that comes forth from (or is constructed in) struggle itself.

5   Note that at the backdrop of these differences between Holloway's and Negri's analyses, one can perceive a significant contrast on a more ontological level: whereas Holloway thinks from a strongly Hegelian–Marxist (and, hence, dialectical) perspective, Negri departs from a Spinozist approach.

6   It needs to be stressed, however, that the term 'particulars' in this context is far from unproblematic. As Hardt and Negri argue in *Commonwealth*, 'The common cuts diagonally across the opposition between the universal and the particular. Normal usage of the terms "common sense" and "common knowledge" captures some of what we have in mind insofar as they extend beyond the limitations of the particular and grasp a certain social generality, but these terms generally view the common as something passive, already given in society. We concentrate instead, following Spinoza's conception of "common notions," on the production and productivity of the common through collective social practices' (Hardt & Negri, 2009: 120–21).

Hence, my depiction of 'commons' as the particulars of 'the common' depends heavily on quite what Hardt and Negri intend by 'diagonally'.

References

Breines, W. (1982). *Community and Organisation and the New Left 1962–1968, The Great Refusal*. South Hadley: J. F. Bergin/ New York: Praeger.

Casaroni, C. and Negri, A. (2008). *In Praise of the Common: A Conversation of Philosophy and Politics*. Minneapolis: Minnesota University Press.

Day, R. (2005). *Gramsci is Dead: Anarchist Currents in the Newest Social Movements*. London: Pluto Press.

De Spinoza, B. (1955). 'The Ethics', in *On the Improvement of Understanding/The Ethics/Correspondence* (trans. R. Elwes). Mineola, NY: Dover.

Franks, B. (2003). 'The direct action ethic from 59 upwards', *Anarchist Studies*, 11(1): 13–41.

Franks, B. (2006). *Rebel Alliances, the Means and Ends of Contemporary British Anarchism*. Edinburgh: AK Press.

Gordon, U. (2008). *Anarchy Alive! Anti-Authoritarian Politics from Practice to Theory*. London: Pluto Press.

Graeber, D. (2009). *Direct Action, an Ethnography*. Edinburgh: AK Press.

Hardt, M. (1991). 'The anatomy of power', in *The Savage Anomaly: The Power of Spinoza's Metaphysics and Politics* (trans. M. Hardt). Minneapolis: University of Minnesota Press.

Hardt, M. (2010). 'The common in communism', *Rethinking Marxism*, 22(3): 346–356.

Hardt, M. and Negri, A. (2000). *Empire*. Cambridge, MA: Harvard University Press.

Hardt, M. and Negri, A. (2004). *Multitude: War and Democracy in the Age of Empire*. London/New York: Penguin.

Hardt, M. and Negri, A. (2009). *Commonwealth*. Cambridge, MA: Belknap Press.

Holloway, J. ([2002] 2010a). *Change the World without Taking Power*. London: Pluto Press.

Holloway, J. (2010b). *Crack Capitalism*. London: Pluto Press.

Klein, E. (2011). 'You're creating a vision of the sort of society you want to have in miniature', *The Washington Post*. At http://www.washingtonpost.com/blogs/ezra-klein/

Knott, A. (2011). 'Multitude and hegemony' (PhD thesis). Brighton.

Laclau, E. (2005). *On Populist Reason*. London: Verso.

Maeckelbergh, M. (2009). *The Will of the Many, How the Alterglobalisation Movement is Changing the Face of Democracy*. London: Pluto Press.

Negri, A. (1991). *The Savage Anomaly, the Power of Spinoza's Metaphysics and Politics* (trans. M. Hardt). Minneapolis: Minnesota University Press.

Negri, A. (1999). *Insurgencies, Constituent Power and the Modern State* (trans. M. Boscagli). Minneapolis: Minnesota University Press.

Negri, A. (2004). 'The *Political Treatise*, or, the foundation of modern democracy', in T. Murphy (Ed.), *Subversive Spinoza, (un) Contemporary Variations* (trans. T. Murphy, M. Hardt, T. Stolze and C. Wolfe). Manchester: Manchester University Press.

Negri, A. (2005). *Time for Revolution* (trans. M. Mandarini). London: Continuum.

Negri, T. (2010). 'John Holloway's change the world without taking power'. At http://antonionegriinenglish.wordpress.com/

Nonini, D. (2007). 'Introduction: the global idea of "the commons"', in D. Nonini (Ed.), *The Global Idea of 'The Commons'*. New York/Oxford: Berghahn.

Polletta, F. (2002). *Freedom is an Endless Meeting: Democracy in American Social Movements*. Chicago: University of Chicago Press

Tronti, M. (1979). 'Lenin in England', in *Red Notes, Working Class Autonomy and the Crisis: Italian Marxist Texts of the Theory and Practice of a Class Movement: 1964–79. London*: CSE Books.

Van de Sande, M. (2013). 'The prefigurative politics of Tahrir Square – an alternative perspective on the 2011 revolutions', *Res Publica*, 19(3): 223–239.

Chapter 2

Realising the common: the assembly as organising structure[1]

Elise Thorburn

Introduction

In the fallout from the financial crisis of 2008, there was a moment of silence. When global financial services firm Lehman Brothers folded, filing for Chapter 11 bankruptcy protection in the wee hours of 15 September 2008, it seemed that the left held its collective breath. And as the financial crisis – coming on the heels of a burst housing bubble in 2006 and a global food price crisis in 2007 – spiralled, the imagined spontaneity of multitude that Hardt and Negri (2000, 2004) had ecstatically theorised at the turn of the century did not immediately appear. History, it seemed, was not on the radical left's side. Or perhaps the left simply lacked organisation, the appropriate structures to realise its politics at this adventitious moment. Indeed, it is neither unkind nor unfair to assert that in the aftermath of the economic crisis, for a period, all was quiet on one front of the class war. Labour did not engage while capital furiously raged against the working class, reshaping the world in its own favour even as it entered the twilight of neoliberalism.

In times past, until the 1980s and the neoliberal reordering, the unions had provided the dominant mode of organisation for the left; however, this was rooted in heavy industry and the composition of the working class in previous eras. Now, by 2008, thrust into the interstices of a crumbling economy, many of those living in the United States and Canada were struggling to survive on low-paid part-time jobs in the retail and service sector and in an ever weaker labour movement (indeed, many more quickly became part of this increasingly disposable working class in the economic aftermath of the financial crisis). Thus, while the decade leading up to the crisis, and its aftermath, had seen cycles of struggles – including the 2006 immigrants' rights marches that brought half a million demonstrators onto the streets in Los Angeles (and more across the US) and an anti-war movement that brought millions of people onto the streets on a single weekend[2] – these were generally not driven by or even had the mass participation of organised labour or radical parties of the left as an institutional bedrock. In fact, something new and experimental was emerging, something that also finally enabled the radical left's response to the post-2008 period, which began with the Occupy Wall Street protest.

In many ways, the Occupy movement that grew from the Wall Street action epitomised the experimentation with new forms of organisation. Centred on shared labour and struggle, this was an amorphous body attempting to challenge the hegemony of financial capital whilst simultaneously attempting to create a reproductive common.[3] Occupy was both the result of transformative politics coming from the struggles of 1968 and earlier experiments in bottom-up organising and also a particular response to the shifting political and technical composition of the contemporary North American working class, referred to by terms such as the 'global worker' (Dyer-Witheford, 2010) as well as Hardt and Negri's (2000, 2009) 'multitude'.

The Occupy movement was only one example of a proliferation of experiments in organisational structure that have been taking place quietly – and not so quietly – across the landscape of North America, Europe, North Africa and Latin America over the last several years. In this chapter, because it is the context in which I live and work, I will focus my attention on the experiments taking place in North America.[4] This is not, however, to mistake the North American situation for an isolated or even unique one. From the international exposure and extension of Occupy in 2010–11, the model of the assembly has been expressed globally, in projects of a similar infrastructure in the squares, for example, of Athens and Madrid, and outside the West.[5] In short, the radical proliferation of assembly projects across the globe points to an emergent mode of organising in a new era of class composition. Appearing to prefigure a possible infrastructure of the common, this asserts a new organisational form with historical precedent but unique to this particular historical conjuncture.

The assembly as the organising model of the common escapes the nexus of party/union that is particular to most organising throughout the history of capitalism – which is not to suggest that these models are dead, but rather that new experiments are necessary to bring new subjects into revolutionary organising. In this contemporary moment, old political concepts and practices – such as the vanguard party and the masses – may *not* be permitted to re-emerge as hegemonic and disrupt or co-opt the struggles of the working classes from below. This moment allows us to examine that which Negri sought to illuminate in his discussion of the transition from the mass worker to the social worker in his analysis of class composition: a framework of incipient new values, existing at a mass level, able to repurpose dissent into a new model for the construction of a communist future (Negri, 1989). In this article, I propose that the assembly is an emergent mode of organising in the contemporary class composition. I seek to analyse this emergent mode in detail through the model of the Greater Toronto Workers' Assembly (GTWA), as an example of a political organisation attempting to contend with the changed class composition of the contemporary mode of capitalist production.

Class composition is a dissident adaptation of Marx's organic composition of capital, as discussed in Volume 1 of *Capital*. The organic composition of capital is the ratio of constant capital to variable capital in production or, more clearly, the correlation of materials, tools and machines for production and the labour power or workers necessary in that production.[6] Class composition, however, represents at a theoretical level the central, historical importance of class struggle. It is the combination of political and material characteristics that make up, on the one hand, the historically given structure of labour power as configured by the productive forces and relations occurring within capitalism, and, on the other that working class as a dynamic subject and antagonistic force, which is 'tending towards its own independent identity in historical-political terms' (Negri, 1989: 209). It refers to 'the process of socialisation of the working class, and the extension, unification, and generalisation of its *antagonistic tendency against capital*, in struggle, and *from below*' (Negri, 1991: xi); and it defines the power and organisation of labour as it is configured antagonistically in relation to capital.

Class composition is also the way in which the technical composition of labour (the capitalist organisation of labour power) corresponds to various behaviour patterns constituting particular openings amongst workers, which then permits a reading of the forms of action and organisation possible at various historical conjunctures (Negri, 1991; Cleaver, 1998; Nunes, 2007). It follows, therefore, that forms of struggle are expressed in terms of a particular composition of the working class, and that the specific historical forms of struggle depend upon the conditions of production. For activists, this means that the form or structure of organising class struggle changes alongside changes in the composition of the working class – how one can organise is itself dependent upon the primacy of certain configurations of capital within capitalism. Class composition and the attendant modes of organising are transitory. As struggle pushes capital to change, so class composition and organisational models change with it.

In certain transitory periods, workers go beyond old organisational models – for example, with syndicalism in response to Fordism – but in the still current period of neoliberal globalisation, they had not, until recently, 'reached a new organisation in a vacuum of political organisation' (Tronti, in Roggero, 2011). Now, at the present conjuncture, I suggest, previously prevailing modes of organising the class struggle – particularly the party model, both revolutionary and parliamentary, and the bureaucratic trade union model – should no longer be considered the exclusive representative or hegemonic form of working class struggle. We have passed through the 'vacuum' stage of political organising and a new political institution, that of the assembly, is emerging.[7]

The assembly as it is constituted today – especially in the various Occupy movements, the Quebec student strike, square seizures and public protests against austerity and state power – is explicitly *not* the general assembly of various institutional (e.g. state and parliamentary) bodies, for those are the forms of representative politics; nor, for that matter, is it the assembly of the union, which also operates in terms of power exclusion (with a hierarchy of representation). The contemporary assembly rejects the politics of simple representation and rather seeks to describe and build an actually existent political organisation of the common; it moves beyond multitude, what Hardt and Negri saw as the class composition in a regime of biopolitical production – the new nature of productive labour, which moves away from mass production in a factory setting and is centred around more immaterial modes of the production of surplus value (Hardt & Negri, 2000) – but which was, I believe, a phase of transition.

Multitude as described by Hardt and Negri is lacking. I contend that a description of and impetus to class struggle through a detailed discussion of the assembly form can flesh out, expand and move beyond multitude as a concept by providing us with a framework for thinking new modes and forms of class struggle in the present. In an era of ever-increasing austerity and intensified class warfare, the attempt to evince a coherent, non-authoritarian communism capable of producing the common must be simultaneous with the search for a new institutional and political form that is up to the task of such a long-term project and programme. This new political form must be able to reconstitute and organise the nodes in varying circuits of struggle, so that they are robust enough to become the channels for the circulation of the common. The assembly as a political formation can provide both the means for beginning to seriously engage with the production of the common and the organisational terrain for the common politics to come.

In order to demonstrate the value of the assembly as an organisational formation in the contemporary context, we need first to establish the theoretical terrain on which to situate it. Here, we can state that the political and theoretical tradition of *operaismo* or autonomist Marxism contributes to an understanding of revolution as, by necessity, driven by the producers and reproducers of the social and economic realm – workers, broadly construed. Then, the specific historical and contemporary instantiations of the assembly as a constituted political organisation of the common can be clarified. It is here that the possibility the assembly form holds for potential models of post-party politics comes to life. In the following, I will briefly outline some of the historical lineages of the assembly form and then focus on a contemporary example – the Greater Toronto Workers' Assembly – in order to elucidate the historical connections and political possibilities, with a focus on rethinking working-class organising as a project of political experimentation that can contribute to the creation of spaces for networked entities to struggle for a shared, common world.

Theoretical lineages: operaismo, autonomism and the ancestry of multitude

Autonomist Marxism concerns itself with the autonomy of human subjects. It is a Marxism centred on the conflict between producers and appropriators, between labour and capital, with labour being the active subject in the relation. In elaborating on Marx's account of the relationship between labour and capital, Western Marxisms have tended to focus on the dominant logic of capital itself, but autonomists sought to affirm the power of labour and the subsequent responses of capital to class struggle, inverting the dialectical relationship between labour and capital. This Copernican turn (Moulier, 1989: 19), first theorised by

Tronti (1979), sees all changes in the mode of production within capital as an outcome of workers' struggles. Thus the perspective of autonomist theory is located in the struggle of the worker and the political history of capital is the 'history of successive attempts of the capitalist class to emancipate itself from the working class' (Tronti, 1979: 10, quoted in Trott, 2007: 205). For this reason, autonomism provides us with the best vantage point from which to examine critical modes of organising in an era of austerity where the common cannot come soon enough. Additionally, an autonomist perspective is crucial to understanding new modes of worker organising that rely not on the state, or on parties, or on top-down bureaucratic union structures, but which are rather self-generative, autonomous and developed horizontally through networks both technological and biological.

Class composition is also a concept derived from autonomist Marxist theorising, with specific forms of struggle developing according to variations of class composition. In response to these forms of struggle, capital attempts to impose several changes designed to restore discipline; this discipline forces a 'decomposition' of the class, which then gives rise to new struggles and a new class composition (Trott, 2007). In this way, class composition is connected to the circulation of struggles and how these struggles are organised. Multitude is the political composition of the working class within biopolitical capitalism, as elaborated by Hardt and Negri in their trilogy (2000, 2004, 2009).

In terms of its depiction of the contemporary working class, the concept of multitude and its attendant descriptors has been thoroughly critiqued. The concept evacuates work, and especially reproductive work, of its gendered character, for example, while its connecting notions of affective and immaterial labour imagine that contemporary labour requires emotions but not materiality, something Federici excoriates when she states that, for example, elder care 'demands a complete engagement with the persons to be reproduced, a relation that can hardly be conceived as "immaterial"' (Federici, 2012: 122). Furthermore, notions of multitude are characterised as the composition of the class in a contemporary regime of biopolitical production.

The notion of biopolitical production is important for conceptualising the new assembly movements because it signifies a new spatial locale for resistance: no longer situated exclusively in the factory, the sites of resistance become the workers' very bodies, the home, the social realm. In a regime of biopolitical production, all labour is immersed in the relational elements that define the social but simultaneously activate the 'critical elements that develop the potential of insubordination and revolt through the entire set of labouring practices' (Hardt & Negri, 2000: 28). It is both production and reproduction. It is also, however, employed by Hardt and Negri in their assertion that the technologies of the present movement create a spontaneous communism, ignoring 'the cooperation we can develop among ourselves, starting from those of us who must face the most vulnerable time in our lives without the resources and help they need, a hidden but no doubt widespread form of torture in our society' (Federici, 2012: 125).

The inadequacies of multitude are manifold, then, but can also be helpful in leading us to consider more expansive and directional forms of struggle, such as those we find in the assembly. In order to understand the contemporary moment in the light of the past, a working through of the phases of class composition, as outlined by Negri, will prove helpful. The first composition of the class under capital is identified as the phase of large-scale industry, the late industrial revolution. In this phase, the skills and activities of a previously artisanal workforce were beginning to be narrowed and subordinated to the functioning of machine technologies and the 'professional worker' constituted the hegemonic working class subjectivity. The interests of this industrial proletariat were represented by the vanguardist workers' party (Bowring, 2004), an organisation with a mass membership and an intellectual leadership.

Capital responded to the class struggle of the 'skilled professional worker' through a decomposition of the workforce with the introduction of Taylorist production practices and Fordist regulation. These practices subdivided labour into simplified, deskilled and individualised tasks that only together formed a complex whole, making the worker a mere human appendage of the assembly line and giving rise to what Negri called the 'mass worker' (Negri, 1992; Bowring, 2004). The mass workers' labour was truly that of the 'abstract labour' of Marx – 'labour which is independent of the particular concrete form it takes at any given time' (Bowring, 2004: 106) and, divided and separated from the end product created, 'reduced to mere abstraction and activity' (Marx, 1973: 693).

The machine rose to new heights of importance in production. As Marx notes, it is not 'as with the instrument, which the worker animates and makes into his organ with his skill and strength, and whose handling therefore depends on his virtuosity', but rather 'it is the machine which possesses skill and strength in the place of the worker, is itself the virtuoso, with a soul of its own in the mechanical laws acting through it' (Marx, 1973: 693). Increasingly moved into densely populated urban environments and concentrated in large factories, workers became newly empowered with a class subjectivity. From this, novel forms of class organisation developed and new, radical workers' movements came to the fore – anti-reformist trade union groups and militant workers' associations arose alongside older formations such as the Communist party.

The general strikes and mass movements of the mass worker were managed by capital through crisis and the attempt to 'revalorise work through *social command*, i.e., to enforce the wage–work nexus and unpaid surplus work over society by means of the State' (Negri, 1992: xii). Responding to the growing power of the mass worker, capital aimed to destroy its political composition in two ways: one, by the introduction of more machine technologies and automated production, minimising human labour needs and leading to further deskilling and proletarianisation; and two, by capital extending itself outside of the factory walls, beyond the boundaries of the workplace (site of commodity production) and into the sphere of the social reproduction of capital, into reproduction itself, wherein social relations as a whole become increasingly subordinated to a capitalist mode of production.

First, as Marx has it, labour became merely a 'conscious organ', something 'subsumed under the total process of the machinery itself' and becoming 'only a link in the system' (Marx, 1973: 393). Then, according to Tronti, this system expanded beyond the factory and into the very realm of social life. The social itself emerged as a plane of capitalised activity in the development of the 'social factory' and 'social worker':

The more capitalist development advances, that is to say the more the production of relative surplus value penetrates everywhere, the more the circuit production–distribution–

exchange–consumption inevitably develops; that is to say that the relationship between capitalist production and bourgeois society, between the factory and society, between society and the state, become … more and more organic. At the highest level of capitalist development, social relations become moments of the relations of production, and the whole society becomes an articulation of production. In short, all of society lives as a function of the factory and the factory extends its exclusive domination over all of society. (Tronti, 1962, cited in Cleaver, 1992: 137)

With increasing technological advances and decreasing geographical space for capital to colonise, the social and even the biological realms of life became sites of valorisation for post-Fordist capital. Labour became even more abstracted (in the Marxist sense), with its focus turning to high-tech communication, transportation and information, and with the withdrawal of the welfare state (which in some ways had socialised elements of reproductive labour). The mass worker of the Fordist era soon became the 'social worker' of post-Fordism.

The social worker was defined by Hardt and Negri (1994: 274) as 'characterised by a hybrid of material and immaterial labour activities linked together in social and productive networks by highly developed labouring cooperation'. Today, capital draws upon a 'basin of immaterial labour' which 'dissolves back into the networks and flows that make possible the reproduction and enrichment of its productive capacities' (Lazzarato, 1996: 136–7). Again, the notion of immateriality is something roundly critiqued by feminist theorists as 'sidestepping the rich problematic that the feminist analysis of reproductive work in capitalism uncovered' (Federici, 2012: 122). This is not to say that value is no longer created at the point of production, but rather that the point of production is spread out through the circulatory networks of capital, expanded into widely varied areas of life, including even the production of life itself – although, from the perspective of labour, the reproduction of human beings differs from the production of commodities.

With capital thus moving the point of production beyond the factory in 'capturing' surplus value in every realm of life that it can, so too is the mass of people who are considered workers expanded far beyond the traditional scope of 'worker'. Negri argues that as the process of capitalist exploitation now takes place society-wide, socially and economically marginalised groups such as students, the unemployed and casual labourers are also part of the proletariat. For workers in the new class composition of the social worker, battles circulate around 'anything which bears the work relation without the wage' (Negri, 1992: xii). For feminist theorists critical of the ease with which this 'multitude' drops commitments to gender, race, age and class, the force of understanding reproductive labour as a productive moment for capital but not to be confused with production commits us to shifting our very social relations so that the valorisation of capital 'no longer commands social activity and reproduction becomes a collective process' (Federici, 2012: 122). This is the power that assembly experiments can bring to new understandings of organisings – the demand that the work of politics begins with the ways in which we *are* together; how we *practice* the common in our very organisational structures.

Of course, the three distinct phases of class composition as outlined here are never so smooth or distinct. Distinguishing characteristics of one phase flow into the next, just as many of the practices of earlier forms of production find themselves in later instantiations, while new characteristics, compositions and practices of both class and capital also emerge. Sergio Bologna (cited in Bowring, 2004: 113), for example, has criticised Negri's 'tendency to ignore counter-trends and exaggerate class unity'. The shifts and waves and changes within the working class and leftist political organising are important to note and key to an argument wherein these organisational forms have traded places back and forth, often in line with changes and shifts in the modes of production. Just as elements of industrial production techniques coexist with biopolitical production regimes, so too, I argue, is it necessary to consider some elements of earlier, more vertical organisational tactics in respect of contemporary, horizontal organising. At the present juncture, we can see lines of organisational development converging in a less dialectical and rather multilateral movement towards some sort of organised yet diffuse, structured yet flexible affinity.

As noted, the claim is that multitude, through the cooperative nature of its labouring self, will give way to spontaneous and elementary forms of communism as it is itself a 'form of political organisation that, on the one hand, emphasises the multiplicity of the social singularities in struggle and, on the other, seeks to coordinate their common actions and maintain with equality in horizontal organisational structures' (Hardt & Negri, 2009: 110), which is problematic and unconvincing. One failing seems to be an underestimation of capital, or non-reckoning of its well-established dynamic. While seemingly cooperative, even in an era of production that requires greater degrees of communication and collective labour, capital continues to divide workers through 'an unequal division of labour, through the use of the wage, giving the waged power over the wageless, and through the institutionalisation of sexism and racism' (Federici, 2012: 92); the realities of contemporary work-life simply cannot be ignored.

Much like Marx, who in some ways saw technology as a liberating force for workers, conceptions of multitude rely too heavily on a technologistic concept of revolution – working classes brought to a revolutionary moment through the cooperative uses of digital technologies and not through their embodied togetherness in organising structures and the process of commoning. Because recent years have shown general increases in inequality, overwork, unemployment and personal debt, while migrant workers, students, youth and women bore the brunt of cascading economic crises, it is difficult to assume the optimism of Hardt and Negri and the theory of multitude which argues that 'the new forms of production the global restructuring of the economy has created already provide for the best possibility of more autonomous, more cooperative forms of work' (Federici, 2012: 106). What this autonomous cooperation is meant to look like remains unclear, and the need to devise a theory of the assembly as the political formation of a common struggle becomes ever more urgent.

Contrary to the spontaneity that Hardt and Negri espouse, an examination of past and present political movements makes it clear that any political formation – any movement with political directionality – does not arise from nothing, but rather must be consciously moved in this activated, revolutionary direction. Indeed, the liberatory possibilities of multitude have already been thoroughly discussed in critiques of immaterial production (Nunes, 2007; Trott, 2007), and it is evident that multitude is not *necessarily* emancipatory, but must be *made* thus. New figures of struggle, new subjectivities, are produced in the latest phase of struggle and capitalist response, but they do not in and of themselves necessarily possess any greater impetus to coalesce and transform into communism. Although effective communication, coordination and collaboration may be a source for radically new forms of democracy (Hardt and Negri, 2004, 2009; Virno, 2004), that these conditions are totalising and already immanent to the practices of labour today 'appears as nothing more than a tragically flawed proposition' (Trott, 2007: 226).

Furthermore, it is important to remember that mass manual labour in the automated production context still exists alongside distinct modes of production, the immaterial labour associated with the tertiary sector, even if obscured in today's 'technological age'. From this it follows that the politics implied in the era of the mass worker remain useful, including, of course, its organisational forms. The continued performance (exchange) of this labour points us to the absence of a sharp contrast between phases of class composition and regimes of production, and highlights the need to invoke internally heterogeneous practices of politics and organising.

The common may arise through struggle and the production of alternatives, as Hardt and Negri themselves suggest, but the requisite subjectivities and organisations can only materialise through more directional, defined structures. The assembly stands as one of these, a radical left institution that does not become the 'Modern Prince', the erstwhile party or the tired vanguard. Riding a line between Leninist discipline and late-autonomist spontaneity, the assembly suggests itself as the form through which the flaws of multitude can be repaired and its potential realised. To deny this possibility, to carry on practising the same old politics, to avoid invigorating experimentation in the face of life as a mix of powerlessness, confusion and fear, to concede power to the usual agents at their usual sites – this simply promotes the continuation of that combination of anarchy and oligarchy that marks the rule of capital. In promoting assembly, however, it is important also to understand the contemporary class composition as maintaining within it elements of the old and to see our tactics, strategies and structures as both innovative and connected to, as a development of and within, a historical lineage of struggle.

The common as a political concept redefines the terrain of contemporary struggle, breaking through the duopoly of public versus private, state versus market. The statist model of revolution 'that for decades sapped the efforts of radical movements to build an alternative to capitalism' (Federici, 2012: 139) has waned, while the neoliberal impulse to subsume every form of life to market logic is increasingly and actively resisted. Indeed, it is in the very (neoliberal) attempts to enclose commons where we find that 'new forms of social cooperation are constantly being produced', including 'in areas of life where none previously existed' (Federici, 2012: 139). As an alternative to the state–market duopoly comprising both 'the common wealth of the material world' (Hardt & Negri, 2009: viii) and the sociality necessary for production in post-Fordism, are things such as knowledge, culture, language and historical remembrances (Mattei, 2011) – the common is not imagined with humanity as a separate entity outside of nature. Moreover, humanity is not seen as the exploiter or caretaker of the common, natural or social.

This is not a conception that posits a subject (a human, corporation or government) that rules over an object (a good, organisation or territory), but rather one that sees human beings as integrally networked into the world around them, as entities inhabiting a shared world. No longer specified by a particular life sphere (the natural commons) that can be set aside and preserved, the common as an idea confronts the ways in which the whole species is subsumed within capital and looks to how this is open to various practices of resistance. Ultimately, this goes beyond conflict with the expression of accrued surplus held by the few and extends to an exploration of our humanity. It is thus a fitting political project for the multitude.

This is a seductive notion, asserting as it does that the common is immanent in our contemporary ways of being, including labouring in post-Fordism. What it neglects, however, is where the possibility of creating the common comes against its limit. This is first, Federici (2012) suggests, in its effusive belief in the technological foundation of common politics – that digital labour is inherently cooperative and thus leads us fairly directly to instantiation of the common. Focusing on the technological ignores the material basis of Internet technology – the rape and pillage of the planet necessary to extract the rare earth minerals used in digital technologies and the obscene labour conditions in both the raw-material mining and product manufacture (of computers, smart phones and tablets, etc.). This may seem a relatively minor and certainly conditional matter, but it represents just the kind of material consideration that the common/multitude thesis stands accused of overlooking.

Then, fetishising technology, information and knowledge production as the basis of the common makes invisible the reproduction of everyday life and the important role that this plays in alternative political and economic projects. Federici notes that this is not unusual to common discourses, which are often not written from a feminist perspective, and thus generally focus 'on the formal preconditions for [the common's] existence but much less on the possibilities provided by existing commons, and their potential to create forms of reproduction enabling us to resist dependence on wage labour and subordination to capitalist relations' (Federici, 2012: 142). Again, however, this critique provides points of entry for the assembly as an organisational form, with its emphasis on embodied being-with as the foundation of its trust and solidarity, and with that embodiment as the foundational ground for the creation of the common.

Instituting the common is a fundamental task in the era of neoliberal globalisation as the common (ecological and social) becomes increasingly obscured through the dominant capitalist ideology and hegemonic state policies. In today's politics of privatisation and austerity, liberal notions of the commons that do not break with the established duopolies risk reproducing 'the traditional mechanistic view, the separation between object and subject and resulting commodification' (Mattei, 2011). While overwhelming empirical evidence shows that cooperative property arrangements, for example, do not bring about Hardin's *Tragedy of the Commons*, since such organisations among individuals have actually been quite successful (Ostrom, 1990), what liberal conceptions of the commons do not contend with is that corporations and states *do* behave in ways that produce the tragedy of over-extraction and exploitation.

It is markets and states that produce the tragedy of the commons, markets and states that 'tend to operate as relentless and merciless maximisers of short term interest' (Mattei, 2011). It is the conventional governmental forms of shareholder control and nation-state democracy that organise this to the common harm, with property laws, public and private alike, mere justifications for and expediters of the power of 'dominant sovereigns over weaker subjects in a process of brutal exploitation' (Mattei, 2011). As a result, liberal notions of the commons such as those forwarded by Ostrom do not overcome commodification, but, on the contrary, contribute to the lineage of modernist thought that denies the possibility of the radical break from commodification ever occurring and thereby materially assists the further destruction and erosion of the common.

It is my contention that a politics of the assembly can help us find an organisational form for the new epistemic and political projects of emancipation. The idea and practice of the common lies in the terrain where we see ourselves as the common, as part of an environment, natural or cultural. In this conception of the common, we can see what has been called 'multitude' as inseparably linked to communities, to ecosystems, to knowledge and to political institutions. The assembly as a political form allows us to do just this – to cut across competing political ideologies, to understand the common as something that develops together through collaborative efforts that are a part of our labouring conditions, but also from our resistances to that dominant ideology and our creative expressions in these anti-capitalist political projects, and from our lived experiences as workers sharing and collaborating with each other in ways that are outside the officially sanctioned paradigm of work. In fact, it is my contention that the assembly as a form contributes to bringing about the common but also *is* the common itself, becomes the common in its very constitution.

The assembly past and present

The assembly as a means of forging political directionality for groups of workers is not new. The contemporary incarnations of assemblies such as in the Occupy movement, or in the GTWA, carry with them a long history of other experiments in workers' democratic control and working class self-liberation. From the early soviets of the first and even second Russian revolutions through the factory councils in Turin in 1918 to the assembly movement in Spain in the 1970s, organisational forms have existed which, in their very construction, resisted the top-down politicking of parties, vanguards and parliamentarianism. As a form of decision-making, assemblies were often a component part of anarchist and Marxist traditions like the Council Communist movement. And like 'council' then, 'assembly' now can be considered something of a catchall term for a 'form of organisation renewed at different times and across different countries by groups of workers often unaware of this kind of structure or of previous historical precedents' (Cohen, 2011: 48).

Workers' councils and assemblies have tended to operate with directly democratic decision-making structures focusing on the self-activity of workers and building unofficial and cross-union forms of worker organisation. These assemblages of workers also helped to forge class unity in that they often incorporated unionised workers with their non-unionised counterparts. Indeed, assemblies are, broadly speaking, a form or mode of organisation that prioritises and is a direct vehicle for class struggle. Forms of direct democracy are fundamental to these movements, and can be seen in the mass meetings, delegate structures and, occasionally, the creation of accountable, revocable 'local leaders'. Features of direct democracy have been seen in even the earliest workers' uprisings under capitalism, for example in the Chartist movement (1830s and 1840s Britain) and even in the earlier tradition of 'cross-trade conferences' held as early as 1810 (Cohen, 2011). Directly democratic structures were often threatening to traditional, bureaucratic trades unions as they allowed decision-making to take place at the site of labour, by workers themselves, and did not require waiting for directives from labour's leadership. This is evident, for example, in the Great Upheaval of the 1870s in the United States (Brecher, 1999), wherein railroad workers walked out in a mass strike action against wage cuts and developed delegate committees 'ignoring the leadership of their national unions' (Cohen, 2011: 49).

The assembly form is simple in that it develops out of the material conditions of workers – it is not 'plucked from thin air' (Cohen, 2011: 48) – while in practice it remains work. There are claims to the naturalness of this form, as councils and assemblies have been repeated throughout various cycles of class struggle, often in movements with little knowledge of past precedent. The combustion of radical energy from workers in the form of councils, soviets and assemblies should not necessarily be considered a spark which ignites a fire, but rather a fire that grows out of embers already lit – this is to say that 'workers independently and repeatedly learn and put into practice class-based lessons' (Cohen, 2011: 54), and the practices that arise develop out of the concrete needs of workers over long periods of both struggle and stagnation. While there is spontaneity, then, there is also coordination – the long smouldering embers of workers' discontent eventually burst into flames, usually after the assembly form has already been constituted in a specific location.

As political structures for the emancipation of labour, councils and assemblies strive to overcome the division between the economic and political spheres – they make struggles over the wage not simply an economic struggle but also a political one.[8] This makes them inherently revolutionary, insofar as this division between the economic and the political means 'in fact, overcoming the capitalist state itself' (Bonnet, 2011: 66). While unions had historically struggled in the economic sphere and (left-wing/socialist) parties in the political sphere – pitting each against owners/managers and (right-wing/conservative) parties – councils resisted this ossified dualism and worked to overcome the division. This desire for innovation in form helps explain why councils and assemblies as movements that condensed power into the bodies of workers themselves have historically been so stalwartly resisted by labour unions and traditional left-wing parties, as much, almost, as by those on the right.

That said, there has always existed a minority current into which assemblies and council movements have fitted, from the Paris Commune as depicted by Marx, through council communism, elements of Trotskyism, anarcho-syndicalism, *operaismo*/autonomism and other 'heretical' left-wing currents that have seen 'workers control and councils as the basis of a self-determined socialist society' (Ness & Azzelini, 2011: 2). The assembly movement in Spain during the 1970s provides an example of the use of assemblies as an experimental, directly democratic organisational form resisting more authoritarian organising measures that has recent historical relevance and also serves to illustrate some of the dynamics in play within the left as a whole.

The workers' assembly movement that arose in Spain during the waning of Franco's dictatorship described itself as the 'independent manifestation of the proletariat' (Amoros, 1984). Catalysing resistance to anti-Franco opposition groups, this was not simply a movement against the Franco dictatorship or merely in support of his replacements, however, but an 'upraising against all forms of exploitation that escaped the narrow framework of bourgeois politics intended for the containment of workers' (Amoros, 1984). Rejecting vanguardism, electoral politics and trade union reformism, these assembly movements sought rather to invoke practices of solidarity, self-defence, direct dialogue and the general strike as their specific methods of struggle. Although they did not begin as a particularly coherent movement, the assemblies soon forged ahead as institutions for the defence of the everyday interests of different workers, serving as spaces to discuss labour problems and strategies around employment issues. They formed in different domains of public life, taking the shape of meetings and colloquiums, street occupations and public engagements and actions.

Through the process of self-education and expansion, the Spanish assembly movement eventually shed its purely spontaneous character and was able to sharpen itself in a necessary evolution from the previously fragmentary politics into a coordinated self-defence body, with aligned activities and actions. Through a commitment to horizontal, democratic engagement and diverse memberships, locations and tactics, the Spanish assemblies of the 1970s never developed into the strict, inflexible party structure of the earlier political mobilisations of, say, the soviets under the Bolshevik party. For a moment, workers' assemblies in Spain became a true counter-power, independent and with enormous force, and full of apparent possibilities. In fact, even as it lost energy, 'worn down, without general goals, without being able to deliver decisive blows [and lacking] a definite revolutionary current', the movement served to define Spanish democracy post-Franco as 'all the existing political forces that attained influence [did so] precisely by virtue of their struggle against that movement' (Amoros, 1984) – and this included the trade unions and the Communist party, as well as centrist and right-wing organisations and groupings.

In the same way that Hardt and Negri discuss multitude as the new, creative social subjectivity of the post-Fordist era of biopolitical production, so too are assemblies and councils about the unleashing of human creativity in the search for and discovery of new ways of being – and producing – together, in common. Councils and assemblies as organisational forms and structures of working class power came from the shared experience of the early capitalist labour process, from the unity and solidarity forged through work, often factory work taking place in the same geographical space. That spatial unity, that locational solidarity, is not as totalising today – which is not to say that it does not exist at all, but rather that older forms of organisation need to mesh with and blend with the newer forms, so as to develop a politics capable of creative resistance.

The reinvigorated assembly contains within it the lineage of those earlier assemblies of the era of the mass worker. The contemporary assembly as an organisational form also speaks to those engaged in the locationally specific, industrial-scale work that does still exist today in the West, as in urban environments worldwide. Contemporary assemblies are heterogeneous; they do not seek to eradicate difference, as did the philosophy of unity that drove much of the Leninist-style organising of earlier eras, but rather use the sectarian, gender, racial and class differences contained within the assembly as a creative force for the advancement of a dialectical political vector. Thus can the assembly model be seen as an institution of simultaneous dissent and action that may manifest the common. Characterised by inclusiveness, non-sectarian identity and a horizontal, participatory structure, the assembly registers the dissent of growing numbers of people dissatisfied with hierarchical modes of organisation and politics, and thus, albeit slowly and often clumsily, builds a new politics and society that can be considered an emergent common.

The Greater Toronto Workers' Assembly

Formed in the autumn of 2009, the GTWA was developed out of a series of consultations with a variety of differently situated activists and organisers on the anti-capitalist, labour and social movement left. These consultations were aimed at illuminating the differences between, on the one hand, various activist projects and, on the other, the labour movement (in particular, they sought to bring together labour organisers based in auto factories with activists in the social movement-oriented Ontario Coalition Against Poverty). The intention was to build strong relationships of solidarity between these two often opposing forces, in order to highlight and examine the relationship between class and other forms of oppression and social determination. The tensions between labour bureaucracies and activists that had existed throughout the history of radical movements[9] were also at play in left-wing organising in Toronto.

The GTWA is imagined as a place where tensions on the left can be sorted through and alleviated. It is narrow enough to limit its membership to those identifying with the anti-capitalist left, but broad enough to encompass anarchists and socialists, labour activists and social movement organisers, autonomists and communists, Trotskyists and dissident members of Canada's social democratic party, the New Democratic Party. As a space of reflection and action for disparate and often disconnected actors, the assembly hopes to defragment struggles and build larger collectivities for work that might address the limits of earlier modes of organising. This opens the assembly up to the possibility of realising itself as a living body engaged in the creation of the common, even if it does not directly self-identify thus. Much of what connects the assembly to the concept of multitude is largely unrecognised by the organisation (as autonomist thought is not the prevailing political tendency within the project), but it is these connections that, if deepened, may best support and nourish the development of the GTWA as a radical and revolutionary institution.

The Occupy movement, too, used the model of the assembly in unique and important ways – the General Assembly (GA) was the centrepiece of most Occupy encampments, with GAs often taking place twice daily during the active occupations. The complexity of Occupy's engagement with the assembly process points us to some of the difficulties embedded within the notions of both 'the common' and 'multitude'. General assemblies in various Occupy sites were points of contention, and varied sites took different approaches to the use and structure of the GA. The New York City General Assembly, struck before the Occupy encampments began, agreed upon the following definition of the General Assembly on 3 September 2011:

> NYC General Assemblies are an open, participatory, and horizontally organised process through which we are building the

> capacity to constitute ourselves in public as autonomous collec-
> tive forces within and against representative politics, cultural
> death, and the constant crisis of our times. (Quoted in Holmes,
> 2012: 152)

Occupy sites used GAs as decision-making bodies and informa-
tion-sharing sites over the course of a spatial occupation – they
were open to anyone at any time without any specific membership criteria, thus often involving actors with competing politics
and priorities. By October, however, when the Occupy Wall
Street encampment was just a month old, some argued that the
'General Assembly was becoming a form of entertainment' and
that it 'could not withstand the pressures of a constant public
and permeable space' (Holmes, 2012: 155). Contrary to its original intentions, the GA was becoming a 'machine of the mob'
(Holmes, 2012: 155).

Another assembly movement, the coalition of student associations, CLASSE,[10] which drove much of the 2012 Quebec student
strike (against a hike in tuition fees), imagined the assembly as
the political space in which organisers and participants would
come together, discuss politics, debate and decide upon strategy in a movement of diverse political actors grounded by a
shared political demand. Here, while the assemblies were open
for observers, votes could only come from those affiliated with
member organisations. For example, only members of the Geography department at Concordia University could vote in the
assembly held by that departmental association.

The differences between these three examples are subtle
but important – together, they can be characterised as illus-
trating the difference between the assembly as a tool and as a

mode of being. There is a distinct difference between the use of assemblies, as by Occupy and CLASSE, and the assembly as the predominant form of a political body on the left centred around a baseline of generally shared politics, as in the case of the GTWA. For the GTWA, the assembly is the form through which a non-sectarian, open and heterogeneous politics are conducted by political actors of varying tendencies for which strategies and tactics form the largest deviation. In attempting to think through new forms of left-wing working class organising in Toronto, the GTWA has begun the process of creating a new organisational common; it has taken initial steps forward in expanding and deepening processes of struggle in the city through attempted convergences of competing and differing visions of radical left organising. It has raised the level of discourse and debate alongside the level of collaboration.

Protracted internal debate is an essential component of an assembly. This commitment to debate and dialogue can make conclusions slow to arrive at, but this does not have to derail the process of decision-making entirely. GTWA meetings are forums for debates that are otherwise not had on the left in general. With just over 300 members, the assembly does not operate on the basis of consensus, and instead uses voting as its decision-making tool. The GA is the highest authority of the GTWA, and no decisions can be made or passed unless they go through discussion, debate and voting by the assembly as a whole. In this way, assembly politics can begin to actively rethink the dichotomy between vertical and lateral organising in favour of more hybrid models, recognising the necessity of working with diverse subjects and groups, while maintaining a commitment to continued struggle through practice, debate and action. An assembly, therefore, attempts to strengthen political communication for the multitude.

If we are to see networking and dialogue as a series of situational negotiations based around the possibility of changing both one's own viewpoint and that of another, an assembly offers a foundation for this with a spatial and temporal togetherness yet without the necessity of drawing clean demarcation lines. Inevitably, disagreements do arise, and the GTWA has not yet discovered ways to move forward in the face of serious political polarities. As time goes on, certain positions within the assembly harden, certain tendencies calcify and certain segments of the GTWA population – mostly more horizontal activists, anarchists and autonomists – feel less 'at home' within the greater body, due to concerns over the direction of the body as a whole. But many of these activists still feel a commitment to the work they carry out in the committees or campaigns where, after all, the main part of their activities are centred. This opens up a serious issue with regard to the level of democratic engagement on the part of the membership and impedes any easy understandings of the assembly as a model simply for improving democratic organising. However, provision of a space to begin to work through these disagreements – to talk across tendencies – is an important first step in building mass movement organisations that can avoid re-inscription of the oft-committed errors made by more vanguardist-type organising models.

As noted, most of the GTWA's action-oriented work takes place in its various committees and campaigns which include the Public Sector Defense Committee (PSDC), the Feminist Action Committee, the Internal Education and Political Development Committee, the Culture Committee and the Free and

Accessible Transit Campaign. These committees and campaigns have autonomy to carry out political activity in the way that they deem most valuable, and their actions then lay the foundation for broader political debate and commentary. For example, in the winter of 2012, the Public Sector Defense Committee intervened in a dispute between a labour organisation and a social movement organisation.

As Toronto's city council prepared to vote on a highly contentious austerity budget that would see cuts to social programming and the outsourcing of many unionised jobs, social movement activists sought to take action, organising a demonstration outside City Hall on the evening of the vote. The labour organisation initially did not respond to calls for collaboration, and when finally it did, it attempted to control the planned demonstration. The social movement activists sought to enter City Hall and engage in a process of non-violent disruption of the council meeting. The labour organisation disagreed with these tactics, but went further, attempting to thwart the social movement activists and community members from proceeding with their action by threatening to take over the rally and cut social movement activists out. The (GTWA) PSDC felt it inappropriate for organised labour to dictate the terms of protest to social movement and community groups, but remained cognisant of the fractious history in activism that this conflict was replaying – a history of disagreement around tactics between labour unions and social movements that is in no way limited to organising in Toronto.

As a clarification of its own politics, and through long discussions, the committee drafted a letter to the labour organisation highlighting three issues at the heart of the current manifestation of the conflict between social movements (less hierarchical) and unions (more hierarchical), including (a) the legitimacy of certain social movements as a significant community voice, (b) the role of certain social movements in rallies, protests and demonstrations and, most importantly, (c) labour organisations' claims to unilateral authority in determining the tactics of others. The committee felt that the conflict between the labour organisation and the social movement was a key sticking point in a history of struggles as they have manifested in varying geographic locales, and it needed resolution.

Whenever there is collaboration between more horizontal and more vertical organisations, there is a question of surrendering some autonomy in the name of common strategy, and this needs to be respectfully negotiated. One group cannot assert dominion over the tactics of others, and the committee felt that limiting class struggle to 'polite' tactics is neither effective nor in tune with the ways labour has acted in the past, nor with the prevailing political conditions, such as the recent actions of Occupy, which helped to inaugurate bold and audacious actions onto a mainstream political stage. This intervention led to conflict within the broader organisation as a whole – some members agreeing with the committee's intervention, others virulently disagreeing. The end result was a fruitful, powerful and important political debate and discussion that helped the assembly further delineate its own politics and positions, bringing not unity to a multitude, but rather the negotiation of difference.

For Hardt and Negri's multitude, there is no unity, no centrality, no homogeneity. Multitude is heterogeneous, the opposite of previous forms of communism which relied on a homogenous subjectivity around which the politics could cohere. A contemporary politics of the common relies on a rather different social subjectivity, an internally differentiated but unseparated heterogeneity. In a way that the concept of multitude is unable to, the notion of an assembly as a coming together of bodies and subjects into politicised space creates a *form* of unity without necessitating an absolute unity of agreement. In the GTWA, debate rages over structure and practice regarding the future directions of the project. Should the assembly intervene in electoral politics or develop a political platform? Should it become a more active force in organising or focus on strengthening political debate and changing political conversations? As these debates are resolved or not – and yet regardless of which – the important work is already underway: creating the common space for these conversations to take place.

The GTWA also represents a common politics by bringing together different segments of the working class, segments that have been divided by 'the pressures of neoliberal policies and labour markets' (Rosenfeld, 2011) and isolated both in their workplaces and in their homes. Isolation is a large part of post-Fordist capitalism, as workers are less and less convening in large factories but are separated in precarious work conditions (labouring on contracts, working from home or in others' homes, often located in alienating suburbs).[11] But the isolation of workers in post-Fordist capitalism is not only spatial, since the divisions that are part and parcel of the new, post-Fordist workforce have created rancour within the working class itself.

Now, workers are pitted against other workers for jobs and, in times of austerity, those perceived members of the labour aristocracy with union protection who labour for higher wages and greater benefits are taken by many members of the non-unionised working class to be an obstacle to greater wealth distribution and thus a different kind of class enemy.[12] In Toronto, for example, the working class is very mixed, with a dramatically declining industrial base and the financial sector, real estate and public services as the economic drivers of the city. The working class itself is divided into 'highly segmented clumps of concentrated numbers: construction; upper-end manufacturing; lower-end manufacturing; servicing the financial services cluster, as well as the retail centres and the entertainment complexes' (Rosenfeld, 2011). Deeper internal divisions within the working class continue with the trajectory of neoliberalism. Such divisions reveal themselves to be highly gendered and racialised in Toronto. Real wages across the city, meanwhile, have declined over the last decade (see Hulchanski et al., 2010), as much work has been consistently outsourced, privatised and restructured. Transnational immigrants – of whom there is a high density in the Toronto population – make up key elements of the commercial capitalist class, but these communities also make up 'an increasingly cheapened and precarious segment of the working class' (Rosenfeld, 2011), this being particularly true in the case of migrant women.

Conclusion: multitude and the assembly as common

What we are seeing, then, is less the autonomist circulation of struggles than the segmentation of struggles amongst disparate groups. The concerns of the employed are counterposed to those of the welfare recipient; a white middle class positioned against new immigrants; the taxpaying private sector maligns and competes with a public service perceived as parasitic; the fully contracted become a salaried elite for those in precarious labour conditions. This momentum does not recompose struggles in circulation, as earlier autonomist theories suggested took place in the era of the mass worker, for example. Rather, a de-compositionary antagonism of struggles (Dyer-Witheford, 2012) is underway, and it is into this trajectory that the assembly – assemblies of the multitude in general, and that of the GTWA in particular – can intervene and serve as a new political force for the creation of the common.

The assembly is and can be the organisational mode and conceptual framework for a politicised multitude, one with a strong commitment to class analysis that simultaneously recognises the differing experiences of those interpolated into the body of the working class/multitude. As outlined here, the GTWA, especially through the work of its committees, exemplifies the taking of the first steps towards the creation of an organisation of the common that is centred in a class analysis of capital, but able also to see the tendrils of capitalist exploitation that radiate outwards, throughout the social factory.

This base-building through action is integral to the longevity of assemblies as political movements. Such bases make the assembly an institution of the common that can develop and maintain a circulation of struggles long past the invocation of a revolutionary moment but throughout the very core of a new common social future. Earlier movements of multitude, in particular the anti-globalisation movement of the late 1990s, were mostly unsuccessful in the Western context of creating long-lasting institutions – but this was not, generally, their aim. Rather, as some have suggested (Katsiaficas, 2002, 2006; Nunes, 2007), the movements of the 1990s were meant to be momentary, spectacular, tangential – and then dissipate. With movements as moments, the main 'institutions' that arose were largely in the ephemeral, virtual world of the Internet.

With its multipolar means of production and circulation, the Internet was a way to massify information and open movements up to horizontality and transparency. As Nunes (2007: 301) notes, 'it is only within the horizon of a social life that has become networked that a politics of networking as such can appear'. Moving beyond the thrill of late 1990s organising around the Internet and then recent ecstatic claims of Facebook and Twitter revolutions, the GTWA marks a turning point in the relationship between communications technology and radical political organising.

In its monthly coffeehouses, which offer space for members and the general public to discuss a specific theme or issue in its campaigns and general membership meetings, the GTWA attempts to create new spaces for people to meet together in person, to create the persistence and physical connection which seemed to be missing from overreliance on virtual communication. At the same time, the assembly pursues very sophisticated digital communication strategies, using the Internet for flexible and quick decision-making, communication and promotion, but without losing sight of the importance of face-to-face contact and debate. It is this strategy of melding the concrete and the virtual that operates to overcome the ephemerality and temporality of anti-globalisation movements, and yet still permits the flexibility and spontaneity that were smothered by inflexible party structures of older forms of organisation.

In the era of crisis and austerity and uncertain 'recovery' in which we now find ourselves, devising new political strategies and experimenting with new political forms is not only beneficial but a necessity. Developing tactics and movements from below will be the only way to bring about the common and challenge what has been called the revolutionary potentiality of multitude. The assembly as a political form can be seen as that structure through which radical politics, politics of the common, can be formulated and developed. Certainly there is much to be learned from past movements, and as political subjects we must be aware of these histories; the assembly form takes us a stage further, allowing us to remain sufficiently flexible to adapt to contemporary conditions, respond to contemporary crises and allow space for a diverse range of subjects and actors so as to make radical social change – the coming of the common – a true possibility.

Notes

1   An earlier version of this essay appeared in *Interface* 4(2) as 'A Common Assembly'.

2   CNN.com: http://www.cnn.com/2006/US/05/01/immigrant.day/index.html; BBC.co.uk: http://news.bbc.co.uk/2/hi/europe/2765215.stm_

3   While Hardt and Negri (2000, 2009) utilise the common to mean the networks of knowledge and communication that reside at the centre of many contemporary modes of production and shape the capacity to think and communicate, to reproduce the social, Federici (2004, 2012) argues that the reproductive labour in which we are engaged requires a concrete engagement with one another, something material, and thus a reproductive common requires a coming together, a being-with in space that Occupy and assembly politics attempts to emulate (see also Caffentzis, 2012).

4   A partial list of recent North American experiments in assembly politics could include the People's Movement Assemblies growing out of the World Social Forum and US Social Forum, the Southern Movement Assembly, the Southern Workers' Assembly, the People's Assemblies Network alongside the better known Occupy assemblies, the student and neighbourhood assemblies in Quebec's

'Maple Spring' and the assembly under discussion here, the Greater Toronto Workers' Assembly.

5   Acknowledging the dangers of overgeneralisation, this can be argued *because of* rather than despite some very different contexts (e.g. those centred in Cairo, Budapest, Rio and Kiev), where assembly has emerged in battles against state authority defined by a wide range of sociopolitical and economic issues, fissures and fault-lines but nevertheless structured by the same neoliberal(ising) class framework. In Istanbul, for example, following the police suppression of the protests in Gezi Park and Taksim Square, which largely originated in marginalised opposition to neoliberal government policies, a series of open, unled, generally unstructured discussion gatherings was held at night in parks across the city.

6   See Chapter 23 of *Capital* (Volume 1), 'The General Law of Capitalist Accumulation'.

7   Actually, we could say that the assembly is *re*-emergent: assemblies are not a new form of organising political struggle. There are, though, considerable differences between today's assemblies and their historical forebears (below).

8   For elaboration on this, see Negri (1989).

9   Much of which is outlined in Ness and Azzelini (2011).

10   *Coalition Large de l'ASSE* (the Broad Coalition of Associations for Student Union Solidarity).

11   This is most especially the case for women, often racialised women, engaged in care work. Much of this has been discussed by autonomist feminists such as Dalla Costa, Rosa and James (1973), Fortunati (2007), Federici (2012) and the Spanish feminist collective, Precarias a la Deriva (2009).

12   This can be seen in the comments sections of newspapers on a regular basis.

References

Amorós, M. (1984). 'Report on the assembly movement.' At https:// libcom.org/history/report-assembly-movement-miguel-amoros

Bonnet, A. R. (2011). 'The political form at last discovered: workers' councils against the capitalist state', in I. Ness and D. Azzellini (Eds.), *Ours to Master and to Own: Workers' Control from the Commune to the Present*. Chicago: Haymarket Books.

Bowring, F. (2004). 'From the mass worker to the multitude: a theoretical contextualisation of Hardt and Negri's *Empire*', *Capital and Class*, 83: 101–132.

Brecher, J. (1999). *Strike!* Cambridge, MA: South End Press.

Caffentzis, G. (2012). 'In the desert of cities: notes on the occupy movement in the US', in K. Khatib, M. Killjoy and M. McGuire (Eds.), *We Are Many: Reflections on Movement Strategy from Occupation to Liberation*. Oakland, CA: AK Press.

Cleaver, H. (1992). 'The inversion of class perspective in Marxian theory: from valorisation to self-valorisation', in W. Bonefeld, R. Gunn and K. Psychopedis (Eds.), *Open Marxism Volume 2: Theory and Practice*. London: Pluto Press.

Cleaver, H. (1998). *The Zapatistas and the Electronic Fabric of Struggle*. At https://webspace.utexas.edu/hcleaver/www/zaps.html

Cohen, S. (2011). 'The red mole: workers' councils as a means of revolutionary transformation', in I. Ness and D. Azzellini (Eds.), *Ours to Master and to Own: Workers' Control from the Commune to the Present*. Chicago: Haymarket Books.

Dalla Costa, M. and James, S. (1972). *The Power of Women and the Subversion of the Community*. At http://radicaljournal.com/books/maria_dalla_costa_power/

Dyer-Witheford, N. (2001). 'The new combinations: revolt of the global value subjects', *The New Centennial Review*, 1(3): 155–200.

Dyer-Witheford, N. (2010). 'Digital labour, species becoming, and the global worker', *Ephemera*, 10(3/4): 484–503.

Dyer-Witheford, N. (2012). 'Net, square, everywhere', *Radical Philosophy*, 171. At http://www.radicalphilosophy.com/commentary/net-square-everywhere

Federici, S. (2004). *The Caliban and the Witch: Women, the Body, and Primitive Accumulation*. Brooklyn, NY: Autonomedia.

Federici, S. (2012). *Revolution at Point Zero*. Brooklyn, NY: Common Notions/AK Press.

Fortunati, L. (2007). *The Arcane of Reproduction: Housework, Prostitution, Labour, and Capital*. Brooklyn, NY: Autonomedia.

Hardt, M. and Negri, A. (1994). *The Labour of Dionysus: Critique of the State-Form*. Minneapolis: University of Minnesota Press.

Hardt, M. and Negri, A. (2000). *Empire*. Cambridge, MA: Harvard University Press.

Hardt, M. and Negri, A. (2004). *Multitude*. New York: Penguin.

Hardt, M. and Negri, A. (2009). *Commonwealth*. Cambridge, MA: Belknap Press.

Holmes, M. (2012). 'The centre cannot hold: a revolution in process', in K. Khatib, M. Killjoy and M. McGuire, *We Are Many: Reflections on Movement Strategy from Occupation to Liberation*. Oakland, CA: AK Press.

Hulchanski, D. J. et al. (2010). *Toronto Divided? Polarizing Trends That Could Split the City Apart* (Report for Cities Centre at the University of Toronto).

At http://www.urbancentre.utoronto.ca/pdfs/gtuo/TorontoDivided-PolarizingTrends-CUI-January2010.pdf

Katsiaficas, G. (2002). *The Battle of Seattle* (Ed. E. Yuen and D. Burton-Rose). New York: Soft Skull Press.

Katsiaficas, G. (2006). *The Subversion of Politics: European Autonomous Social Movements and the Decolonization of Everyday Life*. Oakland, CA: AK Press.

Lazzarato, M. (1996). 'Immaterial labour', in P. Virno and M. Hardt (Eds.), *Radical Thought in Italy: A Potential Politics*. Minneapolis: University of Minnesota Press.

Marx, K. (1973). *Grundrisse*. New York: Penguin.

Mattei, U. (2011). 'The state, the market, and some preliminary questions about the commons', *Human Rights of People Experiencing Poverty*, University of Turin (DGIII Social Cohesion of the Council of Europe). At http://dupublicaucommun.blogspot.com/2011/03/contribution-dugo-mattei-pour-le-seance.html

Moulier-Boutang, Y. (1989). 'Introduction', in A. Negri, *The Politics of Subversion: A Manifesto for the Twenty-First Century*. Malden, MA: Polity Press.

Negri, A. (1989). *The Politics of Subversion: A Manifesto for the Twenty-First Century*. Cambridge: Polity Press.

Negri, A. (1991). *Marx beyond Marx*. New York: Autonomedia.

Negri, A. (1992). 'Interpretation of the class situation today: methodological aspects', in W. Bonefeld, R. Gunn and K. Psychopedis (Eds.), *Open Marxism, Volume II: Theory and Practice*. London: Pluto Press.

Ness, I. and Azzellini, D. (2011). *Ours to Master and to Own: Workers' Control from the Commune to the Present*. Chicago: Haymarket Books.

Nunes, R. (2007). 'Forward how? Forward where? Post operaismo beyond the immaterial labour thesis', *Ephemera: Theory and Politics in Organisation*, 7(1): 178–202.

Ostrom, E. (1990). *Governing the Commons: The Evolution of Institutions for Collective Action*. Cambridge: Cambridge University Press.

Precarias a La Deriva (2009). 'Political bodies vs. bodies politic', *Turbulence Magazine*, December. At: http://turbulence.org.uk/turbulence-5/t-10/bodies/

Roggero, G. (2011). 'Organised spontaneity: class struggle, workers' autonomy, and soviets in Italy'. At http://libcom.org/history/organized-spontaniety-class-struggle-workers-autonomy-soviets-italy-gigi-roggero

Rosenfeld, H. (2011). Workers' assemblies: a way to regroup the left', *MRZine*. At http://mrzine.monthlyreview.org/2011/rosenfeld280711.html

Tronti, M. (1962). 'La fabbrica e la societa', *Quaderni Rossi*, no. 2: 1–31.

Tronti, M. (1979). 'The strategy of refusal', in Red Notes (Ed.), *Working Class Autonomy and the Crisis: Italian Marxist Texts of the Theory and Practice of a Class Movement: 1964–79*. London: Red Notes and CSE Books.

Trott, B. (2007). 'Immaterial labour and world order: an evaluation of a thesis', *Ephemera: Theory and Politics in Organisation*, 7(1): 203–232.

Virno, P. (2004). *A Grammar of the Multitude.* Los Angeles, CA: Semiotext(e).

Chapter 3

Instituting the common: the perspective of the multitude

Sonja Lavaert

Introduction

In this chapter, the theme of the common(s) is discussed from the perspective of the multitude. As Negri played a key role in the reintroduction of the concept of multitude, using the term in his first book on Spinoza, the focus is on his texts and the context of the Italian revolutionary movement of the *operaismo* (workerism). In the content, form and production process of his texts, it is argued, Negri illustrates the creative, participatory logic of the common that he is attempting to invent, realise and theorise. This means that his ideas and concepts are not just individual imaginings, but the result of a collective work. There are many who apply the theoretical praxis, or who are practising the theory and instituting the common. I try to visualise this collective work of the multitude, presenting the genealogy of the concept in two steps: going back in history to the two authors who inspired Negri, namely, Machiavelli and Spinoza, and referring to two contemporary philosophers, Agamben and Virno, who were inspired by Negri but also, in turn, inspired him, who shared thoughts but also presented particular points of view.

In *Commonwealth*, the conclusion of their trilogy, Michael Hardt and Antonio Negri develop the political project of instituting the common. Finding a new space for politics in our globalising world ravaged by war, misery and exploitation is a necessary and urgent task; Hardt and Negri seek this new space for politics not outside but within our shared experience, across the false divides of private/public and capitalist/socialist. We need new forms to overcome the false progressivity, which assumes a hierarchical conservatism and furthers rather than eliminates oppression and social inequality. A reflection in terms of the common promises an ontology that not only enables analysis of the present but also prepares fertile ground for real emancipatory thought and democratic politics.

By 'common', Hardt and Negri mean the common wealth of the material world that is not made by humans (the air, water, natural resources) and also, more significantly, the results of social production ('such as knowledges, languages, codes, information, affects, and so forth'); instituting the common, then, becomes a project of democratic action investigating the art of self-rule of the 'multitude', within and against the 'empire', relying 'entirely on the immanence of decision making within the multitude' (Hardt & Negri, 2009: viii, xiii). The ultimate core of the project is not the production of objects but the production of subjectivity, which consists precisely in the construction of knowledge, affects, linguistic expressions or signs.

Prior to *Empire* and *Multitude*, Hardt and Negri's *Labor of Dionysus* (1994) can be considered as a preparatory outline treating all the major issues of the trilogy: labour, state institutions, the immeasurability of human practice in the production sphere and in politics. For Negri, however, the project of instituting the common within the multitude was initiated already in the early 1980s with the publication of his book on Spinoza and has been developed throughout in his philosophical research.

Although the theme of the common is widely discussed in the trilogy, in this article the focus is on the emergence of the concept of multitude in Negri's oeuvre. Paradoxically, this will allow a shifting from individual identities to the political space and forms of the multitude, which is what 'common', 'the common' and 'commons' is about. The problem with an immanent analysis – as attempted by Negri – is that means and aims coincide, that content and form are inextricably related and subjectivity attains reality only in the process of becoming: when fixed – for instance, as an object of representation – it disappears. The production of subjectivity is therefore only available for scrutiny while it is being practised. This is not an argument against the experiment – on the contrary – but it does have consequences for the method of research and of exposition. Focusing on the emergence of the concept of the common will enable us to contextualise the issues in play here as a historical materialist discussion.

In order to institute the common, or, in other words, to achieve real democracy, we need a production of subjectivity or forms of the multitude characterised by a network structure and a different view of the logics of causality. To understand what these forms are, I will also focus on how the perspective of the multitude is proposed by Paolo Virno. Both Negri and Virno lived through the experience of the *operaismo* and the Italian revolutionary movement of the 1970s. For a number of contextual reasons, and to the extent that he expressed his thoughts as fitting for a preoccupation with the common, Negri took up a key position. He appropriated, in an anomalous, subversive way, concepts of the cultural tradition and linked criticism and resistance to the imagination and invention. As a result, his method became exemplary for a range of contemporary thinkers, including Virno. But this also worked the other way round. Confirmed in his approach by the use of the concept of the 'multitude' by thinkers like Virno, Negri, in turn, was influenced. In the variations of the concept, as well as in the shared modalities, lies great significance.

As the perspective Negri developed is connected to contextual, historical factors, his ideas will be considered here in the context of his life and the *operaismo*. Negri questions objective knowledge and advances both the ethico-political and epistemological effectiveness of perspectivist knowledge. In light of the multitude as a restless expression of the entirety (the collective as a whole), this raises the question of how a partial and antagonistic perspective can pretend to universality, a question that foreshadows Virno's analysis (see below). Negri's terminology derives from the works of Spinoza and Machiavelli; engagement with these authors, therefore, facilitates enumeration of the crucial topics of a non-hierarchical, non-exclusive, creative vision of the common: namely, the antagonism between power of resistance and institutional power, the procedure of reversal, the cause as a convergence of factors, the role of the imagination, a materialist view of time, the profanation of religion and the junction of love and art with politics (see Mack, 2010: 3–5).

Virno's attention, meanwhile, shifts towards art, knowledge and language. He adopts Negri's paradigm to include a historical materialist point of view on matters of experience and temporality. This leads to a critique of teleology, which is explored in some of its applications. Virno launches the concepts of 'transduction' and 'trans-individuality' while looking for the multitude in the ambiguous, undefined nature of human beings and in the phenomenology of current forms of labour. The pluralistic 'multitude' is understood in opposition to the one 'people'; the singular 'universal' is replaced with the embracing 'common'.

Through a presentation of these major issues in Negri's and Virno's thoughts, I will also show some structural similarities and analogies with the work of Giorgio Agamben, who can be seen as a link between the two and clarifies various methodological aspects of the common. Agamben is also interesting because he underlines another textual source for the emergence of the multitude concept, namely the Averroist philosophy and particularly Dante (see Casarino & Negri, 2008; Lavaert, 2011).

Why philosophy, biographies and words?

In recent times, the concept of the multitude first emerged in *L'anomalia selvaggia* (*The Savage Anomaly*), Negri's book on Spinoza published in 1981. From that moment on, the immanent perspective began to appear in texts of political theory and epistemological and ontological matters in terms of 'multitude' or 'common'. For Negri, the book on Spinoza marked the start of a new style of writing – a philosophical one – and of a new type of enquiry – also philosophical. What does this mean? When he wrote this book, Negri was in prison. This was a traumatic experience with which he felt he could only cope by writing and, more particularly, by writing this book. Deprived of his freedom, independence, time and work, and to endure this without losing his sanity, Negri focused on philosophical questions (Gielen & Lavaert, 2011: 189). The search for multitude forms, the investigation of Spinoza, the struggle to maintain his self-integrity against the unjust deprivation, and the immanent perspective all come together and consistently reappear together in the philosophical oeuvre of Negri, from his earliest to his most recent work. In this context, three elements need to be emphasised as hypotheses motivating the present text.

First, philosophy is not a science accessible only to specialists and scholars, nor can it limit itself to treating specific matters in a particular domain. On the contrary, it belongs to everyone, can be practised by everyone and comprises a questioning of issues that concern everyone at the general level of principles. Philosophy goes beyond time and does not depend on specific contexts – although it does deal with particularities of the present and the ordinary life, which means that it features a tension between the universal and the singular, and also between critical analysis and the synthetic, or even artistic, approach. Philosophy searches after the neutrality of knowledge, which is useful for the many and, precisely for this reason, has to consider subjective experiences. The tension proper to philosophical research is the same tension that characterises the quest for the common. In this ordinary sense, philosophy is already and pre-eminently connected to the common and the multitude.

Second, Negri's imprisonment has to be considered in the context of the declaration of the state of emergency in Italy and the introduction of exceptional measures. Negri was arrested because of his participation in the *Autonomia* (autonomism) movement. His arrest and imprisonment did not take place within the normal frame of justice and constitutional civil rights. I am not just referring to his innocence concerning the charges levelled against him (terrorist acts, murder, leading a widespread criminal organisation, etc.), but rather to his sense of his imprisonment as an unjust, constitutionally illegal, in fact criminal attempt by the state to reduce him to silence, negate his will and destroy him as a human being.

Negri was one of 1,500 people arrested in Italy on 7 April 1979, while, according to Virno ([1986] 2011: 5), some 5,000 political activists passed through Italian prisons between 1979 and 1985. Negri's individual experience was thus part of the persecution suffered by the entire revolutionary movement; he underwent an experience shared by many and also functioned as an example in the production of philosophy (or subjectivity, to use his term) for a range of authors, especially those who were undergoing the same experience, and particularly Virno. Related to the historical context and biographical experiences, their shared intellectual space becomes all the more interesting and demonstrates the underlying logic of networking that is characteristic of their approach. Life narratives can illuminate complicated theoretical issues, such as, here, the tension between particularities, (the) common(s), generalities and the universal – or at least they can illustrate what the production of subjectivity is about.

Third, in this study, attention will be directed to methodological questions, forms and words. This means that we first have to determine how to consider the linguistic term 'common'. Following the 'most comprehensive attempts to produce a concept of the common', namely Hardt and Negri's *Multitude* and its successor *Commonwealth*, the word will be considered 'in terms of communication rather than in terms of community … For the common is that which is always at stake in any conversation: there where a conversation takes place, there the common expresses itself'; in other words, the common is considered linguistically and 'relatively' – that is, deriving meaning from and giving meaning to other words and signs with which it is connected (see Casarino & Negri, 2008: 1, 12, 14).[1]

This linguistic approach suits the philosophical categories used in the texts from which the term has emerged, going from Hardt and Negri, Virno and Agamben back to Spinoza, Machiavelli and even Dante. The linguistic reflection on the semantic fields of the languages themselves – Latin, but far more the vernaculars, Italian and Dutch – in which the concept emerged (eventually translated), reveal additional meanings. Finally, it also suits the transposition operated – again, following the authors mentioned – of the concept of 'common' with the perspective of the 'multitude'.

The context

The contemporary concept of the multitude emerged in a nexus of events and readings: Negri's thinking is intimately linked with the revolutionary movement, the *operaismo*, with Marx, Spinoza and Machiavelli and with the traumatic events in his personal life. This combination led him to discover analogies and to opt for a discontinuous, historical materialist approach. His theoretical research is always situated in the current context, upon which it focuses in a realistic way – it is ontology – and yet by doing so it changes the context – it is revolutionary. Here, I shall try to clarify just how and where this all began.

The Italian Communist Party (PCI), in which many critical intellectuals with links to the resistance movement sought refuge after World War II, was not only characterised by an authoritarian structure and subservience to the Soviet Union, but in the 1960s it also abandoned the idea of revolution and opted for the path of governmental participation. It failed to understand that the concrete situation of the workers and production had changed (see below), and as a consequence of this failure it had no response strategy. This led to a rift within the party and the birth of a new movement. The *operaismo*, in contrast to the PCI, remained focused on revolution and made the interrelated nature of theoretical research and political struggle central to its programme. For the movement and for Negri, the search for knowledge is situated in the context that one seeks to change. Negri wanted to know what was really happening in the factories and, to this end, he adopted the subjective perspective of the *operai* (labourers), emphasising an experiential knowledge rather than abstract production. The school of phenomenology played a significant role in the formation of this unique form of perspectivism or collective subjectivity.

As a student of Enzo Paci, who had reread Husserl and Heidegger in the light of Marx, Negri in turn read all texts through a phenomenological lens and criticised scientific or positivistic objectivism.[2] In *Marx oltre Marx* (*Marx Beyond Marx*), Negri ([1979] 1998) wrote a commentary on the *Grundrisse*, arguing that this sort of active, collective subjectivity was precisely what Marx had also aimed at. In the chapter on the machines in the preparatory outline to his famous critique of political economy, Marx (1983) had observed that the 'general, social knowledge' becomes the immediate force of production.[3] Human potentiality itself falls under the control of general knowledge. As Negri ([1997, 1977–78] 2006: 6) asserts, from the very moment the *Grundrisse* was translated into Italian in 1970, the book acquired a paradigmatic value in the movement. But *Marx oltre Marx* also acquired a paradigmatic value: acting/theorising as Negri does means using Marx to go beyond Marx. It also means going beyond Negri.

In the late 1970s, Negri published a series of booklets with publisher Feltrinelli, the famous *opuscoli*, in which he studied the transition from the hegemony of the Fordist labourer to the hegemony of the social labourer and searched for a social organisation that would correspond to the new class composition and the new reality for the workers.[4] He interpreted the transition as the replacement of the abstract labour typical of the Fordist period by subjective, particularised and socialised labour (see below). This interpretation was inspired by the distinction made by Marx between abstract and concrete labour, but it also went beyond Marx in that it revived the phenomenology of the labour organisation and the labourer's struggle against labour, which completely overcomes the tendencies analysed and predicted by Marx. This leads to a revision of all the traditional practices of the labour movement, ranging from an attack on the reformism of the party to a critical confrontation with the terroristic tendencies of the movement. The struggle must target administrative and social structures. The workers' autonomy, which Negri translates into 'collective subjectivity', thus moves towards a 'constituent subjectivity', or, in other words, into the 'production of subjectivity' (Negri, [1997, 1977–78] 2006: 13–15).

An illuminating insight into the *operaismo* perspective and proof of what was to become a preferred mode of expression for Negri was provided by his 1978 interview (Negri, [1979] 2007a). As lively interaction and bringing together a multiplicity of perspectives, the conversation emerges as a paradigmatic expression of the common (Casarino & Negri, 2008: 1). The conversation is a natural way of collective writing; indeed, Negri never considers himself the protagonist of an interview, or rather, to him the interviewer is equally the protagonist.[5] An interview also has the advantage of being read easily and being accessible to a larger public. This must be one of the reasons why

Dall'operaio massa all'operaio sociale (*From the Mass Labourer to the Social Labourer*), rather than the somewhat tight, highly theoretical and difficult *opuscoli*, became a reference text for the militants of the *Autonomia* movement as well as for their opponents, who soon became the persecutors of the movement.

The story of the transition from the mass labourer into the social labourer begins with the social struggles of the early 1960s, related by Panzieri, first of all, to the reading of the *Grundrisse* of Marx (Wright, 2002; Balestrini & Moroni, [1988] 2005: 128–43; Trotta & Milana, 2008). This history has been described more than once from an immanent narrative perspective – that is, by the people who experienced and participated in the movement.[6] It can be summarised in the following key moments.

First, the mass worker – who incarnates the abstract notion of labour as a living machine, a 'biomachine' – becomes the central figure in production. The mass labourer is operating in exactly the same way as the machines he attends to, without autonomous thoughts or linguistic expression. The machines are the result of technology and science, which are part of capitalism. This means that scientific knowledge is completely subsumed to capitalism and that the struggle against capitalism requires a renewed project, one with a different research agenda and knowledge base. It also means that machines do not emancipate, but, on the contrary, empty work of its content; moreover, the more machines there are, the more the pace of work is forced to increase. Hence, the idea arises of the self-organisation of workers, instead of their representation by party or trade union, and, later on, the idea of the rejection of work and the exodus from the factory.

With the riots of Piazza Statuto in Turin in 1962, a new political subject emerged – the immigrant from southern

Italy – and this emergence marked the start of the transition (Balestrini & Moroni, [1988] 2005: 135–6). The unskilled mass workers employed as pure manpower for a high capital return in the lowliest stages of the production process and working at a destructive pace were generally immigrants, mainly recently arrived young men from the south. They emigrated from southern Italy to the north and had no affinity with the organised, collective struggle of the communist tradition formed in the Resistance movement. They were ungovernable for both the authorities and the unions, without pride in their factory or discipline at work. They moved the site of action outside the factory, to the city streets and squares: thus, rather than mass labourers, they were social labourers, and the labour force had undergone a fundamental transformation. Of course, the concept of social labourer has to be connected with production, but in this transition the production was also changed. From a mere economic matter, it now became a biopolitical reality, a form of life, and exploitation became a corruption of the social life.

This brought Negri to the more radical claim of self-organisation and self-valorisation, which informs the principle of autonomist thought. The class struggle has to be fought from within the class of workers just as the search for knowledge has to be conducted from within the perspective where the conflicts or questions arise. The radical claim of self-organisation sharpened Negri's position in the discussion (with Tronti first of all) on the autonomy of the political and on the usefulness of the party, and it finally led to a rift within *operaismo*, which in turn led to a radicalisation of Negri's concept of 'difference'. Moving parallel to the introduction of the concept of the multitude, as Zanini (2007: 97) recounts, the emergence of the revised concept of difference announced the end of the *operaismo*. The historical moment at which the rift – an end and a new beginning – occurred is not unimportant; it was the point at which the capitalist 'counter-revolution' got underway and the state of emergency was declared.

However there is also a clear sense of continuity. It is clear that *operaismo* was the starting point and that the artistic, creative dimension with which, especially today, Negri is experimenting in his search for forms of the multitude, was present right from the start.[7] There is an overflow and a continuity following from the biopolitical idea of philosophy that has to be practised for a common life. Negri uses exactly the term 'biopolitical' to indicate how philosophy must be/is: analysing existential questions and experiences. He uses this term in contrast with that which he criticises, namely the 'biopower', which refers to the oppressive power of governments, systems, regimes, institutions, ideologies and capitalism.

Negri's perspective

The continuity inspired by the biopolitical motivation – knowledge research in praise of the common life – unifies the different stages of Negri's work that thus represents a cohesive whole and can only be understood if considered as such. The events of the 1970s are explained through the analysis, and, conversely, the events inspired extension of the analysis. Negri's readings of Spinoza gave a context to the traumatic personal experiences just as much as the reverse. Discovering similarities in Spinoza's fate with his own, Negri began to consider Spinoza as an example and turned to philosophy. Equally, it was prison that enabled Negri to understand the revolutionary content of Spinoza's thought –

namely that there are always two antagonistic perspectives, one related to the institutional power of the authority and the other to the resistant power of the multitude.

Prison helped Negri to understand the Machiavellian idea of time, the changeability of apparent destinies that often ends in tragedy. Prison also gave him a personal experience of the principle of capitalism as existing in the suppression and deprivation of captivity itself (Negri, 1981: 19). Capitalism consists in the robbery of one's lifetime, he realised. Being in prison, cut off from his teaching at university and in the factory, and far from the distraction of social pleasures, Negri thought he would finally have the time to restudy Spinoza.[8] He felt the need to do so because a lot had been published since the 1960s, and a new, French school of interpretation had presented the author of the *Ethics* as a materialistic, immanent philosopher, as the ground-breaker of democracy in a radical way. However, Negri soon realised that in prison he had as little time as before, an experience that gave him his insight into the real nature of captivity and a society ruled by capitalism. Nevertheless, he did manage to reread Spinoza.

Negri was struck by the anomaly the thinker represented, an anomaly that first appeared to be systematic – still matching the controllable measurability of rationalist metaphysics – and then became wild and immeasurable – transgressing ontology and moving to resistance, politics and change. The ideas of Spinoza went against the major tendencies of his time, against Cartesian rationalism, against the institutionalised academic science and against the Hobbesian belief in the definitive overcoming of the state of nature. But still they were modern, illuminating, emancipatory ideas. Crucially, Negri saw that the history of modernity is not that of a continuous and harmonious evolution rather comprises the discontinuous result of conflicting perspectives and powers. Spinoza represents an alternative modernity in that he considered the political significance of ideas, which necessarily – to have a common sense and potential/power (*potentia*) – are related to the *conatus*, the life instinct and vitality that we humans carry in us. Connected in each of us through the affects to the imagination, this life instinct is expressed by the production of subjectivity.

The *potentia*, *conatus*, imagination or subjectivity cannot be standardised from the outside. Spinoza's is an immanent perspective, which also features the alternative modernity. His subversion consists in the transposition of the ethical research from the past and inner world of the intentions towards the future of consequences and expressions as they evolve over time, from transcendent ideas towards the immanent world we live in and from the rational calculable measure to the immeasurability of the affects and the imagination. In the difference he demonstrates between established government power (*potestas*) and the power of the multitude (*potentia*), Spinoza illustrates a subversive, underground, anomalous line of alternative modernity that is shaped by the actions of the multitude.

In *L'Anomalia selvaggia*, where he elaborates on this reading, Negri (1981: 217–25) mentions the multitude in the context of this difference. He emphasises the rupture within Spinoza's work between a belief in calculable rationality at first and the wild subversion of the imagination later. This rupture occurs when terrible things are happening around one: war, violence, attacks on the democratic institutions. According to Negri, Spinoza felt impelled to express his indignation and anxiety, to caution about what was at stake, to protect the republican rules that were under pressure, and to prevent the further erosion of liberties. The perspective of the multitude appears in Negri's text when he is discussing the wild anomaly of Spinoza's illuminating imagination; the multitude appears but at this stage is not further developed.

In *Lenta ginestra* (*Slow Broom*), his commentary on the (early nineteenth century) poetry of Leopardi, Negri ([1987] 2001) traces a line back to Machiavelli in order to formulate a critique on modernity and its faith in technological progress, but also to underscore pessimism with regard to nature. Negri's critique of modernity has nothing to do with a romantic anti-modernity or counter-Enlightenment, but rather with the assertion of historical materialism and even more so with an indignation about the persistence of social inequality and injustice, despite modernity. The point of his critique is to demolish all illusions, because freedom from illusion and insight into the nothingness that surrounds human existence, in other words atheism, creates a space for social solidarity.[9]

With its slow and cautious progression, Negri's essay reads as a literary novel and illustrates the production of subjectivity. Through his analysis, we also discover interesting comments by Leopardi on the metaphorical character of language, the directness of poetry, the political significance of dramatic texts and, within those, the role of the choir. The choir is the voice of the many, the public commenting in third person. It stands for the ethical principle, the voice of conscience, the general and impersonal anonymous. It is the choir that is judging the actions of the actors, and without its approval (or refusal), the play does not even exist. The choir presents the voice of the common multitude.

In his work on revolution, *Il potere costituente* (*Insurgencies: Constituent Power and the Modern State*), an alternative line of modern thought (Machiavelli, Spinoza, later Marx) is identified and contrasted with the modernity of Hobbes, which lays the foundations for state sovereignty, representative institutions and capitalism (Negri, [1992] 2002b). In the years between his 1981 book on Spinoza and the publication of this essay in 1992, Negri had published *Arte e multitudo* (*Art and Multitude*) in which he explicitly focused on the 'multitude' in relation to labour and, of course, art (Negri, 1990). In social or living labour, the same challenges are at stake as in the artistic production and in the search for common forms by the multitude. The question is how, departing from singularities and differences, to achieve generality and validity for the many. This quest has various aspects associated with the political institution of a commonwealth as well as with the construction of an enlightened, emancipatory knowledge. In artistic production, theory and practice concur. Many texts were published in the 1980s and early 1990s accepting the same challenge, and all played a role in the slow genealogy of the multitude, including books by Virno, Vercellone, Piperno, Lazzarato and Illuminati, and journals such as *Futur Antérieur* (edited by Negri) and *Luogo commune* (edited by Agamben and Virno). One could say that in Italy in the 1980s and early 1990s was constituted 'a kind of laboratory for experimentation in new forms of political thinking that help us conceive a revolutionary practice in our times' – and in this was prepared the space for the 'potential politics' of the multitude(s) as common people, both many and plural (Hardt in Hardt & Virno, 1996: 1).

In *Il potere costituente*, Negri asserts that talking of constituent power is the same as talking of democracy, and the problem of the multitude power is now set in terms of the antagonism between the constituted power of state institutions and the constituent power (Negri, [1992] 2002b: 11). The *potentia* of the multitude is a constituent power. Machiavelli's quest for *verità effettuale* (effective truth) in political matters is conducted explicitly from the perspective of people of lowly origins, the multitude, Negri emphasises. His reflections focus on the formation of new political orders, which, of course, is what a revolution is about. The constituent power is averse to utopia; this fits with the contingency, mutability and material foundation of history. Negri's attention is directed towards the matter of time, the moment of change and its conditions: Machiavelli's significance lies in his vision of time, which he frees from the constraints of continuity, thus allowing for the possibility of change and determination of one's own fate.

The emergence of the multitude in Spinoza

In contrast to the rupture identified and emphasised by Negri, I think it is important to underline the coherence in Spinoza's oeuvre and anomaly. There is consistency in Spinoza's view on cause and experience of time, with implications in the fields of ethics, politics, epistemology and ontology. The theory he elaborates is praxis, and the practice he depicts is theoretical, as in Negri's work, for which it functions as an example. The cause is considered as a connection, a confluence in time of different factors, and it represents a reciprocal movement that affects the encountering factors: it is a bidirectional movement. This cause is at work in all human relations, which means, for example, in the experience of time, knowledge, communication, political and social practice, power and friendship or love. It affects the factors at stake with conditions or consequences, redirecting the attention from the individual terms to the relation or connection.

Of course, the most relevant consequence of this concept of reciprocal bidirectional movement is the idea of the 'multitude' related to the 'empire', two terms that are introduced explicitly by Spinoza (1677a: 278–9) in the *Tractatus Politicus* (*Political Treatise*). It is not without significance that Spinoza uses the word 'empire' for the rule or dominion, whatever its form (monarchical or regent board). It reminds us of Dante. As says Agamben, the word 'empire' is used by Dante, not specifically for a type of monarchical government but to indicate in a neutral way things related to the world, occurring in the limited arc of time of human life, in other words, the ethico-political. Dante also was the first to use the term 'multitude' in an explicit and significant way (Agamben, 2005a: 249–67; Dante, 1965: 249–67).

At this point, I want to suggest that Spinoza introduces the (not so) new terminology of 'empire' and 'multitude' in two movements: on the one hand, following Machiavelli and the authors who inspired him, especially Dante, in an act of profanation, as Agamben calls it (see below), and on the other, polemicising with Hobbes, in whose terminology one can read the apology of the one sovereign and a theory that tries to eliminate the changeability of time experiences. These two movements are intertwined. Machiavelli, whose major issue was the contingency paradigm of *fortuna* and *virtù*, and whose political message is republican, talks about the multitude in an obvious, self-evident way. For Spinoza this terminology must have suited his anti-Hobbesian vision well.

Spinoza uses the word 'multitude' (Latin: '*multitudo*'), forged by the Italian vernacular of Machiavelli and by the Dutch translations of his circle, to indicate the many 'common' individuals (*gemeen, menigte*), and also indicating the many different factors (*veelheid*) at stake in human world affairs.[10] Interesting is Spinoza's attempt to formulate the idea of democracy – equality, material wealth, peace, freedom of thought and expression – not as a specific form of governance, but as the condition for politics in the general interest, starting from the empire/multitude pairing. The empire depends on the multitude in the reciprocity (albeit asymmetric) between the ruling and the ruled: 'right' is the power of the multitude (Spinoza, 1677a: 278–9).

In the *Tractatus Theologico-Politicus* (*Theological-political Treatise*) Spinoza (1670, 2002) relates religion to fear and obedience, which are at odds with democracy.[11] Pursuing this line of thought, we arrive at a defence of disobedience and freethinking. The reversals in his work are exemplary. People are part of nature, in which there is no good or evil. They do not strive after anything because they think that it is good but, conversely, think things are good because they strive for them. This relativism is not an obstacle to ethics: on the contrary, it is the basis on which ethical questions can be formulated. In a democracy, people do not transfer their power to a government to such an extent that they are unable to deliberate: those in power are, therefore, always subject to fear.[12] Spinoza polemicises against philosophers who see passions as defects and thus fail to recognise them as a reality. Political theory must take these passions as its starting point. Thus, he makes an attempt to understand human nature, in order to discover what to do about war, absolutism and people's tendency to act against their own interests, and hence how to fight for freedom and independence.

The role of the imagination is essential to this endeavour. Imagination is not just a negative illusion and the cause of fear. In a neutral way, it is associated with lust, desire and passions; it is part of the human condition. Moreover, it is the basis of hypothetical intuitive thinking, and so has the positive power to inspire change. This threefold function of the imagination is connected to the three types of knowledge that Spinoza distinguishes in the *Ethics* and to the concept of the multitude he introduces in the *Political Treatise*.[13] Importantly, the new terminology only makes proper sense when read as a critique of Hobbes' justification of the absolutist sovereign principle and as a resumé of the fresh Renaissance humanism of Machiavelli, for whom the multitude was still a self-evident concept and perspective.

The perspective of Machiavelli

So, it is right to see Machiavelli as the predecessor of Spinoza, and it is also right that Negri claims the core of Machiavellian thought to be the paradigm of 'virtue and fortune', which equates to the experience of time, the changeability of human affairs, and the how-to issue of directing change (or making a revolution) within the order of nature or without violating the laws of nature. One may criticise Negri, however, for not sufficiently emphasising the topic of 'perspective' in Machiavelli's *Il Principe* (although he does rely on its ontology). This theoretical under-valuation of perspective and its consequences, I would argue, induces a loss of concreteness in Negri's reading. The hermeneutics of the virtue-and-fortune paradigm clarifies our historical research of the common, but a more elaborated interpretation of Machiavelli's description of the social revolt in his *Istorie fiorentine* (*History of Florence*) can enrich and bolster this research. Besides, it is Negri ([1992] 2002b) who puts us on this track.

From Machiavelli's texts, with their concepts of multitude and perspective assumed as self-evident (a self-evidence that surely extends to Negri and explains his vagueness on the subject), we can learn how revolutionary change actually happens; exemplary is his description of the urban social insurrection of 1378, the Revolt of the Ciompi (Machiavelli, [1525] 2005: 443–6). Machiavelli shows that the content of politics is social, that the form is struggle, and that the subject is the multitude of ordinary people. In the case in question, he identifies with the populus through the underclass of (unguilded) wool workers, literally, as the grammatical subject of his narrative recounting the historical event. In Machiavelli's ([1513] 1997) descriptions of the various sociopolitical cases and the many different stories he recounts, I would argue, two thoughts appear which seem to acquire an axiomatic value.[14] First, there are always two perspectives that conflict with each other: the perspective of the 'have-nots' and the perspective of the 'haves', be it wealth or established governmental power. Second, everything is relative and changeable. The second axiom is applicable to the first, which means that the two conflicting perspectives are mobile.

Another Machiavellian insight is that political affairs are not just cognitive but also affective and as an object of knowledge thus require imagination. This is associated with an essential human ambiguity: people are both good and bad, human and animal, and, as animal, fox and lion (roughly, fox for intelligence, lion for force). This is also associated with a historical vision based upon the nothingness of the beyond, an immanent materialist vision. *Verità effettuale* (effective knowledge) concerns finding the opportune moment to enact changes, and then about ensuring that the newly introduced form endures. Whereas Spinoza, with his analysis of the affects, highlights the ambiguity of the multitude, which fails to use its power and is an accomplice to its own servility, we learn from Machiavelli about the revolutionary power, which is unable to maintain itself after the revolutionary moment and or even transforms into its opposite: the stronghold of established sovereignty, the threats, violence and terror. The story often ends in tragedy, leaving the multitude with only knowledge, love and laughter.

Love, laughter, art and multitude

Laughter has always been extremely important to Negri. He has dedicated an entire chapter to the effect of laughter in *Il lavoro di Giobbe* ([1990] 2002a, 2009b). 'The theme of laughter as a potency is also very much present in Spinoza', he says (Gielen & Lavaert, 2011: 191). Laughter is always knowledge and resistance. Knowledge is also potency and resistance when it becomes common or general. And common knowledge is analogous to art, which is always the result of general intellect:

> [The general intellect is] a sort of subjective machine in motion, formed through the interaction of a great many singularities, of their ideas and products. It is an active collective, a multitude. Whenever we find a general intellect, we also discover a multitude of subjects who form this intellect, in the immanence or in the historical situation. This is the way in which we have to imagine the general intellect – as a multitude of subjects. (Gielen & Lavaert, 2011: 173)

Negri considers the relation between art, knowledge, production and power in *Arte e Multitudo*. His idea of art approximates to the multitude also with regard to the issue of time, experience and the causal relationship. As he says, art is about a new view on things, but also 'a genuine insertion, an entering, a connection'; it concerns 'physical contact, hence the image of entering the water and submerging oneself' (Gielen & Lavaert, 2011: 167). The artistic production is living labour, collective, purposeful – the literal meaning of '*ad arte*' being intentionally, knowingly – but, nonetheless, its purpose is general and unfulfilled by a predefined design; its logic is free of teleology. In this sense, it is an open and free activity, and here is another analogy: with love. Negri clarifies that we have to make a distinction between art and non-art. To him,

> non-art is essentially seen in the naturalistic and individualistic reduction of the collective working that is produced by art. Non-art is where this naturalistic reduction to the individual takes place. This can be fully compared to the romantic and religious love that is locked up in the family and, as a result, completely reduced to a function and therefore an identity, which equals non-love. Parallel to that, art is reduced to non-art to the extent to which it is reduced to individual, natural identity. (Gielen & Lavaert, 2011: 179)

Art is purposeful, knowing, deliberate, as is love, but it is also an anomaly, an immeasurable resistance, going beyond any fixed identity, natural *telos* or function.

Negri concretises the analogy between the power of the multitude and love in *Commonwealth*, where, with Hardt, he again presents the analogical thought experiment as a critique of identity and teleological thinking (Hardt & Negri, 2009: 179–88; see also Gielen & Lavaert, 2011: 177–9). The artificial common produced by humans is a solidarity that arises from conflict, through and in the clash of passions, a multiple and conflict-laden tendency that he calls 'love'. This love has nothing to do with religious, romantic or bourgeois love, which are necessarily linked to marriage, family, propagation, calculation and competition and are based on the idea of exclusivity and thus identity or a union of identities. To clarify what he means, Negri uses Deleuze and Guattari's (1980) imagery of the bees and wasps.[15] Bees make love to flowers for the sake of pollination, with a defined function, as identity, in a fixed pattern of natural efficiency. Wasps make love to orchids without function or identity but simply for the pleasure of the experience. While doing so, because they enjoy it, loving for the sake of the experience of love, the wasps create a 'contra-natural common'.

The philosopher insists upon the non-naturalness, which we have to understand in the Leopardian way as critical both to the romantic vision of a harmonious nature and to the belief in determinist progress. Nevertheless, the non-naturalness represents a problematic theoretical topic in Negri's reflections and leads to polemics with, for instance, Virno (see below). Here, I want to draw attention to the problematic terminology: at this point, Negri is not insisting upon the idea of inserting while resisting, or resisting while inserting, as he does when he speaks about art – one could call this the 'naturalness' of art – but his critique is directed against the teleology and the functional way of social thinking. Negri presents his love reflections as an example of creative hypothetical thinking, but underlines that he is also speaking about common, ordinary love (Gielen & Lavaert, 2011: 178). Everyone understands the idea of love for the simple pleasure of the experience and that love only exists in the shared space of different (human or animal) beings.

Agamben's perspective between Negri and Virno

Despite the fact that the concept of the multitude arrived relatively late in his writings and continued to be voiced only implicitly in his analysis, Agamben's shift of attention to art and linguistic practices sheds further light on various aspects of the issue. It is even plausible to consider his entire oeuvre as an argument for the thesis that real common thought, and consequently real democratic forms, can be experienced only on the basis of an internally contrasting plurality of elements and on condition that the relationship is regarded as taking priority over the terms – with respect to time, cause and human relationships.[16]

In Agamben (2007), the emphasis is on principles and epistemological methods, such as the paradigmatic method, into which he introduces new and critical content. As previously mentioned, Agamben's work occupies a place apart from the radical philosophers, primarily because he did not actively participate in the struggle and so did not have any juridical problems with the apparatus of the state. In the hottest years of the revolutionary movement, having previously graduated in philosophy of law in Italy, Agamben lived abroad. He followed seminars held by Heidegger in France, worked at the Warburg Institute in London and read and studied Walter Benjamin, whom he would later translate into Italian. Nonetheless, he did discuss – at the level of principles – the procedures applied to Negri, Virno and the revolutionary movement, and also the concrete actions initiated in response to the procedures. The analogies between Agamben's reflections and theirs are striking, and the mutual criticism between him and Negri represents a corroborating reflection (Agamben, 1995: 49–51; Negri, 2003: 13, 2007b: 109–26, 2007c: 12).[17] One can find in Agamben's idea of network causality and the importance he gives to early Renaissance humanism the same mixture of Marx, Nietzsche and phenomenology, current events, reflections on juridical forms, an aesthetic intuition and indignation about state injustice – each of which was deemed essential.

Agamben (2007: 19–20) states that paradigms obey the analogical logic of the imagination. His theoretical search for the method of knowledge is itself a work of the paradigmatic method, a methodological reflection that thus reveals the specific nature of the imagination. Paradigms, for their part, are living images proceeding in time. They are examples that isolate a particular case in its context and by doing so make a new totality comprehensible in the revelation of particularity. This means that they are not pre-existing factual similarities, but are self-generated by means of a 'bringing together' or 'showing'. It also means that they are not inductive or deductive knowledge methods: they replace the binary 'either/or' logic with a bipolar 'both/and' model following lived realities. Thinking in paradigms means not questioning the temporal origins because there is no origin; or, to be more precise, each phenomenon that appears on the surface is an origin and conversely each image is archaic.[18]

The *arche* that Agamben tracks down is not an origin in time, but makes both the researcher's present and the past of his research object comprehensible. Archaeological or genealogical history writing turns temporal categories on their heads. The temporal structure inherent in philosophical archaeology is not a past but a point of emergence or a beginning, which, however, is only found if one goes back to where this point of emergence was covered by tradition. The point of emergence has the form of a past in the future, a *futuro anteriore*. Relatedly, Agamben (2005a: 365–76) sees the concepts *imperium* and *multitudo* proposed by Spinoza and reintroduced by Negri and Hardt as emerging in the texts of Dante.

Situating the emergence of the concept in the Averroist philosophy of Dante, Agamben clarifies modalities of the multitude perspective, namely its immanence, multiplicity and contingency or temporal discontinuity. Going back to the Renaissance texts themselves, we find that (a) the multitude appears as grammatical subject that is semantically mostly agent, always the immanent cause of the story, gender neutral and pluralistic; (b) the multitude appears together with the empire, which, in Dante's text, is not the image of a specific government or governance, but of the contingent temporal character of political matters, in contrast with the universal character of religious matters (for Dante, this did reflect a political choice, namely against papal power). The *imperium* indicates that common matters are proceeding and passing in time. From the perspective of the multitude, in common (read: political) matters this amounts to finding a rhythm, and art plays a role in this, asserts Agamben ([1970] 1994: 143–56).[19] Art is essential, he argues, because it gives people a place in time, inserting and interrupting. It sets a standard. This is connected with Agamben's argument that imagination is ingrained in experience and that pleasure is the most authentic experience.

Virno, the context, work and (general) knowledge

In Virno also, we see a shift of attention towards art, knowledge and language as he follows Negri's example to include a historical materialist point of view on matters of experience and time. This leads to a critique of teleology, which is explored in processes of labour. In the post-Fordist era, the working class expresses itself not as the people but as multitude, which means a sociological translation in terms of classes and then of class struggle. Also, Virno is searching for 'effective truth'; his aim is a realistic knowledge of current social situations with the potential to change. However, he seems to follow analytical schemes more rigorously than does Negri. This is especially true for *Quando il verbo si fa carne* (*When the Verb becomes Flesh*) (2003) and *E così via, all'infinito* (*And so on, ad infinitum*) (2010) in which the subjects of the analysis are 'trans-individuality', instead of 'collective subjectivity' (Virno avoids the subjective/objective duality), the naturalness of the multitude (seen by Negri as a paralysing determinism) and the ambivalence of the multitude (its impotence before the revolutionary facts, as detected by Spinoza, and its violence after the revolutionary facts, as described by Machiavelli – dangers that are neglected by Negri) (Virno, 2003, 2010). Virno's analytical rigour, related to Kantian and Aristotelian formalism (seen by Negri as determinism), is experienced also in his criticism of 'universality', which he replaces with 'the common'.

Nevertheless, in Virno we see the same contextual nexus as in Negri. On 7 April 1979, he too was arrested, together with other members of the editorial committee of the journal *Metropoli*, of which he was editor-in-chief. He spent three years in prison and one under house arrest charged with further offences, and it was not until 1987 that he was cleared of all indictments, and only in 1988, nine years after his initial arrest, that he was finally acquitted. Virno shared his time in captivity with many friends of the movement, who came together with him to discuss, to think and to write. In *Diario di un'evasione* (*Diary of an Escape*), Negri testifies to these discussions, presenting the article 'Do you Remember Revolution?', co-written by Virno (among others), on the basis of such a collective discussion and published in *Il*

Manifesto on 20 and 22 February 1983, followed by the French translation in 1986, the English in 1988, and after that in various volumes edited by Moroni and Balestrini, Virno and others.[20] The struggle did not stop in prison; quite the contrary, in fact. Thus, while we should dismiss the 'aura' that surrounds sacredness, the uniqueness of particular experiences should be conserved.

Building on a thesis from Benjamin, Virno finds a place for uniqueness in the impersonal and serial. This idea undermines the antagonism between the individual and the collective and brings the experience back to the common. It also represents an answer to the aspirations of a movement in search of a space for politics in the entirety of particularities or a notion of the common emerging from the factual plurality of thoughts and imagination.

Paradoxically, the concept of 'general intellect', which was introduced by Marx (1983: 602) in the 'Fragment on Machines', as it is called, of the *Grundrisse*, is very important to such a materialistic theory. General knowledge does not belong to a defined and concrete individual person like Paolo, Giorgio or Antonio, but is, 'like the air we breathe', a sort of common source of the multitude of human beings (Virno, 2011: 13). General thought is neutrally impersonal, argues Virno, a thought in which *I think* must clear the way for *one thinks*. Moreover, general knowledge is public because it settles in the phenomenal world of appearances and acquires the same characteristics of material facts. It can be as incisive as an act of love, like a kiss or a caress, and as incisive as a revolutionary act, such as the occupation of the streets and squares of a metropolis. When one recognises the importance of the general intellect, Virno continues, the traditional analysis of capitalist society loses truth, as also does the rest of modern political theory.

In the late 1970s, the journal *Metropoli* wanted to reflect on post-Fordism, the crisis of a society based on work, the new forms of subjectivity and the fact that linguistic practice had come to be central to work. In *Convenzione e materialism materialismo (Convention and Materialism)* ([1986] 2011), Virno continues this research and focuses on the epistemological categories that characterise modern intellectual work within social production. The autonomy of the general intellect, it was understood, has irreversibly changed the labour process, but it also offers a possibility of emancipation. Work has become immaterial and, at the same time, social. The consequence is a form of production that is far more complex, and so the law of value ceases to be applicable. Like Negri, Virno insists upon the immeasurability of social labour, from the moment that production includes immaterial goods constituted in the minds of and space between humans (knowledge, affects, codes, languages, etc.), the labour process exceeds the limits of place and time, and its value cannot be measured in temporal units.

Virno's analysis leads to the question of whether, in the current circumstances, it is possible to apply a unified notion of production. The answer is negative: a unified concept is associated with a simple, teleological view in which work activities and linguistic interaction are mutually exclusive. The unified view of labour is based on efficient causality, an idea characterised by a mechanical logic taken from nineteenth century industry (Virno, [1986] 2011: 67–75). Virno sees similarities between the logic of the old mass labour, the causal effect of industrial machines, the efficient causality characterised by a teleological view (coinciding with the final cause) as criticised by Spinoza and the causal effect in linguistic enunciations. The linguistic paradigm reveals that in the efficient (final) cause there are three components: an active agent, a mechanical force and a passive body. These components are completely independent of one another and have no intrinsic features. The operation is silent, and proceeds in one unambiguous direction, which can only be repeated and imitated. There is no reciprocity. This makes the efficient causality unsuitable and unrealistic for post-Fordist production. By contrast, the practice of networking does not seek to replicate the orderliness of machines, but to respond to real effects in order to produce new modes and paradigms. The formal causality is characterised by a formal reciprocity, which is essential for communication, knowledge and language practice. Its components are multiple, various, ambiguous, immeasurable and self-generating. The formal causality matches what is going on in the actual labour processes, from the perspective of the researcher and also from the perspective of the labourer. Thus does the post-Fordist working class express itself as a multitude (Gielen & Lavaert, 2009: 38).

Virno's perspective on the multitude

Essentially, for Virno, the multitude is key to every reflection on current social events. In the genealogy of the concept in its political aspects, Virno (2010: 162–75) is engaging with a debate conducted in the seventeenth century, a period in which much of our ethical and political vocabulary originated.[21] He interprets the assertions of Hobbes and Spinoza as an antagonism between two political perspectives: from the latter, the republican democratic perspective, whilst the former sings the praise of monarchy. According to Hobbes, the natural state is overcome by establishing political institutions and sovereignty. However, says Virno, Hobbes is equally (or even more) concerned with restraining and controlling the use of words, which is among the major sources of conflict and instability. Furthermore, the general human capacity for creating appearance and secrecy with the use of words is troubling for Hobbes. By contrast, a systematic application of the rules, from the linguistic grammatical to civil law, silences any troubling ambiguity. The linguistic natural state reveals an ambiguous, labile, disquieting openness to the world, whereas the Hobbesian civil state brackets openness and creates an artificial environment in which unambiguous habits prevail. This is why, in contrast to Spinoza, for Hobbes the multitude needed to be transformed into 'one' people.

On this basis, Virno argues that the natural state asserts itself in politics when the people return to being a multitude – in other words, a plurality of individuals who no longer obey but who argue, speak, murmur, protest, refute, discourse, commune and suchlike, just as in the Biblical imagery of the exodus (Gielen & Lavaert, 2009: 37; Virno, [1986] 2011: 160–61.).[22] However, the natural state also asserts itself in politics when the sovereign suspends the ordinary laws and declares a state of exception (i.e. a state of emergency requiring exceptional measures). The revolt of the multitude, therefore, corresponds to the state of exception: in both cases, right becomes a factual question and the distinction becomes blurred between the level of the rules and the level of the facts to which the rules must be applied. This shocking intuition is contested by Negri as being far too pessimistic and perverted by Virno's reading of Schmitt, although, on the other hand, it is also corroborated by the genealogy Negri presents in *Multitude*.[23] This strange arguing/agreeing seems to be mediated by Agamben's (2003) presentation of the question of modern sovereignty in terms of sacredness and state of exception, a presentation that was also influenced by the reading of Schmitt.

For Virno, the multitude and the state of exception show the need to regard the link between passions and the use of language as something that is both natural and political. Beyond the rules, there is a prior regularity that forms the anthropological background for any positive law. This regularity exists in the unchangeable basic categories and logical structures of the linguistic human animal, which in themselves are empty and indeterminate. Emptiness and indeterminacy are the conditions for the possibility of filling them up with different contents. in different concrete situations. A theory, seen from the perspective of the multitude, must express the essence of the three levels of human practice: the common, the invention of a determinate rule and the contingent application of this rule. None of the three levels, and application least of all, is immune to so-called evil.[24]

Virno criticises the monopolisation of political decision-making in the hands of a single authority, because this functions according to the rule of repetitive compulsion or because imagination and creativity, essential in experience and application, then become impossible. This critique is based on the assumption that people in general are ambiguous, open and indeterminate, good and bad. Political institutions that definitively outlaw the negative, as is the case when a single authority takes the decisions (but also if they are based on an ideal, a religious dogma or a doctrine), do not protect people but create compulsion, threats, fear and violence. The big issue for democracy is how to arrive at decisions and institutions in favour of the general interest based on the factual plurality of differences and singular interests. Virno finds useful components for this in Simondon's individuation theory, which argues that a living individual constitutes itself in interaction with a pre-individual reality, of which an inchoate residue subsists at any given moment, keeping the process going.[25] The pre-individual reality is the common human nature.

Modern representative democracy as it has developed since the seventeenth century is undemocratic in that it has systematically replaced the common, which can be individuated but cannot be given a predicate, with the universal, which can be given a predicate but cannot be individuated. The universal is identifiable with positive characteristics irrespective of the perspective of the identifier, while the common is not identifiable in a strict way and from outside the space or community in which it constitutes itself. Replacing the common with the universal, imagination and creativity are excluded and the multitude is suppressed by fear, or at best, its (their, our) potency is neutralised. An alternative can be found if, conversely, we focus on the immanent perspective and keep on mustering up the courage to engage in disobedience, freethinking and free speech.

(Non-)conclusion

Negri does not agree with Virno's thesis of the naturalness of the common or with his focus on purely linguistic forms or the multitude's so-called evil.[26] Their discussion is interesting to review because it reveals a great deal of truth, not in the form of conclusive judgements such as who is right or wrong, but in the arguments that appear in the discussion itself. Indeed, their discussion is a philosophical questioning, criticising and searching, which means that it cannot be concluded: the decisions are to be taken within the practice of the movements. Virno likes to underline the fact that his point of view is pessimistic. Because of the ambiguity and naturalness, the power of the multitude is not a guarantee and the story can turn out sour. In Negri's assertions, optimism apparently pervades the potency of the multitude, but it is a realistic optimism. Their reciprocal critiques can be used to help understand the question and to become aware of the traps and confusions that lie in wait.

To clarify his position in the optimism/pessimism debate, Negri often uses a witticism of Gramsci in which he reverses the terms. What we need, he says, is 'optimism of the knowledge and pessimism of the will' (Negri, [1983] 2009a: 193–4). Optimism of the knowledge undoubtedly has the advantage of the enthusiasm it can raise, and, with the necessity of an accompanying pessimism of the will, Negri in fact confirms the ambiguity of the multitude. The pessimism of the will is explicitly expressed against the degeneration of revolutions and, more specifically, the comrades of the autonomist movement who chose terrorist violence – a choice he compares with that of the revolutionary governments of councils that became dictatorial in the Soviet Union and the power of the resistance movement that evolved into the authoritarian hierarchy of the PCI.

One could say that the discussion concerning the ambiguity of the multitude runs within the oeuvre of Negri itself, namely where he distinguishes the rupture (where he follows Althusser) in the work of Spinoza, and perhaps even where he sees a contradiction in Machiavelli's writing of history – that is, between an old pessimistic vision and the discovery of a new method.[27] What this discontinuity is really about can perhaps best be understood, again, when contrasted with the assertions of Virno. The question of a radical rethinking of the multitude (and of how to achieve democracy, equality, social justice, commonwealth, etc.) is that of how to consider the production of the common if the perspective of the multitude is partial, antagonistic and not to be determined in a universalistic, scientifically objective way. This seems paradoxical: is not the multitude expressing the potency of the common without a residual? It is, but in an ambiguous, vivacious and mutable way. Placing the multitude at the core of their research, Agamben, Negri and Virno challenge our conceptions of theoretical and political objects: the multitude is an open concept, disposed to being reshaped by political praxis over and over again. This leads to materialistic, ethical, political, critical theorising, not opposed to imagination and affects, but conversely, using imagination and affect in order to build a real democracy, where the abstract universalism of state sovereignty is replaced by the effective construction of common yet multitudinous forms from within. The *potentia* of the multitude in Spinoza has to be carefully confronted and compared with the theory of the two conflicting perspectives of Machiavelli, and the optimism of knowledge to be combined with pessimism of the will, each time again, in every concrete situation – surely a complex and difficult task. But, in Negri's terms, 'the possibility is real' (Gielen & Lavaert, 2011: 184).

Acknowledgements

I want to thank Tuomo Alhojärvi, Andy Hilton, Joost Jongerden, Pieter Lemmens and Guido Ruivenkamp for their constructive questions, comments and suggestions given during the drafting of this article.

Notes

1   The conversation reported took place when *Commonwealth* was not yet published. My hypothesis is that this conversation between Negri and Casarino, who noticed the absence of the concept of 'communism' in the first two parts of the trilogy, played a role in its translation into the terminology of the 'common'.

2   Antonio Paci, a former disciple of the phenomenologist Antonio Banfi, taught Negri and a whole generation of Italian philosophers, such as Maurizio Ferraris, Pier Aldo Rovatti and Carlo Sini. In 1951, he founded the magazine *Aut Aut*, which was important for phenomenology in Italy. In his Marxist existentialism, we recognise some of the thoughts of Agamben, Negri and Virno, like the status of the principle of relationship and the importance attributed to the negative.

3   We read in Marx's original text a mixture of German and English words: 'das allgemeine gesellschaftliche Wissen, knowledge', the last word translated in the footnote 'Kenntnisse'; and, further, 'general intellect', translated in the footnote 'allgemeinen Verstandes' (Marx, 1983: 602).

4   The *opuscoli* (pamphlets), published by Feltrinelli between 1977 and 1978 (*Crisi dello Stato-piano*; *Partito operaio contro il lavoro*; *Proletari e Stato*; *Per la critica della costituzione materiale*; *Il dominio e il sabotaggio*), were withdrawn from circulation by the publisher in the early 1980s and for a long time were unavailable. They have since been republished in a single volume, *I libri del rogo*.

5   I experienced myself on the occasion of an interview on art and common that Negri regards interviews as conversations, in which he is as curious to know the ideas of the interviewer as the interviewer is to know his. This reciprocity continues in the stage of writing, which he also considers to be a collective process, as testified by Cesare Casarino (Casarino & Negri, 2008; see also Gielen & Lavaert, 2011).

6   For further sources on the *operaismo*, see also Bori, Pozzi and Roggero (2005), Zanini (2007) and Zanini and Fadini (2001); all these texts were written collectively and present testimonies of the protagonists themselves.

7   See Negri's experimentation with political drama in the three plays of *The Trilogy of Resistance* (Negri, 2009b).

8   Similarly, Negri's focus on Spinoza represented a continuity in his philosophical production from *L'anomalia selvaggia* to *Spinoza et nous* (Negri, 2010b; see also Negri, 1981: 225–37).

9   Talking about atheism, I go beyond Negri; there is a humanistic atheism in all of Negri's thoughts but he rarely expresses it in explicit terms.

10   In the translations into Dutch produced in Spinoza's time by friends of his circle, the Latin '*multitudo*' is translated as '*menigte*' and/or '*veelheid*'. Cf. *Staatkundige Verhandeling* in the *Nagelate Schriften* (Spinoza, 1677b); *De rechtzinnige theologant, of Godgeleerde staatkundige verhandelinge* (Spinoza, 1693). The dictionaries of the time are even clearer, giving the two terms systematically (see Koerbagh, 1668; Meyer, 1663).

11   In this representation of Spinoza's thoughts, I remain within the scheme of Negri's interpretation but I also go beyond, or in other words, I present my own reading of Spinoza.

12   This idea is developed in the *Tractatus Theologico-Politicus* (Spinoza, 1670: 180–205).

13   See Chapter II in the *Tractatus Politicus* on 'natural right' (Spinoza, 1677: 270–84), in which he gives the key to reading the *Theologico-Political Treatise* and the *Ethics*; of course, this is a big thesis, to be argued in an independent study which is the current work in progress of the author and was schematically presented in 'Radical Enlightenment, Enlightened Subversion, and Spinoza' (see Lavaert, 2014: 49–102).

14   I present my own reading of Machiavelli, not as opposed to Negri's but as a going beyond; this is especially the case for the conclusions about what we can learn from Machiavelli and Spinoza on the (im)potency of the multitude.

15   Deleuze and Guattari themselves resumed the imagery launched by Bernard Mandeville in *The Fable of the Bees*.

16   This thesis is largely argued in Lavaert (2011).

17   The criticism of Agamben and Negri is also present in Casarino and Negri (2008).

18   The Auschwitz paradigm, it may be noted, is often mistaken for a hypothesis that explains modernity in an analytical way, and as such, it is criticised as an abuse; the same goes for the paradigms of the bare life, sacredness and the state of exception. Besides *Homo Sacer*, in

which is developed the paradigm of bare life and sacredness, the other works exemplary of this method are Agamben (1998, 2003).

19   Agamben's debut, this was perhaps the most important text in Virno's philosophical formation and is crucial to understand Virno's place in Agamben's oeuvre.

20   'Do you Remember Revolution?' was signed by Lucio Castellano, Arrigo Cavallina, Giustino Cortiana, Mario Dalmaviva, Luciano Ferrari Bravo, Chicco Funaro, Toni Negri, Paolo Pozzi, Franco Tommei, Emilio Vesce and Paolo Virno (see e.g. Negri, [1985/86] 2010: 35–49; Virno, 2005: 639–59).

21   In fact, Virno does not say a lot about Spinoza, but goes directly into discussion with Hobbes. Spinoza is systematically implicit in his discourse, however, in the same way that the antagonism to Hobbes is implicit in Spinoza. Like Negri, Virno also applies reversals and, along with the term 'multitude', he resumes the socio-political necessity of dystopia and the idea that the natural state never ends.

22   In *Exodus and Revolution*, Walzer (1985) reads the biblical Exodus text as a paradigm for revolutionary politics using 'paradigm' in the same way as Agamben, so Exodus is not a theory of revolution but a narrative for common use intended for recurrent re-readings and analogical applications. *Exodus and Revolution* was translated into Italian in 1986, which thus surely played a role in the use that the Italian radical philosophers made of the image (see also Iluminati, 2003).

23   In *Multitude* Hardt and Negri (2004) distinguish the concept of 'exception' in both its German and American origin as a key factor for understanding the current global state of war.

24   Virno (2010: 162–75) gives to these experimental reflections collected in the second part of *E così via, all'infinito* the title 'The so-called evil and the criticism of the state'. Part of the experiment is again the procedure of the reversal: he uses the arguments of Carl Schmitt to construct an argumentation from the politically opposite perspective, to criticise the state form, and consequently reverses the results of Schmitt (see also Lavaert, 2013: 117–40).

25   Simondon influenced Deleuze and, even more interestingly, Bernard Stiegler and Gilbert Hottois, as they identify the pre-individual domain with the human 'technical condition'. This means that there is an intrinsic relationship between techniques and common human nature, and it also endorses Virno's thesis on 'natural history' and on 'creativity' (see Simondon, 1989).

26   Each made clear his point of discussion in the interviews (Gielen & Lavaert, 2009: 34–6, 2011: 170–71).

27   In *L'anomalia selvaggia*, Negri (1981) speaks about the systematic rupture, which at a later stage becomes a wild rupture or 'anomaly'. The idea of a systematic rupture recalls Althusser's 'epistemological rupture' in Spinoza. In *Il potere costituente*, Negri ([1992] 2002b) reads Machiavelli's *Istorie fiorentine* as the result of a tension between two methods related to two views on the capacity to intervene in history, a rather conservative pessimistic view and a positive revolutionary view. I do not completely agree with this presentation of the conflicting theory, and prefer to express the conflict and tensions as belonging to reality rather than to the individual theories of Machiavelli and Spinoza, which would have first been blind and later enlightened. (Insisting on the contradiction between a first and a second Machiavelli or Spinoza, one risks having to discuss less important academic questions instead of the more urgent material issues, capturing history in its past instead of relating it to our present and future.)

References

Agamben, G. ([1970] 1994). 'La struttura originale dell'opera d'arte', *L'uomo senza contenuto*. Macerata: Quodlibet. (In English [1999] as *The Man Without Content*. Stanford, CA: Stanford University Press).

Agamben, G. (1995). *Homo Sacer. Il potere sovrano e la nuda vita*. Turin: Einaudi. (In English [1998] as *Homo Sacer: Sovereign Power and Bare Life*. Stanford, CA: Stanford University Press.)

Agamben, G. (1998). *Quel che Resta di Auschwitz. L'Archivio e il Testimone (Homo Sacer III)*. Turin: Bollati Boringhieri. (In English

[1999] as *Remnants of Auschwitz: The Witness and the Archive*. New York: Zone Books.)

Agamben, G. (2003). *Stato di Eccezione. Homo Sacer II, I*. Turin: Bollati Boringhieri. (In English [2003] as *State of Exception*. Chicago: University of Chicago Press.)

Agamben, G. (2005a). 'L'opera dell'uomo', *La Potenza del pensiero*. Verona: Neri Pozza. (In English [2007] as 'The work of man', in M. Calarco and S. DeCaroli (Eds.), *Giorgio Agamben. Sovereignty and Life*. Stanford, CA: Stanford University Press.)

Agamben, G. (2005b). *Profanazioni*. Rome: Nottetempo. (In English [2007] as *Profanations*. New York: Zone Books).

Agamben, G. (2007). *Signatura Rerum. Sul Metodo*. Turin: Bollati Boringhieri. (In English [2009] as *The Signature of All Things: On Method*. New York: Zone Books.)

Balestrini, N. and Moroni, P. ([1988] 2005). *L'orda d'oro 1968–1977. La Grande Ondata Rivoluzionaria e Creativa, Politica ed Esistenziale* [The Golden Horde 1968–1977. The great revolutionary and creative, political and existential wave]. Milan: Feltrinelli.

Bori, G., Pozzi, F. and Roggero, G. (2005). *Gli Operaisti*. Rome: Derive Approdi.

Casarino, C. and Negri, A. (2008). *In Praise of the Common. A Conversation on Philosophy and Politics*. Minneapolis: University of Minnesota Press.

Dante, A. (1965). 'Monarchia'. In *Tutte le Opere*. Florence: Sansoni.

Deleuze, G. and Guattari, F. (1980). *Mille Plateaux* [A thousand plateaus]. Paris: Minuit.

Gielen, P. and Lavaert, S. (2009). 'The dismeasure of art. An interview with Paolo Virno', in P. de Bruyne and P. Gielen (Eds.), *Being an Artist in Post-Fordist Times*. Rotterdam: NAi Publishers.

Gielen, P. and Lavaert, S. (2011). 'Art and common. A conversation with Antonio Negri', in P. de Bruyne and P. Gielen (Eds.), *Community Art. The Politics of Trespassing*. Amsterdam: Valiz.

Hardt, M. and Negri, A. (1994). *Labor of Dionysus. A Critique of the State-form*. Minneapolis: University of Minnesota Press.

Hardt, M. and Negri, A. (2000). *Empire*. Cambridge, MA: Harvard University Press.

Hardt, M. and Negri, A. (2004). *Multitude. War and Democracy in the Age of Empire*. New York: Penguin Press.

Hardt, M. and Negri, A. (2009). *Commonwealth*. Cambridge, MA: Harvard University Press.

Hardt, M. and Virno, P. (Eds.) (1996). *Radical Thought in Italy. A Potential Politics*. Minneapolis: University of Minnesota Press.

Iluminati, A. (2003). *Del Comune. Cronache del General Intellect* [On the common. The chronicles of the general intellect]. Rome: Manifestolibri.

Koerbagh, A. (1668). *Een Bloemhof van Allerley Lieflijkheyd Sonder Verdriet* [A flower garden of all kinds of loveliness without sorrow]. Amsterdam: n.p.

Lavaert, S. (2011). *Het Perspectief van de Multitude. Agamben, Machiavelli, Negri, Spinoza, Virno* [The perspective of the multitude. Agamben, Machiavelli, Negri, Spinoza, Virno]. Brussels: VUB Press.

Lavaert, S. (2013). 'Bartleby's tragic aporia', in P. Gielen (Ed.), *Institutional Attitudes. Instituting Art in a Flat World*. Amsterdam: Valiz.

Lavaert, S. (2014). 'Radical enlightenment, enlightened subversion, and Spinoza', *Philosophica*, 89.

Machiavelli, N. ([1513] 1997). *Il Principe. Opere I* [The prince. Works I]. Turin: Einaudi-Gallimard.

Machiavelli, N. ([1525] 2005). *Istorie Fiorentine. Opere III* [History of Florence. Works III]. Turin: Einaudi.

Mack, M. (2010). *Spinoza and the Specters of Modernity. The Hidden Enlightenment of Diversity from Spinoza to Freud*. New York: Continuum.

Marx, K. (1983). *Grundrisse der Kritik der Politischen Ökonomie. Marx Engels Werke Band 42*. Berlin: Dietz Verlag.

Meyer, L. (1663). *Nederlandsche Woordenschat* [Dutch vocabulary]. Amsterdam: Jan Hendriksz Boom.

Negri, A. (1981). *L'Anomalia Selvaggia. Saggio su Potere e Potenza in Baruch Spinoza*. Milan: Feltrinelli. (In English [1999] as *The Savage Anomaly*. Minneapolis: University of Minnesota Press.)

Negri, A. (1990). *Arte e Multitudo*. Milan: G. Politi. (In English [2011] as *Art and Multitude*. Cambridge: Polity Press.)

Negri, A. ([1979] 1998). *Marx oltre Marx. Quaderno di Lavoro sui Grundrisse*. Rome: Manifestolibri. (In English [1992] as *Marx Beyond Marx: Lessons on the Grundrisse*. New York: Autonomedia/Pluto Press.)

Negri, A. ([1987] 2001). *Lenta Ginestra. Saggio sull'Ontologia di Giacomo Leopardi* [Slow broom. Essay on the ontology of Giacomo Leopardi]. Milan: Mimesis Eterotopia.

Negri, A. ([1990] 2002a). *Il Lavoro di Giobbe*. Rome: Manifestolibri. (In English [2009] as *The Labor of Job*. Durham, NC: Duke University Press.)

Negri, A. ([1992] 2002b). *Il Potere Costituente. Saggio sulle Alternative della Modernità*. Rome: Manifestolibri. (In English [1999/2009] as *Insurgencies: Constituent Power and the Modern State*. Minneapolis: University of Minnesota Press.)

Negri, A. (2003). 'Il frutto maturo della redenzione', *Il Manifesto*, 26 July.

Negri, A. ([1977–78] 2006). '1997: vent'anni dopo. Prefazione alla seconda edizione', in *I Libri del Rogo*. Rome: Derive Approdi. (In English [2005] as *Books for Burning: Between Civil War and Democracy in 1970s Italy*. London: Verso.)

Negri, A. ([1979] 2007a). *Dall'Operaio Massa all'Operaio Sociale. Intervista sull'Operaismo*. Verona: Ombre corte.

Negri, A. (2007b). 'The discreet taste of the dialectic', in M. Calarco and S. DeCaroli (Eds.), *Giorgio Agamben. Sovereignty and Life*. Stanford, CA: Stanford University Press.

Negri, A. (2007c). 'Quel divino ministero per gli affari della vita terrena', *Il Manifesto*, 9 May.

Negri, A. ([1983] 2009a). *Pipe-line. Lettere da Rebibbia*. Rome: Derive Approdi. (In English [2015] as *Pipeline. Letters from Prison*. Cambridge: Polity Press.)

Negri, A. (2009b). *Trilogie de la Différence*. Paris: Stock. (In English [2011] as *Trilogy of Resistance*. Minneapolis: University of Minnesota Press.)

Negri, A. ([1985] 2010a). *Diary of an Escape*. Cambridge: Polity Press.

Negri, A. (2010b). *Spinoza et Nous*. Paris: Galilée.

Simondon, G. (1989). *L'Individuation Psychique et Collective* [Psychic and collective individuation]. Paris: Aubier.

Spinoza, B. (1670). *Tractatus Theologico-Politicus* [Theological-political treatise]. Hamburg: Apud Henricum Künrath/ Amsterdam: Jan Riewertsz.

Spinoza, B. (1677a). *Opera Posthuma* [Posthumous works]. Amsterdam: n.p.

Spinoza, B. (1677b). *Nagelate Schjriften*. Amsterdam: n.p.

Spinoza, B. (1693). *De Rechtzinnige Theologant of Godgeleerde Staatkundige Verhandelinge*. Hamburg: Henricus Koenraad/ Amsterdam: Jan Riewertsz.

Spinoza, B. (2002). *Complete Works* (with translations by Samuel Shirley, edited, with introduction and notes, by Michael L. Morgan). Indianapolis/Cambridge: Hackett Publishing Company.

Trotta, G. and Milana, F. (Eds.) (2008). *L'Operaismo degli Anni Sessanta da 'Quaderni Rossi' a 'Classe Operaia'* [Sixty years of workerism: from 'red notebooks' to 'working class']. Rome: Derive Approdi.

Virno, P. (2003). *Quando il Verbo si fa Carne. Linguaggio e Natura Umana* [(In English [2015] as When the Word Becomes Flesh. Language and Human Nature. Cambridge, MA: The MIT Press.)]. Turin: Bollati Boringhieri.

Virno, P. (2005). 'Do you remember revolution?', in N. Balestrini and P. Moroni, *L'orda d'oro 1968–1977. La Grande Ondata Rivoluzionaria e Creativa, Politica ed Esistenziale*. Milan: Feltrinelli.

Virno, P. (2010). *E Così Via, all'Infinito. Logica e Antropologia* [And so on, ad infinitum. Logic and anthropology]. Turin: Bollati Boringhieri.

Virno, P. ([1986] 2011). *Convenzione e Materialismo. L'Unicità Senza Aura* [Convention and materialism. Uniqueness without aura]. Rome: Derive Approdi.

Walzer, M. (1985). *Exodus and Revolution*. New York: Basic Books.

Wright, S. (2002). *L'Assalto al Cielo, per una Storia dell'Operaismo* [Assault on the sky. A history of operaismo]. Rome: Edizioni Alegre.

Zanini, A. (2007). 'Sui "fondamenti filosofici" dell'operaismo italiano' [On the 'philosophical foundations' of Italian operaismo], in R. Bellofiore (Ed.), *Da Marx a Marx? Un Bilancio dei Marxismi Italiani del Novecento*. Rome: Manifestolibri.

Zanini, A. and Fadini, U. (2001). *Lessico Postfordista* [Post-Fordist vocabulary]. Milan: Feltrinelli.

Chapter 4

Insolvency/autonomy: what is the meaning of autonomy in the semiocapitalist age?

Franco Bifo Berardi

Introduction

In this short piece, I will focus my attention on a concept that is directly linked to the social and political situation emerging from the European crisis: the concept of insolvency. Apparently originating in the financial sphere, the crisis is actually, I argue, the effect of the final aggression of capitalism – in the form of financial abstraction – against the autonomisation of the productive potency of the general intellect.

In explaining this, first I retrace the history of the struggle between the autonomy of work and capital development, along with the rise of the general intellect in the age of recombinant capitalism. Then, I describe the forms of subjugation of subjectivity, the precarisation of labour and the consequent destruction of social solidarity. Finally, I outline the effects of financial capitalism and the inscription of debt into the fabric of daily life and collective psychology – and I suggest the concept of insolvency as the way to the autonomy of daily life from the slavery of precarious work and financial capitalism.

Autonomy and deregulation

Autonomy can be defined as independence of social time from the temporality of capitalism. Simultaneously, however, social autonomy is the engine of capitalist development, and the main factor in capitalist restructuration.

In the last decades of the twentieth century, workers' autonomy from their disciplinary role provoked a social earthquake which triggered capitalist deregulation. That is, the deregulation that entered the world in the Thatcher–Reagan era can be seen as the capitalist response to autonomisation from the disciplinary order of labour. Workers demanded freedom from capitalist regulation, and then capital did the same thing, in reverse – since which, freedom from state regulation has become economic despotism over the social fabric. Workers demanded freedom from the lifetime prison of the industrial factory, and deregulation responded with the flexibilisation and fractalisation of labour. Thus, the autonomy movement in the 1970s triggered a process that evolved from the social rejection of the capitalist disciplinary rule to this special sort of capitalist revenge, in the shape of deregulation, the freedom of enterprise from the state, destruction of social protections, downsizing and externalisation of production, cuts in social spending, de-taxation and finally precarisation.

Understood like this, we see that the effect of the movement of autonomy was to trigger the destabilisation of the social framework resulting from a century of pressure on the part of the unions and of state regulation. The autonomy movement actually foreshadowed the capitalist move, but in a process of deregulation in which was inscribed the coming capitalist post-industrial development that implied the technological restructuring and globalisation of production.

There is a close relationship between rejection of work, informatisation of factories, downsizing, outsourcing of jobs and the flexibilisation of labour, but this relationship is, nevertheless, much more complex than a simple cause-and-effect chain. Rather, the process of deregulation was inscribed in the development of new technologies, allowing capitalist corporations to unleash a process of globalisation. A similar process occurred during the same period in the media field, for example in radio.

Across Western Europe, the 1970s was a time of free and pirate radio stations. In Italy at that time, there was a state-owned monopoly, and free broadcasting was forbidden, but in 1975–76 a group of media activists began to create small free radio stations, like Radio Alice in Bologna. The traditional left (the Italian Communist party and so on) denounced those media activists, warning about the danger of weakening the public media system and opening the door to privately owned media. It appears that is precisely what transpired, and deregulation resulted in the effective transfer of the state hegemony to private hands, generally controlled by a rather small number of imperial entrepreneurs (such as Berlusconi in Italy).

Should we think today that those people of the traditional statist left were right? I would argue that they were wrong at that time: ethically, freedom of expression is better than centralised media, and materially, the end of the state-owned monopoly was inevitable anyway, because it was inscribed in the evolution of the media technology. The traditional statist left was a conservative force in that moment, and it was doomed to defeat as it desperately tried to preserve an old framework that could not endure in the new technological and cultural situation of the post-industrial transition. We could say much the same about the end of the Soviet empire and of so-called 'real-socialism'.

The liberal democratisation of the Russian polity has seen the destruction of socioeconomic protections and the unleashing of a human nightmare of aggressive competition, violence and corruption. But the dissolution of the socialist regime was inevitable, because that order was blocking the dynamic of societal development and because the totalitarian regime was forestalling cultural innovation. The dissolution of the communist regimes was inscribed in the social composition of collective intelligence, in the imagination created by the new global media, and in the investment of desire. This is why the democratic intelligentsia and dissident cultural forces took part in the struggle against the socialist regime, although they knew that no paradise awaited in the capitalist alternative. Now deregulation is ravaging the former soviet society, and people are experiencing exploitation and misery and humiliation, but this transition has to be seen as a progressive change insofar as it opens the way to the emergence of the social potency of the general intellect.

Deregulation does not mean only the emancipation of private enterprise from state regulation and a reduction of public spending and social protection. It also means an increasing flexibilisation of labour. As indicated, the reality of labour flexibility is the flip side of the emancipation from capitalist regulation, a point that bears repetition: the connection between the rejection of work and the flexibilisation that ensued should not be underestimated. One of the strong ideas of the movement of autonomous proletarians during the 1970s was the idea of precariousness as a good. Job precariousness is a form of (indefinite) autonomy from steady, regular work. In the 1970s, many people used to work for a few months, then take some time off, and then return to work for a while. This was possible in times of almost full employment and an egalitarian culture. That situation allowed people to work as they chose, in their own interest as opposed to that of capitalists. Quite obviously, this could not last forever, and the neoliberal offensive of the 1980s responded, aiming to reverse what was itself a *rapport de force*.

Thus it is that deregulation and labour precariousness have been simultaneously the effect and the reversal of workers' autonomy. If we want to understand what has to be done today, in the age of fully flexible precarious labour, we have to understand how it was that, in the 1980s and 1990s, the capitalist takeover of social desire could take place.

The rise and fall of the alliance of cognitive labour and recombinant capital

Over the last decades, a crucial role in the precarisation of labour has been played by the technological transformation of machinery and introduction of information technologies, together with the intellectualisation and immaterialisation of the most important cycles of production (and concomitant development of these in the so-called tertiary sector as the highest value-adding arena). The introduction of the new electronic technologies and the computerisation of the production cycle gave way to the creation of a global network of info-production: de-territorialisation, de-localisation and de-personalisation of work are the effects of this transformation. Indeed, the subject of work can be increasingly identified with the global network of info-production.

If the rejection of work practised by industrial labourers during the decades of full employment has driven capitalism towards an electronic restructuring, the technical transformation of capitalist production into digital networks has triggered the change in the social composition of labour and the dissolution of the political force of the workers' movement. Industrial workers rejecting their role in the factory and gaining freedom from capitalist domination drove capital towards labour-saving technologies and change in the technical composition of the work process, in order to avoid and expel the well-organised industrial workers and create a new pool of labour that would be more flexible.

The cognitive immaterialisation of labour and planetary globalisation of capital are two sides of the same process. Globalisation does indeed have a material side, of course, because industrial labour does not disappear in the post-industrial age, but rather migrates towards the geographic zones where the lowest wages are paid and regulations are least well implemented. As Mario Tronti (1967: 28) foretold in the last issue of the magazine *Classe Operaia*, the most important phenomenon of the following decades would be the development of the working class on a global planetary scale. This intuition was not based on an analysis of the capital process of production, but rather on an understanding of the transformation in the social composition of labour. Globalisation and computerisation could be seen as an effect of the rejection of work in the Western capitalist countries. During the last two decades of the twentieth century, therefore, a sort of alliance between recombinant capital and cognitive work became possible.

By 'recombinant' I mean those sections of capital that are not territorialised or linked to a particular industrial application but can easily be transferred from one place to another, from one industrial application to another, from one sector of economic activity to another, and so on. Financial capital has taken a central place in politics and in culture since the 1990s precisely because it has the essentially recombinant function of capital. Industrial capital is territorialised, embodied in machines, factories and physical products. Financial capital, on the other hand, has no territory, no material assets; it is composed of pure abstractions, figures, algorithms, signs. Financial venture capital and cognitive work were suddenly able to interweave and combine with near unlimited fluidity when the global network (Internet trading, the virtual economy) made possible the de-territorialisation of productive factors.

The alliance of cognitive labour and financial capital has produced an important and ambivalent cultural effect, namely, the ideological identification of labour and enterprise. Workers have been induced to see themselves as self-entrepreneurs, which was not entirely false in the dotcom period, when the cognitive worker could create his own enterprise, just investing his intellectual force (an idea, a project, a formula) as an asset.

Autonomy as self-organisation of cognitive labour

Due to mass participation in the cycle of financial investment, a vast process of self-organisation of cognitive producers took place in the 1990s. Cognitive workers invested their expertise, their knowledge and their creativity and found in the stock market the means to create enterprises. For several years, the entrepreneurial form became the meeting point where financial capital and highly productive cognitive labour intermingled. The libertarian and liberal ideology that dominated the (American) cyberculture of the 1990s idealised the market by presenting it as a pure environment. In this environment, as natural as the evolutionary struggle for survival among the fittest, labour would find the necessary means to valorise itself and become enterprise.

Once left to its own dynamic, the reticular economic system was destined to optimise economic gains for everyone, owners and workers; the very distinction between owners and workers, moreover, becomes increasingly imperceptible as one enters the virtual productive cycle. This model, however, theorised by authors such as Kevin Kelly (and transformed by *Wired* magazine into a sort of digital-liberal (scornful and triumphalist) *Weltanschauung*, went bankrupt in the first couple of years of the new millennium, together with the new economy and a large part of the army of self-employed cognitive entrepreneurs that had inhabited the dotcom world. This new economy and its ideology went bankrupt because the model of a perfectly free market is a practical and theoretical lie. In the long run, what neoliberal ideology supported was not the free market, but monopoly. While the market was idealised as a free space where knowledge, expertise and creativity meet, reality has shown that the big groups of command operate in a way that is actually antithetical to libertarianism and instead introduce technological automatisms, imposing themselves with the power of the media or money, and finally robbing the mass of shareholders and cognitive labour, (quite shamelessly, in fact).

In the second half of the 1990s, actual class struggle occurred within the productive circuit of high technologies. The development of the World Wide Web has been characterised by this struggle. Information, the key productive means of this technology, is encrypted and communicated as part of the rapidly developing system of exchange, which means that it is not necessarily secret and hence accumulated, or even necessarily very stable. Thus, even as the computer and communications industry has, through the Internet in particular, spawned some of the largest private companies the world has seen, their inherent vulnerability to labour and the general intellect, particularly it seems given the sheer pace of change, mean that the outcome of the struggle remains at present unclear. But we can state unequivocally that this will most surely *not* be determined on the level playing field of the ideologically idealised free and natural market.

The fiction that the market works as a pure environment in which there is an egalitarian confrontation of ideas, projects, productive quality and the utility of services has been vanquished by the bitter truth of a war that monopolies have waged against the multitude of self-employed cognitive workers. The struggle for survival was not won by the best and most skilled, but by violence, robbery, systematic theft and the violation of all legal and ethical norms. The Bush–Gates alliance sanctioned the liquidation of the market: one part of cognitive workers was absorbed by the techno-military complex, while another, the largest, was expelled from the enterprise and forced into the condition of mass precariousness. These workers can be considered as *cognitarians*, since they live in the same social condition of alienation and economic dependence that was the mark of the proletarian condition, but their work is essentially based on cognitive skills. At the cultural level, the conditions for the formation of a social consciousness of the cognitariat are emerging, however, and this could be the beginning of a process of autonomisation of work from the capital domination of the global network.

Dotcoms were the training laboratory for a productive model and for a market. In the end the market was conquered and suffocated by the corporations, and the army of self-employed entrepreneurs and venture micro-capitalists was robbed and dissolved. Thus, a new phase began: the groups that became predominant in the cycle of the Net-economy forged an alliance with the dominant group of the old economy (the Bush clan, we may say, representative of the oil and military industries), and in this phase the process of globalisation changed its nature. With the dotcom crash, however, cognitive labour separated itself from capital. Digital artisans, who felt like entrepreneurs of their own labour during the 1990s, slowly realised that they had been deceived and expropriated, and this became the condition for a new consciousness of cognitive workers expropriated by a minority of speculators only good at handling the legal and financial aspects of valorisation.

The unproductive section of the virtual class, the lawyers and the accountants, is taking possession of the intellectual surplus value of physicists and engineers, chemists and writers. This process is marked by the financialisation of capitalism, submission of production to the mere self-valorisation of money. Financial capital is the abstract form that swallows and destroys the concrete useful content of social knowledge and productive potency. In order to increase the economic power of the financial abstraction, social resources are wasted and the general intellect dismantled. Indeed, although it appears to be merely following the line of new orthodoxy with the dismantling of state care and regulation, in the context of the general intellect especially, it is rather striking how the educational system is currently being de-financed and privatised and research increasingly subordinated to financial profit.

The concept of autonomy, at this point, can be expressed by the separation of the content – the general intellect – from the form that is enveloping and entangling its productive potency and concrete usefulness: financial abstraction. Cognitive labour is looking for a way out from the financial castle of semiocapitalism – essentially, the new form of capitalism constituted by the immaterial systems created from the relationship of information technology with the production and consumption of economic value – in order to build a direct relation with society, with the users. The general intellect is looking for its social body and for the social conditions of a new concrete relationship with a useful destination. In this context, autonomy is to be seen as the disentanglement of knowledge and technology from the capitalist subjugation that takes the form of financial abstraction. We needed to go through the dotcom purgatory, through the illusion of a fusion between labour and capitalist enterprise, and then through the hell of endless war and then, finally, the 2009 financial disaster and subsequent economic recession in order to see the problem emerge in clear terms. The system of financial accumulation and the privatisation of education and research together with productive labour increasingly inscribed in the cognitive functions of society begin to build autonomous institutions of knowledge, of invention and education that emerge from the framework of capitalist domination.

Fractalisation and subjugation of social subjectivity

In the sphere of semiocapitalism, flexibility has evolved into a form of the fractalisation of labour, a fragmentation of time and activity. The worker no longer exists as a person, s/he is just the interchangeable producer of micro-fragments of recombinant semiosis entering the continuous flux of the global network.

Equally, capital is no longer buying the availability of the worker to be exploited for a long period of time and is no longer paying a salary that covers the range of economic needs of a working person. The worker (a mere machine possessing a brain that can be used for a fragment of time) is paid for the fraction of time and the partial performance that is recombined in the deterritorialised space of the global network. The working time is fractalised and then, as an aspect of that, cellularised. Cells of time are on sale on the network, and the corporation can buy as many of them as it needs for any given task. The cell phone is the assembly line of cognitive labour, the technical tool that defines the relation between the fractal worker and the recombinant capital, along with the laptop and tablet and smart TV in the ever more technologically integrated network. Cognitive labour is an ocean of de-personalised time fractals.

As an effect of the flexibilisation and fractalisation of labour, what used to be the autonomy and the political force of the industrial workforce has become the total dependence of cognitive labour on the capitalist organisation of the global network. Industrial workers used to be united because their activity was territorialised and their daily experience manifested as the creation of a community of solidarity. The effect of deterritorialisation and of precaritisation is the fracturing of the workforce: isolation, loneliness and competition take the place of solidarity. And what used to be rejection of work and social autonomy has turned into a dependence of the emotions, and of consciousness: the flow of information is stripping social activity of its self-reliance and submitting mental energies to the accelerating rhythm of capitalist productivity. This is the location of the origin of a nervous breakdown in the times of the dotcom crash, at the turn of the century, and is still fracturing and enfeebling the social body and the collective mind.

The dotcom crash and the crisis of financial mass capitalism can be viewed as an effect of the collapse of the economic investment of social desire. I use the word 'collapse' in a sense that is not metaphorical, but rather a clinical description of what is going on in the Western mind, a truly pathological crash of the psycho-social organism. What we have seen since the period following the first signs of economic crash, since the first months of the new century, indeed, is a psychopathological phenomenon. It was an intense and prolonged economic investment of mental and libidinal energies that created the psychic environment for the collapse, which manifested in the field of economic recession, military aggression and a suicidal tendency spreading worldwide.

The present economic depression can be viewed as a consequence or a manifestation of a psychic depression, which is a side effect of the acceleration of the rhythm of the *infosphere* subjecting the *psychosphere* to hyper-stimulation, and of the exploitation of the nervous energies of the collective body.

Self-organisation of cognitive work is the only way to go beyond the psychopathological present. The dissemination of self-organised knowledge can give birth to infinite autonomous and self-reliant worlds. The process of the creation of the network is so complex that it cannot be governed by human reason; the global mind is too complex to be known and mastered by sub-segmental localised minds. However, while we cannot know, control and govern the entire force of the global mind, we can master the singular process of producing a singular world of sociality. This is autonomy today. But it implies and presupposes the disentanglement of the general intellect, of the living bodies of the uncountable bearers of the general intellect from the technological automatisms of the linguistic machine and the automatisms inscribed in the social mind as an effect of subjugation to the financial abstraction. This subjugation takes the form of debt.

Insolvency

What is debt? According to Maurizio Lazzarato (2011), debt is the subjective engine of the contemporary economy, operating as a dispositive for the submission of individual energies and expectations and simultaneously acting as a capturing machine, as a prescriptive tool and a powerful instrument for the redistribution of resources and revenue – although actually subtracting resources from social life and conveying them to the banking system and the financial class. Debt is the biopolitical imprinting of sin in the collective psyche, the identification of the good life and welfare with a guilt that has to be atoned for. Paying the debt is the general obligation that implies renunciation of everything (education, health, free time, pleasure, conviviality) and total dedication to the sacrificial austerity (less money for the workers, unlimited working time, postponement of pensions, increasing productivity, and therefore precarity, unemployment and misery). Debt is not only economic submission, but also psychic culpability and cultural subjection. Debt is compliance with the linguistic rules of the global machine.

In the sphere of semiocapital, social domination has become totally abstract: the techno-linguistic machine is infiltrating every space of production and communication and submitting daily behaviour and social interaction to automatic rules. The financial abstraction is imposing an automatic rhythm to language, emotionality, expectations. This is essentially the financial dictatorship called 'governance', the techno-linguistic subjugation of every human exchange. Debt is the general frame of this subjugation, reducing social relations to a constant blackmail and making possible the plundering of the physical and intellectual resources of society by the universal creditor: semiocapital becomes the abstract source of the techno-linguistic flow.

The burden of debt is haunting the European imagination of the future, and the Union, which used to be a promise of prosperity and peace, is turning into a kind of threat. Therefore, in our time, autonomy takes the form of insolvency, through refusal to take on the debt and refusal to pay the debt, both symbolically and economically. Social independence from monetary exchange and the creation of forms of exchange based on the mutual trust of the community have to be implemented as a concrete manifestation of insolvency and its rejection.

The concept of insolvency is loaded with philosophical implications: it implies refusal, not only to pay the monetary debt but also to submit the living potency of social forces to the formal domination of the economic code. Reclaiming the right to insolvency implies a radical questioning of the relationship between the capitalist form (*Gestalt*) and the concrete productive potency of social forces, particularly the potency of the general intellect. The capitalist form is not only a set of economic rules and functions; it is also the internalisation of a certain set of limitations, of psychic automatism, of rules for compliance.

Try to imagine for a second the whole financial semiotisation of European life disappearing, that all of a sudden we stop organising daily life in terms of money and debt: nothing will change in the concrete, useful potentiality of society, in the content of our knowledge, in our skills and ability to produce. We should imagine (and consequently organise) the disentanglement of the living potentiality of the general intellect from the capitalist *Gestalt* – intended first of all as a psychic automatism governing daily life.

Insolvency means disclaiming the economic code of capitalism as transliteration of real life, as semiotisation of social potency and richness. In insolvency, the materially useful productive ability of the social body is forced to accept impoverishment in exchange for nothing; the concrete force of productive labour is submitted to the unproductive and actually destructive task of refinancing the failed financial system. If we could cancel every mark of the financial semiotisation, nothing would change in the social machinery, nothing in the intellectual ability to conceive and perform. This is why communism does not need to be called out from the womb of the future; it is here, in our insolvent being, in the immanent life of common knowledge disentangled from the debt of salaried work.

In order to become operational and effective, however, this strength of autonomy does need a reactivation of solidarity. Not moral value or a political idea, but living empathy and the feeling of a body for another body. Solidarity is lacking precisely because the precarious form of work and the virtualisation of communication has stripped social existence of the pleasure of the bodily presence of the other. This is why the current situation is so paradoxical – simultaneously exciting and desperate. Capitalism has never been so close to the final collapse, yet social solidarity has never been so far from our daily experience. It is from this paradox that we must start in order to build a post-political and post-revolutionary process of disentanglement of the possible from the existent.

Chapter 5

The conditions of the common: a Stieglerian critique of Hardt and Negri's thesis on cognitive capitalism as a prefiguration of communism

Pieter Lemmens

> To reclaim political agency means first of all accepting our insertion at the level of desire in the remorseless meat grinder of capitalism. (Fisher, 2009: 15)

Introduction: the comeback of communism

After three decades of neoliberal triumphalism and the collapse of the communist alternative, communism – sometimes renamed as 'commonism' – is back on the agenda of leftist political thought. Since the sold-out Birkbeck conference on communism in London, in 2009, organised by Slavoj Žižek and Costas Douzinas, the idea of communism has seemed to be in the air again, slowly (re)gaining serious attention, and not only within radical academia, but also outside, among a growing population that sees the neoliberal capitalist system as definitively ruined, bankrupt, devoid of all future prospects other than iniquitous austerity, towering debt and further devastation of the social fabric and ecosystems. Especially since the financial crisis of 2008 and the subsequent series of mass protests and uprisings in Europe and the Americas, the call for more radical alternatives to capitalism has returned. In the introduction to the volume of the collected contributions to the Birkbeck conference, Douzinas and Žižek applauded this renewed interest in radical ideas and politics, arguing that it should be answered philosophically as well as politically by a reanimation of the communist idea, as best suited to revitalise leftist political thought as well as action in our time (Douzinas & Žižek, 2010: viii).[1]

Alain Badiou, one of the key speakers of the conference and provider of its title and principal motive, most emphatically argued for the rehabilitation of the communist idea as the guiding principle for the emancipatory struggles currently underway (Badiou, 2010: 236). For Badiou, only communism, whose generic characteristics were laid out canonically in Marx and Engels' *Communist Manifesto* and whose principal telos consists in the collective emancipation of mankind conceived as the proper destiny of the human species, provides a genuine alternative to the selfish and animalistic war of all against all to which the inherent logic of capitalism ultimately reduces the human endeavour (Badiou, 2008: 100). Bruno Bosteels, a disciple of Badiou who wrote a book proclaiming 'the actuality of communism' (Bosteels, 2011), and Jodi Dean, who is deeply influenced by Žižek, also committed themselves to the communist cause, claiming that communism is our 'future horizon'.[2]

Franco 'Bifo' Berardi, a post-Marxist thinker associated with the autonomist tradition, also argued that communism is back on the stage of history, initially due to the new commons-based practices of production made possible by the digital networks but more recently also because of the collapse of the unsustainable growth-and-debt economy of the last decades (Berardi, 2009c). 'Communism is coming back', he claims, because of the increasing commonality of knowledge, the growing irrelevance of private property and the mandatory commonisation of needs in today's conjuncture (Berardi, 2011: 151). The late André Gorz perceived in the Free Software and Open Source practices thriving on the Internet the emergence of a new communist model of production, describing these practices as a kind of 'protocommunism' that has the potential to overcome the capitalist system altogether and create an alternative society based on cooperation, autonomy and sharing instead of competition, exploitation and profit (Gorz, 2009: 14–15, 21).[3] As Jason Smith wrote in his preface to Berardi's book *The Soul at Work*: 'We're starting to talk again about communism these days. We don't know yet what it is, but it's what we *want*' (Berardi, 2009a: 16). Even a postmodern author like Gianni Vattimo, proponent of so-called 'weak thought', argued for a return to communism (Vattimo & Zabala, 2011; Zabala, 2012), along with many other authors who make the case for a reconsideration of the communist project in the twilight of a crippled and crumbling capitalist system.

Hardt and Negri and the coming of communism

While it may be the case that Badiou and Žižek were the prime theoretical instigators of the revival of the communist idea, a 'coming of communism' was already explicitly theorised and passionately affirmed by the post-Marxist duo Michael Hardt and Antonio Negri. Their communism is explicitly related to the notion of the common. In their collaborative works from the mid-1990s, this notion of the common and the possibility of a communist 'revolution' born from the new conditions of labour in the context of today's cognitive capitalism has gained ever more prominence.[4] Although the word 'communism' appears only sporadically in *Empire*, the book that was enthusiastically hailed by Žižek at the time as the *Communist Manifesto* for the twenty-first century, it is increasingly present in the later books of the *Empire* trilogy, *Multitude* and *Commonwealth*. And although references to the common(s) are still scarce in *Empire*, in *Multitude* and a fortiori in *Commonwealth* this notion is ubiquitously present. Thus did it became one of the central concepts of Hardt and Negri's work, together with empire, multitude, immaterial (or biopolitical) labour and production, the general intellect, constitutive power and absolute (or radical) democracy.

In this chapter, I will focus on this recent, post-Marxist strand of discourse on communism, which is explicitly politico-economic in nature, revolves around the notion of the common and perceives today's cognitive capitalism as a prelude to a communist future. I want to critically assess Hardt and Negri's thesis of cognitive capitalism as a prefiguration of communism, their perception of cognitive capitalism as creating a 'communism of capital' that breeds in its own bosom the possibility of a 'communism of the multitude', or, in other words, which creates the possibility of a liberation of the common from capital. Hardt and Negri claim that today's immaterial or cognitive capitalism is generating the socioeconomic and technological conditions that will eventually allow the overthrow of the capitalist order and enable the transition towards another society, one that they frequently identify as communist, a society in which capitalist exploitation and domination will be abolished and in which the global multitude of immaterial workers – today's proletariat – will commonly manage production and rule itself autonomously in a radically democratic way. Cognitive capitalism, so to speak, provides the conditions – or prerequisites – for a transition towards and into communism.

According to Hardt and Negri, but to (post-)autonomist and (post-)operaist thinkers in general – including Virno, Vercellone, Lazzarato, Marazzi and Fumagalli, as well as the already mentioned Gorz, who has been much influenced by the (post-) autonomist tradition – it is the becoming-common of labour in today's cognitive capitalism – as characterised by a growing centrality of immaterial (or biopolitical) labour – that provides the condition for the global multitude to break itself free from its domination by capital and to found another, presumably communist, society. Immaterial labour tends towards communism because cooperation is completely immanent in it: 'In the expression of its own creative energies, immaterial labor … seems to provide the potential for a kind of spontaneous and elementary communism' (Hardt & Negri, 2000: 294).

The increasing centrality of the common, as the ultimate foundation of economic production, opens the way to communism for the multitude. As Negri (2008c: 63) suggests, it is the common at the heart of the multitude that contains the seed of the freedom and autonomy characteristic of a communist society, because it is this foundation in the common that makes the multitude both subjectively efficient and objectively antagonistic to capital. Similarly, Hardt writes in his contribution to *The Idea of Communism* that it is through the increasing centrality of the common in capitalist production – in the production of ideas, affects, social relations and forms of life – that the conditions and the weapons for a communist project are emerging (Douzinas & Žižek, 2010: 143). Because of this explicit reference to the common and the commons, Hardt and Negri's version of communism could be designated as 'commonism', a term perceptively coined by the Canadian autonomist Marxist Nick Dyer-Witheford (2007: 28–9).[5]

Doubtless, today's increasingly 'immaterial' nature of labour and production does, in principle, appear to offer plenty of opportunities for the multitude to wrest itself free from capitalist domination and to assert autonomy. However, one must have serious doubts about the (post-)autonomist assertion that immaterial labour is becoming ever more autonomous vis-à-vis capital in today's conjuncture; I am particularly critical of the seemingly boundless optimism of Hardt and Negri as regards the inherently emancipatory and liberatory potentials of the multitude. In this chapter, I want to question this optimism by critically reflecting on what they designate as the contemporary 'conditions and weapons for a communist project' (Hardt, 2010: 144). Is it really true that the current politico-economic conditions of production are already effecting a transition from capitalism to communism? What is the nature of these conditions according to Hardt and Negri? Are these conditions as described 'real', do they pertain? Is the account of these conditions adequate, and if so, is it also sufficient? And what are the 'weapons' that can be used to fight *against* capitalist domination and *for* the preservation and expansion of the common, with the goal of creating a communist society? What is the nature of these weapons? And how must the 'battlefield' of the 'battle for the common(s)' be conceived?

In the following, I first present Hardt and Negri's arguments for their thesis of today's cognitive capitalism as a prefiguration of communism. Then I criticise these arguments from a perspective derived from the work of the French philosopher Bernard Stiegler and the Italian post-autonomist thinker Franco Berardi. Basically, I show that Hardt and Negri's diagnosis of cognitive capitalism as a proto-communist configuration is far too rosy and fails to adequately address the technological and libidinal conditions for the creation of a communist society. Primarily, it fails to acknowledge – indeed, explicitly denies – the deeply proletarianising nature of cognitive capitalism by remaining blind to what is termed the organological and pharmacological impact of digital networks on cognitive labour. Finally, I argue that a communism of the multitude presupposes a struggle against the processes of proletarianisation that are the prime characteristic of cognitive capitalism's subsumption of the mind under capital.

Cognitive capitalism as a prefiguration of communism? Hardt and Negri on the conditions for communism

To support their thesis of an emergent (or even inherent) communism, Hardt and Negri essentially give three, closely related arguments, the first two of which I will focus on here. The first argument is that, due to the hegemony of immaterial labour and biopolitical production – which is fundamentally based on the common and continually expands it – the multitude becomes ever more autonomous and independent from capital.[6] This argument of the growing autonomy of labour under cognitive capitalism is one of the central mantras running throughout the *Empire* trilogy, especially in *Commonwealth*. Basically, it rests on two premises: (1) the growth of the role of the common in immaterial production as both foundation and product, and (2) the growing excess of the productivity of labour power with respect to the bounds set in its employment by capital (Hardt & Negri, 2009: 151). These two developments increasingly empower the multitude:

> The excedence of production (which has immaterial labor as
> its technical base and the self-forming of the multitudes as its

political base) cannot be enclosed within the form and processes of control which the organisational methods of modern capitalism [have] constructed, in relation to massified or Fordist labor. (Negri, 2008b: 76)

What is typical of immaterial labour is that it is intrinsically social and cooperative, that it 'immediately involves social interaction and cooperation' (Hardt & Negri, 2000: 294). Unlike material labour, immaterial labour organises itself and does not have to be organised from the outside, by external means, as cooperation and communication are immanent to its very activity. The more autonomous immaterial labour is, the more freedom it is allowed and the more productive it becomes. Capital's techniques and strategies of control are in complete contradiction with the necessarily autonomous character of immaterial labour, so capital has to remain increasingly external to the process of production.

Immaterial labour does not need the intervention of capital; it is no longer dependent on the capitalist to be able to produce, as it was in the age of industrial capitalism, when workers could only be productive in the factory environment, where the necessary means of production were uniquely present. In the industrial capitalism of the time Marx was writing, it was the capitalist who provided the workers with the means and the site of production. The progressive deskilling or proletarianisation of workers during the process of industrialisation, in particular since the introduction of the assembly line in the twentieth century, reduced the possibilities for the self-management of labour. Today's post-industrial workers, however, are endowed with all the skills and knowledge necessary for collectively managing production themselves (Hardt & Negri, 2004: 251–2).

Due to its foundation in the common, immaterial labour produces the means of production – that is to say, the means of interaction, communication, collaboration and cooperation – directly and spontaneously. Ideas, knowledges, codes, information, images, languages, affects and suchlike are commonly produced *and* constantly expand the common as the foundation of production. In all forms of immaterial production, 'the creation of 'cooperation has become *internal* to labour and thus *external* to capital' (Hardt & Negri, 2004: 47). As stated in *Commonwealth*: 'People don't need bosses at work. They need an expanding web of others with whom to communicate and collaborate; the boss is increasingly merely an obstacle to getting work done' (Hardt & Negri, 2009: 353).

The self-organising and auto-cooperative character of immaterial labour implies that the control and exploitation by capital frustrate its productivity and creativity, forcing capital to allow it increasing autonomy and to position itself at an ever greater distance from the production process:

> Labour tends to be increasingly autonomous from capitalist command, and thus capital's mechanisms of expropriation and control become fetters that obstruct productivity. Biopolitical production is an orchestra keeping the beat without a conductor, and it would fall silent if anyone were to step onto the podium. (Hardt & Negri, 2009: 173)

Capital is compelled to remain increasingly external to the process of production and its functional role is constantly diminishing. Whereas material, industrial labour functioned heteronomously as an organ contained within the body of capital, immaterial labour is becoming increasingly free and autonomous and capital ever more dependent and parasitic, forced to block the movements of knowledge, communication and cooperation (e.g. through intellectual property rights) in order to survive (Hardt & Negri, 2009: 142). Whereas the multitude 'is the real productive force of our social world', therefore, 'Empire is a mere apparatus of capture that lives off the vitality of the multitude – as Marx would say, a vampire regime of accumulated dead labor that survives only by sucking off the blood of the living'; it is nothing but 'an empty machine, a spectacular machine, a parasitical machine' (Hardt & Negri, 2000: 62). Capital thereby loses its historically progressive force and can continue to exist only through direct expropriation of externally produced value – that is, through expropriation of the common (Negri, 2008d: 64–7).

Immaterial production is structurally 'incompatible' with the logic of capital and therefore cognitive capitalism will ultimately destroy itself through its inherent contradictions. Capitalism's traditional mechanisms of exploitation and control, both the intensive and extensive, increasingly contradict and fetter the productivity of biopolitical labour and frustrate the creation of value. Biopolitical labour in all its forms – cognitive, intellectual, affective, etc. – cannot be contained by the forms of discipline and command that were developed during the era of Fordism. Therefore, the integration of labour within the ruling structures of capital becomes increasingly difficult (Hardt & Negri, 2009: 264, 291). Capital's strategies of privatisation and control destroy the common that is at the base of biopolitical production, so biopolitical productivity is hampered every time the common is destroyed. A good example is the impediment of innovation in agriculture and biotechnology and the blocking of creativity in cultural production due to excessive intellectual property regimes in the form of patents and copyrights (see Drahos & Braithwaite, 2002; Lessig, 2004; Aigrain, 2005; Jefferson, 2006; Boyle, 2008; Hope, 2008; Kloppenburg, 2010).

The disciplinary strategies of precarisation of work and flexibilisation of the labour market are also counterproductive, depriving cognitive and affective workers of precisely the time and freedom on which the creativity and productivity of cognitive and affective labour depends (Hardt & Negri, 2009: 145–7). All attempts of capital to intervene in the production process and to appropriate the common frustrate that which it tries to capture: the productivity of the common. And the more the capitalist economy becomes a knowledge economy, the more it embarks on the path of value creation through knowledge production, the more that knowledge escapes its control and the more it produces and nourishes that which ultimately undermines its own existence: the common.

Of course, as Hardt and Negri admit, ever since Marx uncovered the logic of capital, the critique of political economy has pointed to the contradiction within capitalism of the social nature of production and the private nature of accumulation. However, in the context of today's cognitive capitalism, this contradiction is becoming ever more extreme and consequently ever more destructive for the capitalist endeavour, reaching a point of rupture: 'This is how capital creates its own gravediggers: pursuing its own interests and trying to preserve its own survival, it must foster the increasing power and autonomy of the productive multitude', Hardt and Negri (2009: 311) contend. 'And when that accumulation of power crosses a certain threshold, the multitude will emerge with the ability to rule common wealth.' Indeed, capital today is 'facing increasingly autonomous, antagonistic, and unmanageable forms of social labor-power' which embody an inherent potential for autonomy and have the capacity to 'destroy capital and create something entirely new' (Hardt & Negri, 2009: 136, 288, 311).

The second argument developed in support of the thesis of a new communism claims that, due to the fact that the means of immaterial production increasingly reside on the side of the workers (inside the worker's brains, that is), capital is increasingly unable to control these means, which implies that the so-called 'dialectics of the instrument' (Hegel) no longer functions and, consequently, that the process of proletarianisation typical of industrial material (Fordist) production comes to an end. Although Hardt and Negri are very much aware (and this is especially apparent in *Empire*) of the fact that the emergence of digital networks not only opens up new spaces of liberation and autonomy for the multitude, but has also inaugurated new forms of domination and exclusion, they insist on the inherently progressive and emancipatory character of these new technologies.

Indeed, it almost seems, as Danilo Zolo suggests in an interview with Negri, that Hardt and Negri 'see the technological and digital revolution as the vector of an imminent communist revolution' (Negri, 2008a: 28). What is crucial here is their contention that cognitive capitalism entails 'the *reappropriation of the instrument* of labour' by the workers, and that, moreover, cooperation becomes the crucial factor of valorisation and knowledge and information the most important forces of production. This, Negri claims, is undeniably a positive development with respect to the possibility of a transformation towards commonism (Negri, 2008a: 29). What is meant by the reappropriation of the instrument of labour by Negri is the fact that in cognitive capitalism, the means or capacities of production are (again) on the side of the workers themselves, since they reside in their brains. In cognitive capitalism the principal means of production are human brains.

As already mentioned, the fact that the prime forces or instruments of production have become attributes of living labour in the post-Fordist age implies, for Negri, that we witness a withering away of the 'dialectics of the instrument' – that is, the dialectics between capital and labour *through* the instrument (Negri, 2008a: 65). This is the case because cognitive capitalism is no longer capable of articulating command over the instrument in order to control labourers. In the post-Fordist situation, after all, it is the labourers themselves that are the bearers of the immaterial capacities of production. The instrument of labour (the brain, the human nervous system) is now reappropriated by labour:

> Here one can speak of a reappropriation of the tools of labour by the worker. … Capitalism, according to Hegel, was based essentially on the dialectics of the tool, in other words on the fact that the capitalist offered the worker the instrument of labour and life in common was constructed around this instrumentation. Well, today this Hegelian instrumentation is removed. (Negri, 2008b: 175–6)

Given this reappropriation of the means of production by living labour, Negri argues, capital tendentially loses its ability to discipline individuals and collectives *within* the process of production and reproduction. This means that the process of proletarianisation, which operates via the instruments of production, becomes dysfunctional.

In material labour, the instruments of labour are preconstituted by the bosses and only used by the workers. Labour has to adapt itself to capital's machinery of production, to its logic and to its rhythm: classical material labour relies on the production instruments offered by capital. In this situation, as Marx has shown, labour becomes 'variable capital'; fixed capital (machinery) is imposed upon variable capital and the worker exists *within* capital, he is subsumed under and subject to capital, becoming the object of proletarianisation. However, in immaterial, cognitive labour – the labour of the general intellect – intellectual labour power liberates itself from this relation of subjection, which means that 'the productive subject – the multitude – appropriates for itself those labour instruments that capital preconstituted before' (Negri, 2008d: 167–8). Variable capital now represents itself as fixed capital – or, in other words, labour power has internalised elements of fixed capital, which means that it is henceforth able to circulate and be productive outside of its relationship with constant capital, thereby evading the mechanism of proletarianisation (Negri, 2008c: 66). So it is that, as general intellect, the productive singularities of the multitude contain the potential to break free from the capitalist relation. It has gained the capacity to produce outside of its relation with capital. Its cognitive and social capital can exist independent from the apparatuses of constant capital (Negri, 2008d: 168).

On a similar note, Paolo Virno also argues that the centrality of the general intellect in immaterial production means that the process of proletarianisation is coming to an end.[7] In *A Grammar of the Multitude*, Virno (2004: 109) argues that the traditional distinction made by Marxists between simple (i.e. unskilled) labour and complex (i.e. skilled) labour no longer applies to immaterial labour. Based as it is in the intellectuality of the masses, he contends, immaterial labour is complex, skilled labour throughout. This complexity follows for him from the fact that immaterial labour needs the constant mobilisation of linguistic-cognitive capacities, and although these capacities are generically human, their cooperative quality cannot be reduced to simple labour.

Virno argues that in our day, the general intellect – which Marx conceived of as exclusively an attribute of dead labour or fixed capital (as co-extensive with the 'system of machinery') – has become an attribute of living labour. Today, the relation between knowledge and production is not exhausted by the use of machinery in the productive process (as objectified or materialised knowledge). On the contrary, it is primarily articulated today by linguistic cooperation between workers acting in concert. Post-Fordist workers employ an infinite variety of ideas, procedures, schemes and more on the job that can never be totally materialised, computerised or informationalised into machinery (and thereby turned into fixed capital). Even less objectifiable are the informal knowledges, imaginations, ethical propensities, mind sets, language games and creative capacities that are indispensable to immaterial production. These can only be executed on the spot by a plurality of living subjects. The general intellect of immaterial labour functions as a productive force, according to Virno, 'without having to adopt the form of a mechanical body or of an electronic valve'; it consists of a 'depository of cognitive and communicative skills *which cannot be objectified within the system of machines*' (Negri, 2008d: 106–7).

The third and last argument states that the multitude is becoming ever more political, that it has not only the capacity for autonomous production but also of political decision-making. It is ever more capable of self-rule and embodies the potential for a genuine global democracy in the sense of an absolute or radical democracy, a government by all and for all. Briefly recapitulating this argument (which will not be the main focus of the present critique), what Hardt and Negri basically argue is that the imma-terial (informational, linguistic, communicational, cooperative, etc.) nature of production under cognitive capitalism implies that work is becoming intrinsically social, so it is also becom-ing more political; or the self-organising and auto-cooperative characteristics of immaterial or biopolitical production imply an increasing potential for political self-organisation. Typically, in biopolitical production the economic and the political tenden-tially coincide, since biopolitical production is the production of society itself – of social relationship and subjectivities. Also, the networked form of immaterial production provides a model and an institutional logic for a communist society (Hardt & Negri, 2004: 336, 350; 2009: 174–5).

Now, what I want to argue in the following sections is that although these three claims undeniably register deep evolu-tionary (and crucial) developments in the history of capitalism and the transition to post-Fordism, they nevertheless do not adequately reflect the real, actual conditions of the contempo-rary multitude with respect to capital, that is to say with regard to its possibilities of liberating itself from capital and instituting an autonomously governed, communist society. Basing myself mainly on Bernard Stiegler's account of cognitive – and especially his account of today's consumerist – capitalism, but also on Franco Berardi's recent analyses of the labour conditions of the cognitariat in the context of what he calls 'semiocapitalism', I will qualify these claims and show that Hardt and Negri's analyses of the multitude fail to adequately take into account both the technological and the libidinal conditions (and particularly, their interrelatedness) of today's 'general intellect' and its potential to constitute a true, autonomous common.

A critique of Hardt and Negri's diagnosis

In what follows, I express the view that, first, instead of becoming ever more autonomous with respect to capital, as Hardt and Negri have it, the multitude finds itself ever more subjugated to the heteronomising tendencies of a global technological development largely dictated by the automatically functioning imperatives of financial capital. Second, instead of experiencing the end of proletarianisation, as Hardt and Negri as well as Virno claim, we find a dramatic intensification of the process, and not only on the terrain of production but also on that of consumption and even within the domain of theory, of science. And third, despite its engagement in immaterial work – communicating, cooperating and collaborating all the time – the multitude is *not* becoming more politically capable and assertive. On the contrary, the last few decades have seen a decline in active and especially radical engagement and an increase, rather, in political apathy.

Autonomy and heteronomisation

Far from gaining more autonomy, the multitude seems to become ever more entangled in the automatic operations –

Berardi's automatisms – of the digital networks set up by the biopower and psychopower of capital. It is increasingly fractalised and desocialised due to the fragmentation, cellularisation and precarisation of labour, including the cognitive and affective (Berardi, 2009b: 7, 33, 38).[8] Today the digital networks are predominantly a heteronomising not an autonomising force, as not only Berardi and Stiegler but also authors as different as Nicholas Carr (2009, 2010), Jodi Dean (2010), Jaron Lanier (2010), Mark Fisher (2009) and Giorgio Agamben (2009) have pointed out. Our time is one of massive adaptation, not of increasing multitudinous autonomy.

Berardi shares the autonomist insight that whereas traditional industrial capitalism was based on the exploitation of bodies, today's post-industrial or cognitive capitalism thrives on the exploitation of the intellect or, more comprehensively, on the 'soul'. In cognitive capitalism – or *semiocapitalism*, referring to the valorisation of cognitive labour by capital (especially through informational technologies) – it is the entirety of human beings, referred to in our essence of being as 'soul', that is put to work: 'Not the body, but the soul becomes the object of techno-social domination' (Berardi, 2009a: 200). The soul is the seat of desire and it is precisely our desire, in all the ways it expresses itself (as intelligence, imagination, creativity, sociability, etc.), that is captured and controlled by capital to be submitted to economic exploitation. Capitalist valorisation today is based primarily on the 'channeling of Desire' (Berardi, 2009a: 24).

Although Hardt and Negri will probably not deny this, they never give it much attention or examine its consequences. In general, the libidinal aspects of immaterial production are not dealt with in their work, at least not explicitly. Like Stiegler, however, whose analyses of cognitive and consumer capitalism I will discuss below, Berardi has centralised these aspects in his research; whereas Stiegler concentrates on the libidinal investment in consumption, Berardi's analyses are concerned with the investment of desire in production, that is to say, in cognitive (and to a lesser extent also affective) labour.

Cognitive capitalism involves the exploitation of the libidinal energy of what Berardi calls the *cognitariat*, those who sell their cognitive capacities to capital. When the intellect is set to work, its functions (knowing, creating, imagining, expressing, communicating, collaborating, etc.) are submitted to the goal of capitalist accumulation. The cognitariat does not work for itself but for capital, which expropriates both its cognitive activity and its products: capital expropriates the general intellect. This means that the general intellect becomes alienated and separated from the bodily and social life of the workers, making it increasingly difficult for them to seek autonomous existence outside of capitalist relations. And although cognitive work is certainly less gruelling than was traditional factory work, it also deeply impoverishes the cognitive experience of workers because the submission of cognition to economic imperatives systematically erodes its playful, imaginative and creative characteristics. In general the submission to non-cognitive principles of competition and profit maximisation devalues and degenerates the intellect (Berardi, 2009a: 86–7).

Today, technical automatisms systematically overrule psychic and social autonomy. Workers' and consumers' time and attention are controlled via the virtual networks, especially *the* network, the Net. The real process of capitalist domination today has become automated, exercised through the networks, which have become 'conductors' of blindly operating techno-financial automatisms (Berardi, 2009a: 89). In today's semiocapitalism, Berardi (2009b: 143) writes, the speed and limitless expansion of 'cyberspace' overwhelms 'cybertime' (the limited time of the psyche, of living consciousness):

> Cyberspace is the virtual space of the global Internet produced by all the cognitive workers involved in semiotic production. It is the collective result of the ever increasing productivity of the 'general intellect' and it can – and does – expand and speed up indefinitely. Cybertime on the other hand is the mental time necessary for the processing and interpreting of the semiotic fluxes crossing through the Net. It is intrinsically related to the human psyche and to the conscious and sensitive organism supporting it. Cybertime, i.e., the time of living consciousness, is not available in unlimited quantities and its processing capacity and speed are limited by organic, emotional and cultural parameters.

Because cyberspace is expanding much faster than the human psyche's capacity to process information, cognitive workers are increasingly subjected to an overflow of information and thus an overstimulation and over-solicitation of their consciousness and attention. This induces a constant stress on the psyche which erodes its capability for reflexive elaboration and impoverishes its affectivity. The human psyche simply cannot keep up with the avalanche of information that it is forced to process in ever greater quantities at a constantly accelerating speed. In short, 'Cyberspace overloads cybertime' (Berardi, 2011: 55).

Far from progressively escaping the control of capital, the general intellect is ever more completely captured in the automated fluxes of the global system of digital network technologies, stifling its autonomous potential. It is these new conditions of immaterial labour, as Berardi (2011: 14) explains in the introduction to *After the Future*, that frustrate the process of social recomposition that is a prerequisite for the becoming-autonomous of the multitude.[9] Labour has been too fragmented by the new technologies and precarisation strategies of capital to be able to construct a common ground, to create common cultural flows and common desires and to gain a common consciousness, despite the fact that it is ever more based in the common and despite the constant expansion of the general intellect. In the absence of social recomposition, workers lose their sense of togetherness and solidarity and cannot come to form a collective subjectivity.[10] Neoliberalism, with its relentless programme of privatisation, deregulation, marketisation and universal competition, has destroyed the social fabric as such and it is this that prevents the becoming-autonomous of the multitude.

As Berardi shows convincingly in his analyses, the multitude does not show itself as autonomous at all today but, on the contrary, as increasingly captured in the blind automatisms of the digital networks employed by capital. As a consequence, there is a growing divorce between the cognitive work and social life, or between the general intellect and the social body. Whereas Hardt and Negri insist on a growing autonomy of cognitive labour from capital, Berardi observes the exact opposite: a growing control on the part of capital of the life and the 'social psyche' of the cognitariat, primarily through the reign of automatisms. As he writes in the introduction to *Precarious Rhapsody*: 'In our time of digital mutation, technical automatisms are taking control of the social psyche' (Berardi, 2009b: 7). The development of multitudinous autonomy is severely hampered by chains of automatisms that are first of all technological (but by extension also financial and economic) in nature. Such 'automatisms' are defined by Berardi (2009b: 141) as occurrences in which a succession of two states (of language, labour, society or action) follows an automatic, inescapable logic or appears as one inevitable chain). In cognitive capitalism, the behaviour of human agents is automatically regulated via a whole architecture of such automatisms – economic, financial, political and technological.

Cognitive work is captured inside the automatisms of the digital networks. Although it is true that the multitude produces autonomously in a formal sense, its concrete activity is in fact highly coordinated and controlled *through* the network. It might be non-hierarchically organised and seemingly independent, but it actually obeys a strict command. This command no longer comes from human actors though (from bosses, managers, etc.), it resides in the automatic fluidity of the network: 'Control over the labor process is no longer guaranteed by the hierarchy of bigger and smaller bosses typical of the Taylorist factory, but it is incorporated in the flux' (Berardi, 2009a: 89). It is only an ideological fiction, he argues, that cognitive labour in the networks is independent and spontaneously self-organising, a matter of free and autonomously cooperating singularities. In reality, there is strict interdependence of subjective contributions based on the objective chain of automatisms that act both external and internal to the labour process and that completely control it.

Following this argument, cognitive capitalism has gone beyond the old mechanisms of discipline and control, with network labour directed virtually, mostly via the Net, through diffuse but omnipresent systems of techno-linguistic automatisms. In Stieglerian parlance, we could say that this proceeds from the process of technical individuation. It is through the reign of linguistic and operative automatisms that the process of capitalist valorisation appears more and more as a completely automatic process, functioning independently from human conscious decision and withdrawing itself from political influence:

> Devices of social control are incorporated in automated systems: political governance [is] thus replaced by chains of automatisms and incorporated in the productive, communicative, administrative and technical machinery. The living collectivity has no decisional role anymore, on fundamental issues like production and the social distribution of wealth, since the access to the social game requires the adoption of automated operational systems. At a linguistic level, chains of interpretation are automated in such a way that it's no longer possible to read enunciations that don't respect the preventively inscribed code, that is to say the code of capital accumulation. (Berardi, 2009a: 162–3)

Control through techno-linguistic automatisms is invisible and largely irreversible and therefore cannot be ruled by the multitude. Because these automatisms structure the way the networks function, the multitudinous psychosphere finds its potential autonomy overruled by the heteronomy of the 'technosphere' (Berardi, 2009a: 200).

Proletarianisation

Stiegler explains how proletarianisation – understood as the loss of knowledge and know-how and the dissociation between subjects and the technical milieu in which they operate and on which they depend – extends over the whole of society, becoming characteristic of social life in general, sterilising all social bonds (Stiegler, 2010a: 35).[11] And the multitude, rather than becoming ever more creative and intelligent, is confronted with the destruction of its cognitive and affective capacities and affected by a massive process of 'unlearning' (*désaprentissement*) and deskilling, resulting in stupidity (*bêtise*), disaffection and carelessness (Stiegler, 2010b: 56, 45). In short, cognitive capitalism simply destroys cognition and knowledge (Stiegler & Ars Industrialis, 2006: 123). Contrary to Hardt and Negri and also Virno, cognitive capitalism has not only not liberated itself from constant capital, it is argued, but the place of producers is constantly shrinking and the role of labour (of variable capital) diminishing. The process of automation Stiegler shows as having only widened the field of proletarianisation, which is applied now to theoretical knowledge – the knowledge of scientists, engineers, designers and 'creatives'.

Cognitive capitalism essentially consists in the proletarianisation of the nervous system, the brains of workers, since today's income-earners from the effort of the nervous system (the knowledge workers) are just as deprived of their knowledge and know-how as were the nineteenth and early twentieth century wage-labourers of the muscular system: each were/are proletarians. Indeed, cognitive capitalism leads to the proletarianisation of the cognitive *as such*. According to Stiegler, the cognitive labour of today is a labour devoid of any knowledge. Concretely, this means that the cognitive has been reduced to pure calculability; *logos* has become *ratio*, in the sense of pure calculation. Truly skilled professions hardly exist anymore, and most of the so-called 'creative work' today only consists in entropic adaptation to the market wherein what it creates is only market value. It is not work that opens (*ouvrier*, œuvre) new worlds (Stiegler, 2010a: 45–6).

In their praise for the increasing intelligence of the multitude – 'the subaltern classes are already classes with a fixed capital richer than that of the bosses, a spiritual patrimony more important than what the bosses boast, and an absolute weapon: the knowledge essential for the reproduction of the world' (Negri, 2008d: 178) – Hardt and Negri downplay what Berardi refers to as the exhaustion of the libidinal energy of the cognitariat and Stiegler as the destruction of the libido of the *consumer*. In their analyses of the (power of the) multitude, Hardt and Negri, like all other (post-)operaist thinkers, almost totally neglect the perspective of consumption: what the cognitariat desires to have and to use. Crucially, as Stiegler emphasises, the processes of subjectivation within and among the multitude today are not only, and not even primarily, played out on the terrain of production but also, and more decisively, on that of consumption.

Through the means of marketing and public relations, it is consumption rather than the machines of production that is the principal target of control in today's capitalism; thus, it is not biopower that is decisive today but psychopower: 'It is no longer a question … of controlling the population as a producing machine, but rather as a consuming machine, and the danger is no longer biopower but psychopower as both control and production – production of motivations' (Stiegler, 2009: 131–2). Marketing has become the instrument par excellence of social control today; it is the principal instrument of control of our 'societies of control' (Stiegler, 2009: 181, referring to Deleuze). And thus it is the consumer who has become the prime object of proletarianisation in today's service economies, affecting all of us. As Stiegler writes in the first volume of his *Disbelief and Discredit* (*Mécréance et Discrédit*) trilogy, *The Decadence of Industrial Democracies*: 'The consumer is the new proletarian figure, and the proletariat, far from disappearing, is a condition from which it has become nearly impossible to escape' (Stiegler, 2011: 35).

Taking into account these processes of consumerist (de)subjectivation gives a wholly different, less promising, picture of the prospects of a liberation of the common from capital. The capitalist creation of consumer need – and it very much is a felt need, identified with at the core of being – extends throughout the lifespan, manipulated and managed, for example, through TV ads aimed at toddlers through to sophisticated, systematic presentations of life and health insurance to eradicate danger and minimise the risk of life itself. It does not apply merely to the material and our physicalities, but also to the emotions – capitalising all relationships in present-giving, including our relationships with our environments in home building, wherein our place of residence becomes an expression of self-respect and self-love – and to the intellect and the aesthetic.

Thus the urbane become the consumer of culture, expressed in contemporary colloquialisms such as 'must-dos' (must-see films, must-read books, etc.); in the spheres of education productive of the property of nationally and inter-nationally determined required attainments and certifications; in academia, as with the targets of points scored for publishing; and in the domain of theory, of science, with the technical milieu (below). Ultimately, at the level of the individual, we narrate our lives to ourselves as product, literally in the satisfaction of filled-in curricula vitae and metaphorically through normative life-event milestones that reflect how we judge ourselves to ourselves. And thus, at the level of society, do we fill the ranks of the new proletariat (see below).

Political engagement

Despite its engagement in immaterial work, goes the third counter-argument, the multitude is not becoming more politically capable and assertive. On the contrary, the last few decades have seen increased political apathy and a decline in political interest and participation. The multitude has not, it must be stressed, established any kind of a common ground and developed a common consciousness that might form the basis of its political subjectivation or its 'becoming for-itself'. The multitude is incredibly active and productive, frenetically working to the point of total exhaustion, but it is doing this compulsively, automatically, seemingly blindly, without a shared consciousness of its collective activity beyond that of competition, which merely fuels more of the same. Today's cognitive networkers are extremely productive but they are not conscious actors of their own doing and do not seem able to unite their feelings and thoughts into a common space of consciousness. Effective conscious collective action, therefore, is almost completely lacking today.

The mostly summers of protest on the city streets seen in many capitals may appear to have offered a rebuttal to the Stieglerian counter-thesis and even represent something of a turning point in this regard. Unfortunately for the vision of Hardt and Negri and their ilk, however, this (occasional) phenomenon is rather easily contained and managed, in the end heuristically functioning as a social safety valve, a political catharsis rather than expression. In fact, it is argued, the multitude in general suffers from a loss of the symbolic and linguistic resources needed for genuine political action and has fallen into the grip of a regressive political populism primarily caused by the constant, systemic manipulation of its libidinal energies by the mass media of the programming and culture industries, by what Stiegler (2006a: 14) refers to as an 'industrial populism'. Democracy is overruled by telecracy and capital controls collective and individual desires.

Although Hardt and Negri frequently admit that the digital networks that they usually praise for their autonomising and emancipatory potentials are also ideal instruments for new forms of control and exploitation of labour (they sometimes speak of empire's 'network power' in terms of a 'virtual panopticon'), they nevertheless, I would argue, gravely underestimate the overwhelmingly heteronomising and disempowering effects of these networks under cognitive capitalism, effects which render the prospects of 'a becoming-prince of the multitude' rather bleak to say the least. The networks may indeed provide the primary condition for the formation of the common and the creation of institutions of the common, but they can also act as a barrier to it, and they do obstruct the common and prevent its (self-)organisation and institutionalisation.

The libidinal economy of the multitude and the technological conditions for communism

Even more than Hardt and Negri, I would assume, with Stiegler, that the role of networks (and of technology in general) is and will be crucial to the coming constitution of the common and the emancipation/autonomisation of the general intellect. The global network of digital information and communication technologies indeed represents a crucial condition for the becoming-autonomous of the multitude and for the political project of instituting the common and creating a 'communist' society in the sense of an absolute democracy 'by all and for all'. In order to really understand this condition, however – which is fundamentally and irrevocably ambivalent (below) – it is necessary to realise that the digital networks not only provide the technological infrastructure of the economy of production and consumption but are also the technological supports for the 'economy of desire' that underlies the economy of production and consumption: that is, they are crucial also for the constitution of what Stiegler calls, after Freud and Lyotard, the 'libidinal economy' – sometimes also the 'spiritual economy' or 'symbolic economy' – of which the political is, of course, a central aspect (Stiegler, 2010b: 30).

What is insufficiently taken into account by Hardt and Negri is the fact that the constitution of the desires of the multitude – of the individual and collective libido – is crucially conditioned by the 'mnemotechnical milieu', as Stiegler describes it, the system of mnemotechnologies or 'technologies of the mind' (writing, printing, radio, television, computer, Internet, etc.) that form the material support structure for every 'life of the mind'. Hardt and Negri underestimate the extent to which the systemic annexation of this milieu by cognitive and consumer capitalism is exhausting and ultimately destroying the libidinal economy of contemporary society, thereby annihilating what Aristotle called '*philia*', the 'social energy' that is the 'glue' of every form of social and political life, the 'binding agent' of every form of community (Stiegler, 2006a: 15).

More generally, I would argue that Hardt and Negri's account of the nature and conditions of the multitude, in particular the existing conditions for potential collective struggle, tends to neglect precisely that condition which – as I would like to suggest with Stiegler and Berardi – is the most important, most fundamental with regard to the transformation towards another possible communist society: that of desire, that is to say of individual and collective desire. More precisely, what Hardt and Negri fail to consider or at least insufficiently address, I believe, is the libidinal economy underlying the knowledge economy of immaterial production, and, more specifically, the brutalising and regressive effects of the latter on the former under capitalist conditions.

As Stiegler (2006a: 63) makes clear, capitalism is first of all a libidinal economy and it is the libidinal energy of people – of producers, consumers, entrepreneurs and investors – that constitutes the driving force behind the capitalist dynamic, its very motor. This libidinal energy, according to both Stiegler's and Berardi's diagnosis, has suffered from a process of exhaustion during the last decades due to its continuous mobilisation and exploitation through both managerial and marketing strategies and techniques that seek to enhance workers' performativity and promote and increase consumption. In order to capture the libidinal energy of producers and consumers in the course of the twentieth century, capitalism has taken hold of the so-called mnemotechnological milieu on which society and culture ultimately rest (and which forms the support of all symbolic milieus), transforming it into the global information and communication network that we all know and that almost exclusively serves the goals of capitalist accumulation.

It is through the systemic annexation of the mnemotechnical milieu that capital manages to control the desire of the multitude, as both Stiegler and Berardi show. What these authors also both emphasise is that desire is not a natural given, but something that is constructed, the result of practices of cultivation. Referring to Baudrillard, Berardi (2009a: 118) in particular emphasises that desire is not an inherently positive force, as Hardt and Negri seem to assume under the influence of Foucault and Deleuze/Guattari, but a *field*. More precisely it is a battlefield, one on which many conflicting forces meet animated principally by *techne*, as Stiegler (2010b) has theorised extensively. According to Stiegler (2006b: 13), and this is one of his crucial insights, the formation as well as destruction of desire – as a result of processes of sublimation and desublimation – is technologically conditioned through and through. That is to say, a libidinal economy is crucially dependent on a mnemotechnical milieu, a technical 'milieu of the mind'. This means that intelligence, creativity, sociality and the imagination – the 'faculties' constituting the general intellect – depend on a certain state of the technical milieu (Stiegler, 2006a: 34). As the highest forms of sublimated desire, these faculties are all fruits of a libidinal economy – and they deteriorate under the condition of a desublimatory libidinal economy, or better 'dis-economy', which is characteristic of contemporary cognitive and consumer capitalism as it destroys all objects of desire, Stiegler argues. Today's cognitive and consumer capitalism has turned the libidinal economy into an economy based on drives, of both consumers and speculators (Stiegler, 2010a: 84).

For Stiegler, the individual and collective libidinal energy constitutive of something like a general intellect is formed within processes of psychic and collective individuation or, more precisely, in processes of co-individuation between individual psyches and social groups. These processes of co-individuation, he shows, can only take place within a shared technical milieu that co-evolves with society: psychosocial co-individuation proceeds in tandem with a process of technical individuation on which it intrinsically depends. In other words, the psychic organs can only socialise (co-individuate with the process of individuation of the collective) by passing through the technical organs, by co-individuating with the individuation of the technical system. That is to say, the technical 'organs' that make up the mnemotechnical milieu play a fundamental, decisive role in the articulation of psychic organs and social organisations.

Intelligence cannot be understood as a purely individual phenomenon, as Hardt and Negri rightly emphasise. It is socially constituted. Stiegler, however, emphasises that intelligence is also dependent on the existence of a technical system that *thoroughly* conditions it. In fact, intelligence can only be understood in terms of a process of co-individuation in which three different organ systems permanently interact: psychic organs, social organisations and technical organs. To view intelligence in this way is to view it as an organological phenomenon, in Stiegler's terms. What organology studies is the logical, specifically transductive – that is, co-constituting or co-determining – relationship between these three organ systems and in particular the flows of libidinal energy (constitutive of sociality, intelligence, creativity, knowledge, etc.) that cross between these systems, that is, in the circuits of *trans*individuation constituted by these systems.

The organology and pharmacology of the general intellect and the common

What I want to suggest here is that we consider the general intellect and the 'mass intellectuality' of which Hardt and Negri and the other (post-)autonomists speak, from an organological perspective – and, by extension, that we consider the emergence of the multitude and the common and the prospects of a communist society also from an organological perspective. What is most significant about Stiegler's organological view of intelligence is that it conceives of the technical organs – in particular the mnemotechnologies – in terms of *pharmaka*, meaning that they are intrinsically ambivalent with respect to their conditioning effects on the mind.[12] They can, for instance, be both positive and negative, creative-productive or destructive of social bonds; they can act as instruments of discipline and control, but can also function as tools of self-constitution, self-valorisation, autonomy, emancipation and the elevation of intelligence. According to Stiegler's analyses, today's *pharmaka* function primarily as technologies of labour and consumer control. They are the central factors in the generalisation of proletarianisation and heteronomisation of the multitude. Under cognitive and consumer capitalism, these *pharmaka* have become totally poisonous, thereby liquidating every libidinal economy.

However, the new digital *pharmaka* also offer the possibility of fighting against these processes of proletarianisation and of initiating a process of de-proletarianisation; indeed, they carry the promise of a 'pharmacological turn'. The question is whether and how such a turn might become one towards communism. Following the line of argument expressed here, a liberation of the common from capital and a consequent turn to communism at the very least supposes (and therefore must first of all be thought of) as a process of de-proletarianisation of the multitude. To understand this, it is necessary to approach the problematic of the common and the general intellect from an organological and pharmacological perspective.

A liberation of the common from capital presupposes the constitution of a collective, 'commonist' desire – or at least local circuits of commonist desire – and with this, the initiation of commonist processes of psychosocial individuation or subjectivation counter to the neoliberal processes of disindividuation predominant today. The 'struggle for the common' has to be waged first of all on the plane of desire, the terrain of libidinal economy, and the principal arena of struggle is the global technical system at the basis of this libidinal economy. The liberation of the common from capital and the realisation of autonomy by the multitude supposes first of all the liberation of multitudinous desire from its desublimated and heteronomised state under today's cognitive and consumer capitalism.

A communist society will never materialise when even the basic condition for the manifestation of a society, a common desire for a common future, cannot be realised. As Berardi (2009a: 139) rightly emphasises, politics is first of all a question of the social investment of desire and thus the formation of a political will formed on the basis of flows of the collective desire. Such flows are constructed, in Stiegler's terminology, within processes of psychic and collective individuation. However, and deserving of more attention within the debates about the 'communism to come', these processes are fundamentally conditioned by a process of (mnemo)technical individuation, the individuation of a (mnemo)technical milieu. Politics, according to Stiegler, is above all about the motivation and organisation of psychic and collective individuation processes, which, in our epoch, are produced essentially via information and communication technologies, mainly via television and now, increasingly, via the globalised system of digital networks. Currently, the milieu of information and communication technologies is colonised by the programming and culture industries of capital.

Liberating the common from capital: the need for de-proletarianisation

In order to imagine the potentiality of a 'becoming-prince' of the multitude, to consider the self-emancipation and liberation of the common from capital, it is necessary to think about the construction of a 'communist desire', to use the expression introduced by Jodi Dean, and to consider the possibility of 'communist' processes of individuation. To do this, it is necessary to consider the constitution of the multitude and the common – as well as the general intellect – from an organological and pharmacological perspective. A communism of the multitude first of all presupposes a struggle against the state of generalised proletarianisation – of producers and consumers, but also of scientists, engineers, artists and 'intellectuals' – which is typical of our current societies, notwithstanding Hardt and Negri's assertions to the contrary. This state of generalised proletarianisation is primarily sustained and aggravated through the heteronomising effects of a mnemotechnical system that is exclusively subordinated to the logic of – increasingly short-term – profit which has social systems adapt to its 'development' without allowing for an alternative that would allow the invention/emergence of new modes of autonomy and practices of freedom.

As André Gorz (1982) observed in his *Farewell to the Working Class*, only a de-proletarianised 'proletariat' will be able to collectively appropriate and autonomously manage the production system. Or, only radically changing the system of production – both its structure and its means – will make it collectively appropriable and autonomously manageable. According to Stiegler, the historical failure of communism is principally linked to the fact that it proved unable to think – and therefore to fight against – proletarianisation as the dissociation of the workers and the technical milieu and the loss of knowledge and know-how this entailed (the bureaucratic totalitarianism of the Soviet planner-state being, in fact, a paragon of general proletarianisation); the state socialist model of Soviet communism thus ruined the libidinal economy on an unprecedented scale. Today's market totalitarianism, however, is in the process of creating its own version of a libidinal dis-economy, one that is increasingly drive-based and that eliminates motives and motivations and thereby destroys long-term processes of psycho-collective individuation (Stiegler, 2010a: 60–61).

As Stiegler argues, however, today's digital networks offer a pharmacological opportunity to reverse this tendency. Although still mainly functioning as capitalist technologies of control, the reticular milieu of the digital network – because of its associative, non-centralised and bidirectional characteristics (as an 'associated technical milieu', in the terminology of Gilbert Simondon) – can be appropriated and transformed into supports for new processes of psychic and collective individuation and thence developed as new tools of autonomy, socialisation and practices of freedom. This is what 'ad-option' is, according to Stiegler, as against the 'ad-aptive' mode of relating to technology typical of consumerism (and proletarianised production) (Stiegler, 2010b: 46–8, 79).

The question for a twenty-first century communism is how this process of adoption can be 'seized' by the multitude to turn the digital networks into supports for recomposition (to use a term from the [post-]autonomist tradition) and the constitution of a common – and common(s)-oriented – consciousness and desire. How can the digital networks be transformed into instruments for processes of psychosocial individuation in the form of collective – and commons-oriented – singularisations that empower and elevate the multitude instead of enslaving and brutalising it? How can the new processes of psychosocial individuation principally enabled (but still to be invented!) by the digital *pharmaka* be made into processes of *commonisation*, into processes in which the common is protected from expropriation and exploitation by capital and instead collectively assumed and appropriated? How can these processes form the basis of practices of *care* for the common and the commons?

De-proletarianisation for Stiegler means the restoration of care – of taking care of the world and of the self and of others – and the re-emergence and re-valorisation of responsibility as the central stake of the economy to come (which he opposes to the essential carelessness of today's ultra-capitalism) (Stiegler, 2010a: 108, 2010b: 151). A communist – or commons-oriented – process of de-proletarianisation should translate this into care for the common and the assumption of collective responsibility for the common. And although this may (also) be initiated by public authorities, as Stiegler concedes when he calls for a state-organised 'industrial politics of the mind', it is fundamentally and overridingly important that they be initiated 'from below', by the multitude or cognitariat itself.

Given the exhausted and pathologised state of the multitude's libidinal economy, however, such a politics needs first of all to take the form of a profound therapeutic intervention, that is to say, a sociotherapy (Stiegler, 2010b: 80). This would aim at shifting libidinal energies away from the obsessive and egoistical competitive drive for status, possession and addictive consumption – the key attributes of the neoliberal subject – and refocusing it on more collectively and autonomously lived modes of existence, oriented towards sharing, living in common and taking care of the common. The ultimate challenge here for the general intellect is to conquer the overwhelming psycho-power of the mass media of the culture industry.

For Stiegler, the 'therapeutics' here – or, the weapons for such a politics – are given precisely by the new digital *pharmaka*, provided that they be transformed into supports for a new sublimatory libidinal economy, new 'spiritual' and cultural practices and new emancipatory collective projects. Stiegler argues that current initiatives in commonisation, like free software, commons-based peer-to-peer production and creative commons – which have all originated 'from below', from the practices of production itself – represent pioneering cases of such a therapeutic – and as such de-proletarianising – economic practice. Although these initiatives may be described in terms of 'multitudinous entrepreneurship' (as Hardt and Negri might say), until now they have not been able to mature into genuine sociopolitical projects seriously threatening the capitalist order, let alone into solid harbingers of a new 'communist' society. What is still lacking is a 'common cause' and the sublimation and unification of singular desires into what Stiegler calls a consistency, a long-term protection of infinite 'scope', of a collectively affirmed and lived 'ideal' (Stiegler, 2010b: 85, 94, 105).

The same goes for the so-called 'social networks', which turn out to be mainly supports for hyper-consumerist, addicto-genic and mimetic behaviour patterns today – as well as the communicative life-force of the cathartic street protests that on deeper analysis do little other than facilitate the status quo (i.e. dominance of capital). For the moment, as Jodi Dean (2010: 4) has shown quite rigorously in her *Blog Theory*, social media like Facebook, MySpace and Twitter behave predominantly as desublimatory attractors through which the libidinal energy of the multitude is captured and diverted in 'affective networks' that act as the prime generator of surplus value for what she calls 'communicative capitalism' – in the guise of which capital deftly goes on expropriating and exploiting the 'surplus common' continuously produced by the multitude (Casarino & Negri, 2008: 22). As such, digital networks have come to function as 'circuits of drive', in which the multitude becomes fragmented, dispersed and narcotised instead of unified, concentrated and conscious of itself (Dean, 2010: 124). The true pharmacological potential of these networks is still to be invented and realised. If the great democratic challenge of the twenty-first century, the challenge of radical democracy, is the 'invention of the common' (Negri & Revel, 2008), its foremost task will be to reflect upon its organological – and that is to say, pharmacological – conditions of possibility and fight for their institution.

Notes

1   A second conference entitled 'Potentialities of Communism. Of What is Communism the Name Today?' was held in Paris in January 2010. Another was held in Berlin that June, entitled 'The Idea of Communism: Philosophy and Art'. The fourth conference in the series, 'Communism. A New Beginning?', was held in New York in October 2011, and a fifth in Seoul, September 2013. For the Paris conference, see Badiou and Žižek (2011), and for New York, see Žižek (2013).

2   The expression 'communist horizon' comes originally from the Bolivian sociologist and then vice-president Alvaro García Linera; cf. Dean's (2012) work with this title.

3   As such, according to Gorz (2009: 55), 'cognitive capitalism *is* itself the crisis of capitalism'.

4   Actually, in *Labor of Dionysus. A Critique of the State Form* Hardt and Negri (1994) had already given an analysis of the 'prerequisites of communism' in the current state of the development of the mode of production (see Chapter 7, esp. 270.2–282.3). In this work, although they sometimes refer to the 'multitude of workers', the notion of the multitude had not yet replaced that of the 'social worker'.

5   It must be said, however, that Žižek is also relating the current revival of communism to the struggle for the reappropriation of the various forms of commons (social, ecological, cultural, etc.) that is occurring everywhere nowadays. He thereby explicitly refers to the work of Hardt and Negri; interestingly, Žižek describes the privatisations or 'enclosures' of these commons as processes of proletarianisation in which workers are excluded from their own substance (Žižek, 2009: 91) – but see below.

6   Labour has become immaterial principally due to the informatisation of production. Whereas Fordist or modern capitalism was characterised by the *industrialisation* of production, post-Fordist or postmodern capitalism is (most) characterised by the *informatisation* of production (Hardt & Negri, 2000: 284). Today's capitalist economy is an informational economy in which the so-called 'tertiary sector' has become dominant and where knowledge,

information and communication play a foundational role in the production process.

7   Along with Stiegler (who bases himself on both Marx and Simondon), I understand proletarianisation in this chapter essentially as the loss of knowledge and know-how in human subjects resulting from the passing of this knowledge and know-how – via a process of grammatisation – in technical prostheses, which has the tendency of dissociating these subjects from their sociotechnical environments and thereby engendering dissociated technical milieus (see below).

8   See also Beradi, this volume (Eds.).

9   Originating from the operaist tradition, 'recomposition' refers to a process of (re)unification (of the social body, class, labour, the proletariat, etc.) through the convergence of social flows of desire and imagination.

10   '[T]he expansion of the productive potency of the general intellect coincides with a schizoid fragmentation of the collective brain, incapable of recomposing as conscious subjectivity; unable to act in a conscious, collective way' (Berardi, 2011: 130).

11   For a listing of English language translations of Stiegler's works, see http://www.samkinsley.com/stiegler/stiegler-bibliography/

12   The German (and Greek) '*pharmaka*' refers to medicines, drugs, but also to spells, enchantments.

References

Agamben, G. (2009). *What is an Apparatus? And Other Essays*. Stanford, CA: Stanford University Press.

Aigrain, P. (2005). *Cause Commune, L'Information Entre Bien Commun et Propriété* [Common cause: information between common property and property]. Paris: Fayard.

Badiou, A. (2008). *The Meaning of Sarkozy*. London: Verso.

Badiou, A. (2010). *The Communist Hypothesis*. London: Verso.

Badiou, A. and Žižek, S. (Eds.) (2011). *L'Idée du Communisme: Vol. 2, Conférence de Berlin 2010*. Paris: Nouvelles Editions Lignes.

Berardi, F. (2009a). *The Soul at Work*. Los Angeles: Semiotext(e).

Berardi, F. (2009b). *Precarious Rhapsody. Semiocapitalism and the Pathologies of the Post-Alpha Generation*. London: Minor Compositions.

Berardi, F. (2009c). *Communism is Back but We should Call it the Therapy of Singularisation*. At http://www.generation-online.org/p/fp_bifo6.htm

Berardi, F. (2011). *After the Future*. Edinburgh/Oakland, CA: AK Press.

Bosteels, B. (2011). *The Actuality of Communism*. London: Verso.

Boyle, J. (2008). *The Public Domain. Enclosing the Commons of the Mind*. New Haven, CT: Yale University Press.

Carr, N. (2009). *The Big Switch. Rewiring the World, From Edison to Google*. New York: W. W. Norton & Company

Carr, N. (2010). *The Shallows. How the Internet is Changing the Way We Think, Read and Remember*. London: Atlantic Books

Casarino, C. and Negri, A. (2008). *In Praise of the Common. A Conversation on Philosophy and Politics*. Minneapolis: University of Minnesota Press.

Dean, J. (2010). *Blog Theory. Feedback and Capture in the Circuits of Desire*. London: Polity.

Dean, J. (2012). *The Communist Horizon*. London: Verso.

Douzinas, C. and Žižek, S. (Eds.) (2010). *The Idea of Communism*. London: Verso.

Drahos, P. and Braithwaite, J. (2002). *Information Feudalism. Who Owns the Knowledge Economy?* London: Earthscan Publications.

Dyer-Witheford, N. (2007). 'Commonism', *Turbulence* 1. At http://turbulence.org.uk/turbulence-1/commonism/

Fisher, M. (2009). *Capitalist Realism. Is There No Alternative?* Winchester: Zero Books.

Gorz, A. (1982). *Farewell to the Working Class*. London: Pluto Press.

Gorz, A. (2009). *Auswege aus dem Kapitalismus. Beiträge zur politischen Ökologie* [Outflows from capitalism: contributions to political ecology]. Zürich: Rotpunkt Verlag.

Hardt, M. (2010). 'The common in communism', in C. Douzinas and S. Žižek (Eds.), *The Idea of Communism*. London: Verso.

Hardt, M. and Negri, A. (1994). *Labor of Dionysus. A Critique of the State Form*. Minneapolis: University of Minnesota Press.

Hardt, M. and Negri, A. (2000). *Empire*. Cambridge, MA: Harvard University Press.

Hardt, M. and Negri, A. (2004). *Multitude*. London: Penguin.

Hardt, M. and Negri, A. (2009). *Commonwealth*. Cambridge, MA: Harvard University Press.

Hope, J. (2008). *Biobazaar. The Open Source Revolution in Biology*. Cambridge, MA: Harvard University Press.

Jefferson, R. (2006). 'Science as social enterprise', *Innovations*, 1(4): 13–44.

Kloppenburg, J. (2010). 'Impeding dispossession, enabling repossession. Biological open source and the recovery of seed sovereignty', *Journal of Agrarian Change*, 10(3): 367–388.

Lanier, J. (2010). *You Are Not a Gadget. A Manifesto*. New York: Alfred A. Knopf.

Lessig, L. (2004). *Free Culture. The Nature and Future of Creativity*. New York: Penguin Press.

Negri, A. (2008a). *Reflections on Empire*. London: Polity.

Negri, A. (2008b). *Empire and Beyond*. London: Polity.

Negri, A. (2008c). *The Porcelain Workshop. For a New Grammar of Politics*. Los Angeles: Semiotext(e).

Negri, A. (2008d). *Goodbye Mr. Socialism. In Conversation with Raf Valvola Scelsi*. New York: Seven Stories Press.

Negri, A. and Revel, J. (2008). 'Inventing the common', *Multitudes*, 13 May.

Stiegler, B. (2006a). *La Télécratie Contre la Démocratie. Lettre Ouverte aux Représentatives Politiques* [Telecracy against democracy]. Paris: Flammarion.

Stiegler, B. (2006b). *Mécréance et Discrédit 3. L'esprit Perdu du Capitalisme* [Disbelief and discredit]. Paris: Galilée.

Stiegler, B. (2009). *Taking Care of Youth and the Generations*. Stanford, CA: Stanford University Press.

Stiegler, B. (2010a). *For a New Critique of Political Economy*. London: Polity.

Stiegler, B. (2010b). *Ce qui fait que la vie vaut la peine d'être vécue. De la pharmacologie* [What makes life worth living: on pharmacology]. Paris: Flammarion.

Stiegler, B. (2011). *Disbelief and Discredit, Vol. 1. The Decadence of Industrial Democracies*. London: Polity.

Stiegler, B. and Ars Industrialis (2006). *Réenchanter le Monde. La Valeur Esprit contre le Populisme Industriel* [Enchantment of the world: the value of the human spirit vs. industrial populism]. Paris: Flammarion.

Vattimo, G. and Zabala, S. (2011). *Hermeneutic Communism. From Heidegger to Marx*. New York: Columbia University Press.

Virno, P. (2004). *A Grammar of the Multitude*. Los Angeles: Semiotext(e).

Zabala, S. (2012). 'Being a Communist in 2012', *Al Jazeera English Online*, 9 February. At http://www.aljazeera.com/indepth/opinion/2012/02/201223111316317303.html

Žižek, S. (2009). *First as Tragedy, then as Farce*. London: Verso Books.

Žižek, S. (Ed.) (2013). *The Idea of Communism 2*. New York/London: Verso Books.

Chapter 6

Grounding social revolution: elements for a systems theory of commoning[1]

Massimo De Angelis

> We never see the enemy because we can't see ourselves clearly.
> (Sun Tzu, The Art of War)

Introduction

Starting from the position that we should not confuse the commons with resources held in common, I approach commons as social systems in which resources are pooled by a community of subjects who *also* govern these resources to guarantee their sustainability (if they are natural resources) and the reproduction of the community, and who engage in commoning, a form of social labour that has a direct relation to the needs, desires and aspirations of the commoners. Thorough commoning, subjects create conditions of resilience and self-organisation and may develop from grassroots into more all-encompassing systems. Thus, commons come in many shapes and sizes.

In terms of a political definition of commons, what is crucial is the fact that, as systems, commons are defined not only by their own internal relations – from which, for example, Elinor Ostrom (1990) derived her principles of sustainability of commons – but also in relation to their environment. The commons environment includes other systems. In the first place, this means ecosystems. Many commons rely on the natural environment for their resilience, so have a special interest in developing ecologically sustainable practices and struggling against the 'externalities' of other systems, especially that of capital. Second, commons relate to other social systems. These are of several types, related to other commons, and in different ways, as well as to the state and to capital: the typology of commons systems is quite broad in range. It must be remarked that, at this preliminary stage, the commons seem to have an ontological equivalence to social systems such as state and capital. To the extent that they are all *social* systems this is correct, but as soon as we begin to investigate their own processes, key ontological differences emerge.

The phenomenology of commons is grounded in daily life. Households are one example of commons, when patriarchal hierarchies do not turn them into micro-states, that is, or corrupt commons, as in Hardt and Negri (2009), or in the vernacular, and from the perspective of subaltern subjects, 'fucked up' commons. Networks of supporting friends are another sphere of commons, consisting of life-long connections or ephemeral relationships: temporary commons are still commons.[2] Community organisations, housing co-ops and social centres, self-managed workshops, community gardens and water associations, these are all forms of commons systems, as are peer-to-peer (P2P) networks in cyberspace for sharing codes, files and documents (so music, books, etc.) and generally promoting all forms of digital cooperation. As the listing of friendship and virtual networks implies, commons may occupy a social space rather than physical place; they do not need to be situated in a particular locality, although those that are have the additional strategic task of claiming a territory.

Importantly, I argue, we should not think of commons as a third sector, beyond state and market. Or, if we want to do this, then we should not think of the sectors as discrete divisions operating alongside of or in parallel with one another. Commons are 'inside' the state and capital, and, to the extent that states and capital influence the subjectivities of commoners reproducing commons, states and capital are inside commons. Thus, we also find commons in private enterprise, on the shop-floors of factories and in the canteens of offices among co-workers supporting one another, sharing their lunch and developing forms of solidarity and mutual aid; and we find commons inside state schools and universities, often divided along hierarchical lines: the management commons, the teachers' commons, the students' commons (literally, in the 'common room').

Therefore, not only are the commons related to pooled resources governing rivers, coastlines, forests and rivers and their ecosystems, as studied by Ostrom and many of his associates at the International Association for the Study of Commons; nor, moreover, are they only found outside of and in opposition to capital (and state), as in the unemployed squatting in empty houses and sharing tricks on how to fool the benefits office, but also they are within and at the heart even of capital, such as among the rich and privileged. Bill Gates, for example, becomes a commoner with respect to his family and his class, even though his peculiar family commons is part of that 1% of society that concentrates 50% of the world's wealth (Oxfam, 2015) and the physical siting of his commons systems is most likely protected by barbed wire and security cameras that warn armed security guards transforming a commons boundary into a border that keeps the poor and their commons systems out. Indeed, the relation among commons is not something given, but must be politically constructed through boundary commoning (see below).

Both commons and capital may employ high or low tech, make use of oil or not and have functions that require a certain level of authority. Nevertheless, commons and capital are two distinct, autonomous social systems: that is, they both struggle to 'take things into their own hands' and self-govern on the basis of their different, and often clashing, internally generated codes, measures and values. They also struggle to be distinct autopoietic social systems, in that they not only aim to reproduce their interrelations but also the pre-production of their components through their internally generated codes and values. They do this, of course, in a clear, distinctive way. Capital reproduces itself through profit and its accumulation, commons through a set of interrelated values referring to resources and community that define a sharing culture. Commons are generated insofar as subjects common (become commoners), insofar as their social being is enacted with others, at different levels of social organisations, through a social practice that is essentially horizontal and may embrace a variety of forms depending on circumstances (implying the broad typology), but ultimately grounded in community sharing, doing in common and participatory democracy. Capital, by contrast, tends to objectify, instrumentalise and impose hierarchical order.

When we consider commons, we are not (should not be) indicating utopia and pointing to capital as a dystopia. It may appear clear that capital cannot bring us to utopia, since its own *conatus* of self-preservation (De Angelis, 2007) is boundless accumulation, and the processes for realising this are not only environmentally destructive, but also socially divisive and exploitative. It is equally the case, however, that we cannot claim (should not imagine) that commons will lead us to utopia, since utopias are not made of concrete structures contingent on particular situations. What we can claim, though, is that the autonomy and autopoiesis that commons and capital struggle to achieve have a distinct and conflicting character.

Commons and capital/state are often linked, coupled through the buying and selling site of the official market: that is, the 'economy'. Both capital and the commons produce and trade, regulated by state laws (of contract, taxation, health and safety, etc.) and enforced by the state policing and judicial/penal systems.[3] Even in this official linkage, however, they have fundamentally different priorities. Capital buys in order to sell, at a profit – in the case of commercial capital, or as means of production, to turn resources into commodities (add value). Commons, on the other hand, when engaged in market operations, tend to sell commodities in order to buy means of sustenance and reproduction. For example, one or two members of a household sell their labour power to gain an income in order to be able to purchase the goods necessary for the process of reproduction of that household; or an association engages in petty trade to fund itself, or a social centre sells beer at a concert to purchase the materials to build a kitchen. In the case of capital, quantity is paramount: greater production and higher sales imply increased returns; for commons, however, it is sufficiency that is required (there is no internal logic of expansion).

Buying in order to sell and selling in order to buy are two opposite praxes, as they have been from the time of Aristotle, the former governed by a life-activity ultimately wasted in accumulation and the latter governed by the needs and desires of reproduction (subject to market constraints). In other words, and as this chapter explains, while the reproduction of labour power is a feature of the commons' production (of the commodified labour power) that is sold to capital, capital does not necessarily control (or controls only in part through the state and the education system) the labour of reproduction that is fundamental to the commons. The constitution of selling in order to buy that is typical of the labour-power circuit is only the market moment of a commons social system. It is certainly here that labour power is reproduced – but not only labour power.

The various commons all reproduce certain basic elements, at least in their general sense. Thus, at a general organisational level, in order to have commons – of whatever type – we need to have at least three constituent elements, the dry specification of life-enhancing, organic development, a socio-ecological, metabolic process in which cultures of sharing are (re)produced:

- Pooled resources (material or immaterial);
- A community of commoners: that is, subjects willing to share, pool and reproduce the resources that are necessary for their own reproduction (not necessarily a local community in the classical sense of village, territory, etc.);
- Commoning.

Fundamental to all systems as the basis of their dynamics, the concepts of stocks and flows apply to this listing also. The first two elements here (resources and commoners) are stocks categories, referring to that with which any commons begins its reproduction (the resources as object, or target, and commoners as subject, or agent), while the third, commoning, is a flow category, allowing the transformation of the resources into new or renewed forms.[4] Commoning is a social process occurring within a domain that even in the most homogeneous contexts articulates a diversity of values – inducement to social force – to produce a common goal – a force-field oriented in one direction (Lewin, 1997). In commoning, these two aspects (diversity of values and common goals) are not aligned through top-down discipline as in centralised organisations and political systems associated with capital and the state. Rather, the series of stock-flow relations are accompanied by reinforcing and balancing feedbacks, of which the commoners are aware, that they value and recognise and for which commons institutions are created or develop (consensus procedures, swarming, assemblies, inter-mediation, conflict-resolution procedures, etc.).

Regarding the first of the three constituent elements, mate-rial resources include anything physical, or tangible (from food, houses, warehouses and transport to tools, IT, DNA and energy), however obtained (purchased or donated, loaned or occupied). Immaterial resources, on the other hand, comprise the skills, qualities, knowledge and know-how of the subjects involved in the commons – the commoners – who have obtained these through their life histories, which means these include Bourdieu's (1986) symbolic, social and cultural capital (or rather, perhaps, social, symbolic, cultural wealth, since the purpose of pooling them, unlike for capital, is not accumulation).

In the epistemology of the commons, the second element, the community of commoners, might be understood as the collection of subjects and their interrelations as commoners, that is, as sharers (protectors, developers, etc.) of the resources (or of a particular subset of this collection). This presupposes a particular set of interrelated meanings and values that are shared (understood, performed and/or evocative) – in short, some common ground, even if only at an initial, limited and tentative stage. This constitutes a common power – a given social force and the possibility that a given collectivity has of inducing one in specific circumstances (following Lewin, 1997). Clearly, an initial common ground and common power may, through a series of commoning iterations, come to develop, mutate and strengthen the living force that enables the community of commoners to (further) develop that power and their connections with other commoners.

This chapter takes the third element as its subject, the flow concept, commoning, through which wealth is reproduced and extended and comes to serve as the basis for a new cycle of commons (re)production. The discussion presupposes the existence of some common wealth, substantiated in any form (material and immaterial) to whatever degree and regardless of its source at the origin of its pooling. Thus, in tackling the question 'What is commoning?', I first look at some historical pointers in order to distinguish categories for analysis and theoretical development. For this, I concentrate on Middle Ages English peasantry commoning as reported by the work of Linebaugh (2008).[5] Then, in the main sections of this work, I offer some reflections on the senses and implications of commoning as an autonomous and autopoietic activity. In the last section, I discuss in general terms the crucial dynamic of boundary commoning, the type of commoning that occurs at the boundary of the commons and that is the condition for any development of the commons as a social system of production and reproduction and thence as grounding for societal transformation.

Commoning

In his book *The Magna Carta Manifesto*, historian Peter Line-baugh (2008) traces the origin and development of this crucial constitutional text as emerging from the commoners' struggle to have their rights to the commons recognised and acknowledged by the state. In this context, commoning is the activity of the commoners in organic relation to the 'commons' (as pooled resources that need to be sustained and reproduced) and to one another. This implies that commoning is an activity that develops relations preoccupied by their (re)production and therefore – to use a modern term – crucially founded on their own 'sustainability'.

What is also very important to us today is that commoning is constituent of rights, commons (or more generally, common) rights, which should not be confused with legal rights. The latter are granted within the context of the state, by the powerful; common rights instead originate in their being exercised, so the state can only acknowledge and confirm them (or else deny, restrict, etc.). This recognition is precisely what happened in the history of the freedom charters discussed by Linebaugh – the 1215 Magna Carta and the 1225 Charter of the Forest – in which rights were taken by the people, which forced the king to acknowledge them. For the state (the king) to reach the point of confirming commoners' rights (legislate for the common) implied, in fact, that the commoners were already commoning; people were taking their lives into their own hands before commons rights were granted.[6] Equally today, therefore, the state does not only (and, in fact, does not tend to) grant common rights, but (rather) confirms rights (if it does) already exercised by the commoners, as in the case of the customary rights confirmed in thirteenth century England.

If the origin of common rights is in commoning, as an element of commons, we are in the presence of a social system generated by its own operations, codes and values, discussed below in terms of autonomous and autopoietic systems. Inevitably, these are framed by the context of their circumstances. Thus, from the perspective of the medieval English commoners, the right to common was embedded in a particular ecology and corresponding local husbandry (Wolcher, 2009). The issues that preoccupy the commoners are thus moments of a reflective stance grounded in the needs of resource and social relational sustainability. Commoning is actualised through communication processes, performances, affective circuits and social labour that act on and arrange the material. Commoners do not think first in terms of who owns property but rather of human need. What can we grow on this land? How shall we use the water? Research and exploration is central to the practices of commoners.

Commoning is not only arranging selections through communication, however; it is also communicating through actions, through labour. Going 'deep into human history' – as far, in fact, as that history goes – 'commoning is embedded in a labor process; it inheres in a particular praxis of field, upland, forest, marsh, coast'; therefore, 'Common rights are entered into by labor', 'commoning is collective' and, 'being independent of the state, [it] is independent also of the temporality of the law and state' (Linebaugh, 2008: 44–5). It follows that the definitional elements of commoning must include autonomy and direct action and relational modes among commoners and the commons that are 'organic'.

Commoning as struggle for autonomy and self-reliance

The first constituent element of commoning in this working definition is that of autonomy: this is a striving of communities to take things into their own hands in respect of certain material or cultural aspects of their (re)production. Autonomy has different meanings, depending on the domain in which it is applied. It can refer to a state or institution's right of self-government, or to a community's self-government. It may indicate a Kantian notion of the freedom of the will giving itself its own laws or class autonomy vis-à-vis capital. But commons are not individuals, or states or classes, although they can relate to them all.

In order to understand commons autonomy, I am inspired by the biological definition of autonomy at the cellular level, from which I derive – with due caution – an understanding of autonomy in the commons. There, autonomy refers to a condition, the condition of autonomy, of some organic unity controlled only by its own laws and not subject to any other. With respect to a social system, two senses of autonomy can thus be derived. The first is from the perspective of a social system in relation to others, where autonomy defines a commons dynamic vis-à-vis (other) systems in their environment, namely, the state and capital. At this level, autonomy is pretty much understood as a political struggle and does not require much elaboration. It means first of all the establishment of an autonomy in relation to heteronymous pressures coming from outside, in terms of measures, in terms of cultures, in terms of what and how production processes and ways of life should be.

Politically, today, this means establishing an autonomy from (against, in response to, thus defined by) the values and rationales of capital. Institutionalised capital wants us to eat GM food.

Commoners develop commons that promote agroecology and community networks that support them. European capital enforces austerity in terms of basic as well as consumer needs. Commoners develop solidarity economies linking different commons in order to meet needs and reframe desire, as in Greece since 2009 (see below). This autonomy has both quantitative and qualitative dimensions. The former concerns the amount of commons resources and numbers of commoners mobilised within a given space, and the fact that the latter is still in a minority in relation to the capacity of mobilisation of capital is simply a strategic condition and problem of its development. The latter refers to the second sense of autonomy.

As well as understanding autonomy as a relational aspect in terms external to the commons, we must ask how 'its own laws' are generated. For a commons to establish autonomy vis-à-vis capital and the state is not simply a matter of going onto the street and protesting – however difficult is the organisation of such events – since the organisation of other production processes vis-à-vis capital in the manner of resistance is a social, economic and political matter as well as a question of establishing new forms of governance and non-state 'rules', and this in the context of social and cultural fields dominated by capital/state forms of production. At this point, the question of autonomy posed by biologist Francisco Varela for biological unities is as relevant for socioeconomic systems such as capital – Marx asked incessantly about the 'laws of capitalist development' – and the commons. Thus, for Varela, autonomous systems are

> defined as a composite unity by a network of interactions of components that (i) through their interactions recursively

regenerate the network of interactions that produced them, and (ii) realise the network as a unity in the space in which the components exist by constituting and specifying the unity's boundaries as a cleavage from the background. (Varela, 1981: 15)

From the perspective of a social system, autonomy is the property generated by the interaction of components across a social network in such a way that the network that produced those interactions is regenerated. The network, therefore, is reproduced through a recursive loop. Recursion here generally means that an object – a network of interaction among components – is produced (regenerated) by the network itself. Thus, the network of interaction can define a boundary vis-à-vis the outside and thereby constitutes a unity. It is this unity identity – continuously reshaped and redefined by the recursive interaction – that gives the commons system its autonomy.

The components of commons networks – the subjects and the resources, the latter comprising immaterial wealth and the elements of commons material wealth available to the pool – will lie dormant in their respective locations, locked in the human memories and in the physical and virtual places of origin unless and until they are metabolised, transformed from material and immaterial elements of common wealth, into utilisable common wealth. In a forest common (for this and many other traditional commons examples, see Princen, 2005), in order to share the wood of a forest for construction or to burn it to create heat in the houses of a town, it is necessary not only to share the trees but also the logs, which obviously involves a collective process to produce them (as an empirical fact, if not a logical necessity). A collective production process is at the same time both a process of social labour – the mental and physical exertion of energies towards a goal – and of social relations among the commoners. In this light, commoning is thus the recursive life activity that regenerates and develops the social relations constituting the commons; it is the socially defined life activity that reproduces the social relations among subjects and their metabolism with the common resources.

Networks were regenerated and developed, for example, in solidarity movements in Greece during the height of the recent crisis, when unemployed communities blocked access to the tribunal where dispossessed houses were auctioned and where they reinstated electricity to poor households when this was disconnected. And networks at the basis of commons are regenerated and developed as well as their components when workers threatened by redundancy occupy their factory, convert it, connect it to newly created solidarity networks to sell their produce, and open up the space for children and other community activities. To each of these and many other events corresponds a social activity, in which a network is regenerated and developed and a boundary is drawn.[7]

But what, then, are the interacting components of commons as social systems? Not resources and community, but *common* wealth and commoners – that is, resources and people that bear the mark of commons components, that are recognised as such, that are socially 'initiated' into, as belonging to the system of meaning and values constituted and reproducing the commons. The actual physical resources and the actual psycho-physical (biological) individuals are only the punctuated bearers, the signifiers of the commons signified, the ontologically subsequent that only later constitute the components of systems. Thus, commoners can reproduce themselves only via the medium of common wealth, and common wealth can reproduce itself only through the medium of commoners. Commoners are not objectively defined, but relationally defined – so the commoner who abandons the sphere of commons and enters the sphere of capital or the state just disappears, magically turned into workers, commodity labour power, employees, civil servants, administrators, at whatever level of significance we are looking for, even if they have the same body and knowledge. The commoning recursive loop is broken, at least momentarily.

It is the same for the common wealth. The ostensibly same (im)material things and knowledge and experience (know-how) of individuals transforms from common wealth into capital (or public goods), insofar as some agents aim to 'invest' it into (or subsume it under) a capitalist (or statist) production process, defined by another recursively generated autonomy and another unity. And it follows from this as a fact of everyday life that people, we, as (self-conscious) subjects daily bouncing in and out of commons and capitalist and statist circuits, bear witness to this: it is we, the self-same subjects who go to work in a company factory or government office by day, for example, who go commoning in a social centre or a local bar – and at home – by night. Our subjectivities change, our identities become multiple, and we shift between them as we move between qualitatively different circuits (the circuit types of capital/state and commons), which may require certain types of skill and lead to forms of psychic fracturing.

Just as production in capitalist/statist circuits secretes capitalist/statist value, so does production in commons systems secrete commons values. The recursive character of social interrelations throughout the network is possible only through values. Capital-ist/statist values geared towards the production of commodities/ ideologies have a dominant dimension. Capital exchange value, hence cost minimisation and maximisation of profit, is broadly obtained through a range of strategies based on intensification of labour (relative reduction of its cost), while in the case of the state, value is attributed to and derived from hierarchy, through obedience to rules and principles (applied to regulate behaviour in state-defined ways). Commons production through common-ing, on the other hand, secretes a variety of values, among which selection is collectively made through feedback mechanisms (informally through the process of production and formally in moments of group decision-making). Commoning thus relies on a dance of values on the floor of community sharing. Internal autonomy reproduces relationships through a variety of values but reproduces the commons as a whole unit, with a character that in terms of value production distinguishes it clearly from capitalist statist unities.[8]

To the extent that commoners pool a common wealth (i.e. the components of network), and to the extent that common-ers interact with one another qua commoners – establishing, thereby, broadly horizontal relations (adjusted, of course, to the shifting authority of some in given contexts due to their contingent know-how) – each of these components recursively interacts, they regenerate the commons networks and define its boundaries. System autonomy implies that subjects of the community constitute the systems of interactions as a unity, recognisable in the domain in which the process exists, and this implies the constitution of a boundary between the systems of interactions and the environment. Of course, the existence of a boundary does not mean that nothing passes through; rather, it operates as a filtering membrane, in this case connecting a common to its environment – which means also that this boundary often becomes the frontline for (and that defines) the clash with state and capital.

Communities giving shape to commons around the world have taken things into their own hands in the double sense of autonomy, both through regenerating and developing their own value practices and through generating communities of struggle and resistance. In particular, over the last two decades we have witnessed the emergence of an activist commoning, a form of grassroots movement that makes horizontality and direct action two key principles of their political praxis. This is a politics grounded in the particular circumstances of the current phase of the neoliberal capital–state dynamic. Continuing organisation across networks has defined clear boundaries between them, as communities of resistance, and the privatising and enclosing 'enemy' – large (especially multinational) companies – taking away community land to build a dam or establish new mining operations, for example, or patenting the genes of living species. Also, they take things into their own hands and develop a life of their own, such as when city youth acquire an empty building and turn it into a self-organised social and cultural centre for the local community.[9]

Here, networks of activists are first generated through the concentration of forces on a new goal, acquiring and securing the place, whose walls physically institute the common, functioning as a protective and insulating boundary, which then further expands and regenerates further networks through its activities. Both senses of autonomy – the one established in oppositional relationship to capital/state forces and the other recursively established through the activity of commoning – constitute and (re)produce the network boundaries. In the first case of autonomy especially, the boundary might be an immediately antagonistic frontline, as in the case of squatting, but establish filtering mechanisms like anti-racism and anti-fascism. Then, with solidarity activities with migrants, state migration laws and organised xenophobic forces confront the established commons. In the recursive sense of autonomy, the boundary may instead take a more symbolic or cultural form and the new commons generate a cultural opening of new horizons for generations permeated with mainstream values where it is possible to engage in artistic, socioeconomic and other forms of experimentation.

In all these examples, the very ability to point to phenomena implies their definition as unities constituted through autonomous doing in common, through commoning. In other words, the contexts and sitings for the actualisation of a resisting struggle for autonomy and the common urge for self-reliance are potentially endless, and the actual social form that actualises this struggle depends – more or less – on strategic choices of the commoners in given contexts.[10]

Further observations on autonomy

The autonomous force based on commoning often encounters issues of legality. For example, many self-organised social centres in Italy began their journey of commoning outside the law, by squatting. Where they gained a sufficient degree of legitimacy in the community, they also acquired a certain power to negotiate with the state for their permanence on the site, perhaps through a legal tenant's contract, usually at a low cost. Legitimacy is thus the first resource that must be generated and accumulated by the practice of commoning. This involves the participation of widening circles of communities within the extending boundaries of a common – that is, an intensification among as well as expansion of the domain of interaction of the components of a network through the creation of social values clearly recognised as such by a wider community and other networks. Legitimacy is thus an acquired common wealth that can be contrasted to legality and its state instrument of force, up to the point of legalisation of a commons practice.

It is important to point out, therefore, that, notwithstanding general observations made with respect to the relationship between commoning and the state (between granting and acknowledging rights), in combination with the relational aspect of commoning (its characterisation as oppositional), we should not see the issue of autonomy and self-reliance as something necessarily sited outside a given legal framework. This would be forcing the argument onto an ideological ground, forgetting that in many concrete situations there is plenty of space in which things are not done and could be done within the existing laws, in the interstices of the capitalist/state system, such as in the recursive production employing 'detritus' from capital's systemic interactions.[11]

In the case of disused buildings, for example, the alternative to squatting of pooling money collected through donations and fund raising (financial commoning) so as to rent represents a strategic choice, a developmental trade-off between what many perceive as an ultimately impractical (unsustainable) radical ideological correctness and what others see as a 'selling out' for some degree of bourgeois stability and peace of mind so as to organise a free space in relative comfort. In other words, the choice about how to obtain and hold the means to take things into one's hands, to take direct action in respect of one's own life, involves contextualised options specified by the relation of forces on the ground, by tactical shrewdness and, especially, by strategic ambition. What is certain, however, is that regardless of the manner in which one gains and maintains access to the means for collective direct action, commoning autonomy requires the imagination of independence – or 'doing direct action is simply disregarding existing power structures and doing it ourselves', as one activist of the Grow Heathrow projects in London puts it.[12]

Indeed, commoning is expressing a struggle for autonomy and self-reliance that often contrasts with the depressed (oppressed) condition of detritus and alienation in which communities are living before the activity of commoning. This autonomy and self-reliance is actualised by a process that creates and revitalises communities, through some form of access to the means of production – whether through squatting, renting, pooling or redistribution – and the creation of material, social and psychic rewards, which feed back into the system in multifarious ways, including the human motivation to continue, to enter further into the commoning relations, which in turn energises the recursive. The rewards are not – must not be – just individualised payoffs, even though these are important precisely for reducing people's dependence on capitalist markets and increasing state benefits that blackmail them back into low-waged and precarious work; commons also reward through the communal, through staying together and learning from one another, through the forming of intimately human links to replace the tenuous, formal or alienated connections that exist in the neoliberal city that is always on the run, through the bonding made of relations between people as subjects expressing their selves.

We have in this autonomy also a first element with which to understand the relationship between commoning and the quality or state of being worthy of esteem and respect, or dignity. If esteem in the capitalist market is established with the outer symbols of conspicuous consumptions (Veblen, 1973) and under state tutelage through formalised positions in its apparatus, then in commoning it is established by the daily struggle to overcome detritus. In the same way that bio-mass decomposition by millions of diverse biological and chemical iterations in ecosystems supports soil fertility and allows the growth of new plants, so does commoning turn detritus into a social humus in which new ideas can flourish into new organisational practices and bloom with new wealth.

Commoning as a generative force of autopoiesis

Another aspect of commoning, beyond autonomy, is auto-production, or autopoiesis. Autonomy and autopoiesis are related but are not the same: autopoiesis is a particular aspect of autonomy, one that coincides with a higher degree of resilience, in which not only the interaction among components of a system are regenerated but also the components themselves, namely, here, the commoners and the common wealth. In autopoietic commons, therefore, not only are the relations among subjects and the metabolism between subjects and wealth produced, but also these components themselves:

> An autopoietic system is organised (defined as a unity) as a network of processes of production (transformation and destruction) of components that produces the components that

> 1. Through their interactions and transformations continuously regenerate and realise the network of processes (relations) that produced them; and
>
> 2. Constitute it [the system] as a concrete unity in the space in which [the components] exist by specifying the topological domain of its realisation as such a network. (Varela, 1979: 13)

With the components of commons being commoner communities (relationships of subjects qua commoners) and common wealth, commoning (re)produces the bodies and subjectivity of commoners as commoners and the wealth as common wealth. It does not matter whether some material aspects of the wealth come from outside the commons or if the subjects have a predominantly non-commoner subjectivity, as long as (and to the extent that) the recursion established by commoning recreates subjectivities and resources as components of the commons. Or, in other words, while commons autonomy – as we saw – refers to a condition of commons systems controlled only by their own laws and relations, commons autopoiesis adds to this condition the production of the components of the systems: the knowledge, the mind and bodies of the commoner subjects, the material and immaterial resources.

Here, an analogy with capitalist circuits is helpful. In a capitalist circuit, the sum of the exchange values of, on the one hand, the physical components of capital (raw materials and tools, understood and valorised as capital) and, on the other, labour power (the capacity to work, sold for a wage), provides the whole capital invested (at the beginning of a capitalist circuit). Both of these elements have a price tag that makes it possible to measure their cost, in spite of the fact that they constitute quite different (categorically distinct) things.[13] The final result is a new product, which, if sold to the market, would autopoietically reproduce the components of the capitalist system for the next round of capitalist production, that is capital (through profit and amortisation) and labour power (through wages).

In this example of the autopoiesis of capital, the system's components are not machines and labour power, but constant and variable capital – which, as Marx identified, is the value expression of those commodities – and only insofar as it is expected that their use will bring more value at the end of the labour process, a profit. Therefore, the process of accumulation reproduces these components *as* capital. Analogously, albeit through radically different measures, the autopoiesis of commons is obtained through commons circuits that reproduce the common as a social system. After the pooling of a set of resources and gathering of commoners who will at one point engage in commoning as determined by their collective engagement and internally generated values (establishment of a common), autopoiesis of the commons involves the reproduction of the resources and subjects involved in the commoning as further or new common wealth and commoners, agents of these commoning circuits.

The fact that some resources pooled as common wealth do not have (are not measured as) a common monetary exchange value, simply because at no point have they been commodities, does not affect their utility in the commoning process. For those resources that the commons has to buy on the market, it will be necessary to find a source of monetary income – one would need discussion of the type of market, which limitations of space preclude here – however, the budget of the financial ins and outs only describes a relatively minor aspect the overall health of the commons. The fact is that for a household common, the selling of labour power and the buying of consumer goods is only one moment of reproduction of the household – the other being the labour of reproduction, just as for the commons at a greater scale that still depends on some form of market exchange. The commons have other goals than profit (even if some revenue may be one of the goals) and other measures than those impelled by capital's relative and absolute surplus value strategies. If the commons must trade commodities, this is generally done in order to buy other commodities necessary for the commons reproduction, or to give revenues to communities with which they hold solidarity links, and not to accumulate. Exchange value is a measure that appears only in those commons that have to relate to the market, and even then it is routinely subordinated to other features that contribute to the measure of commons (the value expression), such as equity and sharing, solidarity and conviviality. Indeed, the fact that the financial resources utilised are pooled makes them also (reproduces them as) components within that common. The health of a common depends on an appropriate density and balance of all relational circuits, including mutual aid, solidarity and affective circuits.

A characteristic of both autonomous and autopoietic systems is their organisational closure, which does not mean that they do not interrelate with the environment – obviously they do – but rather that their organisation is characterised by processes such that

1. the processes are related as a network, so that they recursively depend on each other in the generation and realisation of the processes themselves, and

2. they constitute the system as a unity recognisable in the space (domain) in which the processes exist. (Varela, 1979: 55)

This implies that autonomous systems – and the autopoietic as a part of them – change their state in response to external events and are realised and propagated only within the networks of processes that produce them and, therefore, through the value(s) that these networks set in operation.

Boundary commoning as a recomposing and generative force

From a political perspective, the autonomy and the autopoiesis of commons initiated and developed by commoning are a necessary but insufficient condition for overcoming the capitalist hegemony as a mode of production and the existing socioeconomic divisions of the proletariat generated by capitalist processes and statist orderings and selections. They are necessary, in that the production of new systems of life and production requires the development of social systems like commons that exercise their autonomy and autopoiesis vis-à-vis capital and the state – that is, by positing their different measures, values and senses of things in praxis, by engaging in the construction of another common sense and another material life. This parallels Marx's idea that social rather than political revolution is a primary condition for overcoming the capitalist mode of production and its state apparatus. But it is not enough.

Solidarity and mutual aid – to list two measures used in the commons that are opposed to the values of capital praxis – are also practices that shape their own boundaries. How boundaries are constructed, and the type of values used to filter interactions across commons and subjects in the 'multitude' and for what purpose are also important questions from an emancipatory perspective. Thus, for example, oppressive, hegemonic power constructs may be expressed, like conventional (patriarchal) forms of gender relations, by various overt and covert exclusions from a co-op's decision-making or membership even applied to women or non-heterosexuals (LGBT-identifying groups and individuals); or a political organisation may organise a momentary commons by distributing food to a crisis-hit population but only to those who belong, say, to a particular nationality or ethnic group – as the neo-Nazi group Golden Dawn has done in Greece.[14] Also, and less aggressively, community organisations of all types are formed that do not ask for a record on people's stance on things like human rights but that organise on some type of affinity: football fan clubs, some youth subculture circles, affinity groups of all types, in fact, reproduce their distinct symbolic identities.

Even while becoming a medium for the development of diverse subjectivities, these types of commons and activities of commoning will not bring about a fundamental transformation of the capitalist-statist system, only of its structural development.[15] Again following terminological usage in biology, by 'structural development' I mean to say that only the components of the capitalist system change – the types of subjectivities and technologies for example, or its models of state governance in any case predicated on the reproduction of hierarchies – and not its fundamental organisation of social production, based on abstract labour, enclosures and exploitation. The emergence of the 'network society' (Castells, 1996) may represent a more fundamental, structural development. Of course, contextualised by the age of neoliberal capital, it has served to extend capitalist relations globally and allowed the utilisation of new technical components and know-how in social and economic processes to this end – but it has also opened up opportunities for new organisations of the commons and new commoning practices – p2p in cyberspace is one important example – and it has also amplified the potential for commoning across commons, or boundary commoning, given the time–space compression that comes with the globalised condition of daily life (Harvey, 1990).

In some areas this structural development of the last thirty years has also absorbed *some* of the anti-authoritarian, anti-racist and feminist demands of the 1970s, for example by expanding a black middle class in the US and facilitating access to a wage (and an equal wage) for women in many areas of the Global North. These 'progressist', inclusive and non-discriminatory practices create new 'components' in global systemic interactions in capitalist and statist circuits and hence structural change, but not new socioeconomic organisational unities beyond capital and the state, with new goals and new social relations. Indeed, the structural changes in these circuits have also forged new, and deeper, hierarchies, both inside world regions and countries and across the globe. Neoliberal capital and state absorption of the struggles of the 1970s have run parallel with a deep wave of new enclosures that continues today alongside a renewed concentration of wealth, expanding to an unprecedented global scale. Ultimately, though, the world is still divided between capital/state loops and commons loops, the former enforcing enclosures, exploitation and abstracting (precarious, low-paid labour), and the latter aiming at various forms of fulfilment and justice while valorising labour power through non-profit values of solidarity and mutual aid.

Structural change of this partial nature, which diversifies components in capital's loops, is only a condition for a mutation of social systems – to maintain the biology parallel – in the sense that it can favour the overcoming of capital and amplifies the mutation of societies towards a commons hegemony. Such a mutation of society can occur only when the commoning interactions reach a sufficient network extension and density, a sufficient autopoietic level to balance (resist, oppose) capital enclosure and reinforce the resilience of commons while drastically reducing capital's loops to below a resilient critical level. In other words, such a mutation corresponds to a change in the DNA of social reproduction, when the measures and codes through which social labour appropriates and metabolises nature evolve in the direction of principles such as, for example, 'from each according to her/his capabilities and to each according to her/his needs'.

The way towards this mutation, I think, is twofold. First, it is, of course, necessary to continue the ongoing struggles for any aspects of structural change acknowledging the capability, needs and dignity of all, both generally and specifically with regard to the commons. This includes issues related to race, gender and sexual orientation and disability, to which list we have learned in recent decades to add ecological considerations and the key responsibility that social systems have to face the consequences of social action in respect of climate change and environmental degradation and destruction. Also fundamental are structural changes that redistribute wealth and reduce the wealth gap, and any changes that open up a greater measure of resource sharing. This range of structural change can only be pursued through a dialectic system (feedback process) between grassroots struggles and the state, pushing to move away from a neoliberal Plan A of capital to negotiate a more redistributive and ecologically sensitive Plan B. But such a Plan B is not in itself a solution since it tends to co-opt structural change imposed by previous waves of struggle into capital's loops unless it opens a space for extending commoning outside those loops.

This extension of commoning, I argue, is a necessary condition of emancipatory social change, whatever the plan of capital. It is predicated on what I call boundary commoning, which is the commoning that produces a structural coupling between and among different commons; by structural coupling I mean the continuous interrelations among systems, in this case commons systems, such that these come to construct something new, a wider sphere of commons that grow dependent on one another, resulting in an enlarged, internally interdependent commons. This constitutes the second route to a mutation of society: through the repeated interactions of two or more commons for the development of a wider sphere, a new systems environment emerges.

Structural coupling among different commons systems constituting a commoning systems environment does not simply involve the sharing of goods or information or acts of solidarity among commons. Rather, through the continuous interactions, structural coupling allows 'the boundaries of one system [to] be included in the operational domain of the other' (Luhmann, 1995: 217). For the boundaries of one system to be included within the operational domains of another is for that system to make its own complexity 'available for constructing another system'; and then to make this complexity available for the other system is to make its own 'sense' available to other systems, 'and with it indeterminacy, contingency, and the pressure to select' (Luhmann, 1995: 213). Through boundary commoning, new senses are developed that modify the horizon in relation to which strategic decisions are made. In other words, the structural coupling that boundary commoning implies corresponds to the construction of a commoning sense and the constitution of 'a state in which two systems shape the environment of the other in such a way that both depend on the other for continuing their autopoiesis' (Moeller, 2006: 19).

Through coupled repetition of relations, structural coupling among commons may drift into different social forms, a typology of which has not yet been attempted. If we were to follow the indication of biology, we would identify two general directions for the drift: that of (toward) meta-commonality (meta-cellularity in biology) and of symbiosis (Maturana & Varela, 1998: 88). The meta-commonality way is taken when the recurring coupling among the commons units maintains each common's identity and internal commoning, while at the same time establishing a new systemic coherence among two or more commons. An example could be when reclaimed occupied factories in Argentina or Italy not only change their structural components by changing their production methods and outputs, but also establish ongoing links with the community and its organisations (for childcare, training, festivities, meetings, etc.), thus developing commons outside the reclaimed factories related to the latter for mutual resilience.[16] The symbiosis way is taken with the inclusion of the boundaries of two (or more) commons into one unit. An example might be the case of a self-managed social centre like the Forte Prenestino in Rome, an old fort that was occupied in 1986 and has since been collectively managed by an assembly of diverse groups and projects that share a basic ethical code and are involved in a variety of activities, including an infoshop, music and dance labs, and a wine cellar, bakery and farm market.[17]

I conclude this section with two further examples of the developing commons – the Genuino Clandestino network of farmers and consumers in Italy and water associations in Bolivia – to show how boundary commoning operates in the production of two types of meta-commonality, dubbed conglomeration and second-order commons. The Italian, nationwide, Genuino Clandestino network of farmers and consumers[18] aims to develop a space outside of state-regulated 'organic' certification. In order to obtain the organic label and thereby enter that trading circuit, farmers have to pay a private agency to come and check the land and take a soil sample back to the lab for testing. This certification labelling process has become an expensive procedure for small farmers (costing hundreds if not thousands of euros) and is wide open to corruption (essentially, the labelling can be assured by paying the right agency enough money).

In response to this failing of the state, a commons approach has emerged with the establishment of the Genuino Clandestino network, which operates through relations of trust. These are founded on proximity, as in the village community, where reputation is mainly built or damaged by the quality of foods supplied, and local people can easily check on the farming conditions (the type of fodder used, the living conditions of animals, etc.). In other words, proximity creates reliability of product through trust in the process at the level of human relations and so without the need for state intermediation, a trust that is secreted by commoning processes in a variety of forms in the locality and distributed through networks of friends or acquaintances. Extending the sense of community from the physically located (bound to the land) to the socioeconomically defined (thus unbound), the Genuino Clandestino network then reproduces the conditions of generation of this village-type trust throughout trading networks that extend into urban spaces.

Trust among consumers and producers is maintained through regular meetings – in the first place, in informal conversation at the regular markets. Consumers are also welcome to visit the farms, and in some cases they work on the farm, at harvest or other busy times, especially the farms that they administrate together with farmers. In the case of the Bologna node – called Campi Aperti,[19] organising more than eighty producers and five weekly markets – each market holds monthly assemblies among producers and consumers to deal with questions of boundary, quality and prices, while bimonthly assemblies are held among the five markets for strategic and political decisions. The level of trust is so significant that one cooperative linked to Campi Aperti – Arvaia, in the Bologna area[20] – decided to dispense with boxes and scales. The members of the cooperative just take the fruit and vegetables they need from a warehouse, having paid at the beginning of the year an amount in proportion to the number of the people composing the household so as to guarantee the farmer income.

Thus we have here a situation in which distinct farmer–consumer commons across Italy engage in their autopoietic operations, while at the same time forming structural coupling links with one another that give rise to a network which is not just like a network of acquaintances who occasionally meet but a meta-commonality network that organises a range of campaigns and events and propagates a method and philosophy of doing agriculture based on food sovereignty and trust-building. Thus, through a process of boundary-commoning, many growing commons have come together to form a network of commons with its own autopoietic process scaled up from the autopoietic processes of the individual commons. Finally, within this commons conglomeration, repetitive relations among commons and subjects commoners as subjects give rise to and reinforce ways of interacting within this environment – for a new commoning sense.

Another example of the meta-commonality drift brought by boundary commoning is the relation between two community organisations constituting a third that includes them both in the mode of associations at a second level – or second-order commons. This can be illustrated by the history of a wave of struggle in Bolivia that succeeded in reverting the privatisation of water there, the Cochabamba Water War in the first months of 2000. This massive movement developed out of water commons established in the preceding decades among communities in the poorer south of the city of Cochabamba and surrounding rural areas to deal with the lack of public water provision and escape the usury prices charged by private traders.

Frustrated by the lack of state provision and poor private provision (traders offered water in unsafe water tanks and at three or four times the public water price paid in the wealthier, northern part of the city), communities originally took things into their own hands by digging wells, laying pipes and building systems of urban water storage and distribution (Zibechi, 2009). Through thirty years of activities involving urban migrants and rural networks, commoners established water associations drawing and distributing water communally. Then they established associations to facilitate coordination among local community associations and effective intra-community sharing of resources (water pumps, cistern tracks, skills, etc.) and to constitute institutions of political representation vis-à-vis the state. These associations created for and from the primary associations thus operated as a secondary tier, as second-order commons, representing a form of meta-commonality.

At the end of 1999, a neoliberal-inclined government passed water privatisation laws giving (multinational) water companies the right to claim ownership of all water, including that extracted and distributed by the community plants – a clear form of enclosure not just of a generic right, but of a very specific type of common. The rural indigenous communities in the mountains then descended into the city in protest and kick-started a major process of political re-composition in many social networks, starting from the communal-based water associations in the city, mobilising communal resources and giving rise to what Zibechi (2010) dubbed a 'Society in Movement' – which, in our terms, is another, quite extensive, form of meta-commonality clashing with the state/capital.

After four months of social mobilisation and confrontation with street battles, on 10 April 2000, the national government reached an agreement with the protestors to reverse the privatisation. In what was effectively a U-turn of state policy and collapse of the water capitalisation project, this opened the way to a state recognition of the communal economy, with the commons thereby gaining a place in the new constitution ratified in 2009 (cf. the issue of legality, above). The water associations continue their operations while campaigning for the public water board to invest in water structures still administrated by the communities.

Concluding reflections

In this chapter, I have offered elements for a conceptualisation of the commons as social systems and commoning as the living force of their reproduction, sense-making and development. My overarching preoccupation has been the problematic of social revolution (de Angelis, 2014), of a radical change or mutation of mainstream modes of production and governance based on capital and the state that are generated from the emergence of new modes of production and governance from below. We have reached an age in which the desire for such a revolution is widespread and its need more urgently felt the more the various destructive crises intensify. Fatalism, cynicism, unreformed socialist, communist and anarchist ideologies, divided class conditions and subjectivities and partisan 'rent positions' within the multitudes make it difficult to conceive the historical movement and the social forces underpinning it that have a chance to bring about such a change. Here, however, I dare to offer such a conception through the hypothesis that social revolution is nothing else than the 'accumulation', diffusion and acceleration of commoning, in both quantitative and qualitative (meta-commoning) terms.

Ultimately, the only way to generate commoning social systems that are autonomous (independent of and contrary to the values of capital and the state) and autopoietic (in the sense of being able to produce their own subjectivities, senses, materials, ideas, knowledge and common wealth) is to live a life of joy, abundance and love in action. Social revolution is nothing else than the exponential growth of occasions of boundary commoning across commons, the only way to constitute a social fabric flexible, resilient and strong enough to counter capital and the state. With some luck and determination, we (the commoners, the movers of history) will reach a point at which the old adage will come true and we will be sitting at the gateway of hell singing, 'It will be a laughter that will bury you!'

The argument that I have proposed here only indicates an approach for the conception of societal transformation grounded in alternative social relations and forms of cooperation through values and measures that are unlike those of capital and the state. This is not an approach that normatively posits a specific set of alternative goals, a compass of values to orient action (beyond, of course, the generic of commoning). To do so – to detail a positive programme, or a commons manifesto, for example – is of course also important, and not just from a theoretical perspective but also very much for the given set of 'radical' values upon which decision-making and strategy selection can be based in actual daily practice contextualised by real situations.[21] Rather, the approach outlined here starts out from the observation of systems that set alternative values and that contain a variety of subjectivities in movement.

This method of enquiry allows insight into contradictions within commons and their sets of values inducing or restraining actions on the assumption of commons as systemic rather than universal entities (whether radical or mainstream). It helps to make sense of the fact that the diversity of constituent subjects, cultures and resources and the vast arrays of operational contexts and scales mean that the commons even reproduce within themselves subjects in conflict over the set of values to be adopted in a given situation. Sidestepping the need for a universalisation that tends to essentialise and naturalise, to reduce the commons to some primary properties or characteristics (allowing merely reference to things like 'sharing' and 'solidarity'), a systems theory approach can better get at the intra- and interrelations among commons.

Also, approaching commons as social systems with a unity produced by their operations can prevent their (abstract and material) demise at the hands of other systems, such as capital, through their evolution and adaptation to new conditions. This framework, therefore, allows for a reflection on the commoners' condition, one that has a very long history, far beyond the history of working class organisation and the socialism, anarchism and communism associated with industrialisation since the late eighteenth and nineteenth centuries. Like the indigenous movements around the world reconnecting to a practice of life and struggle that actually reaches up through history and pre-history, the reproduction of commons and commons cultures did – does – not begin with capitalism; indeed, it has mutated several times in different contexts of state despotic and capitalist modes of production.

To see ourselves as commoners reproducing our own communities and networks and then reconstituting them anew, and in so doing becoming workshops and laboratories of value and sense, is not only to become aware of our politically charged connections with other systems, like capital and the state, but also of our historical connections with the past, and the ecologies we depend on. Furthermore, thinking in terms of commons systems allows us to see things strategically: only by seeing ourselves through commoning can we see the commons' historical enemies, capital and the state, as an alien force. In this respect, the pertinent practices of commoning are those that enquire about and experiment with the leverage points in commons systems in which social force can be applied to further develop the practice of commoning, and push capital/state systems back from our lives.

Notes

1   This article contains some passages from De Angelis (2017).

2   See e.g. Bey (1991) on temporary autonomous zones.

3   Both capital and the commons also avoid and evade state regulation, of course, in various ways.

4   The act of commoning is also transformative of the agent, of course: people/communities change as they engage thus.

5   The history of indigenous modes of production around the world would offer another crucial entry point, one that I suspect would have many parallels to that I refer to here.

6   For example, building from Linebaugh, law professor Louis Wolcher discussed the meaning of the commons during 'The Law of the Commons' conference, organised by the Seattle Chapter of the National Lawyers Guild on 13 March 2009. Commenting on the commoning of the English farmers in the fifteenth and sixteenth centuries, Louis Wolcher put it thus: '[T]o common was to engage in a form of life in which you took your life, your subsistence, into your own hands and you did not wait at the table for crumbs to drop from the powerful' (Wolcher, 2009). The use of the past tense here refers

to the history of the commons in England before their enclosure, but this element of 'taking things in one's own hands' is crucial also in contemporary situations, all around the world and at different scales of social action, and help us to understand the relation between legality and legitimacy.

7   On the types of solidarity actions in Greece during the crisis, see Solidarity for All (2013: 13–24).

8   Thus, for example, in my experience of community gardening, the occasional bossiness of some (expressing the value of authority of those 'in the know' regarding how to grow a vegetable and an inherited culture, a *habitus* of hierarchy) is not a recognised practice within a role, so it is tempered by others through open jokes and on the basis of knowledge researched on alternative methods of food production (establishing the value of equity as well as of sharing knowledge) and purchase of tools (greatly dependent on commodity values), while the crop is distributed through sharing principles (the value of community sharing). After a few recursive iterations, bossiness disappears and is substituted with a more humble behaviour, moulded to the community of gardeners, which is also thereby confirmed. If, however, a hierarchy were to ossify, the commons would have started its metamorphosis into something else.

9   See, for example, the case of XM24, a self-organised occupied centre in Bologna, established in 2002 from roots in the anti-globalisation wave of the 1990s. After several years of conflict and negotiation, the council authorities of Bologna granted the right for the centre to exist and administer itself with the establishment of a third authority which vouches for XM24 but does not represent it. This allows the centre to be a heterogeneous space of self-management of everyday life, governed by a weekly general assembly operating through consensus. Among the activities that are organised are a people's bike shop (which also promotes the Bologna Critical Mass against the Bologna Motor Show); people's kitchen, a vegetarian cruelty-free space available for movements to organise fundraising for legal aid, political prisoners and projects; a people's free gym giving access to free yoga classes and other arts in

the neighbourhood; a weekly market operated by *Campi Aperti*, a network of more than eighty small farms and consumers themselves operating through horizontal and participatory practices (see Casey & Foresti, 2014).

10   Thus, commoning is not only a praxis of emancipatory forms, but also of social movements like the Tea Party. Clearly, these differ in terms of objective (to promote a right-wing agenda), conception (libertarianism) and origin (in the Tea Party case, promotion by corporate entities); this is revealed especially in its boundaries (illegal migrants, for example, are refused membership of the Tea Party's 600 local chapters).

11   The detritus of capital consists of negative externalities, such as the by-products of 'development', that accumulate in eco-, commons and psychic systems, where capital produces least (perhaps no) capital wealth; the condition of detritus reproduced by capitalist relations then becomes a stock, a condition that by its own nature produces the material out of which the common can grow, even within a given set of laws (De Angelis, 2007).

12   http://www.transitionheathrow.com/grow-heathrow

13   It is not just any human labour involved in this equation, of course, but abstract human labour, labour expended 'without regard to the form of its expenditure' (Marx, [1887] 1976: 128), work that is only important if and insofar as it increases the amount of surplus value – and thus profit – at the end of the process.

14   See e.g. 'Police shut down Greek-only soup kitchen', Al Jazeera, 2 May 2013. At http://www.aljazeera.com/news/europe/2013/05/201352103715660344.html

15   This goes for the Tea Party case (above), in which the commoning only affirms the capitalist system in its reduction of state.

16   See e.g. Rimaflow, in Milan (http://www.rimaflow.it/), and Officina Zero, in Rome (http://www.officinezero.it/); for Argentina, see Ruggieri (2010).

17   http://www.forteprenestino.net/

18   http://genuinoclandestino.noblogs.org/

19   http://www.campiaperti.org/

20   http://www.arvaia.it/

21   For a compass of values that would distinguish radical commons from others, see e.g. Midnight Notes and Friends (2010) and Caffentzis and Federici (2014).

References

Bey, H. (1991). *Temporary Autonomous Zones*. New York: Autonomedia.

Bourdieu, P. (1986). 'The forms of capital', in J. Richardson (Ed.), *Handbook of Theory and Research for the Sociology of Education*. New York: Greenwood. At https://www.marxists.org/reference/subject/philosophy/works/fr/bourdieu-forms-capital.htm

Caffentzis, G., and Federici, S. (2014). 'Commons against and beyond capitalism', *Community Development Journal*, 49: i92–i105. At http://cdj.oxfordjournals.org/cgi/doi/10.1093/cdj/bsu006

Casey, S. P. and Foresti, G. Z. (2014). 'XM24: survival and inspiration against all odds', *Roar Magazine*, 14 September At http://roarmag.org/2014/09/xm24-social-center-bologna/

Castells, M. (1996). *The Rise of the Network Society. The Information Age: Economy, Society and Culture*, vol. 1. Malden, MA: Blackwell Publishing.

De Angelis, M. (2007). *The Beginning of History. Values Struggle and Global Capital*. London: Pluto.

De Angelis, M. (2014). 'Social revolutions and the commons', *South Atlantic Quarterly*, 113(2): 299–311.

De Angelis, M. (2017). *Omnia sunt communia. On the Commons and the Transformation to Postcapitalism*. London: Zed.

Hardt, M., and Negri, A. (2009). *Commonwealth*. Cambridge, MA: Harvard University Press.

Harvey D. (1990). *The Condition of Postmodernity: An Enquiry into the Origin of Cultural Change*. Cambridge, MA: Blackwell.

Lewin, K. (1997). *Resolving Social Conflicts. Field Theory in Social Science*. Washington, DC: American Psychological Association.

Linebaugh, P. (2008). *The Magna Carta Manifesto: Liberties and Commons for All*. Berkeley: University of California Press.

Luhmann, N. (1995). *Social Systems*. Stanford, CA: Stanford University Press.

Marx, K. ([1887] 1976). *Capital. A Critique of Political Economy*, vol. 1. New York: Penguin Books.

Maturana, H. R. and Varela, F. J. (1998). *The Tree of Knowledge. The Biological Roots of Human Understanding*. Boston/London: Shambhala.

Midnight Notes and Friends (2010). *Promissory Notes: From Crisis to Commons*. At http://www.midnightnotes.org/Promissory%20 Notes.pdf

Moeller, H.-G. (2006). *Luhmann Explained: From Souls to Systems. Ideas Explained Series*. Chicago: Open Court.

Ostrom, E. (1990). *Governing the Commons. The Evolution of Institutions for Collective Action*. Cambridge: Cambridge University Press.

Oxfam (2015). *Wealth. Having it All and Wanting More* (Issue Briefing, January 2015). At http://www.oxfam.org/sites/www.oxfam.org/ files/file_attachments/ib-wealth-having-all-wanting-more-190115- en.pdf

Princen, T. (2005). *The Logic of Sufficiency*. Cambridge, MA/London: MIT Press.

Ruggieri, A. (2010). *Las Empresas Recuperadas en la Argentina* [Recovered companies in Argentina]. Buenos Aires: Programa Facultad Abierta, Facultad de Filosofía y Letras de la Universidad de Buenos Aires. At http://www.autogestion.asso.fr/wp-content/ uploads/2012/10/Informe-Relevamiento-2010.pdf

Solidarity for All (2013). *Solidarity is Peoples' Power. Towards an International Campaign of Solidarity to the Greek People*. At http:// www.solidarity4all.gr/files/aggliko.pdf

Varela, F. J. (1979). *Principles of Biological Autonomy*. Boston: Kluwer Academic.

Varela, F. J. (1981). 'Autonomy and autopoiesis', in G. Roth and H. Schwegler (Eds.), *Self-Organizing Systems: An Interdisciplinary Approach*. Frankfurt/New York: Campus Verlag.

Veblen, T. (1973). *The Theory of the Leisure Class*. Boston: Houghton Mifflin Company.

Wolcher, L. (2009). 'The meaning of the commons', *The Law of the Commons* (Conference), Seattle Chapter of the National Lawyers Guild (13 March 2009). At http://www.commoner.org.uk/blog/?p=204

Zibechi, R. (2009). 'Cochabamba: from water war to water management', *American Program*, 27 May. At http://www.cipamericas.org/archives/1723

Zibechi, R. (2010). *Dispersing Power. Social Movements and Anti-State Forces*. Edinburgh: AK Press.

Chapter 7

Commodification and the social commons: smallholder autonomy and 'rurban' relations in Turkey[1]

Murat Öztürk, Joost Jongerden and Andy Hilton

Introduction

The introduction of neoliberalism into the agrarian sector in Turkey, which began in the 1980s and accelerated in the 2000s, brought unprecedented changes to rural life. The old, state-led development strategy was phased out, in accordance with and as guided by the International Monetary Fund (IMF) and the European Union, and neoliberal restructuring resulted in a squeeze on peasant farming and associated living structures. In addition to the entry and penetration of large-scale producers (especially food manufacturers), the withdrawal of government supports to agriculture in combination with stagnating product prices and increasing input costs led to a markedly increased smallholder vulnerability to market fluctuations.

Meanwhile, the Anatolian countryside has suffered a contraction of the natural commons. Ongoing developments and imminent threats from the state and business and combinations of the two involve millions of hectares already lost to the recent development of infrastructure (river dam projects, industrial zones, roads and housing, etc.) and in grave danger (with plans for the compulsory purchase of meadowland, the transfer of national park management, etc.). This de-commoning is manifested also as restriction and decline of the rural knowledge commons – such as through the increasing control by international corporations of seed production, reproduction and trading – and occurs also at a more abstract level, in terms of reduced autonomy and communalism; at least, that appears to be the case. Against this, however, we argue for a rather different, more positive interpretation of current realities from the commoning perspective, one that focuses on small farmers, emerging peasant strategies and their associated living structures.

Our proposal here is for a socioeconomic analysis that includes forms of the agriculturally based social commons that are maintained in the face of capitalisation but places this in the context of new social commons that are being developed. Identifying two responses to the new economic environment that enable families to keep their land and their farms, we first look at a direct resistance to commodification (both through the maintenance of traditional practices and development of new skills and localised market relations) and then at an indirect, strategic resistance to commodification (primarily through income differentiation).

Basically, the evolution of employment strategies outside of agriculture, retirement revenues and other social security benefits and transfers – in combination with the development of market relations while yet avoiding dependence on these – enables families to keep their land and maintain their small-holdings. This desire to maintain family farms itself represents an exercise of autonomy against submission to capital. Since rural employment opportunities tend to be limited, it is facilitated by urban migration, along with the formation of extended (rural–urban) settlement structures, which involve various types of mobility and novel living structures, or spatial definitions, and comprise a new form of solidarity network-based common. This implies that we need also at look at commoning as a geo-social practice, as a form of re-spatialisation.

Although a (partial) non-entry into markets and, at the same time, development of wage-labour relations appear contradictory, they tend to operate in tandem, combining socially with an integrative synergy premised on migratory and other movements between the rural and urban. Through this double strategy, that is, farming households not only mitigate the squeeze on small-scale agriculture and maintain a certain level of autonomy – by navigating a course somewhat outside of co-option by capital and independently of the state – but also create new socioeconomic spatial structures spanning village and city that function as expressions of a new form of social commons. This commoning constitutes a resistance to capital, not in the sense of political activism – either overt (like demonstrations, riots and strikes, mostly linked to urban contexts) or covert (false compliance, feigned ignorance and a range of other methods applied in peasant struggles) – but in a 'resistance of a third kind': that is, the 'direct intervention in, and alteration of, the processes of labour and production', and 'a wide range of heterogeneous and increasingly interlinked practices through which the peasantry constitutes itself as distinctively different' (van der Ploeg, 2007: 2.1).

The primary purpose of this chapter, therefore, is to present an approach to and notion of social commons in the contemporary context of neoliberalism in agriculture, using Turkey as a case study. First, the basic analytical approach to the idea of commons is introduced. Then, the main features of the resistance to commodification are outlined, focusing specifically on (i) the maintenance and revision of autonomy, and (ii) the re-spatialisation of the social commons via external sources of income and rural–urban mobility. Two main data sources are employed: official Turkish statistics and the results of an original research project. The former are drawn from figures compiled by the Turkish Statistical Institute (TSI or TURKSTAT, TÜİK in Turkish). The latter are based on a research project implemented in two phases during 2010–11 (Öztürk, 2012a). The first phase consisted of focus groups with villagers (in twenty-five villages, nationwide) and in-depth interviews with Ministry of Agriculture district office managers and agricultural input sellers and product traders (in eighteen of the country's eighty-one provincial districts); the second comprised interviews with village households (436) and a village-based questionnaire (seventy-one).

Commons as practice

Three main issues characterise our approach to the recent development of the commons in the social and political sciences and the humanities (Ostrom, 1990; Hess & Ostrom, 2006; Hardt & Negri, 2008; Harvey, 2011). First, we consider commoning as social practice (Reckwitz, 2010: 249). The common is not just a resource external to us, on which we act, but also something (re)created in our actions, the practice by which the resource is produced and reproduced. Second, we position commons beyond the domains of the private and the public. Produced and reproduced on the basis of autonomy, access, participation, cooperation and caring, commoning should be distinguished from both of these. Combining this with the first point, we regard private, public and commons practices as all (re)producing resources in their own particular way; thus, they also similarly (re)produce social relations, as characteristically instrumental – commodified by capital or administratively state-defined or else autonomous and communal.

Third, defined as a practice, the common is more than a remainder of the past or vague hope for the future but operates among us now, even though we tend to be blind to the 'moral economy of common action' (Hardt, 2010: 352; see also Harvey, 2011: 101). Indeed,

> the common is always present, or potentially so … [since it] concerns our capacity to control and reproduce our means of existence, our being in the world … we are this common, making, producing, participating, moving, sharing, circulating, enriching, inventing, restarting. (Negri & Revel, 2008, emphasis added)

Thus, commoning may indeed 'carry people beyond the limits established by the status quo' (Bookchin, 1991: 3) and 'perform new economic hopes' (Gibson-Graham, 2008: 4). This then is an emancipatory notion of the commons, the idea 'that through hard work, cooperation, joint actions and/or over struggle, progress might be wrought' (van der Ploeg, 2008: 274).

Here, this notion of commoning is applied to the smallholder – or peasant (see Hilton, 2012: 13–16) – mode of production, and among rural migrants and urban dwellers with linkages to village and agricultural households. The primary locus lies in practices that connect, as indicated, the rural and the urban (and transnational), and a sense of the communal that is grounded in but no longer limited to a single place. Thus, refer loosely to social ties and networks in the context of commoning – the operation of non-capital and non-state-defined social relations – as a novel form of autonomous communalism.

The maintenance and revision of autonomies

Since the 1950s, the historical 3:1 rural-to-urban population ratio in Turkey has inverted to today's 1:4. This marks the 'success' of a state policy initially aimed at an urban-based economic growth led by industry and services. At first, the demographic change was slow and gradual: the urban population simply increased more quickly than the rural. Then, with the initial introduction of market-oriented reforms in the 1980s, the absolute rural population started to fall, a trend that accelerated sharply after the turn of the millennium, when neoliberal policies were introduced into the agrarian sector.

The removal of the centralised system of structural supports constructed over the previous half-century was effected through the 2001–06 Agricultural Reform Implementation Project (ARIP), sponsored by the World Bank, which saw huge cuts in and/or the ending of a range of state production facilities, price control mechanisms (including fixed price purchases and high import duties) and input subsidies (such as subsidised fertilisers and cheap credit through the state Agriculture Bank), combined with the facilitation of land transfer and international capital entry (Aydın, 2010; Öztürk, 2012b). Largely as a result of this economic strategy, while the total population of Turkey during this period rose by 4%, its rural population dropped by 12%, from around 24 to 21 million, approximately half a million people per year. Within the space of less than a decade, that is, one in eight of all rural dwellers departed, and the village population returned to a level last seen forty years previously (TÜİK,

2000, 2008). In simple terms, the main narrative is of a massive assault on peasant agriculture, leading to urban migration and a demographic earthquake: as the young and healthy moved to the cities to find work and start new families – especially young women, for whom education and employment in the service sector offered liberating opportunities – the ageing and elderly stayed in the village (TÜIK, 2011).

The agrarian base of the old Turkish economy, it was understood, needed to be changed to a secondary/tertiary economy in order to increase value addition for economic growth. In this new model, agrarian-related value was to be added by the processing industry, and farmers were supposed to deliver higher yields for relatively lower costs. Since most farms had been small-scale, family operations, it followed that the recent huge change should lead to a similarly massive reduction in the number of smallholdings. Intriguingly, however, while the smallholder share of total agricultural land *has* fallen quickly – as agribusiness consolidated its holdings – in terms of the *number* of family farms, only that of the very smallest (up to two hectares) has declined. Indeed, half of all holdings in 2001 were still plots of 2–10 hectares, and yet by 2006 this figure had actually increased a little. Actually, this only follows historical trends since the 1950s, and by 2006, when the bulk of the most recent rural-to-urban migration wave had occurred (it continues still, but much more slowly), around four in five holdings (around three million) were still less than 10 hectares in size (Öztürk, 2012b: 77).

Thus, although simple subsistence farming is largely gone now, this is by no means the case for small-scale enterprise, and although the relative importance of small-scale enterprise in the food production system as a whole may be diminishing upon the entry of capital, the effect of this on rural social life in general has been significantly mitigated. Looking more closely, we see that nearly all of these small farms were inherited (around 95% were on family land) and a majority (around 60%) engaged in mixed agriculture (Gürsel & Karakoç, 2009, citing TÜİK, 2008), suggesting low-level capitalisation – market-oriented perhaps, but supported by self-sufficiency and including arable farming for winter livestock feed. This is broadly the situation that we find today, based on data for rural household food supply, with over half of primary foods – bread and dairy products, along with *tarhana* (a traditional soup base) – still produced at home, on the farm.[2]

Self-produced food may be regarded as one of the commons of rural life. First, the basic material inputs, such as grain and milk, are mainly uncommodified, created outside of the market economy. Farmers use corn and cows raised from the previous generation of corn and cows with few or no external (state or private) inputs. Second, production skills, both on the land (raising animals, growing plants) and in the kitchen (making cheese, preserving vegetables), are maintained in village life, passed down through the generations. Food-making knowledge is acquired and shared, not purchased. Home-made foods are, therefore, produced for daily or seasonal consumption within village and family structures, mainly outside of the social relations of the market and its producer/consumer and employer/employee relations. The peasant mode of production is essentially autonomous and communal, representing a social common.

The traditional peasant way, as it may be characterised, centres on the maintenance of a non-commodity circuit (van der Ploeg, 2008: 29) in the production process, through which smallholders assert control over the reproduction of their own farms independently of markets. Contrary to what is referred to as subsistence farming, however, the (contemporary) peasant method of production also involves a commodity circuit; in combination with the non-commodity circuit there thus develops a novel dual circuit system (Figure 7.1). When the commodity circuit starts to dominate, the farm becomes structured by the logic of capital (Figure 7.1, relation a), a development indicated by the importance of the relation of inputs to outputs in the farm as a whole (Figure 7.1, relation b). Peasant struggles for food sovereignty, as, for example, in Via Campesina, are characterised by the fight to maintain and develop autonomy through the non-commodity circuit. Furthermore, and in contradistinction to the anonymous markets of abstract exchange that mark the modern consumer society, a product becomes valued not only in terms of price, but also through the way the product is produced. Consumer relations in the contemporary peasant way are not governed by low price but by fair price, and the economy of exchange is expressed as a moral economy.

It should be noted that, from this perspective, even the agricultural marketing strategies of smallholders to maintain their farms should not necessarily be evaluated in terms of individual decision-making processes of market actors, but may be more relevantly considered in terms of the development of different social relations of production. Thus, in contrast to the process of increased external control constituted by heightened dependency on markets, many smallholdings in Turkey have survived partly through strategies that in some way support the non-commodity circuit, which is sited in the living social structures of family, friends and neighbours, of people with whom rela-

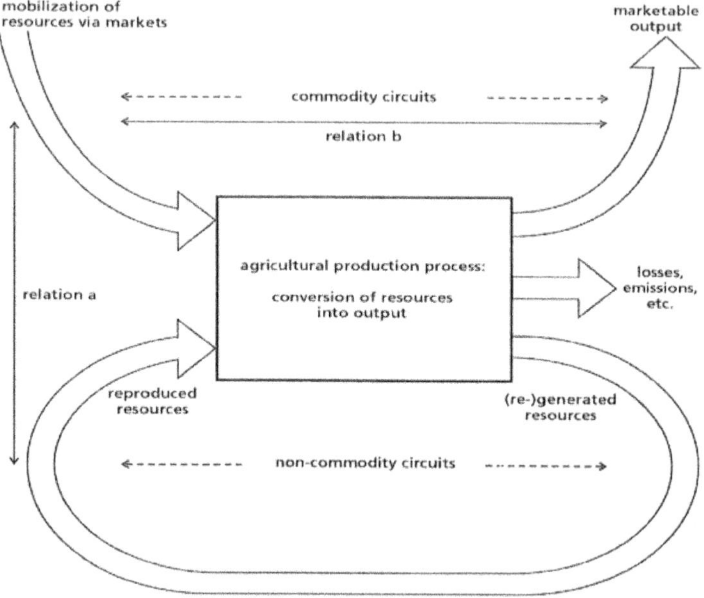

Figure 7.1. The contemporary peasant way: a dual-circuit system
Source: Van der Ploeg (2008: 29).

tionships are based on interconnecting and multivalent human and locality (territorial) ties rather than their positioning in the linear and functional framework of commodity production–distribution and purchase–sale.

Commodification and autonomy are constantly under negotiation on the farm through countless decisions about how to organise the circuits of commodities and non-commodities. Certainly, a creeping commodification is manifested, for example, in rural consumption (see below). The cash or credit required for this is partly accessed through borrowing or sales – sometimes of assets but primarily of agricultural produce supported by labour power – as well as through transfers (in which some of the wealth produced by the operation of capital generally is moved to smallholdings through personal entitlements, such as old-age pensions). The point to note here, though, is that it is precisely the access to such goods that enables the survival of the village and, thus, the maintenance of traditional social commons (expressed economically as the peasant way, the non-commodity circuit), and which also thus characterises the role of the village in the expression of what might be dubbed a post-modern common (the dual circuit).

Essentially, a peasant mode of production remains a transformative reference point in the rural social landscape where social commons not only endure, but through which new modes can emerge. Thus, a dialectical relationship manifests itself, as the very commodification that slowly eats into the social commons of village life enables its revival in altered form. Indeed, given the recent rise in GNP in Turkey and its causally associated urban migration, the number of village farmers would surely have already been decimated had they not gained sufficient entry into the market to compete well enough in order to survive – one way or another. A few brief examples of how commodification has entered traditional rural practices and how commons have not only declined but also been reformulated can serve to illustrate some of the complex socioeconomic dynamics at play here.

The uptake of consumer durables (Table 7.1) shows that farming families become tied into capital through the need to access financing, especially for vehicles, which are particularly important for people living and working on the land but very expensive. In addition to general purpose vehicles, ownership of tractors and other farming equipment, such as for ploughing and harvesting, is also widespread now. We observed that around half of households possess their own tractors, a proportion in line with the official national average. There are forms of commoning even in this capital acquisition, however. First, extended families (two or three nuclear clusters) regularly pool resources, clubbing together to purchase, maintain and share usage of the goods. Then, vehicles and equipment are also sometimes shared with other families, perhaps paid for in kind – in around a third of cases (households and villages), we found this to occur. And then, when tractors (most commonly) are rented out for daily payments, the traditional independence and communal structuring of rural social relations means that the financialisation of sharing does not include profiteering and typically does not involve formal payment arrangements (people tend just to pay when they can).

Table 7.1. Rural household penetration of selected consumer durables (%, n = 436)

Durables	Present	Absent
Mobile phone	94	6
Washing machine	90	10
Vehicle*	44	56
Dishwasher	23	77

* Car, pick-up, truck

Source: Öztürk (2012a).

This entry of financial transfers (cash payments) does, neverthe-less, represent a commodification of daily life that manifests itself in many ways, and older villagers do complain, for example, that 'people don't share anymore'. Again, though, lest it be too easily overlooked, the social commons continue to be enacted despite, and developed through, this commodification. In many moun-tain settlements, for example, it used to be a traditional practice for the whole village (and adjoining hamlets) to move their bovine (buffalo and cattle) herds together for summertime pasture on higher land, whereupon some villagers would stay in the mountain settlement (*yayla*) to look after the animals, while the rest returned to harvest the corn and scythe the grass for hay. This involved a range of communal social activities (the timing of the move would be decided by informal consensus, people would look after one another's herds, etc.) – and it still occurs, with modernising developments. Journeys are made by private vehicle now, includ-ing minibus trips (private enterprise) up and down the mountain, enabling the villagers to descend and return in a day, cutting and baling their grass for winter feed between the dawn and dusk herding and milking in the *yayla* – which, in turn, allows smaller numbers of people to maintain properties and farming activities, a vital development in the context of reduced populations.

Another aspect of commodification is observed in the ways in which agricultural inputs are obtained. In addition to mechanical hardware and the necessary fuel and maintenance, farmers purchase not only inputs like fertilisers (74% of small-holders) and pesticides (67%) – for which state subsidies have now been significantly reduced – but also certified seed (47%) and seedlings (20%). With regard to the latter, state restrictions, albeit loosely applied, limit farmers' rights to produce and sell their own seeds, subject to legislation introduced by ARIP in accordance with EU regulations. The multinational operations of agribusiness are thus legally enabled to introduce patented seed products and related biotechnologies – millions of tons of genetically modified seed (corn, rape/oilseed and cotton) now enter Turkey, where they are converted into the constituents of several hundred food products. Here, though, the legislated construction of dependency meets with a relatively politicised resistance in the form of seed barter festivals, especially in the western (Aegean) region. At these festivals, farmers exchange seed in non-financial transactions, thus circumventing not only the new legislation but also the capitalised market. Even though the room for manoeuvre in the practice of independent farming is reduced, and with it the social commons restricted, therefore, it is re-engaged by an independent, communal response.

The purchase of tractors, fertilisers and seeds – and of washing machines and mobile phones, along with payments for fuel and health and education needs (Turkey has a reasonably well developed but not entirely free system for social welfare) as well as for all manner of other expenses – obviously requires smallholders to enter the market with cash or credit. Traditionally, when farmers/villagers needed access to goods, they would seek them in communal solidarity (without financial payment) or, if money was required, by localised, personal borrowing (from family, neighbours and friends). This grounding in communal social relations is also changing to one of capitalist commodity relations, as traditional methods decrease and credit relations grow. Thus financialisation constitutes another dimension of the commodification process. Again, however, there is a crucial caveat: bank loans are quite difficult for smallholders to secure, and around a fifth of the households and villages we questioned borrow on the basis of human rather than capital relations, while another fifth would not, or simply do not, take loans, opting instead for other, belt-tightening and asset-realisation approaches, such as by reducing consumption and/or farming activities and renting out land (Table 7.2).

Table 7.2. Preferred credit/barrowing sources (household, *n* = 171)

Preferred credit source	Proportion (%)
Bank	35
Family/neighbours	21
Agriculture credit co-ops	12
Private ('loan shark')	7
Farmer's union	4
Nowhere (do/would not borrow)	21

Source: Öztürk (2012a).

In the quest for solvency, farmers may indeed attempt to transform assets into capital or make savings rather than raise money. Our research shows that around half of villagers draw on their savings in times of need; they certainly hold out against selling land, the preferred option of only 3%. At the same time, in another expression of the dialectic referred to above, the departure of people from the farms for jobs in the city, thereby entering into full capital relations, also has the effect of releasing the pressure on smallholding production capacity by reducing household consumption demand, indefinitely.

Whereas in the past, the loss of labour supply, of young people in particular, would have outweighed the gain for the farm of lower consumption, now, with the entry of capital, and when labour needs can be so reduced by mechanisation, this becomes a positive factor: labour loss becomes labour sale, with remittances contributing to the survival of family smallholdings and the traditions they maintain.

Another interesting contemporary strategy is that of investment in solar power. Very popular among smallholders now, this medium-term investment option not only enables savings in electricity costs but also contributes to rural development, reducing the pressure on environmentally damaging energy sources. Taking farmers away from national grid dependency, it also, of course, contributes to their autonomy. Indeed, we found that making savings – reducing farming expenses and cutting consumption generally – is practised, as necessary, by some 50–60% of farmers. Inevitably, however, smallholders cannot endure indefinitely with just scaling-down and stop-gap measures, such as belt-tightening and borrowing, and even long-lasting efficiencies, such as the departure of family members and introduction of cheaper energy supplies, will not stem the relentless tide of capital.

External income and rural–urban mobility
Eventually, if family farms and the associated social commons are to survive the vicissitudes of the market, they must either capitalise more fully for market efficiency, or develop other relations with markets such as through value addition ('deepening'), engaging in non-agricultural on-farm activities ('broadening') or reducing costs and finding non-farm, non-agricultural

sources of income ('re-grounding') (van der Ploeg & Roep, 2003). Among the positive market relations related to value addition – deepening – and the moral economy aspect of the peasant way is the adoption, by whole villages even, of a single, high-value product. This assumes two forms. One is general, the application of generic terms and techniques, such as 'organic', which are increasingly attractive to the urban middle class. The other is specifically related to quality definition via the branding of produce by locality, such as honey (parts of Turkey are ecologically rich in native flower varieties for pollen sources for bees) or cheese made from unpasteurised milk (e.g. in the Kars region of north-east Turkey). In the latter case, of a product that has both intrinsic quality value and a localised production structure, a recent initiative is now striving for recognition and protection under the geographical indication regulation of the EU to promote and protect quality agricultural products and food.

These examples of the emergence of embedded or 'nested' markets (Aguglia et al., 2009) represent informal and localised farmer-based developments, rather than determinations by distant and anonymous enterprises ordered by the logic of agribusiness. Although they are integrated into capital and dependent on markets, this is much more on local people's own terms than, for example, the medium-sized entrepreneurs of central Anatolia who produce potatoes to order for supermarkets to be converted to crisps, where the varieties, quantities and prices are all fixed by the industry, which also gains the most added value (through the secondary production process). On the one hand, these nested markets valorise community as bottom-up initiatives and through their need for and, thus, support of local skills and knowledge sharing; on the other hand, they buttress independence through the development of what tend to be individually articulated markets with highly tailored yet flexible infrastructures that are inherently resistant to takeover.

Something else that contributes to rural development by enhancing the value of the common as a locality-based resource – the pluriactivity of broadening – involves the turn to tourism. The contemporary phenomenon of *yayla* tourism, essentially by urbanites touring the countryside as an alternative summer holiday, offers opportunities for income generation in various spheres, such as hotel and restaurant provision, in which localised entrepreneurial activities are currently expanding quite quickly. Again, although operative within the general context of commodification and market-driven, this also combines with smallholder practices to provide a combination of subsistence/ livelihood inputs that afford families relatively high levels of control – to organise, for example, the particular mix of incomes received according to a range of factors that are self-determined (by individual preference and family changes).

Investment activities require external income sources, just like inputs into the commodification process to develop smallholdings in the market, or, for that matter, the mere maintenance (survival) of 'inefficient' family farming enterprises. For re-grounding, there are two main sources other than formal (bank) or informal (fellow villager) credit – namely pensions and wages/salaries. The relatively high proportion of elderly people living in villages and their increased coverage by state pension schemes nowadays means that this is a major contribution to the rural economy as a whole and certainly supports farming families – the contribution is typically pooled if they live in a single household and otherwise informally shared according to need across households. Although clan-type and extended-family single-residence arrangements are no longer the norm, the more communal arrangements of large families remains usual – including multiple generation and adjoining homes. Pensions thus tend to go 'into the pot', with (ostensibly private) family arrangements operating as (relatively restricted) commons (see below). Obviously a more lucrative source of income, however, and preferred in almost half (46%) of the villages we surveyed, is paid employment.

Like borrowing, wage labour results in commodification and financialisation. It also leads to a dissolution of collective work, inter-work, loan work and solidarity via labour support, especially to the elderly: simply, one who sells their labour has less time for kinship/communal work. This is a de-commoning effected by the commodification of human relations at the level of agriculturally based social practice. Farmers cannot maintain their farms for any length of time simply through the addition of income from their paid employment, however, since their farms also demand their labour. Thus, families organise in ways that enable the maintenance of their smallholdings through the external financial inputs of some members and the on-farm labour of others. Official figures show rural employment outside of farming to have constantly increased, by over 50% since 2004, and now standing at nearly 40% of all paid labour in the country-side (TÜIK, 2013).

Although inputs into smallholder farms may come from local employment, in the nearest town perhaps, it more often comes in the form of remittances from work in a large city or metropolis, or abroad, and involves a rural-to-urban, or transnational, change of residence. In terms of time period, this move may be a permanent one or else a temporary arrangement (e.g. seasonal, semi-annual), followed by return(s) to the village; so, rather than specify urban migration, we need to talk more generally about movements and mobility. Return to the village is also a function of overall economic activity: during a downturn, people in the city become unemployed and a proportion head back 'home'. Thus, while agricultural employment fell by nearly 15% in the period immediately prior the 2008 economic crisis, it then rose by a quarter. During periods of reduced employment, when capital – the market – fails, agriculture offers an alternative, a fall-back means of sustenance, an escape route for recent urban migrants in particular, who are typically marginalised in conditions of precarious labour.

Obviously, it is usually younger people who tend to engage in such wage labour, impelled not only by family needs and local economic capacity limitations, but also individual, life-course-associated desires to engage with the cosmopolitan, the wider world. Essentially, this is a function of modern mobility, enabled by local road and regional highway construction, in tandem with automobile ownership and a massive nationwide network of bus services, as well as, now, affordable, nationwide flights. Socially, it is organised around kinship, although it also involves lineage more broadly – especially clans (in Turkey, especially in the south-east, the Kurdish region) – and ties of place (villages, districts and beyond).

Kinship (and lineage/locality) may be regarded as an alternative mode of order. Although it is very much tied in with capital (e.g. in respect of inherited wealth) and tends to function for the social organisation of private property, it is also historically pre-capitalist and stands outside the market, from a social relations perspective. In terms of social practices, kinship thus works as a common, on the basis of shared resources. Of course, we should not idealise kinship networks, since they operate, traditionally and to this day, in ways that privilege some, typically males and elders, over others, thus giving these groups greater access to the common wealth of the group. Indeed, insofar as kinship is bound to the private (as family wealth), we may also analyse it from an external perspective as structurally operative in ways defined by capital. Nevertheless, from an internal perspective (within families), kinship organises social practices on a communal basis. Its resources are fundamentally inaccessible to outsiders, but intrinsically open to those within, as commons. Kinship constitutes community in a way that, importantly, is not defined by capital, or, for that matter, the state, and thus persists autonomously.

Kinship is an important socioeconomic and cultural configuration. Practices of residence and resource mobilisation in Turkey are at least partly kinship-based or mediated, and especially in the rural contexts of agriculture. As Belge (2011) showed in reference to the Kurdish situation and the continuing contemporary efficacy of its clan structures, kinship networks may function as an important reservoir of resistance against a repressive and interventionist state – and from the perspective of the commons and social practice, the state is routinely repressive and interventionist, denying autonomy and the communal. The advance of capital may be considered to undermine and diminish kinship relations, as evidenced in the contraction of the primary family unit (from extended to nuclear). Essentially, this consists in the reduction of the overarching patrilineal unit as a multiple household – a hierarchical structure strongly related to the pre-modern era of human development, generally organised around a male head, in which women are part of the extended family of their father, or an older brother, until their transfer upon marriage to the newly formed extended family of the husband (Kovanci, 2005).

This kinship-based societal system not only continues to form the bedrock of social relations in rural areas and heavily informs urban living patterns in Turkey, but also, as indicated, takes new forms of expression through resistance rooted in agriculture, the efforts of people and groups to maintain autonomy and their communal basis of human connectivity oriented to farming. Notably, in this context, the financial inputs from employment (engagement with capital) that enable the continuation of small-holdings are also skewed towards empowering, through wage employment, the young and also women (working especially in the growing service sector, such as in local supermarkets, banks, etc.). As another aspect of the multifaceted dialectic, capital thus has a liberating effect on the common.

Crucially, an extended family can develop an extended settlement pattern. Again, this is impelled by the operation of capital (as people are attracted to its centres) on the common (kinship structure) – or extended settlement patterns develop as a resistance of the common to the dominion of capital that informs new socioeconomic forms and practices. In addition to the weakening of traditional age and gender practices, this implies the development of communal living structures, which span rural and urban environments as out-migration causes families to spread from home village to towns and cities and maintain ties of solidarity to hold this social fabric together.

Composed of an indeterminate number of households, an extended family network commonly comprises a small number of households in the village and several in towns and cities – thus incorporating, one might argue, rather than being defined by, the paradigmatically capitalist, nuclear form. In addition to its constrictive (external) definition in terms of the private, this structuring has a tendency to function on the basis of shared resources, without these being pooled as such. We may understand them in terms of material commonalities, of accessible goods, finances and labour, rather than a simple commons. For example, male members of an extended family sometimes decide to cultivate the land to which they are entitled together and share the revenues, while household income generated from other work, like wage labour in the city or income from (other) entrepreneurial farming activities is not shared, or only partly (Jongerden, 2007: 28–9). Indeed, bonds of blood and locality have been reformulated rather than dissolved as a result of the entry of capital.

What has emerged in Turkey today, therefore, is an extended settlement pattern based on traditional, agrarian social relations of kinship and community that, linking the rural to the urban, serves to support village smallholders through diversified income-generating strategies. This we may refer to as a solidarity-network-based common. As a result of mobility and migration, this solidarity, or sharing, does not take place in a context of the village and agriculture, but in the context of mobilising resources across the rural–urban divide. From the village perspective, as a smallholder strategy of having household members working in the city, it is partly a response to decreasing incomes and insecurity in the countryside. Therefore, we can comprehend smallholder families engaging with wage labour in the city as a strategy to gain or maintain autonomy through communal social practices, one that enables the small family farm to survive and yet also withstand the pressure to organise according to a purely capitalist logic. In other words, the solidarity-network-based common supports the dual-circuit economy of the contemporary peasant way. Thus are traditional commons maintained and new ones created, not only despite but also because of and in tandem with the development of capital.

For the several million people who have been pouring into Turkey's cities, we should also mention that access to housing in cities is mainly organised on the basis of relations of locality (*hemşehrilik*), in which those born in the same village or region help each other. Newly arrived urban migrants usually start out by living with family already based in the city and most typically in a part of the city where their home district *hemşeri* are located. Through these community-rooted relations, referring to place as well as family, housing and work are secured, as well as credit (gifts and loans to facilitate the establishment of a new life) (Karpat, 1976: 85; Kovanci, 2005). This constitutes a grouping together for urban networks of support that is even visible at the level of apartment blocks, in which members of the same lineage rent or buy flats on different floors of the same building, or even join together to build it.

The importance of these kinship- and locality-based solidarity networks – or communalism – has not diminished in Turkey over the last decade; on the contrary, it has increased, for two main reasons. First, compared to earlier migrants, recent arrivals have fewer housing opportunities due to de-commoning practices. Until the 1980s, migrants could occupy land relatively easily, create their own housing and add value, but this changed during the 1990s, as the urban periphery morphed into the commuter belt, making land a scarce commodity that the state, municipalities and private construction and investment companies develop (the Turkish '*rantiye*', from 'rentier', is now in popular usage). Today's city newcomers generally cannot find land on which to build their own dwelling and instead become dependent on the private housing market. Second newcomers now have to accept the conditions of precarious employment. Previously, the urban poor worked for the state or local authority in official jobs with low salaries but job security. This has been radically undermined by the neoliberal downsizing of the state since the 1980s, with restricted employment in the public sector contributing to an excess supply of labour accompanied by a diminishment of the labour unions – all of which has depressed wages.

Obviously, this mostly affects the least powerful in the labour market, who are disproportionately urban migrants. Research on people who have migrated to twenty large cities in Turkey over the last two decades shows that slightly over a quarter (28%) are in casual or temporary employment and slightly under a quarter (22%) are 'self-employed', which tends to mean engagement in a low-level (insecure, low remuneration) enterprise or just street-hawking. Approximately half of these city migrants, therefore, are in marginal forms of employment. Some come from towns and other cities, but the majority, about two-thirds, are from villages. Their employment conditions do mean, therefore, that they are relatively free to move between city and village, as economic circumstances dictate, which offers at least a minimal level of autonomy. Further to this, white-collar workers and even professionals are also observed to be engaged in village farming and dual-residence living patterns, suggesting that factors like independence and maintenance of close contact with the land may be actively valued and not just the result of economic necessity (Öztürk & Topaloğlu, 2013).

For the less fortunate, the increased difficulties of leaving their villages for the city means that, rather than sending remittances to their families in the village, it is they who need support to get established. This comes in both financial and other material forms (food, bedding) and through different avenues (e.g. produced at home, sent by bus). The net result is a complex picture of interaction, wherein solidarity network commoning operates in multiple expressions of a two-way movement of money and goods (Table 7.3).

Table 7.3. Migrant solidarity forms (*n* = 436)

Direction	Solidarity form	%
Rural-to-urban	Migrants produce own needs in village when visiting	35
	Basic necessities sent to migrants	28
	Financial aid sent to migrants	11
	Migrants borrow	7
Urban-to-rural	Financial aid sent to families	28
	Goods sent to families	20
	Aid sent for communal (village) needs (e.g. school)	8

Source: Öztürk (2012a).

Several other dynamics may be observed in the development of the new commons. Further compounding the blurring of urban and rural space, for example, is the incidence of urban agricultural practices. State figures show that a small but increasing proportion of agricultural labourers (now over three-quarters of a million people) live in towns and cities; also, as we have observed, there is a category of urban–rural farmers who either work their land from a town or city or who make land-use or sharecropping arrangements with villagers and return as necessary to manage the planting and harvesting. Another tendency is that of the village youth living with relatives in towns/cities where they go to school and of whole families similarly moving for education. Such arrangements are, of course, intrinsically temporary and subject to a variety of social patterning dynamics.

Also, in respect of capital movements, accrued wealth is not only sent in the form of rural remittances to support farming and ageing relatives and maintain family properties but also invested in village home rebuilding and extensions, particularly with retirement in mind. Further to the return of migrants, there is a significant flow of people to the countryside for the 'good life', both back to village homes and to new ones, especially in later life. In fact, people engage in a variety of rural-directed movements. These include retirement, with reverse (sometimes transnational), counter-urban (urban-to-rural) and even 'trans-rural' (rural-to-urban-to-rural) migration, along with dual-place residence, where people oscillate between city and village, typically escaping village winters (for the elderly) or city summers (going back to village roots for extended family holidays, perhaps, or just going home to help out on the farm). This seasonally based movement is a marked feature of rural life in contemporary Turkey, with village populations doubling and trebling during the summer. In general, the phenomenon of village return is particularly productive of a rich variety of village residence-oriented dual- and multi-place (hybrid) living structures (Öztürk, Hilton & Jongerden, 2013).

Premised on mobility, these movement dynamics fudge the dichotomy of rural/urban; they involve the production of what may be dubbed the 'rurban', to borrow a term from the Turkish socialist Nusret Kemal Köymen (1940), whose novel conceptualisation of spatial settlement attempted to synthesise agriculture and industry. These spatial living structures and the social relations by which they are defined today are significantly determined by smallholder farming. Insofar as they are grounded in peasant ways and specified by communal ties of kinship and locality in a fundamentally a-statist and a-capitalist context, they invoke a social praxis that valorises commonalities. Thus, they may be deemed to fall under the original category of 'rurban' mobility as an agriculturally based social common – or an importantly 'ruraland' agriculturally oriented re-spatialisation that may be characterised as a novel, relatively autonomous communalism.

Conclusion

Despite the ancient history of property and its control, the massive encroachment of both state and market that we see in everyday life now is a relatively new phenomenon. Neither public nor private capital determined the centre from which order radiated across much of the world for most of its history. Social relations and the daily practices riding on them were rather organised around and through rural locality and family, on the basis, that is, of kith and kinship. Related to this communal arrangement was a human or moral economy as opposed to a command or market economy. Now, however, family networks, the community and moral economy have been transformed worldwide in the drive for 'development', with neoliberal state policies and the commodification of agriculture and the rurality both causing and being facilitated by mass urban migration. Technological restructuring along with the financial advances of globalisation have produced sociopolitical expressions of capital that have profound implications for the commons – with de-commoning as an aim, indeed an instrumental necessity, rather than just tangentially operative.

Regarding the present state of social commons in the countryside, the snapshot presented in this chapter is a mixed one. The massive and ongoing outflow of population, market pressures on farmers, and partial collapse of traditional village life may all be cited in support of an arguably depressing thesis. Against that, however, the striking resilience of smallholder subsistence enterprises, with, on the one hand, both the maintenance of old and development of new autonomous practices and strategies and, on the other, the extension of family- and also community-based 'rurban' space and its material commonalities, all go to suggest an alternative reading. On the capitalist accumulation side, the commodification imperative operates as a function of the demand for profit, of course, but on the side of the common, ordinary human intent leads us to continually strive to determine our own social relations and maintain basic values even under the sometimes oppressive conditions of our lived environments. The balance of these contradictory vectors emerges as a synthesis, whereby even as commodification appears to overcome the common and convert everything to a value for exchange, the common is enabled, both through the continuation of the 'natural' order based on communalism and autonomy and also as a constant rescuing of relations from the hegemony of capitalist logic.

Despite so many signs to the contrary, therefore, the analysis presented here suggests that the force of the common is not just a romantic nostalgia projected as a fanciful ideal for a future never to be realised. On the contrary, it represents a way in which the human spirit, as the drive for autonomy and need for community, emerges, like weeds ever-growing through the concrete of external, divisive, dehumanising controls, and thus in an unending dialectic with capital. Not only do families in Turkey manage to maintain rather than sell out and cash in on their land, but, as a result of the squeeze of the market and the underlying migratory pull of the urban sourced by capital through the terms of trade, their desire to farm has contributed to an extension of kinship and other communal ties across socio-geographical space in the production of new social forms.

Thus, the networks of support interconnecting cityscape and countryside observed here are, to a large extent, directly produced by the present neoliberal thrust. And even as they operate in the context of the village deteriorating from thriving community to shelter for the weak, aged and infirm unable or unwilling to compete in the urban labour market, so, equally, do they involve reverse movements of people and other material and immaterial resources from the city that help to sustain small-scale agriculture and rural life, including both the maintenance of non-commodified practices and human relations and the development of new ones. In the present development and evolution of the social commons, therefore, previously disparate spheres of human activity now span and integrate the rural–urban divide to produce re-spatialisation as a contemporary, novel form of social re-commoning.

Notes

1   This is a revised version of an article published in *Agrarian South: Journal of Political Economy* 3(3).

2   Around a third of farming households produce their own fruit and vegetables, but this masks huge variations, dependent on local farming conditions, which in turn determine consumption levels; meat is traditionally regarded as a luxury in many areas and relatively little consumed.

References

Aguglia, L., Henke, R., Poppe, K., Roest, A. and Salvioni, C. (2009). 'Diversification and multifunctionality in Italy and the Netherlands: a comparative analysis', *Wye City Group Conference* (second meeting), FAO, Rome (11–12 June 2009). At http://edepot.wur.nl/13897

Aydin, Z. (2010). 'Neo-liberal transformation of Turkish agriculture', *Journal of Agrarian Change*, 10(2): 149–187.

Belge, C. (2011). 'State building and the limits of legibility: kinship networks and Kurdish resistance in Turkey', *International Journal of Middle Eastern Studies*, 43(1): 96–114.

Bookchin, M. (1991). 'Libertarian municipalism', *Green Perspectives*, 24. At http://dwardmac.pitzer.edu/Anarchist_Archives/bookchin/gp/perspectives24.html

Gibson-Graham, J. K. (2008). 'Diverse economies: performative practices for "other worlds"', *Progress in Human Geography*, 32(5): 613–632.

Gürsel, S. and Karakoç, U. (2009). *Türkiye'de Tarımın Yapısı Değişiyor* [The changing structure of agriculture in Turkey]. Bahçeşehir

Üniveritesi, Ekonomik ve Toplumsal Araştırmalar Merkezi, Araştırma Notu 24, Istanbul: BETAM.

Hardt, M. (2010). 'The common in communism', *Rethinking Marxism*, 22(3): 346–356.

Hardt, M. and Negri, A. (2008). *Commonwealth*. Boston: Harvard University Press.

Harvey, D. (2011). 'The future of the commons', *Radical History Review*, 109: 101–197.

Hess, C. and Ostrom, E. (2006). *Understanding Knowledge as a Commons: From Theory to Practice*. Cambridge, MA: MIT Press.

Hilton, A. (2012). 'Foreword', in Murat Öztürk (Ed.), *Agriculture, Peasantry and Poverty in Turkey in the Neo-liberal Age*. Wageningen: Wageningen Academic Publishers.

Jongerden, J. (2007). *The Settlement Issue in Turkey and the Kurds: An Analysis of Spatial Policies, Modernity and War*. Leiden/Boston: Brill Academic Publishers.

Karpat, K. (1976). *The Gecekondu: Rural Migration and Urbanization*. London: Cambridge University Press.

Kovanci, O. (2005). *Kinship, Woman Labor and Gender Relations in Turkey*. Ankara: Ankara University Working Papers Series, 86.

Köymen, N. K. (1940). 'Köy sosyolojisi. Ziraat – sanayi – köy – şehiri' [Village sociology: agriculture, industry, village, city], *Ziraat Dergisi*, 1(1).

Negri, A. and Revel, J. (2008). *Inventing the Common* (trans. N. Lavey). At http://www.generation-online.org/p/fp_revel5.htm

Ostrom, E. (1990). *Governing the Commons*. Cambridge: Cambridge University Press.

Öztürk, M. (2012a). '1980 sonrası yıllarda Türkiye'de tarımda ve kırda dönüşüm dinamikleri' [The dynamics of agricultural and rural change in Turkey since 1980]. Unpublished research report, funded by Kadır Has Uniersity, Istanbul.

Öztürk, M. (2012b). *Agriculture, Peasantry and Poverty in Turkey in the Neo-liberal Age*. Wageningen: Wageningen Academic Publishers.

Öztürk, M. and Topaloğlu, B. (2013). *Sonrasında İç Göç Eğilimleri İç Göç Türleri Nedenleri ve Yerleşim Yerleri ve Nüfusuna Etkilerinin*

Ekonomik ve Demografik Yönleri [After internal migration: varieties, trends, and reasons for settlement location and settlement effects on economic and demographic orientations]. Unpublished research report, Kadır Has University, Istanbul.

Öztürk, M., Hilton, A. and Jongerden, J. (2013). 'Migration as movement and multiplace life: some recent developments in rural living structures in Turkey', *Population, Place, Space*, 20(4): 370–388.

Reckwitz, A. (2010). 'Toward a theory of social practices: a development in culturalist theorizing', *European Journal of Social Theory*, 5(2): 243–263.

TÜİK (2000). *Genel Nüfus Sayımları* [General population census], 1927–2000. Ankara: TÜİK.

TÜİK (2008). *Tarımsal İşletme Yapı Araştırması 2006* [Agricultural holdings structure research 2006]. Ankara: TÜİK.

TÜİK (2011). *Adrese Dayalı Nüfus Kayıt Sistemi (ADNKS)* [Address-based population record system]. At http://www.turkstat.gov.tr

TÜİK (2013). *Hanehalkı İşgücü İstatistikleri, 2012* [Household labour force survey, 2012]. At http://www.turkstat.gov.tr

Van der Ploeg, J. D. (2007). 'Resistance of the third kind', *ESRS Conference*, Wageningen (23 August 2007). At www.jandouwevanderploeg.com/EN/publications/articles/resistance-of-the-third-kind/

Van der Ploeg, J. D. (2008). *The Peasant Principle: Struggles for Autonomy and Sustainability in an Era of Empire and Globalization.* London: Earthscan.

Van der Ploeg, J. D. and Roep, D. (2003). 'Multifunctionality and rural development: the actual situation in Europe', in G. van Huylenbroeck and G. Durand (Eds.), *Multifunctional Agriculture. A New Paradigm for European Agriculture and Rural Development.* Burlington, VT/Aldershot: Ashgate.

Chapter 8

The square as the place
of the commons

Ruud Kaulingfreks and Femke Kaulingfreks

Introduction

Squares have always been a distinctive feature of the city. They form the centre of gravity of urban life and have been of paramount importance for social interaction through different times and across a variety of cultures.[1] As Cutini (2014: 248) states, 'A square is a public open living space, the meeting and relation space par excellence, where people do meet and gather day by day'. In the Italian language, Cutini explains, various expressions evoke the square as a symbol for the people: 'to go down to the square' means to revolt, and 'to listen to the square' means to sound out public opinion, so even in everyday speech the square becomes 'the physical representation of its community meaning'. The square is the place where public life is concentrated and social value is created.

All kinds of encounters can occur on the square, often at the same time. It is a place to meet and to converse, to buy, to protest, to feast or watch a spectacle, to be lazy, to flirt, to drink and to play or just to wander about. It operates as a site of contestation and transformation, a place where institutions are confronted, new forms of organising emerge and hierarchical power structures are rearranged. The square has this potential because it is an open, delineated but inherently undefined urban space. The square is an empty place in the city, a white spot on the map simultaneously incorporating all colours. It is, therefore, a place where anything can happen and anyone can reside. Its very multipurposeness is what makes the square a common space for everybody and therefore a place where a sense of community can arise. Squares embody communality. They are the locality of the commons and represent a space that cannot be exclusively appropriated, because this space is open to the public.

In this chapter, we want to demonstrate the openness of the square as an embodiment of the commons. The spatial features of the square – its accessibility, centrality and emptiness – make it inviting for a variety of people and activities. Squares allow for a multiplicity of manifestations of togetherness without requiring these to be forced into any one definition. The square is the place to be singular–plural, in the words of Jean Luc Nancy (2000). This allows for the emergence of spontaneous and transient communities in which an awareness of shared interests is expressed. Our analysis of the square as the place for community focuses mainly on the writings of Jean Luc Nancy since, we believe, he presents a novel way of analysing the social that is of particular interest when dealing with pluriformity.

Besides being the place of fairs and festivals, squares all over the world have a history of protest and repression. The public (re) claims the square, one might say, in oppositional acts of political performance, directed against central power. Our analysis of the square therefore implies an analysis of struggle between attempts to control the square and the contestation of the disempowered. In recent years we have seen a striking rise of protests against anti-democratic, neoliberal and capitalist economic structures and political governance characterised by gatherings on the square as their focal point (Lopes de Souza & Lipietz, 2011; Dhaliwal,

2012; Schiffman et al., 2012; Stavrides, 2012; Marom, 2013; Örs, 2014). On the square, people experiment with new forms of real and direct democracy; the square becomes the space in which the concept of the commons is actualised.

An open space in the city

When wandering through a city, one often ends up at a square – sometimes accidentally, but very often intentionally, since cities are largely known by their squares (Cutini, 2014: 248). Indeed, as Moughtin (2003: 90) explains, it is typically 'only when the main square of most old towns is reached that one has really "arrived"', because 'all the streets lead naturally to this focal point' which 'dominates the town in size and grandeur' and ultimately 'gives meaning to its existence as a place distinct from other places'. The square is a fissure in the city, where the dense construction of buildings cracks open (e.g. the Piazza del Campo in Siena). In cities built according to an Italian Renaissance design, the main square is located right in the geometric centre of the settlement, complemented by a number of smaller squares scattered around (Cutini, 2014: 253).

In modern cities, squares function as traffic nodes, and important public buildings are often grouped around the square (Moughtin, 2003: 93). Also, in cities with a more modern urban design, squares are often a central place for social interactions. These light and open spaces are attractive places to meet, since spatiality is an important aspect of social traffic. Interactions do not take place in a void. The *topos* where we meet influences the character of the interaction, so we tend to prefer a place that fits the encounter. Which interests (should) play a part in the meeting? Who is allowed to set the parameters and who should adapt to the situation? Do we invite the other over to our terrain? Who is the guest and who is the host? Such questions are resolved by the neutrality of public spaces, sites without private ownership, which are accessible to all and therefore facilitate more symmetrical relations. Squares are places that can be temporarily used by anyone.

Although in English the name is 'square' – even when they obviously are not always square (e.g. Times Square, in New York) – in almost every other Western language they are just called 'places':[2] *place* in French (Place de la Concorde, Paris, for a while the Place de la Révolution), *Platz* in German (Potsdamer Platz, Berlin), *plaza* in Spanish (Plaza Mayor, Madrid), *piazza* in Italian (Piazza Navona, Rome). The Dutch word *plein* is derived from the Latin *planum*, as in the English 'plane' and 'plain', signifying a flat space without any particular content (Het Plein in the Hague does not even need a specific name). However, as Heidegger (1971: 141 ff.) explained, a place is the location of something, a thing, a person. It is a distinguishable position in the vastness of the world, a location, as opposed to the indistinctiveness of empty space. A place indicates an opening to a labyrinth of possibilities. Heidegger gives the example of a bridge. Along the shores of the river many points may be indicated that could be occupied by something. One of these points becomes recognisable as a place because of the bridge; it becomes a place because the bridge leads to it. A place is always the place of something. The essentially empty space of a square becomes a place in relation to its use by the people and in relation to its surroundings.

Socioculturally, the square indicates the place within the city where community can be actualised. This location thus becomes a locality, allowing for different kinds of use and different forms of appropriation by different people. Mattias Kärrholm (2005) speaks of the 'territorial complexity' that is generated in the square. Various groups of people develop a certain personal relationship with a place, because of the way they identify with and use it. Simultaneously, top-down, planned and impersonal territorial strategies are enacted to delimit or control it. It is symptomatic of this that most redesigned modern squares are ordered spaces, sectioned into units, each with its own purpose, even when designed for the relaxation of citizens, as is the case with numerous squares that have been reclaimed from traffic (Gehl & Gamzoe, 2006). Nevertheless, people tend to appropriate such ordered spaces in unexpected ways. The use of the square by buskers and homeless people are examples, which are consequently regularised in response. It is this constant interplay of territorial tactics and strategies, formal and informal markings of a place, exercised by a variety of groups and actors, which leads to the territorial complexity. Squares are characterised by a complex interplay of different power struggles, different uses and people. Unlike, for example, shopping malls, which are regulated spaces designed with one form of use and activity in mind, there is not a single territorial strategy dominating the square (Kärrholm, 2005: 16).

Physically, the empty space of the square becomes a locality through the contrast with its surroundings. The large buildings around the square, the shops and cafés with terraces, perhaps a town hall, often a church or cathedral at the head (see below), define the square because they attract visitors (e.g. the Grote Markt/Grand Place, in Brussels). Hence, paradoxically, the limits to the open space of the square define its inviting character. The buildings around the square both guard it and keep it together. An equilibrium is needed, however, between the central open space of the square and the surrounding urban texture that defines it. There is a delicate balance between a space that is open to all and a limitless, impersonal expanse. The former is cosy and invites one to dwell in it; the latter overwhelms and disorients us.

The atmosphere of the square takes shape in the interplay between the open space and the buildings on the periphery. Urban designers have researched the ideal physical features of the public square, taking into account aspects such as solar access, wind flow, thermal comfort, noise and pedestrian movement (Giddings, Charlton & Horne, 2011). Architects have discovered an ideal relationship between the height of the surrounding buildings and the sides of the square (Moughtin, 2003: 100) – which, unsurprisingly, is 1/3:2/3, the Golden Ratio. If the adjacent buildings are too high, the square becomes pompous and authoritarian; it makes us feel small and insignificant (as at Potsdamer Platz). If they are too low or the surroundings are too open, the communal space becomes an anonymous place (like the Plaza de la Revolucion in Havana); people tend to feel lost in the vastness of the space if there are no protecting boundaries (such as the Praça dos Três Poderes in Brasilia).

Historically, early urban settlements tended to feature an open, common place in a closed, built environment. This early incarnation or forerunner of the modern city square was of great importance to the community for protection. In castles located in rural settings, as well as in walled cities, there was an open space left within the tight fabric of buildings, where peasants and their animals could enter and seek shelter in case of attack. The inhabitants of the neighbouring countryside were brought inside the walls when the enemy was approaching. Since walled cities could not expand outside the walls, they grew inside. The medieval city became a dense maze, with every inch utilised. Despite the lack of space, however, areas were left unoccupied in order to accommodate large crowds of people. In these places, people gathered for common purpose. During the Middle Ages and the Renaissance, squares were used for commercial purposes, as marketplaces, as well as for public festivities and executions.

Nowadays, as through the centuries, the square occupies the metaphorical and, often enough, still literal centre of the city for its populace, the physical siting of the urban cultural communal. It forms a spatial opening where public encounters can take place, surrounded by the dense tissue of private places in streets and alleyways, nooks and crannies that can be easily appropriated. It is this contrast between the darkness and secrecy of the niches in between houses, and the wide openness and light of the square that makes the latter so attractive. In the square, the gaze is free and horizontal. The square is therefore a place of light, where one can see the other in reciprocity. There are no hiding places in the middle of the square, and there are no vantage points where one can observe without being seen. In the square, the gaze is democratic and egalitarian – it therefore contests power structures of discipline and control. The square takes a political stance inherent in its sociocultural, physical and historical positioning.

As explained by Foucault (1991), disciplinary power works through an asymmetric gaze, by seeing without being seen and in this way attaining control over subjects who are exposed, as objects – while the centre of power, from whence the gaze emanates, remains hidden. Because of its openness and accessibility, the square can facilitate different relationships of power.

In contrast to hierarchical, asymmetric power production, the power of the commons is exercised on the square in the open horizontal gaze of its users. They qualify to share in power through their embodied presence. Literally and physically, those who meet on the square stand on the same level, all exposed to one another. This horizontality and equality comprises a crucial, defining feature of the commons.

The place of the commons and community

Like common land, the square is a general place for use by the community, not owned by anyone in particular. In the Middle Ages, the herd of the whole village flocked and grazed on the common fields, as they were used by all without distinction or exclusion (Coop & Brunckhorst, 1999). In an urban setting, the square can have a similar function to the rural common. Since the square is of everybody, it is a free space where the community holds sway, rather than an individual owner, or a single family. It is for the public, not the private. The square brings people together and hence speaks of a communal economy, an economy of sharing instead of exclusive property. Here, value is created through cooperation and collective use, rather than through the competing trade of commodities. Even on the marketplace, where each stall is individually owned and operated, the sellers share the marketplace itself. The marketplace itself is the embodiment of the commons.

The square offers space to a kind of entrepreneurship that is not based on the entitlements derived from private craftsmanship, but on the shared efforts of a community. In the square, one organises collectively, making use of shared resources and adhering to public regulations. The results of the enterprises undertaken on the square thus benefit the community as a whole. The space itself, where these enterprises take place, cannot be claimed by particular individuals or groups. The market may dominate on certain days, but it never makes a continuous and permanent claim on the space; the square as a common is never defined by one activity or by a single selection of people with a particular identity.

As an open space of the commons, the square is not uniform, but serves multiple, constantly changing purposes; it is everyone's because it can be anyone's, wherein lies its essential pluralism. The square itself is public and therefore it has no particular identity in the sense of a substantive significance. As an unsanctioned right, everyone can take the square, precisely because it belongs to nobody. Since the square is an inherently non-prescriptive place, it simultaneously opens up and binds together. It is nobody's home, but it can be a place where everybody feels at home. The square is communal, but this does not mean it defines the common: it is not a common denominator of sharing and feeling part of a group or club. In this sense, the square can be seen as the place where community emerges, as envisioned by Jean-Luc Nancy. This community does not consist of the aggregated sum of autonomous individuals or subjects, but is rather the expression of an inherently shared being, which is always already singular–plural, irreducible to separately existing entities. It emerges spontaneously in encounters, without a premeditated organisational model or identity, and the square is the place for this par excellence. The square is a place where common meaning is created, which constantly transforms with the then present (emergent, expressed) community.

For Nancy, the concept of community does not indicate a homogeneous entity. Our sense of community rather originates in a shared coexistence in the world, something that happens unexpectedly. Nancy (2000: 29) emphasises that everything that exists always exists together with something else. In existence, therefore, we always share the world. We are always already together with others. Even when we define ourselves as unique and autonomous subjects, we have to do this by distinguishing ourselves from others. Being, therefore, always takes place in diversity, instead of unity. The 'with' is at the core of being itself. Being-with others is not a relation that is added onto a pre-existing, autonomous state of being by itself, as the origin of being often tends to be misunderstood, according to Nancy (2000: 30–31). Rather, since being always means coexistence, we always already think and interact within a certain form of community.

This notion of community should not be essentialised or reified as a natural or original entity that forms a certain foundation for social interactions and the political formation of a society, as one can find in romantic interpretations of Rousseauian ideas about a 'natural community':

> Such a thinking constitutes closure because it assigns to community a common being, whereas community is a matter of something quite different, namely, of existence inasmuch as it is in common, but without letting itself be absorbed into a common substance. Being in common has nothing to do with communion, with fusion into a body, into a unique and ultimate identity that would no longer be exposed. Being in common means, to the contrary, no longer having, in any form, in any empirical or ideal place, such a substantial identity, and sharing this (narcissistic) 'lack of identity'. (Nancy, 1991: xxxviii)

The feeling of 'loss of communitarian intimacy' plays an important role in our historical understanding of the relation between community and society, according to Nancy (1991: 9); where society is a construct formed in order to deal with political interests, as 'a simple association and division of forces and needs', community is often seen as some kind of pure body in which people are bound together by sincere intimacy and harmonious relations. In contrast to this romantic notion, Nancy understands community as essentially ungrounded in its lack of identity. We do not produce community as if it were a piece of work, an opus, but we rather experience it in its 'inoperativeness', or its 'unworking' impact – community simply 'happens to us in the wake of society', neither as a pure form of shared intimacy, nor as a deliberately constructed agreement (Nancy, 1991: 11, 31). Nevertheless, one should add, this sense of community, which can spontaneously emerge on the square, can move people to act out politically and strive for the transformation of society.

For Nancy (1991: xxxvii), a sense of community and a sense of the political are inextricably bound to each other: 'the political is the place where community as such is brought into play'. However, just as Nancy associates an inherent lack of identity with community, political agency is also not based on a pre-established, strong subjectivity or ideology in his interpretation. The political is not based on a shared organisation, programme or identity that brings individuals together in a collective body, but on the understanding that we necessarily coexist with others, with whom we share no necessary similarities beyond a certain basic humanity and spatio-temporal concurrence. Political agency is not an act of the formation of a people around a specific programmatic claim, but rather the initial affirmation of the equality of all in irreducible difference. For Nancy, political agency begins with the awareness that we share the world on an ontologically equal basis. This initial state of being is the only state of being in which we are together on a completely equal basis. An experience of the commons can highlight this ontological equality.

Nancy is interested in the conception of the 'commons' as a drive for political agency, and traces the origin of this notion back to the cloisters in the fourteenth century.[3] The monastery used to be, in the first place, the communal possession of the community of monks, before individual monks could claim part of this possession on the basis of their membership of the monastic order to which the cloister pertained. Before monks had rights of possession, that is, they only had rights to usage. Since that period, the notion of the commons, argues Nancy, has been used to speak of the collective possessions of a community *apart* from its individual members. The idea of the commons, therefore, implies a shared coexistence that precedes individual claims to ownership, identity or governance. This understanding of commons becomes relevant for political agency, when it enables us to say 'we' without implicitly indicating a shared political programme, a shared national character, or a shared citizenship status. Nancy speaks of an experience of the commons that can literally open a space between and for people, without becoming a fixed ideology or designed blueprint for society. This space that is opened can enable us to ask questions like 'How can we think about society, government, law, not with the aim of achieving the *cum*, the common, but only in the hope of letting it come and taking its own chance, its own possibility of making sense?' (Nancy, 2010: 150).

We can encounter others, who live fundamentally different lives, at a specific place where we share a certain situation which suddenly makes us aware of the fact that we experience a common condition in one and the same world. Such an encounter can inspire collective political agency, and usually takes place in the social arena of public space. The public nature of the square, in contrast to places of private ownership, has such political implications. Traditionally, the square is therefore the designated place for the self-governance of the people. In the European tradition, we can certainly trace this back to the *agora* as the birthplace of democracy in ancient Greece, the square where the *demos* gathered to discuss the matters of the *polis*. As the site for the determination of the general interest, the *agora* spatially designated a form of direct democracy performed by all men with citizenship rights.

Today, the square still functions as the place where people go to claim direct influence on matters of governance. It is no longer a place where those with exclusive citizenship rights alone can raise their voice, but also for those who are not treated as equal citizens and hence wish to claim their rights. People who wish to militate for equality and justice in a broader sense beyond the liberal, enabling rights of citizenship, also convene here. Contestation against state authorities that are seen as not properly representing the people often takes place on the square.

David Harvey (2012: xvii) emphasises the intimate relation between the contemporary urban and citizenship, which holds a dynamic and revolutionary potential, particularly in the context of a class analysis. Harvey argues that capital, as the central authority, imposes itself nowadays as a process of homogenisation in cities through the high added value of property. Because of this process, the more central areas in the city become ever more expensive and thus inaccessible to people with lower incomes, as well as to non- or anti-capitalist alternative practices. However, the capital value of the central squares of cities is not realised, because they remain essentially undeveloped. They are therefore paradoxically positioned as centres of opposition to the hegemony of capital at the very heart of capital, the city centre. In a structural reading, squares could be seen as heterotopic spaces in the Lefebvrian sense, where a radically different political organisation can be imagined and enacted, both as demand and as an alternative. They are the social spaces where disparate groups can – and do – come together in a spontaneous moment of irruption to engage in collective action.

Colonisation of the square

The spontaneous community formation on squares is difficult to manage. Historically, institutional and governing powers have always considered squares to be dangerous meeting places of the people, the crowd, the mob, the rabble. The physical assembling of large numbers of people in public space has proven to be an effective method to pressure state powers by those who cannot make use of institutional infrastructures: 'One means by which insurgent groups overcome their general inferiority in resources is to take advantage of one resource they have – the force of numbers' (Sewell, 2001: 58). Squares therefore have a long history of colonisation, of attempts to prevent the possible empowerment of the masses.

From the edges of the square, governing powers can cast a hidden gaze over the crowds on the open plane and hence exercise a form of control. Some powers have tried to gain control over the commons by building large structures overlooking the square. These are vantage points, as Dale and Burrell (2008: 43ff.) have pointed out. According to them, the domination of the skyline is equated to the domination of the market and economic competition, once literally, now metaphorically. Architecture is used by political leaders to seduce, to impress and to intimidate. Dale and Burrell (2008: 170) develop this analysis with the example of the Vasari corridor in Florence. Typifying an architecture that separates and divides, it 'provides a superior route between office, church, garden and home for the powerful, whilst separating them physically and symbolically from the general populace below'.

In an urban environment significantly determined by its development within the framework of Christianity, the Church often arrived first at the square. While a church or cathedral dominates many squares, it is important to note that the square existed before the church. Originally, churches had no open space in front of them. Houses were built leaning against the church, using the church walls as props, as we still can see in the case of several medieval churches (e.g. the Santa Maria del Mar in Barcelona). Later, churches were built next to squares, where large crowds of people could gather for religious ceremonies. The common space became a semi-sacral arena, where the community stood in the shadow of the church. The square then became the outside portal of the cathedral, where one could admire its splendour from a distance. After the church, the king – and later the state – built palaces and halls opposite the church, thus making the square a front yard for the home of the governing authorities (e.g. the Piaza della Signoria in Florence). Then, also, the square was transformed into a place to hold military exercises, hence the common Spanish name '*plaza de armas*', which can be found in several Latin American capitals (e.g. Santiago de Chile, Lima and Havana). The crowds could thus be controlled by the military, as directed from the palace.

Given the history of squares and the attraction of this central gathering site for markets, it is unsurprising that capital – the market supreme – moved in and another, increasingly hegemonic, colonisation of the square became exercised by commerce. Originally, during the European Renaissance, warehouses and palaces of rich merchants were built around the square in order to keep an eye on the market. Nowadays, we see that banks and corporations take over squares and preside very distinctively over the communal space, privatising it and transforming the social into a space of consumption and for consumers, where one has to comply with the regulation of the owner (Potsdamer Platz has been dominated by banks since it was remodelled in the 1990s). Cafés and terraces claim a monopoly on the way one is supposed to spend time on the square (Kohn, 2004). The same generic Starbucks cafés emerge everywhere; in many squares, one is effectively no longer allowed even to eat one's own food, let alone exercise one's own activities.

The commodification of the city (above) has been furthered by the privatisation of public space, where nowadays commercial activities are favoured over other social forms of gathering. Investors as well as local authorities generate profit and income from the privatisation of the public through the taxation of its space and the arrival of private enterprises. In order to minimise the risk of unmanaged gatherings on the square, access is ever more regulated and social control tightened through regulatory measures, 'security' enforcement and privately owned urban development projects (Minton, 2006). The square as a site of contestation is rebutted by the hegemonic order through financial means, as well as other forms of disciplinary power.

In sum, the square is overlooked and controlled by the church, the government, the bank and (partially) filled in with terraces (e.g. the Zocalo in Mexico City, with the cathedral, the presidential palace and the central bank all around the same square). However, this colonisation is never complete. The square still attracts spontaneously emerging communities, which often directly oppose the powers colonising the square. Squares are not politically innocent. Since they are the place where social value arises and the public interest is defined, they are also the place of protest against dominant powers and discontent with existing injustices and inequalities (Örs, 2014: 492). The square remains the place to meet and discuss for those who are not allowed inside the palace and are thereby confined to speak from outside (as the name of the Piazza del Popolo in Rome suggests). In the contemporary context, as we know, uprisings certainly still take place in the square.

Contestation on the square

Because it is the material and symbolic place of the governing power of the people, the revolution often starts in the square, in both Western and non-Western cultures. In fact, the square tends to become synonymous with the revolution, and, in successful cases, the square is even named after it, as in the French and Cuban examples (above). It is remarkable how they still attract protestors and uprisings, even when squares have been transformed into large and anonymous expanses, as in the case of Tiananmen Square in Beijing, or when the open space is choked with traffic, as in the case of Tahrir Square in Cairo. Known for their recent cycles of protest and repression, both squares are, incidentally, the places where a previous revolution began – Mao opened the doors of the Forbidden City (and after the revolution built the headquarters of the Central Committee) on the square, and Egyptian independence from the British empire was proclaimed at Ismailiyya Square, renamed Midan al-Tahrir (Liberation Square) – indicative of a sociocultural tradition wherein the revolutionary meaning of the very name of the place becomes deeply etched into a national psyche.

In the Tiananmen and Tahrir cases, the spatial features of the square have facilitated this symbolic political function. Both places were first 'desacralised' before they were 'resacralised' in the name of the people (Sewell, 2001: 66). Tiananmen Square, for example, was a place of vertical communication between the Communist Party leadership and the anonymous masses, before it was reclaimed as a space of horizontal self-governance during the student uprising. The Tiananmen and Tahrir cases also both exemplify the loss of the people's square in its plurality, as attempts to reclaim the square were eventually violently oppressed by the authorities. In the case of Tiananmen Square, the authorities' fear of the symbolic power of the square is a reason why it is no longer used for official, ceremonial gatherings, and now functions mostly to attract foreign visitors, while anniversary gatherings for the revolution at Tahrir Square are forcibly prevented.

Nevertheless, as stated, the square remains 'a locality', an open space where horizontality reigns, despite attempts of a vertical gaze of power to colonise it. The square continues to be the main place where sparks of a sense of the commons and of political change are ignited. The occupation of squares in the context of, for example, the Indignados movement, Occupy and the Arab Spring have aimed to create space and visibility for the commitment to the commons of ordinary people, contrary to the occupation of squares by the state and hegemonic centres of power: the Church, the Crown, the army, the stock exchange. Taking place in the all-embracing, globalising phase of neoliberalism, these occupations have aimed at both top-down imposed state ideologies and capital in its urban form, protesting at the denial of heterogeneous and communal space.

In addition to the iconic squares that became symbols for a movement, occasionally other communal, public spaces in the city have also been reclaimed during recent protests, such as in city centre parks. Occupy Wall Street in New York used Zuccotti Park as a home base, which physically appears very much like a square with trees, while the Taksim Square protests in Istanbul originated and ended at the adjacent Gezi Park, a formalised, fairly open, rectangular space that operates somewhat as an extension of the square.

The occupation of Zuccotti Park during Occupy Wall Street did not only take place in reaction to the economic crisis, but also in response to the extensive segregation and policing of public space in New York City (Smithsimon, 2012). Due to gentrification, public plazas were increasingly designated for the richer segments of the population; stop-and-frisk tactics by the police filtered out undesired bodies from the public space. While the Occupy Movement reopened public space to a wider variety of people, the protests in Istanbul established a week-long common. Also in this case, the occupiers attempted to collectively reclaim a square with strong symbolic power associated with state ideology.

The Gezi Park/Taksim Square site was originally constructed on a vast plain where army barracks were located during the Ottoman empire (Örs, 2014: 492–7). As in the Tiananmen and Tahrir cases, it had been the site of an early revolutionary moment, when the barracks housed a counter-movement against the overthrow of the sultan during the establishment of the Turkish Republic. The recent protest arose when the ruling Justice and Development Party (*Adelet ve Kalinma Partisi*, AKP) attempted to impose a certain neo-Ottoman identity on the area as part of a large-scale redevelopment project. The protesters envisioned a more inclusive urban landscape and republican imagination that, following violent dispersal by the police, evolved into a process of night-time assemblies in parks around and outside the city. Here, as in the Occupy case, we see how the square can form a starting point for solidarity and for political alternatives.

A comparable reappropriation of public space for a wider community formation took place during the occupation of Syntagma Square in Greece. As Stavrides (2012: 558) notes,

> Communities create 'common space', space used under conditions decided on by communities and open to everyone. … The community is formed, developed, and reproduced through practices focused on common space. To generalise this principle: the community is developed through communing, through acts and forms of organisation oriented toward the production of the common.

A distinctive quality of the recent protests in squares, underlining the communality of the space and a reappropriation of the public arena, is the absence of specific leadership. A striking feature of recent protest movements that have gathered on squares has been their refusal to be identified with and certainly not represented by a single political organisation defining their programme or mode of communication. On the contrary, these movements have generally been characterised by their leaderless organisational structure and emerged outside of the existing networks of civil society organisations such as NGOs and trade unions, as well as political parties (Ishkanian, Glasius & Ali, 2013). While the space of the square is occupied, the event of the protest is not claimed by a specific institution, party or organisation. No one can exclusively appropriate the expressed critique of existing political and economic governance, which is seen as already for too long framed in exclusive and exclusionary terms.

The recent occupations and expressions of contestation on the square were performed by a multitude that based a 'we' not on a shared ethnicity, nationality, citizenship status or ideology, but on a sharing of the same world at an ontological level, as envisioned by Nancy. This multitude cannot be theorised as a (single) social movement and thus runs counter to a large segment of new social movement theory, where an emphasis is placed on identity claims, made especially in order to plead for equal rights for minority or 'deviant' groups. The struggle of new social movements no longer takes place only in the area of the class struggle, but also addresses social exchange and cultural production (Melucci, 1996). The civil rights, feminist and environmentalist movements, to name some prominent examples, have all employed a shared culture and collective identities in order to push for political change (Castells, 2009). This emphasis on a shared culture and identity, which provides a shared meaning and position to the movement, tends to be absent in the coming together of multitudes on a square.

The non-identitary nature of the multitude was clearly expressed in the case of the Occupy Movement. There, the widely used slogan 'We are the 99%' indicated that the only antagonistic division between friend and enemy was drawn between an elite 1%, unjustly possessing most political and economic power, and everybody else, a highly diverse multitude with wide-ranging backgrounds and sociocultural identities, but importantly unified in some sense of suffering from the economic crisis and lack of political influence:

> 'We are the 99%' highlights a division and a gap, the gap between the wealth of the top 1% and the rest of us. As it mobilizes the gap between the 1% with half the country's wealth and the other 99% of the population, the slogan asserts a collectivity. It does not unify this collectivity under a substantial identity – race, ethnicity, religion, nationality. Rather it asserts it as the 'we' of a divided people, the people divided between expropriators and expropriated. (Dean, 2011: 1)

The multitude does collectively contest injustices and unequal treatment, but not on the basis of a shared culture or identity (Stavrides, 2012: 592–3). Rather, it comes together on the basis of a shared yet heterogeneous perspective on agency. Other than the undifferentiated unity of the masses, the multitude is composed of a set of singularities, whose difference cannot be reduced to sameness (Hardt & Negri, 2004: 99). Community formation, as both Nancy and Hardt and Negri understand it, occurs in a being-together in the world with others who might be radically different from us. The inherent confrontation with difference does not always lead to recognition and consensus, but entails also insecurity and an ongoing discussion of society's features and foundations (Kaika & Karaliotas, 2014). Such a continuous questioning of fixed foundations can be found in the political agency that was recently developed, and continues to be developed on squares all over the world criticising dominant power structures that maintain deep inequalities between economic and social elites, ordinary people and especially marginalised groups.

Recent movements and uprisings – in locations as diverse as Kiev, Bangkok and Hong Kong – have not only opposed central political authority, but specifically critiqued the dominant status quo of neoliberal governance and capitalist economy. Capitalism is critiqued because it is not based on commonality but on the individual, and on ownership in the material sense instead of ownership as a sense of self or singularity that is always co-shaped by others. During the 2014 Rio protests, a whole financial and shopping thoroughfare, Paulista Avenue, was effectively converted into a square as a space of the common. In contrast to the existing power structures, squares offer a place to experiment with political agency, which is based on a notion of the commons. The multitude can act politically, not because it stands as one or has a single identity, but because in its internal diversity it also has a longing for a more just and egalitarian governance, in common.

Harvey (2012: 161–2) speaks in this sense of the creation of a 'political commons' in a central public space, as 'a place for open discussion and debate over what that power is doing and how best to oppose its reach'. In reference to various recent protest movements that occupied public squares, Harvey notes that the collective power of human bodies in public space is still the most effective instrument of opposition when all other means of access are blocked. Dhaliwal (2012) emphasises the same physical occupation of the square with an encampment as an important strategy of resistance in the Indignados movement, a strategy inspired by the occupation at Tahrir. The physical place of Tahrir Square had been crucial in enabling previously dispersed groups of protesters against the Mubarak regime to gain greater visibility and a central, easily accessible place to coordinate their actions.

Patel (2013) hypothesises that the strategies of resistance as applied at Tahrir particularly inspired protests in cities where there was a large, focal square that could be occupied, as was the case in Madrid and Barcelona, where the Indignados movement attracted large crowds of people. New spatial relations were created on these squares through mass public deliberation and horizontal decision-making in general assemblies, as opposed to the dominant, hierarchical structure of the existing political order. However, this enactment of a different form of political decision-making on the square was of a temporary nature. Eventually the camps on the squares in Spain were evicted due to a combination of police repression and the need for people to focus on their lives outside of the square. As in Istanbul the following year, an attempt was made to continue mobilisation through neighbourhood assemblies. Although the question of what sustainable effect may be expected from the efforts of movements such as Indignados remains, this might not be the most important question to ask in relation to protests that evoke the creation of a political commons. Their greater significance may lie just in their enunciation of the possibility of different social relations and forms of decision-making, which can inspire new political practices in other settings, beyond the temporary occupation of the square.

Real and direct democracy

> One of the most remarkable aspects of the Occupy Wall Street movement (OWS) is its capacity to ground itself in a struggle for a public commons. For many involved, including myself, Zuccotti Park was our public commons, our agora, just as the gardens in Union Square have been for so many years in New York. 'The agora was the center of athletic, artistic, spiritual, and political life of the city,' notes OWS activist Morgan Jenness. Yet, today, many suffer from 'agoraphobia … a fear of participating as a full citizen in the commons,' she continues. OWS challenged this logic, grounding itself in the public commons from the movement's very first day. (Shepard, 2012: 21)

The movements that demand 'real democracy' and oppose themselves to human indignation offer a space in the square for people to organise a variety of activities, in which anyone can take part at any time, thus creating a constantly evolving form of organising in which the one person can take the place of the other according to the flow of events. People continue to find inspiration in places where one can transform from a random passer-by to a participant of a general assembly, while simultaneously children are playing in an area of political protest, people doing gardening, reading books, practising yoga and discussing the latest sports results on the streets, and the energy of tense confrontation and liberation ebb and flow like the tides, everything constantly moving and transforming. Many of the protests in squares take place at election time, showing other expressions of political engagement, which form an alternative to voting. An example is the case of Spain, where the first large gatherings on Puerta del Sol took place close to the date of local and regional elections.

The communities that gather on the square typically develop decentralised and open-ended network structures, with participatory and consensus-based practices of decision-making and horizontal modes of organising. In so doing, they open up the possibility for a much more diverse and inclusive practice of democracy in which conflicting identities and opinions flourish, quite differently from the existing systems of representative liberal democracy (Maeckelbergh, 2014: 347). The political agency on the square takes place here and now, as an expression of direct, participatory democracy. Swyngedouw (2014: 123) emphasises that this agency does not articulate specific social or economic demands directed at the elites, but aims at a revisiting of the nature of 'the political'. It can take a peaceful or militant form, but is in general opposed to the rules and regulations of institutionalised security systems, which routinely prohibit large, unregulated gatherings in undesignated public space. In a political moment, any public space can be reclaimed from such regulations: 'The space of the political is to disturb the socio-spatial ordering by re-arranging it with those who stand in for "the people" or the community' (Swyngedouw, 2014: 132).

These protests should not be directly judged on their demonstrable long-term 'outcomes', let alone with respect to their immediate impact on institutional structures. They rather have a value as 'prefigurative politics', as 'a practice, movement, moment or development in which certain political ideals are experimentally actualised in the "here and now", rather than hoped to be realised in a distant future' (van de Sande, 2013: 230).[4] Again, movements of prefigurative politics do not see it as their highest goal to assume some type of durable state power, but rather exhibit an alternative, horizontal community formation (Dhaliwal, 2012: 268); the common space that is opened up in these movements indicates a threshold to new possibilities because it is not 'demarcated by defining parameters' (Stavrides, 2012: 589).

Uruguayan journalist and writer Eduardo Galeano nicely captured this kind of movement in words, while standing on the Plaza de Catalunya in Barcelona during the Indignados occupation.[5] For him, it is the enthusiasm generated in the occupation of the square that is its most important effect. Referring to the Greek origin of the word 'enthusiasm' – *entheos,* to have the Gods inside – Galeano points out that enthusiasm is experience of the intrinsic value of life, which we should not allow to be devalued by political or economic mismanagement. According to Galeano, we are currently living in an uninspired world, but the young people he saw around him during the occupation of the Plaza de Catalunya showed him that we could look beyond the threshold of this world, towards new perspectives.

This opening of a window to another possible world is more important to Galeano than any question about concrete institutional changes to which the protests and occupation of squares might lead. What interests him is what is happening at this moment, a moment in which an endless range of possibilities is announced. He makes a comparison to the experience of love in which eternity is also folded into the moment. When we truly experience love, we feel that we are really alive, and we no longer think about dying. Love is endless in the moment we experience it, as long as it lasts. This experience, Galeano continues, indicates a calculation of time other than the checks and balances that are made in the context of economic efficiency, a political system that is defined by the calculation of profit and loss. The square can thus be a place that nurtures alternative relations to the materialism underwriting the present neoliberal capitalist hegemony.

Galeano's interpretation of the events of protest on the square echoes Nancy's understanding of how unexpected events can contribute to the opening up of another world. Our co-appearance in the world is characterised by Nancy and Bailly (1991: 8) as an event, an event that cannot be grasped in a mode of thought or speech: 'The event surprises or else it is not an event', as Nancy (2001: 167) elsewhere states. The event-ness of the event can therefore never be captured in our thoughts or expectations. The meaning of the world emerges together with us in this event, and is therefore not external to this world (Nancy, 2007: 43). The event is not 'what is produced or could be shown' as the outcome, or even the entry, of guided human interactions, but rather the very happening of the unexpected – which also implies that there is not only one ideal world, but a 'multiplicity of worlds' (Nancy, 2007: 109, 169). No first origin can be designated as the point out of which the world emerged. There is nothing other than the 'happening' of the world itself that takes place in each instant, in each situation. As such, the world itself is also no 'effect of some particular operation of production', but it 'springs from all sides' (Nancy, 2001: 83).

The fact that there are more worlds possible opens the possibility of disagreement with and rejection of the one in which we find ourselves and can lead us to engage in a struggle to improve it. It is precisely the recognition that no blueprint for the world can be made that can form the basis for a struggle against injustices created by an ordering of the world which assumes to assign people to unequal, but seemingly natural positions. A single, 'true' arrangement of the world would be a foundational illusion with the unjust pretention to generate order:

> To create the world means: immediately, without delay, reopening each possible struggle for a world, that is, for what must form the contrary of a global injustice against the background of general equivalence. But this means to conduct this struggle precisely in the name of the fact that this world is coming out of nothing, that there is nothing before it and that it is without models, without principle and without given end, and that it is precisely what forms the justice and the meaning of a world. (Nancy, 2007: 54–5)

Conclusion

Flemish writer Paul van Ostaijen's ([1916] 1982) short story 'The City of Constructors' (*De stad der opbouwers*) narrates what happens in the city of Creixcroll, where the mayor has decided that demolishing buildings is too easy and morally wrong. It is therefore forbidden to tear anything down, and citizens are encouraged to build as much as possible. A building fever takes hold of the city. Everybody starts constructing new buildings. Soon there is no more space available for new buildings, and the people cannot continue to build into the heights. Consequently, the squares are all abolished and filled with buildings. This is not to everybody's liking, and an anti-building movement arises. The leader of the movement is promptly arrested and sentenced to the pillory as an example to anyone wishing to tear a construction down. His sentencing also present an excellent opportunity for a festival. However, the executioner notifies the judge that this is impossible, since there are no longer any squares and hence no place for the pillory and festivities. As soon as the people hear of this, they rebel, since they are longing for festivities. The city council is expelled and the leader of the anti-building movement is freed and named the new mayor. In his first speech standing on the balcony of the city hall he asks: 'What do the people want?' 'Squares!' they respond in unison.

Squares are the quintessential public space. They are the place where a sense of the common is created and reinforced, through a singular–plural sense of community, grounded in an open and accessible, empty and horizontal spatiality. Everybody can be equal on the square. Pluriform and spontaneous communities emerge in this place, inciting a solidarity based on new possibilities for a shared political agency, instead of a shared identity or culture. As the place of the common, squares are the privileged places at which and from where to oppose the powers that be and to imagine new worlds. Politics is not only a matter of ideas and discussions, but also of space and locality. The square is an actor in the making, bringing large numbers of people together, constituting social meaning and enabling the literal 'taking place' of protest. On the square is embedded a resistance to control as well as a sense of togetherness that can take many forms. It materialises a being in common that is not planned or designed other than through its being as a *place* in the full meaning of the word. The square thus becomes the stage of society, where the common is enacted.

Notes

1   Our analysis in this chapter is mainly based on the development of an urban environment influenced by European and Christian traditions. This is not a development, however, that is exclusive to these, and our designation of the square as a locality of the commons is also illustrated by examples from around the world.

2   The Persian-Arabic equivalent of 'square' – Latinised as '*meyd*ân', or similar – with similar forms in, for example, Sanskrit, and etymologically traced as the proto-Indo-European '*méd*ʰ*yos*' – cf. Latin '*medius*' – has a meaning of 'middle', thus specifically referencing the central siting of the square in the urban settlement.

3   Cloisters are literally the enclosed open spaces of monasteries (attached to a church), which obviously links closely to the present subject (the words 'cloister' and 'enclosure' have the same Latin root, '*clausus*', past participle of '*claudere*').

4   See van de Sande, this volume (Eds.).

5   See http://www.youtube.com/watch?v=IcCo_DbbiHo

References

Castells, M. 2009. *The Power of Identity: The Information Age: Economy, Society and Culture*, vol. II. London: Wiley-Blackwell.

Coop, P. and Brunckhort, D. (1999). 'Triumph of the commons: age-old participatory practices provide lessons for institutional reform in the rural sector', *Australian Journal of Environmental Management*, 6(2): 69–77.

Cutini, V. (2014). 'Spatial analysis of urban squares', *Tema, Journal of Land Use, Mobility and Environment*, University of Naples (special issue, June 2014).

Dale, K. and Burrell, G. (2008). *The Spaces of Organisation and the Organisation of Space*. Basingstoke: Palgrave.

Dean, J. (2011). 'Claiming division, naming a wrong', *Theory & Event*, 14(4).

Dhaliwal, P. (2012). 'Public squares and resistance: the politics of space in the Indignados movement', *Interface*, 4(1): 251–273.

Foucault, M. (1991). *Discipline and Punish, The Birth of the Prison*. London: Penguin.

Gehl, J. and Gamzoe, L. (2006) *New City Spaces*. Copenhagen: The Danish Architectural Press.

Giddings, B., Charlton, J. and Horne, M. (2011). 'Public squares in European cities', *Urban Design International*, 16(3): 202–212.

Hardt, M. and Negri, A. (2004). *Multitude*. London: Penguin.

Harvey, D. (2012). *Rebel Cities: From the Right to the City to the Urban Revolution*. London/New York: Verso.

Heidegger, M. (1971). 'Building, dwelling, thinking', in *Poetry, Language, Thought*. New York: Harper Collins.

Ishkanian, A., Glasius, M. and Ali, I. (2013). *Reclaiming Democracy in the Square? Interpreting the Movements of 2011–2012*. London: London School of Economics and Political Science.

Kaika, M. and Karaliotas, L. (2014). 'The spatialization of democratic politics: insights from indignant squares', *European Urban and Regional Studies*, 23(4): 556–570.

Kärrholm, M. (2005). 'Territorial complexity, a study of territoriality, materiality, and the use of three squares in Lund', *Nordic Journal of Architectural Research*, 1: 99–114.

Kohn, M. (2004). *Brave New Neighborhoods, the Privatization of Public Space*. New York: Routledge.

Lefebvre, H. ([1970] 2003). *The Urban Revolution*. Minneapolis: Minnesota University Press.

Lopes de Souza, M. and Lipietz, B. (2011). 'The "Arab Spring" and the city', *City*, 15(6): 618–624.

Maeckelbergh, M. (2014). 'Social movements and global governance', in M. Parker, G. Cheney, V. Fournier and C. Lands (Eds.), *Routledge Companion to Alternative Organization*. London: Routledge.

Marom, N. (2013). 'Activising space: the spatial politics of the 2011 protest movement in Israel', *Urban Studies*, 50(13): 2826–41.

Melucci, A. (1996). *Challenging Codes: Collective Action in the Information Age*. Cambridge: Cambridge University Press.

Minton, A. (2006). *What Kind of World Are We Building? The Privatization of Public Space*. London: RICS.

Moughtin, C. (2003). *Urban Design: Street and Square*. Oxford/
    Burlington, MA: Architectural Press.

Nancy, J. L. (1991). *The Inoperative Community*. Minneapolis:
    University of Minnesota Press.

Nancy, J. L. (2000). *Being Singular Plural*. Stanford, CA: Stanford
    University Press.

Nancy, J. L. (2001). *La communauté affronté* [The community
    confronted]. Paris: Galillée.

Nancy, J. L. (2007). *The Creation of the World or Globalization*. Albany:
    State University of New York Press.

Nancy, J. L. (2010). 'Communism, the word', in C. Douzinas and S.
    Zizek (Eds.), *The Idea of Communism*. London/New York: Verso.

Nancy, J. L. and Bailly, J. C. (1991). *La Comparution* [Appearance].
    Paris: Christian Bourgois Éditeur.

Örs, I. (2014). 'Genie in the bottle: Gezi Park, Taksim Square, and the
    realignment of democracy and space in Turkey', *Philosophy and
    Social Criticism*, 40(4–5): 489–498.

Patel, D. (2013). *Roundabouts and Revolutions: Public Squares,
    Coordination and the Diffusion of the Arab Uprisings*. Ithaca, NY:
    Department of Government, Cornell University.

Schiffman, R. et al. (Eds.) (2012). *Beyond Zuccotti Park: Freedom of
    Assembly and the Occupation of Public Space*. Oakland, CA: New
    Village Press

Sewell, W. H. (2001). 'Space in contentious politics', in R. Aminzada,
    J. Goldstone, D. McAdam, E. Perry, W. Sewell, S. Tarrow and C.
    Tilley (Eds.), *Silence and Voice in the Study of Contentious Politics*.
    Cambridge: Cambridge University Press.

Shepard, B. (2012). 'Occupy Wall Street, social movements, and
    contested public space', in R. Schiffman, R. Bell, L. J. Brown and L.
    Elizabeth (Eds.), *Beyond Zuccotti Park: Freedom of Assembly and
    the Occupation of Public Space*. Oakland, CA: New Village Press.

Smithsimon, G. (2012). 'A stiff clarifying test is in order: occupy and
    negotiating rights in public space', in R. Schiffman, R. Bell, L. J.
    Brown and L. Elizabeth (Eds.), *Beyond Zuccotti Park: Freedom of*

Assembly and the Occupation of Public Space. Oakland, CA: New Village Press.

Stavrides, S. (2012). 'Squares in movement', *The South Atlantic Quarterly*, 111(3): 585–596.

Swyngedouw, E. (2014). 'Where is the political? Insurgent mobilizations and the incipient "return of the political"', *Space and Polity*, 18(2): 122–136.

Van Ostaijen, P. ([1916] 1982). *Music Hall.* Amsterdam: Bert Bakker.

Van de Sande, M. (2013). 'The prefigurative politics of Tahrir Square – an alternative perspective on the 2011 revolutions', *Res Publica*, 19: 223–239.

Chapter 9

Transition towards a food commons regime: re-commoning food to crowd-feed the world

Jose Luis Vivero-Pol[1]

> There is nothing like a dream to create the future.
> *Utopia today, flesh and bone tomorrow.* (Víctor Hugo)

Introduction

Air, water and food, the three essentials our human body requires to function, vary in terms of their public–private status. Air is still considered a commons, although its commodification has already begun, with creative accounting for emissions trading schemes and quotas essentially operating as private entitlements to pollute (Bohm, Misoczky & Moog, 2012). Water is assumed as a public good, although widely being transferred to the private domain through absolute commodification of the good itself and the state transfer of consumer supply and waste-water treatment enterprises (Franco, Mehta & Veldwisch, 2013).[2] Food, however, is largely regarded as a pure private good, although wild foods could perfectly well be considered a commons but with genetic rights now an issue.

This has not always been so, and it remains less true than one might suppose, but it does represent the dominant reality in the world today. The value of food is no longer based on its many dimensions that bring us security and health, values that are related to our foundations in human society (food as culture) and the way food is produced (food as a sustainable natural resource) as well as to human rights considerations based on its essential nature as fuel for the human body (so, ultimately, the right to life). Instead, these multiple dimensions are combined with and superseded by its tradable features, thus conflating value and price (understanding the former in terms of the latter).

It is certainly true that the industrialisation and commodification of food has brought humanity many important positive outcomes, such as accessibility (by lowering prices), availability (by sufficient production to feed us all) and economic efficiency (in cultivation techniques); but it has also yielded many negative externalities and unfulfilled promises, such as pervasive hunger and mounting obesity, environmental degradation, oligopolistic control of farming inputs, diversity loss, knowledge patenting and neglect of the non-economic values of food. Here, these issues are reviewed and a transition path to a new food system outlined. Essentially, what I propose is a radically different approach to food and a better balanced governance system.

An iniquitous, inefficient and unsustainable food system

The industrial technology-dominated food system achieved remarkable outputs during the second half of the twentieth century in the form of massively increased food production and food access for millions of urban and rural consumers. Global crop output was tripled, yields raised and food prices lowered with the move away from traditional habits and skills to more systematically organised production methods in tandem with the introduction and extension of a wide range of agrarian and technical developments (UNEP, 2009; Bindraban & Rabbinge, 2012). This represented a huge achievement, with massive reductions in the numbers of poor and undernourished people in the world (FAO, IFAD & WFP, 2015). Manifestly, the increase in food production outpaced population growth, benefiting most people in the world and the poor in particular. However, this commodification of the industrial food system did not come for free, and many undesirable externalities are now evident.

The most relevant systemic fault lines in the current food system – even, that is, within its own mono-dimensional framework – may be identified as inequality, inefficiency and unsustainability within the planetary boundaries.[3] Crucially, these cannot be reversed or corrected by simply applying lip service to a system – or food regime – based on sustainable intensification that focuses on technological challenges but obscures social and power imbalances (Godfray & Garnett, 2014).

Iniquitous: many eat poorly to enable others to eat badly and cheaply

In global terms, we have a troublesome relationship with food, since so many people in so many parts of the world have food-related health issues. In all but two countries in the world, for example, significant parts of the population suffer from three common forms of malnutrition: stunting, anaemia and obesity (IFPRI, 2014). In fact, an estimated 2.3 billion people globally, fully one-third of the world's population, are either overweight or undernourished (GAIN, 2013). Even as hunger continues to be the largest single contributor to maternal and child mortality worldwide, with more than three million children dying every year from hunger-related causes (Black et al., 2013), obesity causes some 2.8 million deaths annually (WHO, 2012), with well over a billion people expected to be classified as obese by 2030 (Kelly et al., 2008). Despite years of international anti-hunger efforts and rising levels of gross national income and per capita food availability in a world that already produces enough food to adequately feed all, the number of hungry people has only been declining at a very slow pace since 2000 (FAO, IFAD & WFP, 2015).[4]

Among the painfully ironic paradoxes of the globalised industrial food system are the facts that half of those who grow 70% of the world's food are hungry (ETC Group, 2013), yet food kills the wealthy. Moreover, an ever greater share of the food supply is being diverted to livestock feeding and biofuel production, and, most shockingly of all perhaps, a third of the total global food production ends up in the garbage every year, enough to feed 600 million hungry people (FAO, 2011). Agriculture is also highly demanding of water – using 96% of world non-marine supply (de Marsily, 2007) – but it makes poor use of it, while the industrial system diminishes the nutritious properties of many foods, through cold-room storage, (over-)peeling and boiling, and transformation processes (Sablani, Opara & Al-Balushi, 2006). Consequently, the overemphasis on the production of empty and cheap calories that renders obesity a growing global pandemic is set alongside highly energy inefficient food production, as we need 10 kcal to produce 1 kcal of food (Pimental & Pimental, 2008). This is not to mention profound and growing issues related to a range of ecological issues, including soil degradation and biodiversity loss.

Inefficient: oil-based food systems are nothing without state subsidies

Agronomically speaking, the industrial food system is not performing much better than did the traditional, pre-industrial one, insofar as productivity gains have been uneven across crops and regions (Evenson & Gollin, 2003) and global increases in output have been confined to a limited range of cereal crops (rice, maize and wheat), with smaller increases in crops such as potato and soybean (Godfray et al., 2010). Increased cereal production has supported the increase in chicken and pig production, but also led to less diverse, overly meat-based diets, with a concomitant increase in the ecological footprint. It also appears that yield improvements are already reaching a plateau in the most productive areas of the world (Ray et al., 2013). Thus, many scientists and agri-food corporations are calling for a 'Greener Revolution' or 'Green Revolution 2.0' (Pingali, 2012), led by genetic engineering and urban-based production, including alternative (e.g. hydroponics) production systems.

In fact, a closer examination reveals that the industrial food system is not more efficient in material or financial terms than the more sustainable food systems (traditional or modern organic, permaculture, etc.), as it is heavily subsidised and greatly favoured by tax exemptions (e.g. through national fertiliser subsidies.the EU Common Agricultural Policy and the US Farm Bill).[5] The great bulk of national agricultural subsidies in OECD countries are mostly geared towards supporting the intensive use of chemical inputs and energy and helping corporations lower the prices of processed foods. Yet, and contrary to popular wisdom, alternative, organic systems are more productive, both agronomically and economically; they are more energy efficient, have a lower year-to-year variability (Smolik, Dobbs & Rickerl, 1995) and depend less on government payments (Diebel, Williams & Llewelyn, 1995). Strikingly, small and medium-sized family farms tend to have higher agricultural crop yields per hectare than larger farms, mainly because they manage resources better and use labour more intensively (FAO, 2014).

We need to go beyond price in the market, where the major driver for agri-businesses in the mono-dimensional approach to food-as-commodity is merely to maximise profit. We need to value the multiple dimensions of food for human beings. This is highlighted by the issue of inequality and social justice, with the 1.2 billion poorest people presently accounting for just 1% of world consumption, while the billion richest consume 72% (UN, 2013).

Unsustainable: eating our planet and beyond

Since the Industrial Revolution in the latter part of the eighteenth century, humans have been altering the Earth on an unprecedented scale and at an increasing rate, radically transforming the landscape, using (up) natural resources and generating waste (Hoekstra & Wiedmann, 2014). Our human society is living beyond its means, and the current environmental effects of human activity are just not sustainable. For example, the appropriation of natural resources is currently exceeding available biocapacity by 50% (Borucke et al., 2013). Many respected researchers are warning of an apocalypse triggered by climate disruption and resource scarcity within this century (Motesharrei, Rivas & Kalnay, 2014).

On this road to perdition, food production (largely, the industrial food system) has become a major driving force pushing the environment beyond its planetary boundaries. Agriculture, as the largest user of land (Ramankutty et al., 2008), is now the dominant force behind many environmental threats, including biodiversity loss and degradation of land and freshwater, while it is responsible for 30–35% of global greenhouse gas emissions (Foley et al., 2011). Of the two – global water and total ecological – footprints analysed in the 2014 'Living Planet' report, food systems account for 92% (WWF, 2014) and a third, respectively.[8] Human society is quickly approaching two planetary thresholds associated with unsustainable food systems: land conversion to croplands and freshwater use (Rockstrom et al., 2009). This situation will only worsen as growing water and food needs due to population growth, climate change, consumption shift towards meat-based diets and biofuel development exacerbate the already critical challenges to planet boundaries. If we extrapolate current food consumption and production trends, humanity will need three Earths by 2050 to meet demand (Clay, 2011).

The commodification of food

The conversion of goods and activities into commodities has been a dominant force transforming all societies since at least the mid-nineteenth century (Polanyi, 1944; Sraffa, 1960), a process that has led to today's dominant industrial system that fully controls international food trade and is increasingly exerting a monopoly over agricultural inputs (seeds, agro-chemicals, machinery), while both feeding and failing the world's population, and in an unsustainable manner, as indicated (above). Essentially, food has evolved into a private, mono-dimensional commodity in a global market of mass consumption. The mechanisms of enclosure, or restriction and privatisation of common resources through legislation, excessive pricing and patents, have obviously played a major role in limiting access to food as a commons, while the social construct of food as a commodity denies its non-economic attributes in favour of its tradable features, namely durability, external beauty and the standardisation of naturally diverse food products, leading to a neglect of nutrition-related properties of food alongside the emphasis on cheap calories.[9] These cheap calories not only come at great cost to the environment (the sustainability issue) and human health (the obesity issue) but have also lowered prices for producers and promoted cheap rural labour, forcing small-scale farmers to flee to urban areas (Roberts, 2013). Increasingly, the result is a mass transformation of the rurality into paradoxically barren, depopulated zones of production.

Under capitalism, the value in use (a biological necessity) is highly dissociated from its value in exchange (price in the market), giving primacy to the latter over the former (McMichael, 2009). Food as a pure commodity can be speculated in by investors, modified genetically and patented by corporations, or diverted from human consumption just to maximise profit, the latest twist on this being the substitutionism of food commodities (Araghi, 2003), whereby tropical products (sugar cane, palm oil, etc.) are replaced by agro-industrial (and pharmaceutical) by-products (for high fructose corn syrup, margarine, etc.). Ultimately, industrial food systems alienate food consumers from food producers in socially disembedded food relations, and in so doing, it is argued, they damage societal well-being (disconnecting us from nature and deeply undermining a holistic sense of life). Indeed, the development of food as a pure commodity radically opposes the other dimensions, rather important for our survival, self-identity and community life: as a basic human need to maintain vital functions (Maslow, 1943), as a pillar of every national culture (Montanori, 2006), as a fundamental human right that should be guaranteed to every citizen (UN,

1966) and as a part of a wider ecological context involving sustainable production. This reduction of the food dimensions to one of a commodity explains the roots of the failure of the global food system (Zerbe, 2009). Moreover, market rules not only put prices to goods, but, in doing so, markets corrupt their original nature (Sandel, 2012). The commodification of food crowds out non-market values and the idea of food as something worth caring about.[10]

It is becoming obvious to many that the reliance on massively distorted (imperfect) market forces, industry self-regulation and public–private partnerships to improve public health and nutrition does not result in substantial evidence to support any major claim for their effectiveness in preventing hunger and obesity, let alone in reducing environmental threats (Fuchs, Kalfagianni & Havinga, 2011; Hawkes & Buse, 2011). On the contrary, trans-national corporations are major drivers of the latter two of these – in the case of obesity epidemics, for example, by maximising profit from increased consumption of ultra-processed food and drink (Monteiro et al., 2011). The conventional industrialised food system, dominated by mega-corporations, is basically operating to accumulate and under-price calorie-based food resources and maximise the profit of food enterprises instead of maximising the nutrition and health benefits of food to all (Rocha, 2007; Clapp & Fuchs, 2009).

The increase in consumption of unhealthy food and drinks is occurring fastest now in poorer ('developing') countries, where the food systems are highly penetrated by foreign multinationals (Stuckler et al., 2012) and the state institutions are usually not capable of controlling corporate leverage; but even in advanced countries, the only mechanisms that have clearly been shown to prevent the harm caused by unhealthy commodities are public regulation and market intervention (Moodie et al., 2013). This means more state, not less. Governed by self-interest, markets will not provide an adequate quantity of public goods, such as health, nutrition and hunger eradication, which have enormous benefits to human beings but are non-monetised, as the positive externalities cannot be captured by private actors.

With millions of people needlessly dying prematurely each year from hunger and obesity in a world of ample food supplies, nobody can dispute the need for change. There is a clear and urgent demand for unconventional and radical perspectives to be brought into the debate to look for possible solutions and a transition towards a fairer, healthier and sustainable food system. In addressing this need, the power of food to generate a substantial critique of the neoliberal corporate and industrialised production and service system and to harness multiple and different alternative collective actions should not be underestimated (McMichael, 2000). Food is a powerful weapon for social transformation.

The historical evolution of food governance: from commons to commodity

Historically, human societies have developed different institutional arrangements at local and regional levels to produce, manage and consume food, and the major features of these have often been an unstable balance between private provision, state guarantees and collective actions based on the commons of land, water and labour force.[11] Food has certainly not always been regarded as a pure commodity devoid of other important dimensions. For millennia, indeed, food was generally cultivated in common and regarded as a sacred item in a mythological context;[12] many societies have considered, and still consider, food as a commons, as well as the land and water and its forests and fisheries; and the consideration different civilisations have assigned to food-producing commons is rather diverse and still evolving.

Historical developments and present evidence

While anthropological studies have been reporting on tribal societies with essentially communal hunter-gatherer and gardening arrangements for food since the nineteenth century, historical records indicate commons-based agrarian food-production systems ranging from the early Babylonian empire (Renger, 1995) and ancient India (Gopal, 1961) to medieval Europe (Linebaugh, 2008) and early modern Japan (Brown, 2011). This historical diversity is reflected in the current world's wealth of proprietary schemes for natural resources. Even now, the private arrangements that characterise industrial agriculture are not universally prevalent in large areas of the world, where subsistence, traditional and agro-ecological types of agriculture are still the norm. Actually, in simple population numbers, small, traditional farmers with mixed proprietary arrangements for natural resources are greatly in the majority, with, for example, just 27 million farmers working with tractors as compared to 250 million using animal traction and over a billion working just with their hands and hand-tools.

Across the world, commons-based land and food systems are often found in relatively 'wild', depopulated territories, such as in parts of the Asian interior (e.g. in Mongolia), the hills of Borneo and the Amazon rainforest. In sub-Saharan Africa, about 500 million people still rely on food from communal lands

(Kugelman & Levenstein, 2013), and tribes regard themselves as custodians of the land for future generations rather than its owners, and the land-plots are usually inalienable and legally recognised (Ike, 1984). There are well-documented examples of functioning food-producing commons in Fiji (Kingi & Kompas, 2005) and Mexico's *Ejidos* (Jones & Ward, 1998), while in countries such as Taiwan, India, Nepal and Jamaica, land ownership by ethnic minorities is also granted as common land.

At the other end of the world developmental scale, in the US there are lobster fisheries (Wilson, Yan & Wilson, 2007), in the Scandinavian countries anyone can forage wild mushrooms and berries under the consuetudinary Everyman's Rights (La Mela, 2014), and the Spanish irrigated *huertas* (vegetable gardens) are a well-known and robust institution (Ostrom, 1990), while there are thousands of surviving community-owned forests and pasturelands across Europe where livestock freely range, including the *Baldios* in Portugal, crofts in Scotland, *Obste* in Romania and *Montes Vecinales en Mano Comun* in Spain. In fact, and despite centuries of encroachments, misappropriations and legal privatisations, millions of hectares of common land have survived in Europe.[13]

Historical and modern studies have demonstrated that the traditional food-producing common-pool resources systems were, and still are, efficient in terms of resource management (Ostrom, 1990; De Moor, Shaw-Taylor & Warde, 2002).[14] Common lands have been pivotal for small-farming agriculture everywhere in Europe throughout history, as sources of organic manure, livestock feedstock and pastures, cereals (mostly wheat and rye in temporary fields), medicinal plants and wood. Peasants pooled their individual holdings into open fields that were jointly cultivated, and common pastures were used to graze their animals. In Fiji, the proprietary regime in commons, organised under traditional practices, seems to improve farm productivity and efficiency as compared to modern farming enterprises (Kingi & Kompas, 2005). Many Latin American countries, such as Brazil, Honduras, Venezuela and Nicaragua, have formally recognised the communal rights of indigenous communities to their traditional territories (Robson & Lichtenstein, 2013), with common lands preserving habitats better than privately owned ones (Ortega-Huerta & Kral, 2007). Likewise, in Asia, over 10,000 villages in Vietnam are managing more than two million hectares of community forests with good results (Marschke at al., 2012), while common-pool resources, covering 25.6% of India's territory, are estimated to contribute 20–40% of household annual incomes nationwide (Chopra & Gulati, 2001). The agricultural and related utility of commons to human societies has enabled them to survive up to the present day, despite the waves of enclosure.

The enclosure of the commons

Enclosure (originally 'inclosure') is the act of transferring resources from the commons to purely private ownership (Linebaugh, 2008) or the decrease of accessibility of a particular resource due to privatisation, transferring common properties 'from the many to the few' (Benkler, 2006). The commons-based food-producing systems in Europe started to be dismantled soon after the end of the medieval age, when royal and feudal landowners began enclosing common lands. Through legal and political manoeuvres, wealthy landowners marked and hedged off sections of the commons for their own profit, impoverishing many villagers and ultimately destroying their communitarian way of life in what Polanyi (1944) dubbed 'a revolution of the rich against the poor'.

The latter part of the eighteenth and early nineteenth centuries saw a second wave of enclosures. During this period, of course, enclosure was also globalised, as a feature of the colonising activities of the maritime empires of Western Europe claiming native lands in the Americas, Africa, southern Asia and Australasia. The processes undoing the communal regime continued through the late nineteenth and the twentieth centuries, relentlessly pursued by the state and wealthy private owners realising the value of land for the production of food and other goods (cotton, sugar, rubber, etc.). Internationally, it was first promoted by imperial trading companies supplying to mother countries and then continued in the post-colonial context; in North America, it took the form of the barbed-wire fencing of open range, while in the Soviet Union, land was 'consolidated' in the collectivisation drive of the 1930s; generally, it was propelled by the need for rural areas to supply the growing urban populations and later justified by the idea that communal property was an obstacle to economic growth and did not guarantee conservation of resources (Serrano-Alvarez, 2014). Finally, over the last thirty years, common lands have suffered a third, global wave of commodification and enclosure, 'land-grabbing' spurred by the dominant neoliberal doctrine and competition for non-renewable natural resources and supported now by the evolutionary theory of land rights (Barnes & Child, 2012).[15] Community-owned lands are presently under huge pressure from voracious states and profit-seeking investment funds, backed initially by the IMF and World Bank in the framing of structural adjustment programmes and lately by drivers such as growing populations, shifting (more meat-based) diets, water and soil constraints, climate vagrancies and long-term investments in natural resources with increasing demand (Cotula, 2012).

The third wave of privatisation of food-producing commons systems was theoretically and ideologically grounded on Demsetz's (1967) narrative that considers rising populations to drive property values and communal resources upward, leading to increased demand and disputes over natural resources, which can only be solved through government-led property formalisation. Using this theory, Alchian and Demsetz (1973) stated that the increase in the value of a communal resource will inevitably lead to the enclosure of the commons; and Hardin (1968) wrote his famous tragedy. However, with a varied set of successful case studies of common-pool resources, Ostrom (1990) was able to demonstrate the incorrect assumptions of this approach, both theoretical and practical.

The enclosure and commodification of goods owned by no one or by all is expanded and deepened by capitalism's insatiable appetite through the modern mechanisms of copyrights, permits, restrictive legislation and taxes on specific activities (Lucchi, 2013). For example, plant genetic resources in the form of seeds used to be public goods until scientific and technological progress enabled us to synthesise DNA, modify living organisms and reconstruct genes in the laboratory; now, private enterprises are granted copyright licences for the genes and seeds they develop. Enclosure of the commons can be driven by protection rather than profit-seeking, such as the quotas that are set to address the problem of declining open-sea fish stocks due to overexploitation (Young, 2003) or the licences and seasonal permits that regulate fishing from the seashore and collecting mushrooms in the forest in many areas and certain seasons. Such regulation can also lead to the development of new markets for the services common-pool resources provide, as in the case of polluting air emissions.

Re-commoning food and the food commons regime: theoretical underpinnings

In this scenario, a re-commoning of food would certainly open up the prospect of a transition towards a new food regime in which the several food dimensions are properly valued and primacy rests in its absolute need for human beings. But in order to move in this direction, the very foundations of how economics and social sciences perceive foods and foodstuff have to be reassessed; first, food excludability and rivalry has to be contested. Although foods, as single items or classes, may be rivals, this need not be the case for the category of food as a whole in a condition of plenty, where there is, in fact, enough for all. Food, as a renewable resource, can be unlimited, provided its production matches global consumption. And food certainly ought not to be an excludable good to anyone. The commodification of natural resources essential for human beings can be reversed. Moving from possibility to prescription, a re-commoning of food is argued for here as an essential paradigm shift. It leads us towards a new regime, which could be called the food commons.

The evolution of different food regimes

A food regime is a rule-governed structure of food production and consumption on a world scale, with food regime theory – initially formulated by Friedmann (1987) and further expanded by Friedmann and McMichael (1989) and McMichael (2009)

– standing as a historical and sociological approach aimed at accounting for recent past and present global food systems. This theoretical framework critically analyses agricultural modernisation, underlining the pivotal role of food in the global political economy and describing the main features of stable food regimes and their fault lines, crises and transitions. The regimes approach also considers shifting balances of power among states and private corporations and NGOS, along with the rules and institutions that govern the food system and permit capital accumulation. This type of analysis depicts food as a source of power and domination, a power that lies in its material and symbolic functions linking nature, human survival, health, culture and livelihood. Among the variables that define food regimes, one may mention the role of food in capital accumulation, where and how food is produced and by whom, major patterns of food flows and control of food production.

Implicit in the historical narrative of de-commoning, three major food regimes have been identified, namely the UK-centred colonial-diasporic regime (1870–1930s), the US-centred mercantile-industrial regime (1950s–70s) and the global corporate regime (1980s–2000s), leaving definition of the situation nowadays open, as either the final stage of the corporate regime or a troublesome transition towards something new. The UK-centred colonial-diasporic regime, defined by food imports from settler and tropical colonies to provision emerging industrialisation in the UK and Europe, developed mono-cultures in tropical colonies and national agricultural systems in settler colonies. The US-centred mercantile-industrial regime, during the post-war reconstruction and Cold War, had export subsidies and US food aid as the international mechanism to deter expansion of communism and extend industrialisation in the Global South, when agriculture became more specialised, industrialised (with longer food chains) and commodified (detached from place of origin and non-commercial values), the term 'agribusiness' being coined at Harvard University in the mid-1950s. This regime was also characterised by the technology-driven Green Revolution, land reform schemes to fully privatise community-owned land-plots together with the dismantling of Global South diverse agricultures for their transformation into mono-crop agro-exporting systems, the development of processed durable foods and the anathematising of food self-sufficiency.

Now the global corporate-environmental (neoliberal) regime defines a set of rules institutionalising corporate power in the world food system (Pechlaner & Otero, 2010), deepening the commodification of food by radically undermining its non-monetary dimensions (food as a human need, a human right and a cultural determinant) and developing its tradable features through the transnational financialisation of food; this is expressed in the transformation of food (for fuel and animal feeds) and its substitutionism (food providing foodstuffs) facilitated by international capital (e.g. supply/demand controls through futures markets). Other pertinent features of this regime include the supermarket revolution and the vertical expansion of retail corporations into production, corporate oligopolies that control the major share of food-producing inputs (seeds, agrochemicals, tractors, etc.) and the privatisation of agricultural research and enclosure of food-related knowledge commons by intellectual proprietary rights (patents and lawsuits) – the latter a modernist narrative that sees small-scale farmers and peasants as residuals in furthering commodification, homogenising and decontextualising of the 'food from nowhere' and extending yet greater WTO-style agricultural liberalisation.

This regime, however, has been attenuated by strong, citizen-led, environmental and justice concerns that have advocated for state-regulated governance of corporative activities within the domains of animal welfare, fair trade, organic and healthy products and their land-grabbing and conversion of forestry into arable land and while also partially restraining the absolute commodification of natural resources (e.g. endangered species used as luxury goods and air as carbon trade schemes).[16] 'Sustainable Intensification' and 'Green Growth' are the new narratives developed by the duopolistic neoliberal states and corporations to respond to those concerns (OECD, 2013).

From food sovereignty to a food commons regime

Transitions between regimes stem from internal strains, claims by marginalised groups, power imbalances, outrageous capital accumulation and contradictory relations resulting in crisis and transition towards a successor regime (Le Heron & Lewis, 2009). Currently, the corporate food regime (industrial food system) is coming under increasing scrutiny by aware citizens, combatant grassroots organisations, concerned governments and small-scale stakeholders in the food chain as the major fault lines of inequality, inefficiency and unsustainability become ever more evident. Within this apparently and at least potentially transitional framework, characterised by experimentation, tension and contestation (Burch & Lawrence, 2009), Wittman (2011) has recently posited food sovereignty as an alternative paradigm, a driver of change that is challenging the corporate food regime with the aim of replacing it with a new one, provisionally named the food sovereignty regime.

Although one may be sympathetic to the sociological critique of the corporate regime, however, one cannot ignore the fact that the highly politicised, counter-hegemonic food sovereignty paradigm has only managed to draw a small number of countries to its side (Ecuador, Bolivia, Nicaragua and Mali). Originating from rural organisations and food producers (peasants, small-scale farmers, indigenous peoples, fishermen), this movement has not yet fine-tuned legitimate concerns about healthy and local food, a return to nature and less polluting forms of food consumption by urban citizens and food consumers. Indeed, up to 2013, the leaders of the food sovereignty movement were rather oblivious to the range of recent academic and urban developments that were gaining momentum and beginning to shape urban and national policies in several countries (below). This is gradually changing now.

The worldwide Via Campesina movement, from which the idea of food sovereignty originated, is now becoming appreciative of the strategic importance of urban-based alternative initiatives.[17] This is important, since the predominantly rural social movement of food producers from the Global South and the predominantly urban alternative food networks of food consumers and producers from the North do need to combine if some sort of grand coalition of the counter-hegemonic movement is to coalesce as the key development in the transition towards what could be more appropriately termed a 'food commons' regime.

The food commons regime, as the name implies, would fundamentally rest on the idea of food as a commons, which means revalorising the different food dimensions that are relevant to human beings (value in use) – food as a natural resource, human right and cultural determinant – and thus, of course, reducing the tradable dimension (value in exchange) that has rendered it a mere commodity. This regime would inform an essentially democratic food system based on sustainable agricultural practices (agro-ecology) and open-source knowledge (creative commons licences) through the assumption of relevant knowledge (recipes, agrarian practices, public research, etc.), material items (seeds, fish stocks, etc.) and abstract entities (transboundary food safety regulations, public nutrition, etc.) as a global commons.

The food commons regime will entail a return move from corporate–state control to a collective, polycentric and reflexive governance, a shift of power from a state–private sector duopoly in food production, transport and distribution to a tricentric governance system, where the third pillar would be the self-regulated, civic, collective actions for food that are emerging all over the world. Presently developing a narrative of valuing food as an essential, natural good, produced and consumed with others and thus a bonding tie in human cultures, these alternative food initiatives will be the organisational drivers of change. In short, a food commons regime will be governed in a polycentric manner by food citizens (Gomez-Benito & Lozano, 2014) who develop food democracies (De Schutter, 2014) that value the different dimensions of food (Vivero-Pol, 2013).

Crowdsourcing the transition to food as a commons

At present, the globalised world appears to be at the crossroads of two food transition streams: the well-advanced nutritional transition from vegetable- to meat-dominated diets (Popkin,

2003) and the incipient food transition from oil-dependent industrial agriculture to more environmentally friendly and less resource-intense food systems. This nascent stream can evolve towards re-localised, organic food systems, spurred by non-monetised food dimensions and alternative food movements (Heinberg & Bomford, 2009) or else to a deepening of the globalised, profit-driven path of the industrial food system supported by science and technology developments under the 'sustainable intensification' or 'green growth' paradigms (UN, 2012) (e.g. renewable energy-based hydroponics in city towers owned by retail corporations). The dominant path that emerges from these transitions will determine the new food paradigm.

The proposal here is for a transition towards a food commons regime based on an adequate valuation of all the dimensions of food. This transition path approaches food as a commons, contrary to the history of previous transitions, in which food was first privatised and then commodified. Although some authors have already suggested this (Ausin, 2010), none of the major analyses produced in the last decades on the fault lines of the global food system and the very existence of hunger has ever questioned the nature of food as a private good (World Bank, 2008; UK Government, 2011).[18] Following the mainstream rationality, although the most pressing issue is the lack of food access, this only becomes such an intractable problem due to the assumed private nature of food and its absolute excludability.

While the present proposal may seem to be going against the tide of history, that might be regarded rather as a strength than a weakness; as Einstein noted, problems cannot be solved with the same mind-set that created them. And in fact, the consideration of food as a commons is already in play and increasing, with (a) food-related elements being considered as global or national commons (or global public goods, as they are usually termed) in the context of civil struggles for re-commoning, and (b) an evolving governance of the food system being constructed from bottom-up grassroots urban and rural initiatives.[19] These do, in fact, all point in the same direction, towards a very possible future.

Material and non-material food-related elements already considered as commons

There is a need to reclaim a discourse and a rationale of the commons to be applied to food at global, regional/national and local levels. The good news is that policymakers and academics are already moving from the stringent economic definition of public/private goods to a more fluid idea of global public goods or commons. Regarding terminology here, the former, 'public goods', is more usually assumed in the hegemonic discourse of major institutions, while the latter 'commons' tends more to be taken up by alternative activist advocates, with both variously appended by 'global' or 'national'.

The important thing is that these public goods/commons, however named, are available worldwide, essential for all human beings, regarded as things that need not and should not be treated as excludable and rival, and whose production and distribution cannot be governed exclusively by one state. Such goods need to be governed in a common manner as to be beneficial for all (Kaul & Mendoza, 2003), even if not everybody is contributing to or paying for their provision. In addition to the material commons and related practices already considered, the following represents a (non-exhaustive) list and commentary of aspects of food that are currently considered as global public goods or global commons.

Edible plants and animals produced by nature
Since nature's unenclosed territories (e.g. Antarctica, the deep ocean) are largely assumed as global commons, the natural resources in these are commons as well (including, therefore, fish stocks and marine mammals) (Christy & Scott, 1965; Bene, Phillips & Allison, 2011). Although there are complicating factors depending on national and international proprietary rights schemes, the basic assumption remains in place for fish stocks in coastal areas, as well as for wild foods produced in urban and rural areas.

Genetic resources for food and agriculture
Agro-biodiversity represents a continuum of wild-to-domesticated diversity that is crucial to people's livelihood and well-being and is therefore considered as a global commons (Halewood, Lopez-Noriega & Louafi, 2013). Some authors and many activists and producers demand genetic resources be patent-free to enable innovation, free exchange and peer-to-peer breeding (Kloppenburg, 2010). Seed exchange schemes – to some extent a phenomenon growing in response to private development programmes and enclosure attempts – are considered networked-knowledge goods with non-exclusive access and use conditions, produced and consumed by communities.[20]

Traditional agricultural knowledge
A commons-based patent-free knowledge contributes to global food security by upscaling and networking grassroots

innovations for sustainable and low-cost food production and distribution (Brush, 2005). There is widespread evidence of a growing appreciation of the value of this indigenous traditional knowledge to adapt to climate change (Altieri & Nicholls, 2013) and nurture alternative visions of development (Pretty, Toulmin & Williams, 2011)

Modern, science-based agricultural knowledge produced by public institutions

Universities, national agricultural research institutes and the Consultative Group for International Agricultural Research (CGIAR), UN and EU centres all produce public science, widely considered as a global commons (Gardner & Lesser, 2003). Although there is pressure on the public production of information by corporate interests, research into something as basic as food is not popularly challenged as a common good. Research funds should be directed towards sustainable practices and agro-ecology knowledge developed by those universities and research centres instead of further subsidising industrial agriculture.

Cuisine, recipes and national gastronomy

Food, cooking and eating habits are inherently part of our culture; gastronomy is regarded as a creative accomplishment of humankind, like music or architecture. Recipes are an excellent example of commons in action, and creativity and innovation are still dominant in this copyright-free domain of human activity (Barrere, Bonnard & Chossat, 2012). The culinary and convivial commons dimension of food has received little systematic attention from the food sovereignty movements (Edelman, 2014), although it is being properly valued by alternative food networks (Sumner, Mair & Nelson, 2010).

Food safety

Epidemic disease knowledge and control mechanisms are widely considered as global public goods, as zoonotic pandemics are public bads with no borders (Richards, Nganje & Acharya, 2009). Issues in this domain are already governed through a tricentric system of private sector self-regulating efforts, governmental legal frameworks and international institutional innovations, such as the *Codex Alimentarius*.

Nutrition, including hunger and obesity imbalances

There is a growing consensus that health and good nutrition can be considered as global public goods with global food security recently joining that debate in international forums (Page, 2013). Although this political approach is still at an early stage of development, far from established as a general understanding and certainly without a negotiated global statement as yet, it is an idea that is taking hold, as witness FAO Director General Graziano da Silva in the closing remarks of the International Conference of Nutrition, November 2014.[21]

Food price stability

Extreme food price fluctuations in global and national markets, such as the world experienced in 2008 and 2011, are a public bad that benefits none but a few traders and brokers. The basic fact that those acting inside the global food market have no incentive to supply the good or avoid the bad is increasingly observed, and the need for concerted, state-based action to provide such a global public good as food price stability is gaining traction (Timmer, 2011).

It goes without saying that all governments have a deep concern about food issues, which is why subsidised food production and consumption policies are the norm all over the world (see above, on subsidies to industrial agriculture) and food-related civil unrest is as much a subject of political concern nowadays as it ever has been (Holt-Gimenez & Patel, 2009). For all governments, food is a very particular good as it is an essential need and thus highly regulated and heavily subsidised. Indefensibly, the political discourse of the OECD and WTO calls for a dismantling of national trade barriers and subsidised agriculture in developing countries while developed nations maintain massively subsidised food systems at home. Yet this hypocritical approach merely reflects the incoherence between the dominant narrative of the neoliberal model (food as a pure commodity) and the *realpolitik* most governments pursue (food as a de facto public good). Since food is strategically governed, massively supported and strongly protected by public institutions, provided by collective actions in thousands of traditional and post-industrial collective arrangements (as listed above, with others like farmers' markets, various types of food cooperatives, producer–consumer associations, etc.) and yet largely distributed by market rules, why should we not consider it a commons or public good, as we do with education and health? Shifting the dominant discourse on food and food system governance from the private sphere to the commons arena would open up a whole new world of economic, political and societal innovations

The tricentric governance of the food system as the transition path

Local transitions towards the organisation of local, sustainable food production and consumption are taking place today across the world.[22] Directed on principles along the lines of Elinor Ostrom's (1990, 2009) polycentric governance, food is being produced, consumed and distributed by agreements and initiatives formed by state institutions, private producers and companies, together with self-organised groups under self-negotiated rules that tend to have a commoning function by enabling access and promoting food in all its dimensions through a multiplicity of open structures and peer-to-peer practices aimed at sharing and co-producing food-related knowledge and items.[23] The combined failure of state fundamentalism (in 1989) and so-called 'free market' ideology (in 2008), coupled with the emergence of these practices of the commons, has put this tricentric mode of governance back on the agenda. The further development of tricentric governance will comprise (combinations of) civic collective actions for food, the state and private enterprise.

(a) *Civic collective actions for food* (alternative food networks, AFNs) are generally **undertaken at local level to begin with and aim to** preserve and regenerate the commons that are important for the community (food as a common good). There have been two streams of civic collective actions for food running in parallel: the challenging innovations taking place in rural areas, led by small-scale, close-to-nature food producers, increasingly brought together under the food sovereignty umbrella, and the AFNs exploding in urban and peri-urban areas, led on the one hand by concerned food consumers who want to reduce their food footprint, produce (some of) their own food, improve the quality of their diets and free themselves from corporate-retail control, and on the other by the urban poor and migrants in the developing world motivated by a combination of economic necessity and a desire to maintain their old food sovereignty and links to land. Over the last twenty years, these transition paths have been growing in parallel but disconnected ways, divided by geographical and social boundaries. But the maturity of their technical and political proposals and reconstruction of *rurban* connections[24] have paved the way for a convergence of interests, goals and struggles. Large-scale societal change requires broad, cross-sector coordination. It is to be expected that the food sovereignty movement and the AFNs will continue (and need) to grow together, beyond individual organisations, to knit a new (more finely meshed and wider) food web capable of confronting the industrial food system for the common good.

(b) *The state* has as its main goal the maximisation of the well-being of its citizens and will need to provide an enabling framework for the commons (food as a public good). The transition towards a food commons regime will need a different kind of state, with different duties and skills to steer that transition. The desirable functions are shaped by partnering and innovation rather than command-and-control via policies, subsidies, regulations and the use of force. This enabling state would be in line with Karl Polanyi's (1944) theory of its role as shaper and creator of markets and facilitator for civic collective actions to flourish. This state has been called partner state (Kostakis & Bauwens, 2014) and entrepreneurial state (Mazzucato, 2013).

The partner state has public authorities as playing a sustaining role (enabling and empowering) in the direct creation by civil society of common value for the common good. Unlike the Leviathan paradigm of top-down enforcement, this type of state sustains and promotes commons-based peer-to-peer production. Amongst the duties of the partner state, Silke Helfrich mentioned the prevention of enclosures, triggering of the production/construction of new commons, co-management of complex resource systems that are not limited to local boundaries or specific communities, oversight of rules and charts, care for the commons (as mediator or judge) and initiator or provider of incentives and enabling legal frameworks for commoners governing their commons.[25] The entrepreneurial state, meanwhile, fosters and funds social and technical innovations that benefit humanity as public ideas that shape markets (such as, in recent years, the Internet, Wi-Fi, GPS), funding the scaling up of sustainable consumption (like the Big Lottery Fund supporting innovative community food enterprises that are driving a sustainable food transition in the UK)[26] and developing open material and non-material resources (knowledge) for the common good of human societies. Public authorities will need to play a leading role in support of existing commons and the creation of new commons for their societal value.

(c) *The private sector* presents a wide array of entrepreneurial institutions, encompassing family farming with just a few employees (FAO, 2014), for-profit social enterprises engaged in commercial activities for the common good with limited dividend distribution (Defourny & Nyssens, 2006) and transnational, 'too-big-to-fail' corporations that exert near-monopolistic hegemony on large segments of the global food supply chain (van der Ploeg, 2010). The latter are owned by unknown (or difficult to track) shareholders whose main goal is primarily geared to maximise their (short-term) dividends rather than equitably produce and distribute sufficient, healthy and culturally appropriate food to people everywhere.[27] During the second half of the twentieth century, the transnational food corporations won market share and dominance in the food chain, although space, customers and influence is being regained, spurred by consumer attitudes towards corporate foods and the sufficiently competitive (including attractive) entrepreneurial features of family farming (which still feeds 70% of the world's population) and other, more socially embedded forms of production, such as social enterprises and cooperatives.[28]

The challenge for the private sector, therefore, is to adjust direction, to be driven by a different ethos while making profit – keeping, indeed, an entrepreneurial spirit, but also focusing much more on social aims and satisfying needs. Or, put the other way around, the private sector role within this tricentric governance will operate primarily to satisfy the food needs unmet by collective actions and state guarantees, and the market will be seen as a means towards an end (well-being, happiness, social good) with a primacy of labour and natural resources over capital. Thus, this food commons transition does not rule out markets as one of several mechanisms for food distribution, but it does reject market hegemony over our food supplies since other sources are available, a rejection that will follow from a popular programme for provisioning of and through the food commons (popular in the sense that it must be democratically based on a generalised public perception of its goodness and efficacy).

According to the typology developed by Harvey et al. (2001), food can be provided by four types of agencies, based on different principles: market (based on demand–supply market rules), state (based on citizen rights or entitlements), communal (based on reciprocal obligations and norms) and domestic (do-it-yourself or household provision based on family obligations). By encouraging (politically and financially) the development of non-market modes of food provisioning (state and/or communal) and (similarly, in parallel) limiting the influence of market provisioning, we can rebuild a more balanced tricentric food system (Boulanger, 2010). In plain words, governments will support private initiatives whose driving force is *not* shareholder value maximisation (e.g. family farming, food cooperatives, producer–consumer associations), while citizen/consumers will exert their consumer sovereignty by prioritising food with a meaning (local, organic, fair, healthy) beyond the purely financial (not just the cheapest). The private sector will also, or primarily (depending on the details of any particular tricentric mix), trade undersupplied, specialised and gourmet foodstuffs (food as a private good) and it may also rent commonly owned natural resources[29] to produce food for the market. Enterprises will further emerge around the commons that create added value to operate in the marketplace, but should probably also support the maintenance and expansion of the commons they rely on.

The transition period for this regime and paradigm shift should be expected to last for several decades, a period when we will witness a range of evolving hybrid management systems for food similar to those already working for universal health/education systems. The era of a homogenised, one-size-fits-all global food system will be replaced by a diversified network of regional food-sheds designed to meet local needs and put culture and values back into our food system (The Food Commons, 2011). The big food corporations will not, of course, meekly allow their power to be diminished, and they will, inevitably, fight back by keeping on doing what has enabled them to reach such a dominant position today: legally (and illegally) lobbying governments to lower corporate tax rates and raise business subsidies, mitigating restrictive legal frameworks (related to GMO labelling, TV food advertising, local seed landraces, etc.) and generally using the various powers at their disposal to counter alternative food networks and food-producing systems. To emphasise, the confrontation will continue over decades, basically paralleling and in some ways reversing, in fact, the industrialisation and commodification path that has led us to this point.

Appropriate combinations of self-regulated collective actions, governmental rules and incentives, and private sector entrepreneurship should yield good results for food producers, consumers, the environment and society in general. The tricentric governance schemes will be initiated at both local and regional scales, as they imply a different way of organising the territory: smaller bio-regions with stronger local authorities, community-based civic collective actions and nested markets to supply unmet needs, supported by a partner and also an entrepreneurial state with a better balance of command-and-control measures and reflexive governance tools. Regarding socioeconomic and environmental sustainability, the governance of food as a commons will rest on three premises: (a) the bonds and multidimensional value systems of the food-producing communities, (b) the tricentric governance mechanisms steered by partner states that regulate the food production, distribution and consumption, and (c) the sustainability of the food-producing systems to maintain food footprints within ecological boundaries and to produce good food economically and efficiently.

Concrete proposals for re-commoning the future

In the developmental process of re-commoning food, the initial transition phase should witness greater levels of public sector involvement. States have a vital role to play, as throughout history (De Moor, 2008), by enabling legal and financial frameworks for collective actions to maximise the common interest (e.g. taxing and incentive schemes, public subsidies, relatively relaxed regulations for collective actions). The state must be seen as a funding and operational instrument to achieve society's well-being, including food security. However, the leading role of the state should gradually be shifted to self-initiated collective actions by producers and consumers, as the public provision of food should not surpass the net benefits yielded by the self-organised and socially negotiated food networks (Bollier, 2003). This will be crucial in order to avoid the pitfalls of the old-style socialist command economies. Therefore, there should be a devolutionary emphasis further enabling and promoting local organisation, agents and agencies (local governments, local entrepreneurs and local self-organised communities).

Second, if food is to be considered a commons, the legal, economic and political implications will go far beyond the territories of the hungry, as the food system governance will bring (further) extra-territorial obligations (Kent, 2008), as pertaining to the global nature of this common good. Until now, advocacy for anti-hunger measures has been based on demonstrating the economic and political impacts that hunger imposes on human societies (Grantham-McGregor et al., 2007) or highlighting the links between food insecurity, social unrest and productivity losses (Messner & Cohen, 2008); alternative, non-economic arguments, such as moral obligation, public health considerations, social cohesion and human rights approaches have largely been neglected (Sidel, 1997; Pinstrup-Andersen, 2007). Considering food as a commons will provide the rationale underpinning these non-economic arguments.

Therefore, food will be kept out of trade agreements dealing with pure private goods (Rosset, 2006), and there will thus be a need to establish instead a transnational commons-based governing system for production, distribution and access to food, such as the agreements proposed for climate change (Griggs et al., 2013), future generations (Gardiner, 2014) and universal health coverage (Gostin & Friedman, 2013). This will pave the way for more binding legal frameworks to fight hunger (MacMillan & Vivero-Pol, 2011) and guarantee the right to food for all, as well as reinforce cosmopolitan global policies (Held, 2009) and fraternal ethics (Gonthier, 2000). A scheme for universal food coverage[30] would materialise the new narrative, guaranteeing a daily minimum amount of food for all citizens (HLPE, 2012) and thereby protecting the only human right declared as fundamental in the International Covenant on Economic, Social and Cultural Rights (ICESCR): freedom from hunger. The food coverage will probably need to be implemented as a basic food entitlement (van Parijs, 2005) or a food security floor, similar to the social protection floor proposed by Deacon (2012). As an immediate mechanism, every state should guarantee a minimum wage to a level at least equal to the value of the food basket.

There are legal and ethical grounds for banning futures trading in agricultural commodities, as speculation on food has a major impact on international and domestic prices and only benefits speculators. Considering food as a commons will prioritise the use of food for human consumption, and thus limit non-consumption uses. Additionally, it will serve to backstop the narrative to reverse the excessive patenting of life, helping to apply the principles of free software to the food and nutrition security domain. The patents-based agricultural sector appears to be retarding or even deterring the scaling up of agricultural and nutritional innovations (Boldrin & Levine, 2013), while the freedom to copy positively promotes creativity, as can be seen, for example, in the fashion industry and the computer world (Raustiala & Sprigman, 2012). Millions of people innovating with locally adapted patent-free technologies have a far greater capacity to find adaptive and appropriate solutions to the global food challenge than a few thousand scientists in expensive laboratories and research centres (Benkler, 2006).

Conclusion: crowd-feeding the world with meaningful food

This text posits that a fairer and more sustainable food system that takes food as a commons will revalorise its non-monetary dimensions (as an essential resource, human right, cultural item and tradable asset) as against the dominant industrial food system's mono-dimensional approach to food as a commodity. With the global and local food production and distribution systems no longer exclusively governed by market rules, institutional arrangements based on collective actions, appropriate legal collective entitlements, adequate funding and political support can also be given due consideration by politicians and academics. Self-regulated collective actions for food represent a third pillar of the governance of the evolving food system. The state–market duopoly in food provision will need to re-accommodate this mounting force of citizen actions to reclaim food as a commons. Food can and must be shared, given for free and guaranteed by the state as well as cultivated by many and also traded in the market. The world cannot be fed by profit-seeking corporations treating food as a commodity, as we know now. We all need to be involved in food governance; the world should be crowd-fed by billions of small producers that are also consumers.

Food will be better governed by collective actions than by the rules of supply and demand. Unlike the market, the food commons are about cooperation, sharing, stewardship, equity, self-production, sustainability, collectiveness, embeddedness and direct democracy from local to global. Crucially, they involve civic collective actions for food built upon civic engagement, food conviviality, reducing consumption of ultra-processed foods and increasing seasonal and local products. This invokes a radical paradigm shift from individual competitiveness as the engine of progress via endless growth towards collective cooperation as the driver of happiness and the common good. The inherent sociability of *Homo sapiens* (Fiske, 1991) will enable the *Homo cooperans* to substitute the *Homo economicus* when dealing with our natural essentials.[31]

The de-commodification of food implies a delinkage of commodities and well-being, acceptance of free food schemes as part of the welfare state and increase in the proportion of goods consumed and services utilised outside both the formal market and the public (state) sphere. The re-commoning of food involves a transition towards a new food regime in which primacy rests on the absolute needs of human beings and the different dimensions of food are properly valued. Such a food commons regime is one for which the world is eminently ready.

The institutional arrangements that govern local food systems and people's capacity for collective action will be essential agencies in any reconfiguration of the global food system to render it fairer and more sustainable. Finding the adequate balance between the tricentric institutional setup envisaged in the programme for a food commons regime as sketched here will be one of the major challenges for humankind to address in the coming century. We need to develop a food system that, first, provides for sustainable nutrition for all and, second, provides meaning, and not just utility, to food production, trading and consumption (Anderson, 2004). To achieve such a food system, we need to reconsider how food is regarded by our society, not merely or fundamentally as a privatised commodity but rather and crucially as a common good.

Notes

1   The author gratefully acknowledges co-funding from the Belgian Science Policy Office, under the project Food4Sustainability (BRAIN-be contract BR/121/A5) and the European Commission, under the PF7-projects BIOMOT (grant agreement 282625, http://www.biomotivation.eu) and GENCOMMONS (ERC grant agreement 284).

2   The denationalisation of water provision services has become highly contested in many cities, such as Paris, Budapest, Jakarta and Dar el Salaam; see http://www.remunicipalisation.org; http://www.world-psi.org/sites/default/files/documents/research/dh-remunicipalisation_presentation-ppt.pdf

3   Planetary boundaries: thresholds in Earth-system variables that, if traversed, could generate unacceptable change in the biophysical processes of the world's natural environments (Rockstrom et al., 2009).

4   Malnutrition leads to the squandering of 11% of GNP, but just 1% of total overseas development assistance goes to nutrition programmes (IFPRI, 2014).

5   See http://www.voanews.com/content/fertilizer-subsidy-costs-could-outweigh-benefits/1693403.html; EU (2012); http://ec.europa.eu/agriculture/statistics/factsheets/pdf/eu_en.pdf; http://capreform.eu/the-us-farm-bill-lessons-for-capreform/

8   The latter is an estimate made by the author based on data from the Global Footprint Network, including footprints of croplands, grazing lands and fishing grounds. http://www.footprintnetwork.org

9   Cheap calories: low-cost sources of dietary energy such as refined grains, added sugars and fats, which, inexpensive and tasty, together with salt form the basis of ultra-processed industrial food; the more nutrient-dense lean meats, fish, fresh vegetables and fruit are generally more costly because they are less highly subsidised (Drewnowski & Darmon, 2005).

10   E.g. recipes associated with some types of food, the conviviality of cropping, cooking or eating together, the local names of forgotten varieties and dishes or the traditional moral economy of food production and distribution, materialised in the ancient and now proscribed practices of gleaning or famine thefts.

11   Within these three categories, of course, a wide range of different rights and duties can be identified, related to access, withdrawal, management, exclusion and alienation, being the result of complex societal arrangements by different human groups (Schlager & Ostrom, 1992).

12   Many types of food are still endowed with sacred beliefs (quinoa was sacred for the Peruvian Incas, cows are sacred and inedible for Hindus, etc.) and their production and distribution thus governed by non-market rules.

13   Mostly used for grazing, common lands still cover 9% of the surface of France (Vivier, 2002), for example, more than 10% in Switzerland, 4.2% in Spain (Lana-Berasain & Iriarte-Goni, 2015) and 4% in England and Wales. http://www.nationalarchives.gov.uk/help-with-your-research/research-guides/common-lands/; http://ec.europa.eu/eurostat/statistics-explained/index.php/Farm_structure_survey_%E2%80%93_common_land; http://webarchive.nationalarchives.gov.uk/20130822084033http://www.defra.gov.uk/wildlife-countryside/protected-areas/common-land/about.htm

14   The same can be said of community-managed forests, worldwide (Porter-Bolland et al., 2012).

15   There are currently 1,550 million hectares of cultivated land, a resource that is becoming increasingly scarce (Lambin et al., 2013).

16   NGOs such as Carbon Trade Watch, Carbon Market Watch and Redd Monitor are advocating against the EU Emissions Trading Scheme. See http://www.carbontradewatch.org, http://carbonmarketwatch.orgwww.redd-monitor.org

17   E.g. see the final Declaration of La Via Campesina during the World Social Forum (Tunisia, April 2013). At http://www.viacampesina.org/en/index.php/actions-and-events-mainmenu-26/world-social-forum-mainmenu-34/1405-to-reclaim-our-future-we-must-change-the-present-our-proposal-for-changing-the-system-and-not-the-climate

18   This is evident in the global food security policy documents 'MDG and WFS Plans of Action', the 'CFS Global Strategic Framework for Food Security and Nutrition 2012', the 'G-8 New Alliance for Food Security and Nutrition 2012', the 'G-20 L'Aquila Food Security Initiative', 'The G-20 Action Plan on Food Price Volatility And Agriculture 2012' and the 'World Economic Forum New Vision for Agriculture' (see Vivero-Pol, 2013).

19   Although not yet acknowledging themselves as part of the same movement, grassroots collective-based initiatives related to, e.g., degrowth, food sovereignty, commoners, peer-to-peer, veggies, *buen vivir*, happiness index, open knowledge, occupy and indignados are building a new way of producing, transforming and consuming food.

20   See, e.g., the Open Source Seed Initiative, recently launched at the University of Wisconsin-Madison. http://www.opensourceseedinitiative.org/about/

21   http://www.fao.org/about/meetings/icn2/friday-21-november/en/

22   E.g. food swaps in Australia, food growing and free harvest in Belgium, food gleaning in the UK, food policy councils in Canada (Toronto) and Brazil (Belo Horizonte), food trusts and community-supported agriculture in the US and local food-sheds in New York, and the Slow Food movement originating in Italy and now extended to 150 countries.

23   Peer-to-peer: the ability to freely associate with others around the creation of common value; alternatively, 'communal shareholding': the non-reciprocal exchange of an individual with a totality, being the totality of the commons (Fiske, 1991).

24   A term created by Bauer and Roux (1976) to describe the blurred boundaries between urban and rural spaces in ever-growing metropolitan areas where area-specific economic activities and social relations in urban and rural areas influence each other, the food system being a paradigmatic case.

25   See Silke Helfre's notes in the Partner State entry at the P2P Foundation. http://p2pfoundation.net/Partner_State

26   Making Local Food Work is a five-year £10 million programme funded by the Big Lottery Fund and delivered by the Plunkett Foundation that helps people to take control of their food supply by supporting a range of community food enterprises across England. At http://www.makinglocalfoodwork.co.uk

27   Shareholder value maximisation is detrimental for company performance in the medium and long term insofar as it subtracts money from profits to be distributed to short-sighted shareholders and stock buybacks instead of being used to reinvest in company assets, higher salaries, fair payments to suppliers, research and innovation or social responsibility (Chang, 2011).

28   The total turnover of the food-producing cooperative sector in 2012 was US$0.6 trillion, and growing every year despite

the global financial crisis (International Co-operative Alliance, 2014). This information was collected from 523 cooperatives from 30 countries involved in the production, processing and marketing of agricultural goods for members. The agriculture and food cooperative sector is the second biggest in the world, after finance, and includes some huge enterprises, such as the Japanese National Federation of Agricultural Co-operatives (USD$56.8 billion turnover), the South Korean NH Nonghyup (US$50.7 million, with 2.4 million members and a financing system serving 37 million customers) and the Fonterra Cooperative Group in New Zealand (US$16.2 billion).

29   Owned by trusts (in the US), local communities (in Europe or Africa, see above) or the state.

30   An idea called for by Nobel prize-winner Amartya Sen. At http://www.governancenow.com/news/regular-story/amartya-sen-bats-universal-food-coverage

31   The *Homo economicus* concept, launched in the nineteenth century by the philosopher John Stuart Mill, sees humans as rational and narrowly self-interested actors whose main goal in the market is to maximise utility as consumers and economic profit as producers (Persky, 1995); in contrast, the *Homo cooperans* idea regards people as primarily motivated by cooperation, the common of their society, community or group, and to improve their environment (De Moor, 2013).

References

Alchian, A. A. and Demsetz, H. (1973). 'Property right paradigm', *Journal of Economic History*, 33: 16–27.

Altieri, M. A. and Nicholls, C. I. (2013). 'The adaptation and mitigation potential of traditional agriculture in a changing climate', *Climatic Change*. doi: 10.1007/s10584-013-0909-y

Anderson, M. (2004). 'Grace at the table', *Earthlight*, 14(1).

Araghi, F. (2003). 'Food regimes and the production of value: some methodological issues', *The Journal of Peasant Studies*, 30(2): 41–70.

Ausin, T. (2010). 'El derecho a comer: Los alimentos como bien público global' [The right to eat: food as a global public good],

Arbor, Ciencia, Pensamiento y Cultura [Arbor, science, thought and culture], 745: 847–858.

Barnes, G. and Child, B. (2012). 'Searching for a new land rights paradigm by focusing on community-based natural resource governance', *Proceedings of Annual World Bank Conference on Land and Poverty*. Washington, DC: World Bank. At http://www. landandpoverty.com/agenda/pdfs/paper/barnes_full_paper.pdf

Barrere, C., Bonnard, Q. and Chossat, V. (2012). 'Food, gastronomy and cultural commons', in E. Bertacchini, G. Bravo, M. Marrelli and W. Santagata (Eds.), *Cultural Commons. A New Perspective on the Production and Evolution of Cultures*. Cheltenham: Edward Elgar Publishing.

Bauer, G. and Roux, J. M. (1976). *La rurbanisation ou la ville éparpillée* [Rurbanisation or the scattered city]. Paris: Ed. Du Seuil.

Bene, C., Phillips, M. and Allison, E. H. (2011). 'The forgotten service: food as an ecosystem service from estuarine and coastal zones', in *Ecological Economics of Estuaries and Coasts. Reference Module in Earth Systems and Environmental Sciences. Treatise on Estuarine and Coastal Science*, 12. Waltham, MA: Academic Press.

Benkler, Y. (2006). *The Wealth of Networks. How Social Production Transforms Markets and Freedom*. New Haven, CT: Yale University Press.

Bindraban, P. and Rabbinge, R. (2012). 'Megatrends in agriculture – views for discontinuities in past and future developments', *Global Food Security*, 1–2: 99–105.

Black, R. E. et al. (2013). 'Maternal and child undernutrition and overweight in low-income and middle-income countries', *The Lancet*, 382(9890): 367–478.

Bohm, S., Misoczky, M. C. and Moog, S. (2012). 'Greening capitalism? A Marxist critique of carbon markets', *Organization Studies*, 33(11): 617–638.

Boldrin, M. and Levine, D. K. (2013). 'The case against patents', *Journal of Economic Perspectives*, 27(1): 3–22.

Bollier, D. (2003). *Silent Theft. The Private Plunder of Our Common Wealth*. New York: Routledge.

Borucke, M. et al. (2013). 'Accounting for demand and supply of the biosphere's regenerative capacity: the national footprint accounts' underlying methodology and framework', *Ecological Indicators*, 24: 518–533.

Boulanger, P. M. (2010). Three strategies for sustainable consumption. *S.A.P.I.EN.S*, 3(2). At http://sapiens.revues.org/1022

Brown, P. C. (2011). *Cultivating Commons: Joint Ownership of Arable Land in Early Modern Japan*. Honolulu: University of Hawaii Press.

Brush, S. B. (2005). 'Farmers' rights and protection of traditional agricultural knowledge', *CAPRI Working Paper 36*. Washington, DC: International Food Policy Research Institute.

Burch, D. and Lawrence, G. (2009). 'Towards a third food regime: behind the transformation', *Agriculture and Human Values*, 26(4): 297–307.

Chang, H. J. (2011). *23 Things They Don't Tell You about Capitalism*. London: Penguin Books.

Chopra, K. and Gulati, S. C. (2001). *Migration, Common Property Resources and Environmental Degradation: Interlinkages in India's Arid and Semi-arid Regions*. New Delhi: Sage.

Christy, F. T. and Scott, A. (1965). *The Common Wealth in Ocean Fisheries; Some Problems of Growth and Economic Allocation*. Baltimore: Johns Hopkins Press.

Clapp, J. and Fuchs, D. (Eds.) (2009). *Corporate Power in Global Agrifood Governance*. Cambridge, MA: MIT Press.

Clay, J. (2011). 'Freeze the footprint of food', *Nature*, 475: 287–289. doi: 10.1038/475287a

Cotula, L. (2012). 'The international political economy of the global land rush: a critical appraisal of trends, scale, geography and drivers', *Journal of Peasant Studies*, 39(3–4): 649–680.

De Marsily, G. (2007). 'An overview of the world's water resources problems in 2050', *Ecohydrology and Hydrobiology*, 7(2): 147–155.

De Moor, M. (2008). 'The silent revolution: a new perspective on the emergence of commons, guilds, and other forms of corporate collective action in Western Europe', *International Review of Social History*, 53 (Supplement): 179–212.

De Moor, M. (2013). *Homo cooperans. Institutions for Collective Action and the Compassionate Society*. Inaugural Lecture, Utrecht University, August.

De Moor, T., Shaw-Taylor, L. and Warde, P. (Eds.) (2002). *The Management of Common Land in North West Europe c. 1500–1850*. Turnhout: Brepols Publishers.

De Schutter, O. (2014). *The Transformative Potential of the Right to Food*. Report of the Special Rapporteur on the right to food to the UN Human Rights Council, A/HRC/25/57.

Deacon, B. (2012). 'The social protection floor', *CROP Poverty Brief*. At http://www.crop.org/viewfile.aspx?id=415

Defourny, J. and Nyssens, M. (2006). 'Defining social enterprise', in M. Nyssens (Ed.), *Social Enterprise. At the Crossroads of Market, Public Policies and Civil Society*. London: Routledge.

Demsetz, H. (1967). 'Toward a theory of property rights', *American Economic Review*, 57(2): 347–359.

Diebel, P. L., Williams, J. R. and Llewelyn, R. V. (1995). 'An economic comparison of conventional and alternative cropping systems for a representative northeast Kansas farm', *Review of Agricultural Economics*, 17(3): 120–127.

Drewnowski, A. and Darmon, N. (2005). 'The economics of obesity: dietary energy density and energy cost', *American Journal of Clinical Nutrition*, 82(1): 265S–273.

Edelman, M. (2014). 'Food sovereignty: forgotten genealogies and future regulatory challenges', *Journal of Peasant Studies*, 41(6): 959–978.

ETC Group (2013). 'With climate change … Who will feed us? The industrial food chain or the peasant food webs?' At http://www. etcgroup.org/sites/www.etcgroup.org/files/Food%20Poster_ Design-Sept042013.pdf

Evenson, R. E. and Gollin, D. (2003). 'Assessing the impact of the Green Revolution, 1960 to 2000', *Science*, 300(5620): 758–762.

EU (2012). *Comparative Analysis of Agricultural Support within the Major Agricultural Trading Nations*. Directorate General for Internal Policies. Brussels: European Union.

FAO (2011). *Global Food Losses and Food Waste. Extent, Causes and Prevention*. Rome/Gothenburg: Food and Agriculture Organization/Swedish Institute of Food and Biotechnology.

FAO (2014). *The State of Food and Agriculture. Innovation in Family Farming*. Rome: Food and Agriculture Organization.

FAO, IFAD and WFP (2015). *The State of Food Insecurity in the World*. Rome: Food and Agriculture Organization, International Fund for Agricultural Development-World Food Programme.

Fiske, A. P. (1991). *Structures of Social Life: The Four Elementary Forms of Human Relations*. New York: Free Press.

Foley, J. A. et al. (2011). 'Solutions for a cultivated planet', *Nature*, 478: 337–342. doi: 10.1038/nature10452

Franco, J., Mehta, L. and Veldwisch, G. J. (2013). 'The global politics of water grabbing', *Third World Quarterly*, 34(9): 1651–75.

Fraser, E. D. G. and Rimas, A. (2011). *Empires of Food. Feast, Famine and the Rise and Fall of Civilizations*. London: Arrow Books.

Friedmann, H. (1987). 'International regimes of food and agriculture since 1870', in T. Shanin (Ed.), *Peasants and Peasant Societies*. Oxford: Basil Blackwell.

Friedmann, H. and McMichael, P. (1989). 'Agriculture and the state system: the rise and fall of national agricultures, 1870 to the present', *Sociologia Ruralis*, 29(2): 93–117.

Fuchs, D., Kalfagianni, A. and Havinga, T. (2011). 'Actors in private food governance: the legitimacy of retail standards and multistakeholder initiatives with civil society participation', *Agriculture and Human Values*, 28(3): 353–367.

GAIN (2013). *Access to Nutrition Index. Global Index 2013*. Utrecht: Global Alliance for Improved Nutrition.

Gardiner, S. M. (2014). 'A call for a global constitutional convention focused on future generations', *Ethics & International Affairs*, 28(3): 299–315.

Gardner, B. and Lesser, W. (2003). 'International agricultural research as a global public good', *American Journal of Agricultural Economics*, 85(3): 692–697.

Godfray, H. C. J. et al. (2010). 'Food security: the challenge of feeding 9 billion people', *Science*, 327: 812–818.

Godfray, H. C. J. and Garnett, T. (2014). 'Food security and sustainable intensification', *Philosophical Transactions of the Royal* Society of *London. Series B, Biological Sciences*, 369(1639): 20120273.

Gomez-Benito, C. and Lozano, C. (2014). 'Constructing food citizenship: theoretical premises and social practices', *Italian Sociological Review*, 4(2): 135–156.

Gonthier, C. D. (2000). 'Liberty, equality, fraternity: the forgotten leg of the trilogy', *McGill Law Journal*, 45: 567–589.

Gopal, L. (1961). 'Ownership of agricultural land in ancient India', *Journal of the Economic and Social History of the Orient*, 4(3): 240–263.

Gostin, L. O. and Friedman, E. A. (2013). 'Towards a framework convention on global health: a transformative agenda for global health justice', *Yale Journal of Health Policy Law and Ethics*, 13(1): 1–75.

Grantham-McGregor, S., Cheung, Y. B., Cueto, S., Glewwe, P., Richter, L., Strupp, B. and the International Child Development Steering Group (2007). 'Development potential in the first 5 years for children in developing countries', *The Lancet*, 369: 60–70.

Griggs, D. et al. (2013). 'Sustainable development goals for people and planet', *Nature*, 495 (21 March).

Halewood, M., Lopez-Noriega, I. and Louafi, S. (Eds.) (2013). *Crop Genetic Resources as a Global Commons. Challenges in International Law and Governance*. Abingdon: Earthscan-Routledge.

Hardin, G. (1968). 'The tragedy of the commons', *Science*, 168 (13 December).

Harvey, M. A., McMeekin, A., Randles, S., Southerton, D., Tether, B. and Warde, A. (2001). 'Between demand and consumption: a framework for research', *CRIC Discussion Paper* No. 40. Manchester: University of Manchester.

Hawkes, C. and Buse, K. (2011). 'Public health sector and food industry interaction: it's time to clarify the term "partnership" and be honest about underlying interests', *European Journal of Public Health*, 21(4): 400–401.

Heinberg, R. and Bomford, M. (2009). *The Food and Farming Transition: Toward a Post-Carbon Food System*. Santa Rosa, CA: The Post Carbon Institute.

Held, D. (2009). 'Restructuring global governance: cosmopolitanism, democracy and the Global Order', *Millennium: Journal of International Studies*, 37(3): 535–547.

HLPE (2012). *Social Protection for Food Security*. A report by the High Level Panel of Experts on Food Security and Nutrition of the Committee on World Food Security, Rome.

Hoekstra, A. Y. and Wiedmann, T. O. (2014). 'Humanity's unsustainable environmental footprint', *Science*, 344(6188): 1114–17.

Holt-Gimenez, E. and Patel, R. (2009). *Food Rebellions: Crisis and the Hunger for Justice*. Oxford: Fahumu Books.

IFPRI (2014). *Global Nutrition Report 2014. Actions and Accountability to Accelerate the World's Progress on Nutrition*. Washington, DC: International Food Policy Research Institute.

Ike, D. N. (1984). 'The system of land rights in Nigerian agriculture', *American Journal of Economics and Sociology*, 43(4): 469–480.

International Co-operative Alliance (2014). *World Co-operative Monitor. Exploring the Co-operative Economy 2014*. Trento: International Co-operative Alliance and EURICSE. At http://www. euricse.eu/en/worldcooperativemonitor

Jones, G. A. and Ward, P. M. (1998). 'Privatizing the commons: reforming the ejido and urban development in Mexico', *International Journal of Urban and Regional Research*, 22(1): 76–93.

Kaul, I. and Mendoza, R. U. (2003). 'Advancing the concept of public goods', in I. Kaul, P. Conceição, K. Le Goulven and R. U. Mendoza (Eds.), *Providing Global Public Goods: Managing Globalization*. New York: Oxford University Press.

Kelly, T., Yang, W., Chen, C. S., Reynolds, K. and He, J. (2008). 'Global burden of obesity in 2005 and projections for 2030', *International Journal of Obesity*, 32: 1431–37.

Kent, G. (Ed.) (2008). *Global Obligations for the Right to Food*. Lanham, MD: Rowman and Littlefield.

Kingi, T. T. and Kompas, T. F. (2005). 'Communal land ownership and agricultural development: overcoming technical efficiency constraints among Fiji's indigenous sugercane growers', *International and Development Economics Working Papers idec05-11*, Australia National University. At https://crawford.anu.edu.au/degrees/idec/working_papers/IDEC05-11.pdf

Kloppenburg, J. (2010). 'Impeding dispossession, enabling repossession: biological open source and the recovery of seed sovereignty', *Journal of Agrarian Change*, 10(3): 367–388.

Kostakis, V. and Bauwens, M. (2014). *Network Society and Future Scenarios for a Collaborative Economy*. London: Palgrave MacMillan.

Kugelman, M. and Levenstein, S. L. (2013). *The Global Farms Race: Land Grabs, Agricultural Investment and the Scramble for Food Security*. Washington, DC: Island Press.

La Mela, M. (2014). 'Property rights in conflict: wild berry picking and the Nordic tradition of allemansrätt', *Scandinavian Economic History Review*. doi:10.1080/03585522.2013.876928

Lambin, E. F. et al. (2013). 'Estimating the world's potentially available cropland using a bottom-up approach', *Global Environmental Change*, 23: 892–901.

Lana-Berasain, J. M. and Iriarte-Goni, I. (2015). 'Commons and the legacy of the past. Regulation and uses of common lands in twentieth-century Spain', *International Journal of the Commons*, 9(2): 510–532.

Le Heron, R. and Lewis, N. (2009). 'Theorising food regimes: intervention as politics', *Agriculture and Human Values*, 26: 345–349.

Linebaugh P. (2008). *The Magna Carta Manifesto. Liberties and Commons for All*. Oakland: University of California Press.

Lucchi, N. (2013). 'Understanding genetic information as a commons: from bioprospecting to personalized medicine', *International Journal of the Commons*, 7(2): 313–338.

MacMillan, A. and Vivero-Pol, J. L. (2011). 'The governance of hunger. Innovative proposals to make the right to be free from hunger a reality', in M. A. Martín-López and J. L. Vivero-Pol (Eds.), *New Challenges to the Right to Food*. Cordoba/Barcelona: CEHAP/ Editorial Huygens.

Marschke, M., Armitage, D., van An, L., van Tuyen, T. and Mallee, H. (2012). 'Do collective property rights make sense? Insights from central Vietnam', *International Journal of the Commons*, 6(1): 1–27.

Maslow, A. (1943). 'A theory of human motivation', *Psychological Review*, 50(4): 370–396.

Mazzucato, M. (2013). *The Entrepreneurial State. Debunking Public vs. Private Sector Myths*. London: Anthem Press.

McMichael, P. (2000). 'The power of food', *Agriculture and Human Values*, 17(1): 21–33.

McMichael, P. (2009). 'A food regime genealogy', *Journal of Peasant Studies*, 36(1): 139–169.

Messner, E. and Cohen, M. (2008). 'Conflict, food insecurity and globalization', in J. von Braun and E. Díaz-Bonilla (Eds.), *Globalization of Food and Agriculture and the Poor*. New Delhi: Oxford University Press.

Montanori, M. (2006). *Food is Culture. Arts and Traditions on the Table*. New York: Columbia University Press.

Monteiro, C. A., Levy, R. B., Claro, R. M., de Castro, I. R. and Cannon, G. (2011). 'Increasing consumption of ultra-processed foods and likely impact on human health: evidence from Brazil', *Public Health Nutrition*, 14(1): 5–13.

Moodie, R. et al., on behalf of The Lancet NCD Action Group (2013). 'Profits and pandemics: prevention of harmful effects of tobacco, alcohol, and ultra-processed food and drink industries', *The Lancet*, 381(9867): 670–679.

Motesharrei, S., Rivas, J. and Kalnay, E. (2014). 'Human and nature dynamics (HANDY): modeling inequality and use of resources in the collapse or sustainability of societies', *Ecological Economics*, 101: 90–102.

OECD (2013). *Putting Green Growth at the Heart of Development.* Paris: OECD Green Growth Studies. doi: 10.1787/9789264181144-en

Ortega-Huerta, M. A. and Kral, K. K. (2007). 'Relating biodiversity and landscape spatial patterning to land ownership regimes in northeastern Mexico', *Ecology and Society*, 12(2). At https://www.ecologyandsociety.org/vol12/iss2/art12/ES-2007-2151.pdf

Ostrom, E. (1990). *Governing the Commons: The Evolution of Institutions for Collective Action.* New York: Cambridge University Press.

Ostrom, E. (2009). 'A polycentric approach to climate change', *Policy Research working paper WPS 5095.* Washington, DC: World Bank.

Page, H. (2013). *Global Governance and Food Security as Global Public Good.* New York: Center on International Cooperation, New York University.

Pechlaner, G. and Otero, G. (2010). 'The neoliberal food regime: neoregulation and the new division of labor in North America', *Rural Sociology*, 75(2): 179–208.

Persky, J. (1995). 'Retrospectives: the ethology of Homo economicus', *Journal of Economic Perspectives*, 9(2): 221–231.

Pingali, P. L. (2012). 'Green revolution: impacts, limits, and the path ahead', *Proceedings of the National Academy of Sciences of the United States of America*, 109(31): 12302–8.

Pimental, D. and Pimental, M. H. (2008). *Food, Energy and Society.* Boca Raton, FL: CRC Press.

Pinstrup-Andersen, P. (2007). 'Eliminating poverty and hunger in developing countries: a moral imperative or enlightened self-interest?', in P. Pinstrup-Andersen and P. Sandøe (Eds.), *Ethics, Hunger and Globalization. In Search of Appropriate Policies.* Dordrecht: Springer.

Polanyi, K. (1944). *The Great Transformation: The Political and Economic Origins of Our Time.* Boston: Beacon Press.

Popkin, B. M. (2003). 'The nutrition transition in the developing world', *Development Policy Review*, 21(5–6): 581–597.

Porter-Bolland, L., Ellis, E. A., Guariguata, M. R., Ruiz-Mallén, I., Negrete-Yankelevich, S. and Reyes-García, V. (2012). 'Community managed forests and forest protection areas: An assessment of their conservation effectiveness across the tropics', *Forest Ecology and Management*, 268: 6–17.

Pretty, J., Toulmin, C. and Williams, S. (2011). 'Sustainable intensification in African agriculture', *International Journal of Agricultural Sustainability*, 9(1): 5–24.

Ramankutty, N., Evan, A. T., Monfreda, C. and Foley, J. A. (2008). 'Farming the planet: 1. Geographic distribution of global agricultural lands in the year 2000', *Global Biogeochemical Cycles*, 22: GB100.

Raustiala, K. and Sprigman, C. (2012). *The Knockoff Economy: How Imitation Sparks Innovation*. Oxford: Oxford University Press.

Ray, D. K., Mueller, N. D., West, P. C. and Foley, J. A. (2013). 'Yield trends are insufficient to double global crop production by 2050', *PLoS ONE*, 8(6): e66428. doi:10.1371/journal.pone.0066428

Renger, J. M. (1995). 'Institutional, communal, and individual ownership or possession of arable land in Ancient Mesopotamia from the end of the fourth to the end of the first Millennium B.C.', *Chicago-Kent Law Review*, 71(1): Article 11. At http://scholarship.kentlaw.iit.edu/cklawreview/vol71/iss1/11

Richards, T. J., Nganje, W. E. and Acharya, R. N. (2009). 'Public goods, hysteresis, and underinvestment in food safety', *Journal of Agricultural and Resource Economics*, 34(3): 464–482.

Roberts, W. (2013). *The No-nonsense Guide to World Food* (2nd edition). Toronto: New Internationalist.

Robson, J. P. and Lichtenstein, G. (2013). 'Current trends in Latin American commons research', *Journal of Latin American Geography*, 12(1): 5–31.

Rocha, C. (2007). 'Food insecurity as market failure: a contribution from economics', *Journal of Hunger and Environmental Nutrition*, 1(4): 5–22.

Rockstrom, J. et al. (2009). 'A safe operating space for humanity', *Nature*, 461: 09a/461472a

Rosset, P. M. (2006). *Food is Different: Why the WTO should Get Out of Agriculture*. London: Zed Books.

Sablani, S. S., Opara, L. U. and Al-Balushi, K. (2006). 'Influence of bruising and storage temperature on vitamin C content of tomato fruit', *Journal of Food, Agriculture and Environment*, 4.

Sandel, M. J. (2012). 'What isn't for sale?', *The Atlantic*, February. At http://www.theatlantic.com/magazine/archive/2012/04/what-isnt-for-sale/308902/

Schlager, E. and Ostrom, E. (1992). 'Property-rights regimes and natural resources: a conceptual analysis', *Land Economics*, 68(3): 249–262.

Serrano-Alvarez, J. A. (2014). 'When the enemy is the state: common lands management in northwest Spain (1850–1936)', *International Journal of the Commons*, 8(1): 107–133.

Sidel, V. W. (1997). 'The public health impact of hunger', *American Journal of Public Health*, 87(12): 1921–22.

Smolik, J. D., Dobbs, T. L. and Rickerl, D. H. (1995). 'The relative sustainability of alternative, conventional, and reduced-till farming systems', *American Journal of Alternative Agriculture*, 10(1): 25–35.

Sraffa, P. (1960). *Production of Commodities by Means of Commodities: Prelude to a Critique of Economic Theory*. Cambridge: Cambridge University Press.

Stuckler D., McKee, M., Ebrahim, S. and Basu, S. (2012). 'Manufacturing epidemics: the role of global producers in increased consumption of unhealthy commodities including processed foods, alcohol, and tobacco', *PLoS Medicine*, 9(6): e1001235.

Sumner, J. H., Mair, H. and Nelson, E. (2010). 'Putting the culture back into agriculture: civic engagement, community and the celebration of local food', *International Journal of Agricultural Sustainability*, 8(1–2): 54–61.

The Food Commons (2011). *The Food Commons 2.0. Imagine, Design, Build*, October 2011. At http://www.thefoodcommons.org/images/FoodCommons_2-0.pdf

Timmer, P. (2011). *Managing Price Volatility: Approaches at the Global, National, and Household Levels*. Stanford, CA: Stanford

Symposium Series on Global Food Policy and Food Security in the 21st Century, May.

UK Government (2011). *The Future of Food and Farming: Challenges and Choices for Global Sustainability.* Final project report. London: Foresight, Department for Business Innovation and Skills, The Government Office for Science.

UN (1966). *International Covenant on Economic, Social and Cultural Rights,* adopted on 16 December 1966, General Assembly Resolution 2200(XXII), UN. GAOR, 21st sess., Supp. No. 16, U.S. Doc. A/6316 (1966), 993 UNTS 3.

UN (2012). *The Future We Want.* Outcome document adopted at the Rio+20 Conference. A/Conf. 216/L.1, 12 June.

UN (2013). *A New Global Partnership: Eradicate Poverty and Transform Economies through Sustainable Development.* Report of the High-Level Panel of Eminent Persons on the Post-2015 Development Agenda. New York: United Nations.

UNEP (2009). *The Environmental Food Crisis. The Environment's Role in Averting Future Food Crises.* Nairobi: United Nations Environmental Programme.

Van der Ploeg, J. D. (2010). 'The food crisis, industrialized farming and the imperial regime', *Journal of Agrarian Change,* 10(1): 98–106.

Van Parijs, P. (2005). 'Basic income. A simple and powerful idea for the twenty-first century', in B. Ackerman, A. Alstott and P. van Parijs (Eds.), *Redesigning Distribution: Basic Income and Stakeholder Grants as Cornerstones of a More Egalitarian Capitalism.* The Real Utopias Project Vol. V. London: Verso.

Vivero-Pol, J. L. (2013). *Food as a Commons: Reframing the Narrative of the Food System.* SSRN Working paper series. At http://papers.ssrn. com/sol3/papers.cfm?abstract_id=2255447

Vivier, N. (2002). 'The management and use of the commons in France in the eighteenth and nineteenth centuries', in L. De Moor, L. Shaw-Taylor and P. Warde (Eds.), *The Management of Common Land in North West Europe c. 1500–1850.* Turnhout: Brepols Publishers.

WHO (2012). *Obesity and Overweight Factsheet # 311.* At http://www. who.int/mediacentre/factsheets/fs311/en/

World Bank (2008). *World Development Report 2008: Agriculture for Development*. Washington, DC: World Bank.

Wilson, J., Yan, L. and Wilson, C. (2007). 'The precursors of governance in the Maine lobster fishery', Proceedings of the National Academy of Sciences, 104(39): 15187–89.

Wittman, H. (2011). 'Food sovereignty. A new rights framework for food and nature?', *Environment and Society: Advances in Research*, 2: 87–105.

WWF (2014). *Living Planet Report 2014. Species and Spaces, People and Places*. Gland, Switzerland: WWF, Global Footprint Network, Water Footprint Network and National Zoological Society.

Young, O. R. (2003). 'Taking stock: management pitfalls in fisheries science', *Environment*, 45(3): 24–33.

Zerbe, N. (2009). 'Setting the global dinner table. Exploring the limits of the marketization of food security', in J. Clapp and M. J. Cohen (Eds.), *The Global Food Crisis. Governance Challenges and Opportunities*. Ontario: The Centre for International Governance Innovation & Wilfrid Laurier University Press.

Chapter 10

Seeds: from commodities towards commons

Guido Ruivenkamp

Introduction

Seed production in recent decades has been subordinated to the commodified system of global food chains steered by transnational corporations. The focus of this chapter, however, is on ways in which diverse groups of actors have begun resisting further appropriation by organising alternative and sustainable modes of seed production in common. The production of seeds is discussed as a domain through which the social struggle of commoning against commodification evolves. Referring to a long-developed research focus on seeds as 'politicising products' (Ruivenkamp, 1989, 2005, 2008), the discussion centres on how new alliances between immaterial and agrarian labour are emerging and thereby creating social relations that strengthen the perspectives for producing seeds for food crops as commons.[1]

The first section presents a short overview of the history of the social transformation of seeds as natural commons (external to capital relations) into commodities (internal to capital). The following section looks at the social struggle over commons in the actual epoch of contemporary capitalism and discusses some oppositional movements for the re-commoning of seeds;[2] this comprises a consideration of some of the multiple practices of commoning in seed development and applications ongoing today. The chapter concludes with a reflection on the opportunities for this immaterial and agrarian labour (the common) to produce something genuinely new – not, that is, new seeds as new objects per se, or not primarily this, but rather seeds as representing new social relations external to the social organisation of global food chains and thus creating new perspectives for diversity in producing and living – so diverse forms of life – outside of capital and its commodified relations.[3]

From natural commons to commodities: the social transformation of seeds

There is a long-standing practice among peasants[4] in various regions of the world of exchanging plant genetic materials and seeds. The varieties (landraces) developed through this social cooperation are considered as natural commons, as a common heritage of mankind or at least as a common heritage of the communities in the region or of the nation of peoples. In recent times, however, the safeguarding, exchange and development of the plant genetic materials through the social cooperation of the peasants has been taken over by public and private institutions (see below). Thus, the crop genetic resources has become increasingly externalised, colonised, absorbed and put at the service of privatisation by these institutions, which modified the resources into commodities and made them into products of profit and command.

Through the change of the property regime of the seeds (previously controlled by peasant communities but appropriated by public and private institutions), seeds were transformed from a common natural resource (a natural commons) into commodities and developed immanence in the social organisation of global food production, absorbing the characteristic social relations of that production system (Ruivenkamp, 1989). The modern farming style (van der Ploeg, 1999) thus became what Feenberg (1999) termed 'the cultural horizon' for the further development of seeds, with the selection of specific aspects to be inscribed into the new knowledge-intensive products. The production of these new 'informationalised seeds' (Ruivenkamp, 1989, 2005) was not only aimed at creating new crops, new objects as such, but also at creating *new social relations* in farming and food production. The new seeds mediated (Verbeek, 2000) the social organisation of labour in agricultural production systems and became 'politicising products' (Ruivenkamp, 1989, 2005), reinforcing and creating social relations internal to the capital arrangements of global food chains and controlling at a distance the social organisation of agricultural production. This process involves the transformation of seeds as pre-modern, natural commons into seeds as man-made, commodified products of cognitive labour – the seeds themselves increasingly become subjects, effecting drastic changes in the social organisation of labour in global food chains. It thus becomes relevant to develop insights into the ways through which the work of labour in seed production has been appropriated and transformed by public and private owners, and how a range of social forces are creating antagonistic practices of commoning that move plant-breeding knowledge from a positioning internal to capital to one that is external and relates it to new forms of careful *agri-cultural* production (Lemmens, 2010).[5]

The commodification of seeds

The societal transformation of seeds from an item of common heritage into commodified product is realised by changing the social relations with regard to the objects concerned (the seeds).

Of these social relations, the following three are considered here: the changing composition of labour, the tendential transformation of the immaterial/material composition of seeds and seeds as subjects for social transformation.[6]

The changing composition of labour

An important aspect that contributed to the historic trend of transforming seeds from common to commodity is the gradual change of the social group that holds and acts in relation to the plant genetic materials (the seeds). Originally – for centuries indeed – peasants and peasant communities safeguarded, exchanged and developed the plant genetic materials, managing them with a loose set of rules that were generally established by the cultural norms of the community. Generally these operated environmentally on principles of harmony with nature and socially on the basis of reciprocity and gift exchange (Kloppenburg, 2010; Martinez, 2015). Innovation occurred through this system of 'eco-friendly', *communal* development. The genetic diversity we find within the crop genetic resources today is a result of this sharing and exchange of plant genetic materials over generations. It is important to note that innovation through exchanging, producing and developing plant genetic materials took place despite the fact that there were no market mechanisms to control the production and distribution of the plant genetic materials, and that no community, state or company has had an exclusive proprietary right to claim ownership of them. The plant genetic materials were considered part of the common heritage, safeguarded and developed by the peasants in different ecological regions.

This changed in the nineteenth and twentieth centuries, when the project of modernity in agricultural production was imposed, leading to what has been called the most dramatic change in the second half of the twentieth century: the creative destruction of the peasantry (Hobsbawm, 1995: 289), a social cleavage that forever cut the modern present from the agrarian past. An exemplar for that social transformation was the transfer of the safeguarding and development of plant genetic materials into the hands of public and private research institutions. This creation of a property regime now has its own history, a dynamic force in which there has been a growing awareness of the wealth of the diversity of plant genetic materials, originally conserved and developed *in situ*, on peasants' plots, embedded in their social and cultural relations. In other words, the development of the seed (genetics supply) industry has been based on the recognition and appropriation of the commons, by gradually dissolving the strong interrelationship between crop genetic resources and their social/cultural environment and its associated productive relations. Separated from these social relations, genetic wealth became an object in itself.

This objectified genetic wealth was first transferred and exhibited in botanical gardens and subsequently stored in international agricultural research centres, national research centres and by companies. Through this storage in the gene banks of public and private research institutions, the plant genetic materials came gradually into the possession of state and capital, and through this change of property, regime other social relations were modified. For example, the *ex situ* storage of plant genetic material by public and private institutions devalued the role of its *in situ* conservation by peasants.[7] Moreover the changeover from *in situ* to *ex situ* storage concerned not only a relocation of the storage entity, but also, and more fundamentally, indicated a reinforcement of the trend to disconnect plant genetic materials from their natural, social and cultural environments. The institutional installation of the gene-bank storage system enabled plant breeders to rewrite the plant genetic materials, increasingly referring less to their socio-cultural embedment and expressing the materials in scientific formulae.

As plant genetic materials were stored, evaluated and classified in terms of their genetic composition, only understandable and accessible to the scientific breeders working within the public and private research institutions (Patnaik, 2015, 2016), scientists rather than peasants became the experts in developing crop genetic resources, and they were able to modify these resources into the new 'miracle seeds' of the Green Revolution. Completing a kind of circle, the application of these crops in farming systems now needed to be 'explained to' the peasants – through a new group of professionals, the extension officers – which created new commodities (information, advice, communication) to be sold (or given as part of the seed sale) to the peasant farmers (or 'smallholders' as they had become known), who themselves increasingly became perceived as ignorant and passive receivers of these now externalised and commodified seeds and supporting chemicals.

The transfer of the possession and development of crop genetic resources from peasants into the hands of public and private institutions – referred to as the 'externalisation of agricultural research' (van der Ploeg, 1987) – converged with the industrialisation and commodification of agricultural production, built upon various institutional rearrangements.[8] These rearrangements ensured the social (common-to-commodity) transition of seeds through which they became the products of abstract labour, organised internally by capital relations. The further development and production of these commodified seeds became primarily (re)located within the social organisation of global food production chains, which enabled plant breeders to extend their (indirect) control over agriculture and its associated production process, and thence to further 'improve' the plant genetic materials.[9] The improvement of the genetic composition of global food crops, whether for profit or to solve the global hunger problem, was – is – thus implemented through the inscription of specific traits in the seeds, strengthening the changing composition of labour in their material design and transforming the commodified products into agents for change.

The changing composition of the immaterial and material elements in seeds

In addition to the change in the social groups that hold (possess) and work on (develop) the plant genetic materials, the product itself is also changing. Characterised by their composition of immaterial (environmental, social, cultural, political) and material (physical) aspects, the development of seeds is interwoven with this totality of social relations embedded and expressed in them as an immaterial–material composite. The different environmental situations (cold/hot, dry/rainy climates, etc.) in specific sociocultural contexts (industrialised or small-scale farming) with associated political implications (multinational or peasant oriented) taken as a whole determine which plant characteristics are perceived as desirable to be bred for and thus eventually cause changes in the plant genetic material.

The use of agricultural crops in specific ecological zones and local climates was originally introduced as a process of evolution through the interaction of the plant with its natural environment. Natural selection enabled plants themselves to internalise the requirements for good growth from their environment into their genetic programme (Ruivenkamp, 2005).[10] For this reason some plants grow well at high altitudes, for example, and others at low. Indeed, as Martinez (2015) has shown, the peasantry developed and exchanged the landraces incorporating the different types of environmental and social aspects indicated above; it was this specific content of the im/material composition of the seeds that played a key role in the exchange and breeding activities among peasants

This practice of making use of the existing diversity of the im/material composition of seeds has gradually been replaced by the activities of research institutions aiming to *intervene* in the im/material composition of the seeds. These institutions direct their activities to changing the im/material composition and the narrow relationships between plant growth and natural surroundings. An illustrative example is that of the breeding during the Green Revolution, in which the im/material composition of seeds was changed by introducing other information into their genetic programme, especially for the purpose of higher crop yields. The commodification of seeds concomitant with the Revolution was based on a dualistic development: improved plant-breeding techniques 'freed' the agricultural varieties from the limiting characteristics of their natural surroundings, but replaced this with agricultural research incorporating into the seeds' specific scientific information with related dependencies for inputs like extension officer knowledge and pesticides. It is clear that this transformation – the uncoupling of seed reproduction from its surroundings and re-coupling it to scientific information – has not yet been completed, and offers new opportunities for commoning as well as for commodification.

Much in the same way as common land was claimed in the face of enclosure in Britain, some landraces are nowadays consciously and politically claimed as commons by local, indigenous peoples – such as in the case of potatoes in the Bolivian Andes (Rodriguez, 2010). This illustrates a new social struggle focused on the specific scientific information that may be incorporated in the seeds. Indeed, a division – and contradiction – *is* emerging between, on the one hand, breeding programmes focused on the development of informationalised seeds with their politically loaded, immaterial content (of the socioeconomic organisation of global food chains, i.e. the politicising seeds developed within the cultural horizon of global food-chain capital); and on the other, multiple, alternative forms of seed development in which other social objectives are incorporated and which are referred to through their products as sub-political seeds, developed from inside labour and through practices of commoning (Ruivenkamp & Jongerden, 2013).

The externalisation and scientification of seed production (van der Ploeg, 1987, 2008), referring to the cultural horizon of the modern entrepreneurial farming system embedded within global food chains, has stimulated the continuity of a specific plant breeding trajectory in which, among other practices, seeds are hybridised (Kloppenburg, 1988, 2010). This is a trajectory that has even led to a reproduction of crops that are disconnected from the plants themselves, and replaced in some limited (F1) lines possessed by public and private institutions and used for developing varieties without the vigour to self-propagate, (i.e. sterile, forcing farmers to buy new seed every year). This is a trajectory of the biochemicalisation of seeds (Ruivenkamp, 1989), indicating that the scientific information incorporated in the seeds changes them in such a way that the research institutions become the agents able to control from a distance (through their seeds) not only the reproduction of the seeds but also the cultivation of their crops, programming things like whether the crops should be cultivated with or without herbicide and on a large-scale industrial farm or a smaller setting.

The sense in which seeds are imbued with a political meaning thus becomes perfectly clear: they contain a value-laden, immaterial content that prescribes a choice between referring either to the use of chemicals and high-yielding, hybridised varieties cultivated on mechanised and large-scale farms, or to the development of crops cultivated in farming systems built upon crop rotations on small farms embedded in local food networks. In other words, seeds are transformed into a politically loaded combination of material and immaterial content (politicising seeds) – which also transforms the researchers at public and private institutions into 'political agents' (Ruivenkamp, 2003a).

These researchers play a key role – through the development and manufacturing of the politicising seeds – in changing the social organisation of global food chains. This trajectory does not take place outside but, on the contrary, within an intensive social struggle around the creation of new social relations in the post-Fordist mode of food production, in which increasing opportunities also emerge to make other choices related to the informationalisation of seeds and to re-innovate the means–ends systems of these products. In other words, there is a potential to open perspectives for developing seeds as commons, related to trajectories of sustainable, location-specific developments of agriculture that valorise and prioritise work (human rights), environment (sustainability) and food quality (health). This involves the appropriate introduction into locality-based farming systems of biogenetically engineered seed in a way that valorises well-being.

Seeds as subjects for social transformations

The transformation of seeds from a material into a primarily immaterial and (bio)politicising product has positioned them as a frontier of social change. On the one hand, public and private input-supplying institutions and companies are aiming to control agricultural production from a distance through their design of the im/material composition of the informationalised seeds, delivered to an increasing number of farmers around the globe. On the other hand, the relevance of the immaterial component in the seeds also enables researchers and farmers to create new alliances and develop other trajectories of seed development. Indeed, multiple efforts are being made to de-commodify seed production and to search for different means–ends systems in plant-breeding activities. A variety of strategies are being followed, embedded in quite contrasting systems of knowledge production – centralised versus decentralised, proprietary- vs. sharing-oriented, top-down vs. bottom-up and exogenous vs. endogenous.

It is apparent that the production of seeds can no longer be considered the production of pure products/objects, but that these objects are becoming subjects in the sense of creating new social relations. Considering 'seeds as subjects' implies that they can become a vehicle for social transformations, supporting a range of forces to develop alternative systems of food production, creating 'the event' (Badiou, 2005) of a rupture of the presently operative and dominant production system. This process, moving towards the production of seeds as subjects – or their becoming a human commons, internal to the multitude – can already be discerned in various developments and different practices of commoning.

From commodities to practices of commoning: seed production reclaimed

Three general levels of social struggle and change can be deduced from the multiple approaches to commoning seed production, with efforts made to

- Challenge the mode of ordering imposed by the global food-chain capital of commodified and informationalised seeds;
- Recompose the im/material combined form of seeds to revitalise local natural and social resources for development;
- Common the knowledge production with open-source approaches.

The overall aim of these efforts can be described in terms of a strategy to attune the science and technology of seed production to the perspectives of location-specific agricultural developments ('tailoring biotechnology'), within a broad philosophy of re-territorialisation (Magnaghi, 2005, 2010), re-peasantisation (van der Ploeg, 2008) and agri-culture with care.[11]

In the efforts to go beyond the limits of the imposed ordering of the seed products, social forces are developing a new kind of resistance. No longer a form of (defensive) reaction of 'waiting and refusing' – often exemplified in the approach of NGOs – this is an active form of production, involving the development of social cooperation through the design and implementation of seeds as subjects internal to the multitude. It is a new form of resistance based on innovativeness, on autonomous production between producing and consuming subjects (Negri, 2005; Lemmens, 2010), and on constructing local solutions to global problems by reassembling the resource base of food production within local food networks (van der Ploeg, 2008). It is important to emphasise that these various ways of producing seeds as subjects are not characterised by the desire for a confrontation with the genetics-supply industry, but rather by the work of developing continuously their own specific and dynamic practices. As Gorz correctly emphasises:

> The movement against the commodification does not aim to take power, rather their objective is to change the world without taking power by hollowing out and delegitimizing the power of the institutions and authorities that hold it, by wresting ever larger spaces of autonomy from the planetary grip of capital and (re)appropriating the things capital has taken from people. (Gorz, 2010: 126)

The production of these ever larger social spaces takes place 'from within', with all those subjects who are indignant about and tend to refuse, resist and rebel against the ordering and subjugation of global food chains. It concerns a multitude of social forces, including peasant farmers aiming to reconstruct relations of care in agricultural production, regarding its natural environment, the soil on which crops grow, the landscape, the local varieties, the food quality; peasants/farmers who are inclined also to create new social relations with the urban citizenry, offering holidays, relaxation and health care on their farms. It concerns members of unions reducing the environmental hazards of their agrochemical products and farmers' organisations widening the scope of the social objectives of their members to include the management and production of landscape and of diversity. It concerns researchers, entrepreneurs, consumers and citizens demanding the integration of broad ethical issues of 'justice' to be incorporated in production and consumption and the establishment of socially responsible entrepreneurship. It concerns organisations for animal welfare and many singular contacts between farmers and consumers at local level developing new strategies, from organic vegetable networking and regular farmers' markets to strengthening the trend towards a re-territorialisation of agricultural production and short food production–consumption linkages, and a whole host of other initiatives. It concerns fair trade and solidarity movements, emphasising the politics of food sovereignty and rights to food. It concerns the half-billion peasant-farmers in the world today and the one-third of the world's population that depends on small-scale farming to live.

That is, the practices of commoning seed production refers to a range of social forces that are constantly extending their social spaces within which new forms of seed production can be designed and implemented – seeds which, in their turn, may strengthen the socially transformative orientations of these countless initiatives through the embodiment of another, alternative political content. The co-evolving, transformative processes of the production of seeds from within these different practices enable the creation of new alliances between different, apparently separated but actually closely interrelated actors (scientific researchers, entrepreneurs, workers in the genetics supply industry, farmers, consumers, environmentalists, ecologists, feminists, ethicists, etc.). Alliances emerge that, in their turn, may bolster these social forces to create new spaces for autonomy – 'from inside their institutions, work-relations and domains of social life' (Ruivenkamp & Jongerden, 2013: 306–12) – thus challenging the disciplinary command of global food chains and affording additional opportunities for practices of commoning in seed production. Taken as a whole, this comprises a clear trend towards an increasing variety of 'oppressed voices and location-specific dialects of science and technology development' (Ruivenkamp & Jongerden, 2013: 313–21).

Challenging the mode of ordering imposed by the commodified seeds

Various examples of practices of commoning in seed production have already been described (Ruivenkamp, 2005) and filmed (Ruivenkamp, 2008), but additional remarks need to be made reflecting on the social relevancy of these practices. Stimulated by Feenberg's (1999, 2010) critical theory of democratising technology (also Veak, 2006), different tactics and strategies (Feenberg, 1999: 113, referring to De Certeau) can be discerned through which social forces in different regions struggle to de-commoditify and (re-)common seed production through the embodiment of another immaterial (political) content in seeds.

A concrete tactic of peasants/farmers who are technically managed[12] by the seeds is to cross hybrids with local varieties, aiming to develop and improve the local varieties (landraces) by incorporating traits of the hybrids (e.g. high yield), but keeping the ability of the local varieties to propagate without losing their vigour. Hybrid seeds only give high yields during the first year of their existence; subsequent generations no longer have this hybrid power, so farmers are forced to buy new seed frequently instead of laying aside part of the harvest for sowing in the traditional way. By mixing local landraces with hybrid varieties, however, farmers undermine the embodied political content of the hybrids and thereby create a certain independence of the genetics supply industry, maintaining and mixing the desirable traits of both landraces and hybrids.

Further to these farmers' tactics, national research institutions in collaboration with farmer groups develop strategies to go beyond the embodied political content of hybrids by developing improved but open-pollinated varieties. For example, national research institutions and farmers' groups in northern Ghana have made clear choices to develop not hybrid but rather open-pollinated, enriched local maize varieties (called '*Obatampa*', which means 'good mother' in the local Twi dialect). These enriched varieties – well-embedded within local culture – are cultivated by farmers who deliver their products at the school feeding programme (Quaye et al., 2010), reinforcing the linkage of the improved varieties with local consumption needs and patterns.

Another strategy aiming to go beyond the ordering of hybrids is followed by some researchers making use of the apomictic properties of certain crops (i.e. their ability to reproduce asexually), so as to circumvent the biological protection of hybrid varieties. Cross-breeding apomixes into, for example, hybrid maize varieties may create opportunities to remove the hybrids' biological protection against propagation and thus undermine the command of the genetics supply industry, thence allowing many more of the world's farmers an increased accessibility to seeds without the expensive disadvantage of regular seed purchase. However, this strategy can only be properly realised under one crucial condition – that the apomictic techniques become freely accessible, themselves commons.

Another option, less spectacular but possibly more convincing, are practices of changing the social organisation within which various techniques for breeding and reproducing crops are developed, specifically by modifying the vertical production chain of technology development into a horizontal network. For example, farmers in India together with NGOs and scientists combine science-based tissue culture applications in local tree species in India, such as amla, tamarind, custard apple and karaya, with people-based experiences of applying grafting techniques (Ruivenkamp, 2005). Another example is the cooperation between scientists and farmers in selecting, isolating, fermenting and distributing locally specific *Bacillus Thuriengiensis* (BT) material for their plant protective and growth stimulating characteristics (Vimala Devi & Rao, 2005). Through their social cooperation, scientists and farmers are challenging the ordering of a global production of pesticides by reorganising it into territorialised productions of things like BT sprays, as has been done in the south-eastern Indian state of Andhra Pradesh (Ruivenkamp, 2008).

Not only are the externally produced knowledge-intensive inputs rejected in these efforts, but also other products are produced, by combining traditional and modern knowledge systems through which social identities are regrouped and reconstructed. This makes these scientists and farmers (farming communities) again co-innovators of a new production system within which plant growth protection and plant breeding are socially reorganised. The new varieties and techniques combining modern and traditional systems that are produced within this changed organisational setting actively challenge the social ordering and knowledge base of the entrepreneurial farming system embedded within global food chains.

Recomposing the im/material combined form of seeds to revitalise local natural and social resources for development
In various parts of the world, practices of commoning seeds are evolving with the aim of designing and implementing seeds that strengthen and/or create new linkages between agricultural production and its agro-ecological and social environment. Crop genetic resources are selected and added to scientific information to be introduced into cultivars in order to reinforce the regional quality of agricultural crops and/or refine a location-specific rotation of crops. A concrete example is the development of dual purpose, early maturing sorghum varieties in India, which not only facilitates the generation of additional incomes for farmers but also contributes to the restoration of soil fertility (Rana, 2000).[13]

Another strategy is to recompose the im/material combined form of seeds to reinforce the linkages between local crop development and local food production and consumption. Instead of developing the politicising seeds that disconnect crops from their local context and (re)connect the crop varieties to global food markets, the practices of commoning seeds aim at producing seeds that reconnect them to the territorial (local, regional) potentialities for development. Vroom (2008, 2009), for example, has described how scientists, farmers and consumers in the Andean region are using local landraces to develop pest-resistant potato varieties, tailored to the specific food habits of the region. Another example is the development of the zinc and iron enrichment of local cowpea and maize varieties in Ghana, for which specific supporting measures have also been taken to relate the local cultivation of these crops to the local consumption of national dishes, such as *waakye* and *kenkey* (Quaye et al., 2010).

Various other examples of similar practices in other countries (Ruivenkamp, 2008) also show that research to enrich food crops needs to be strongly embedded within local food habits and actual social relations within which the technical improvements of the seeds are shaped. For example, the dissemination of protein-enriched maize varieties in Ghana cannot be separated from the smooth functioning of seed stations; in such a case, continuous consultation with the client groups is indicated. In Ghana also, farmers have emphasised the importance of maintaining specific traits in the nutritionally enriched maize crops – such as high yield, early maturation, resistance to heat and dryness and open pollination (enabling farmers to select their own varieties to plant after each season) – while local consumers have shown their preference for ease of cooking and fruit (pea) size and colour (Quaye et al., 2011). It is only the attuning of the breeding research goals to these specific needs of the local farmers and consumers that can guarantee the distribution of new crops and differentiate such practices of commoning from the application of similar efforts to enrich food crops (e.g.

golden rice) within a top-down, science-driven approach that links the enrichment of crops to the social relations of global food chains.

The practices of commoning that aim to revitalise local natural and social resources for a regional development has nothing to do with conserving traditional practices or a romantic return to the past. On the contrary, it represents a dynamic, progressive way forward (Manzini, 2005), towards a future of organising open local spaces from within endogenous developments (van der Ploeg & van Dijk, 1995). Concretely, the practices of commoning seeds realise the efforts of the common (the alliances of various forms of labour, the commonality) to restore (create and recreate) a territorial relation between the products of plant breeding and the local environment. This is done in many ways on various levels in different localities and carried out through different forms of partnership.[14]

The multitudinous production of seeds implies a continuing transformative process. Seeds are produced through the social cooperation of immaterial and agricultural labour. The seeds produced stimulate further institutional reorganisations and strengthen the alliances between immaterial and agricultural labour, which in turn creates new opportunities to continue producing seeds as subjects and vice versa. In short, a very dynamic process is set in motion, which includes a focus on changing the institutional base of the knowledge production.

Commoning the knowledge production
The practices of commoning seeds not only affect the embodied political content of the combined im/material form of the seeds, but also the institutional setting within which seeds are

developed as well as the agricultural setting within which they are implemented. In addition to changing the mode of ordering imposed by commodified seed, and further to a recomposition of the seed content, therefore, the practices of commoning also imply a change in the institutional setting within which the commoning of seeds takes place. The multitudinous production of seeds goes hand in hand with a reorganisation of the knowledge production system, hollowing out the power relations of the commodified seeds and global food chains.

It has been emphasised (Ruivenkamp, 2005) that the biopolitical, command basis of agricultural knowledge is built upon the non-transparent, complex setting of knowledge production. The knowledge production of informationalised seeds takes place in complex organisational settings, built upon fluid, hybrid, transnational networks of private/public and fundamental/applied research institutions. The complex organisational form of the knowledge production of the informationalised seeds is instrumental in the construction of an individualised research setting where the immaterial labourers have no opportunities to develop insights into the politicising content of the end products to whose development they contribute.

Although these end products are characterised by their contributions to the creation of new social relations, the very non-transparency of the complex knowledge production system leads researchers to be alienated from the social significance of their work. There is a disjunction or inherent tension between the organisational opportunities offered to the individual researcher to (technically) develop their work and the constraints placed on the individual researcher by the same organisational form with regard to critical reflection on the social content of their work. The highly specialised type of work within these complex, opaque networks implies that the technical potentials of the immaterial production are increasingly separated from a political critical reflection, although that politicising content is, as argued, the single main characteristic of the products delivered.

This decoupling of the technical and politicising content in the production of the informationalised seeds due to the complex organisational form of knowledge production – resulting in an alienation of the immaterial labourers, in the classical (e.g. Sartrian) sense of a separation from the true self (simply, losing one's humanity) – is exactly what is challenged in the multitudinous ways of producing seeds as subjects. It is precisely because the immaterial labourers become aware of the politicising component as the core element of their products that they demand – and increasingly realise – the re-establishment of a direct connection between the technical and political content of their work, which involves, for example, consulting other knowledge providers, such as client groups.

It is important to observe that the multitudinous production of seeds as sub-political subjects occur in socially reorganised production systems.[15] Systems no longer assume the rigid hierarchical and centralised and proprietary-oriented form but are increasingly horizontally organised in flexible and fluid networks built upon constant communication, information exchange, sharing and personal involvement.[16] There is a social reorganisation of knowledge production that enables the immaterial workers to reflect on the means–ends relationship of their scientific research, and in which the consultation and participation of other actors play a crucial role. There is a commoning, that is, of knowledge production, which opens the perspective of developing commons in the world of biotechnology and genomics. It is just this alliance of immaterial and agricultural labourers within the production of sub-political seeds that locates where concrete commoning choices about the specific information to be incorporated in the seeds can be made. This presupposes a dynamic and flexible form of knowledge development based on respect and exchange of different visions and knowledge systems. It also enables a transformation in the knowledge base of agricultural production that might reverse the trend of producing peasant ignorance and convert it into a revitalisation of their earth art, of their craftsmanship and their knowledge.

The radical break from the past that came with the wresting of, the ownership and control of plant genetic resources away from the peasants by public and private research institutionsas outlined above involved also a drastic change in the knowledge base of agricultural production. The original knowledge base of farming practices built upon peasants' knowledge of their (own, pre-modern) farming practices was devalued and its role in the development of new seeds marginalised. As van der Ploeg (1987) observed, this implied that the craft of peasant farming – such as that related to the reproduction of crops – was no longer indispensable or even useful for good farming. The spread of the knowledge-intensive inputs still today 'produces ignorance' at smallholder level. Meanwhile, contemporaneous with the devaluation of pre-modern practice, a new market for information was being created, supplied by a new group of actors,the extension officers. Peasants increasingly became 'workers in the open air' remotely controlled by the life-sciences companies and informed about farming practices by extension officers willing to sell their advice for a 'fair and friendly price' (Ruivenkamp, 1989, 2005).

This changing knowledge base is a dynamic process that can no longer be perceived merely as an imposition, for it has become the result of a common creation by different actors. Whenever the changed knowledge base for agricultural production is institutionalised, wherever the horizon of the modern entrepreneurial farming system is culturally established, the participatory plant-breeding methods within this institutionalised setting may contribute to a furthering of the trajectory of the commodification of seed production (internal to the capital of global food chains); this, in turn, can then integrate the residual informal knowledge systems of peasants into that commodified production of seeds. Still many other initiatives are evolving, as mentioned, that reverse this trajectory, challenge the functional relation of seeds to the modern farming style and change its design and implementation.

Seed production as a common(s) future

The social struggle around commodification and commoning manifests itself particularly in the design and implementation of various forms of seed production. Contrasting developments are taking place in the production of seeds as commodified products (internal to capital relations of global food chains) and seeds as commons (internal to the common, the alliances of immaterial and material labour). We are now witnessing the international consolidation in multi-billion dollar conglomerates of that historical development within which (politicised) commodified seeds are produced through the (literal) incorporation of (specific) scientific information referring to and strengthening the cultural horizon of modern entrepreneurial farming systems embedded within the social organisation of global food chains. Meanwhile, as an alternative to this, there is a range of decreasingly marginalised efforts compelled by a variety of social forces to common and develop (sub-political) seeds, themselves seeding a change in the embodied political content of the combined im/material form of the seeds aiming to reconnect crop development to local natural and social resources. There is a huge struggle unfolding that relates to little less than the future direction of world food production and consumption.

Yet there is no need for hyperbole. The simple, shocking reality of hunger today – approaching a billion 'undernourished' people, one in every seven of the world's population – juxtaposed against science and technology development – some two-to-three billion dollars and euros invested every month in biotech R&D alone – illustrates the enormous gap that exists between those excluded from nutrition and well-being and the socioeconomic organisation of global food chains. Instead of passivity – waiting and hoping for the benefits of the present system to 'trickle down', or for multilateral institutional initiatives to eventually 'manage development' for those who are in need now – this article advocates for the initiatives of farming multitudes acting in common by setting up activities and alliances between immaterial and material labour in the domain of biotechnology and seed production. Peasant farmers around the world, reinforced by a variety of agents and actors, from research teams and consumers' groups to charitable foundations and individual entrepreneurs, are beginning to cooperate in a variety of novel, flexible ways to create social spaces in regional localities and international institutions, aiming to revitalise agriculture by reconnecting it to its local agro-ecological and social, cultural environment – its territory, its communities – with care.[17]

A range of innovative practices can be observed and envisaged through which the 'tragedy of capital', as it may be expressed, of the separation and devaluing of the common, here through commodified and informationalised seeds, is transcended, transformed by the common into seeds as human commons. The effect of this is to challenge the ordering and the embodied political content of the politicised seeds. The initiatives of the common are hollowing out the structure of command of the commodified seeds by deconstructing the abstract and de-localised technological developments and simultaneously rewriting the embodied political content of the seeds. They are changing the intermediate role of seeds as subjects in ways that form other social relations.

In respect of the deconstructive aspect of seed production, it is manifest that the initiatives of the common do indeed pose a challenge to the structure of command intrinsic in the commodified seeds. Instead of accepting the institution of dependence on the genetic supply industry, the production of ignorance on the farm and the detachment of local agriculture from its very ground through the introduction of abstract technological products, the common (the alliances of immaterial and material labour) aims to embody increased autonomy, a revalidation of local knowledge and reconnection of agriculture to local natural and social resources through the introduction of tailor-made artefacts.

In the process of rewriting the embodied political content of the seeds, the common refers to another cultural horizon for their design and implementation. No longer is reference made to a care-less agribusiness but to concerned agriculture, committed to its natural and social environment, the deep ecology. The common aims to design and implement seeds (e.g. dual purpose, early maturing sorghum) that aim to find local solutions for the global problems through a reassembling of the local natural and social resources (van der Ploeg, 2008). The common rewrites the embodied political content of the seeds not only to break through the dependence of peasant farmers on the seed multinationals, such as by restoring to crops their power to self-propagate, but also to weave in other social relations enabling the emergence of alternative forms of agricultural production and new modes of knowledge attuned to the development of local resources. In the production by the common of seeds as subjects is incorporated a dynamic in social relations that facilitates the growth of sustainable styles of agricultural production. No longer globally organised, overspecialised and brutally mechanised, this is rather location-specific and multipurpose-oriented, valuing skilled craftsmanship and bodily techniques. These seeds can also go beyond the urban–rural dichotomy of the conventional monolith of modern development, stimulating urban agriculture and rural food processing.

The deconstruction and rewriting enables the seeds as subjects (as human commons) to contribute to alternative systems in and of agricultural productions. Viewed in its entirety, this offers up the hope of a social transformation, from the uniform agri-business model of mass provision to heterogeneous forms of organic, location-specific agri-cultures that care for local natural and social resources. Crucially, these new forms are embedded in the alternative knowledge base of agrarian human commons. Through the alliances of immaterial and agricultural labour, the production of immaterial (scientific and politicising) knowledge is changing. The production of seeds as subjects is being realised through the collective efforts of the common to constantly create new opportunities and perspectives, or possible autonomies for the common.[18] Situated in the changing settings of agricultural production and consumption, as well as in the changing research settings of developing immaterial knowledge, the seed production as common(s) is characterised by an embodied political content that stimulates constantly transformative processes. Thus, the seed production as common(s) is ultimately a production of subjects, of new social relations; it is a strengthening of the common.

These seeds also reinforce the opportunities for place-bounded agricultures. Specified by the context of territoriality, they establish additional spaces within research frameworks to further develop new seeds, multi-modalities predicated on diversity – in contradistinction to the present sterility of monistic standardisation. These innovations in seed production in turn imply yet further social cooperation between immaterial, industrial and agricultural labour, each incorporating yet more new identities (Ruivenkamp, 2003). The multitudinous production of seeds implies a process of proliferation. The alliances of labour produce seeds (as subjects) and beget institutional reorganisations that yield new alliances and social relations (Ruivenkamp, 2003). In challenging the hegemony, ordering and command of the current biopower system at such a profound level, the political alliances of the multitude convened in the rewriting and development of sub-political seeds can launch the epoch of a democratisation of production. According to Feenberg (2002: 3), this democratisation of technologies is the new challenge for humanity:

> [W]hat human beings are and will become is decided in the shape of our tools no less than in the action of statesmen and political movements. The design of technology contains political consequences. The exclusion of the vast majority from participation in the decision-making process of the design of our tools is profoundly undemocratic.

The practices of commoning are beginning to enable the democratisation of seed production to be realised. A variety of alliances between immaterial and agricultural labour are already established, and multitudinous ways already exist to produce these (sub-political) seeds as subjects, as vehicles for the creation of new social relations, new forms of life. I conclude, therefore, with the statement that instead of asking whether the multitudinous production of seed production directed by the common is possible, it may be more appropriate to ask how these forms of seeds production can – will – become so dominant as to create a Badiouian 'event-as-rupture' from the existing entrepreneurial farming system of global food chains. Where is the tipping point, and how can we best progress from here? This may serve as the starting point for further critical theoretical reflections on how the commoning practices of re-seeding outlined here might continue.

Notes

1   The distinction between immaterial and agrarian labour here relates to the product of labour, where agrarian ('physical') labour – farming – results in material production (crops, etc.) as opposed to immaterial ('mental') labour – e.g. research – which results in cultural production (scientific information, system designs, etc.); immaterial and material productions thus combine in seeds, which gives them their specific 'political' content.

2   According to Silvia Federici (2010), the epoch of contemporary capitalism is structurally dependent on the appropriation and commodification of commons, including the appropriation of natural/cultural and social commons, products of labour and human interaction; here, I reflect on seeds as a juncture of the social struggle of commodification versus commonisation.

3   I refer here to Marxian analysis, that not only objects but also subjects are produced that may create new forms of life: 'Production not only creates an object for the subject, but also a subject for the object; creating new forms of life, a new seeing, a new hearing, a new thinking, a new loving' (*Grundrisse*, cited by Hardt, 2010: 141). Michael Hardt, here, emphasises that actually the object of production is really a subject defined by social relationship, or a form of life, which is the rationale for calling the actual form of production 'biopolitical'.

4   Van der Ploeg (2008: 23) characterises peasants by the way they actively pattern the agricultural production as a self-regulated resource base and an organisation of relations with markets that does not permit the market to become hegemonic (dominant over the production process itself).

5   Lemmens refers to the possibility of integrating care (for humans, work, environment, animals and plants) as well as the cultural diversity of food into a renewed social organisation of agricultural production, which we may thus dub 'agri-cultural'.

6   This tripartite division is stimulated by Pedersen (2010), whose jurisprudential analysis of 'property as social relations' distinguishes three social variables: the relating subject, the related-to object and the relational modality.

7   Although, wherever the *ex situ* conservation was well-established and institutionalised, new opportunities arose for *in situ* conservation – but mostly embedded in the framework of these institutionalised breeding programmes.

8   For the reorganisation of agricultural labour in global food chains, see Ruivenkamp and Jongerden (2013).

9   The improved varieties are better from the point of view of yield and also resistance to environmental pressures in certain conditions – especially irrigation and chemical applications (pesticides/fertilisers) – which implies monocropping for maximum quantity yield to supply markets, and thus the large-scale farming by well-capitalised enterprises (see below).

10   For the relation between genetic programmes and environmental influences, see Nicolosi and Ruivenkamp (2011).

11   See the journals *Tailoring Biotechnologies*, at http://www.ctc.wur.nl, and the *International Journal of Technology and Development Studies*, at http://www.ijtds.com/.

12   Feenberg (1999) differentiates between the tactics of those whose actions are managed by the artefacts and the strategies of those who own and manage these artefacts, which paves the way for discussion about how material and immaterial labour are connected within the practices of commoning.

13   This represents an exemplary project, since sorghum can be used as a food source for both humans and animals (as fodder), thus generating extra income for the farmers. Moreover, the use of early maturing sorghum means that the next crop in the rotation cycle – often used for soil improvement – can be planted earlier, which has the additional advantage that the main crop in the cycle will often need fewer fertilisers and pesticides, thus cutting overall costs. Introducing appropriate information into crops can create multiple social benefits – such as, in this case, improved nutrition, higher income for farmers and lower fertiliser/pesticide consumption.

14   The restoration of territoriality, it should be emphasised, is not the same as the restoration of the traditional practices of any given territory (Magnaghi, 2005). Territoriality restoration *may* involve

traditional practices (these are not rejected per se, any more than are the achieved results to date of biotechnology and genomics), but nor are they privileged (it is true that traditional practices will generally be territorial – locally suitable – and thus valued of themselves, but they are not necessarily very productive, for example, or egalitarian, for that matter).

15   The reorganisation of knowledge production due to open source and knowledge commons has been studied by Archana Patnaik (2016), Mithun Bantwal Rao (2015) and Soutrik Basu (2016) within the Rural Sociology department of Wageningen University.

16   It should be observed that there are simultaneously efforts to re-institutionalise these multitudinous ways of producing seeds into knowledge networks re-linked to capital and social relations of global food chains (Ruivenkamp, 2005).

17   Soutrik Basu has investigated how the scientific workers producing knowledge commons (i.e. drought-tolerant rice varieties) within the CGIAR Generation Challenge Programme in India (mostly) created social spaces to reconnect these knowledge commons to care-oriented agriculture (Basu, Ruivenkamp & Jongerden, 2011); Archana Patnaik has investigated the resistance of women's self-help groups against the dominance of 'miracle rice seeds' and their efforts to set up community seed banks as a vehicle for commoning the millet cultivation in their villages.

18   Berardi speaks about 'possible autonomy' as the translation of opportunities and perspectives of autonomous movements into concrete projects (discussion with Andreas Rostik in *Tageszeitung*, 22 December 1979, cited in van den Oudenrijn (1992: 188).

References

Badiou, A. (2005). *Being and Event*. London/New York: Continuum.

Bantwal Rao, M., Jongerden, J., Lemmens, P. and Ruivenkamp, G. (2015). 'Technological mediation and power: postphenomenology, critical theory, and autonomist Marxism', *Philosophy & Technology* 28(3): 449–474.

Basu, S. (2016). 'Knowledge production, agriculture and commons: the case of generation challenge programme' (PhD thesis). Wageningen University.

Basu, S., Ruivenkamp, G. and Jongerden, J. (2011). 'Open source, commons, and development: a research agenda on common pool of services of Generation Challenge Programme (GCP)', 13th *IASC International Conference*. Hyderabad: India.

Federici, S. (2010). *Feminism and the Politics of the Commons*. At http://www.commoner.org.uk/wp-content/uploads/2011/01/ federici-feminism-and-the-politics-of-commons.pdf

Feenberg, A. (1999). *Questioning Technology*. London: Routledge.

Feenberg, A (2002). *Transforming Technology: A Critical Theory Revisited.* Oxford: Oxford University Press

Feenberg, A. (2010). *Between Reason and Experience: Essays in Technology and Modernity*. Cambridge, MA/London: The MIT Press.

Gorz, A. (2010). *The Immaterial: Knowledge, Value and Capital*. Calcutta: Seagull Books.

Hardt, M. (2010). 'The common in communism', in S. Žižek and C. Douzinas (Eds.), *The Idea of Communism*. London/New York: Verso.

Hobsbawm, E. (1995). *The Age of Extremes: The Short Twentieth Century, 1914–1991*. New York: Penguin.

Kloppenburg, J. (2010). 'Impeding dispossession, enabling repossession: biological open source and the recovery of seed sovereignty', *Journal of Agrarian Change*, 10(3): 367–388.

Lemmens, P. (2010). 'Deproletarianizing agriculture-recovering agriculture from agribusiness and the need for a commons-based, open source agriculture', in *Innovation and Sustainable Development in Agriculture and Food*. Montpellier: HAL-00539829.

Magnaghi, A. (2005). 'Local self-sustainable development: subjects of transformation', *Tailoring Biotechnologies*, 1(1): 79–102.

Magnaghi, A. (2010). *Il progetto locale, Verso la coscienza di luogo* [The local project]. Turin: Bollati Boringhieri editore.

Manzini, E. (2005). 'Agriculture, food and design: new food networks for a distributed economy', *Tailoring Biotechnologies*, 1(2): 65–80.

Martinez-Flores, L. A. (2015). 'Seeds, food networks and politics. Different ontologies in relation to food sovereignty in Ecuador' (PhD thesis). Wageningen University.

Negri, A. (2005). *Public Sphere, Labour, Multitude. Strategies of Resistance in Empire*. At http://www.generation-online.org/t/common.htm

Nicolosi, G. and Ruivenkamp, G. (2011). 'The epigenetic turn. Some notes about the epistemological change of perspective in biosciences', *Medical Health Care and Philosophy*, 15: 309–319.

Patnaik, A. (2016). 'Seeds as biosocial commons. An analysis of various practices in India' (PhD thesis). Wageningen University.

Pedersen, J. M. (2010). 'Properties of property: a jurisprudential analysis', *The Commoner*, 14: 137–210.

Quaye, W., Adofo, K., Buckman, E. S., Frempong, G. Jongerden, J. and Ruivenkamp, G. (2011). 'A socio-economic assessment of cowpea diversity on the Ghanaian market: implications for breeding', *International Journal of Consumer Studies*, 35: 679–687.

Quaye, W., Essegbey, G., Frempong, G. and Ruivenkamp, G. (2010). 'Understanding the concept of food sovereignty using the Ghana School Feeding Programme (GSFP)', *International Review of Sociology*, 20(3): 427–444.

Rana, B. S. (2000). *Annual Report National Research Centre for Sorghum*. Rajendranagar, Hyderabad: Indian Council of Agricultural Research.

Rodriguez, D. P. (2010). *Redesigning Genomics, Reconstructing Societies: Local Sustainable Biotechnological Developments*. Zutphen: Wöhrmann Print Service.

Ruivenkamp, G. (1989). 'De invoering van biotechnologie in de agro-industriele productieketen: de overgang naar een nieuwe arbeidsorganisatie' [The introduction of biotechnology into the agro-industrial chain of production: Towards a new organisation of labour] (PhD thesis). Universiteit Van Amsterdam.

Ruivenkamp, G. (2003). 'Biotechnology: the production of new identities', in W. Koot, P. Leisink and P. Verweel (Eds.), *Organizational Relationships in the Networking Age: The Dynamics of Identity Formation and Bonding*. Cheltenham: Edward Elgar.

Ruivenkamp, G. (2005). 'Tailor-made biotechnologies: between bio-power and sub-politics', *Tailoring Biotechnologies*, 1(1): 11–33.

Ruivenkamp, G. (2008). *Biotechnology in Development: Experiences from the South*. Wageningen: Wageningen Academic Publishers.

Ruivenkamp, G. and Jongerden, J. (2013). 'From prescription to reconstruction: opportunities for subpolitical choices in biotechnological and genomics research', in P. Derkx and H. Kunneman (Eds.), *Genomics and Democracy: Towards a Lingua Democratica for the Public Debate on Genomics*. Amsterdam/New York: Rodopi.

Van den Oudenrijn, F. (1992). *Autonomie: Hoofdlijnen van het Politiek-theoretisch Project van Toni Negri* [Autonomy: core issues in Toni Negri's political-theoretical project]. Nijmegen: Uitgeverij Papieren Tijger.

Van der Ploeg, J. D. (1987). *De Verwetenschappelijking van de Landbouwbeoefening* [Scientification of agricultural practices]. Wageningen: Leuven University.

Van der Ploeg, J. D. (1999). *De Virtuele Boer* [Virtual farmer]. Assen: Van Gorcum.

Van der Ploeg, J. D. (2008). *The New Peasantries: Struggles for Autonomy and Sustainability in an Era of Empire and Globalization*. London: Earthscan.

Van der Ploeg, J. D. and van Dijk, G. (1995). *Beyond Modernization: The Impact of Endogenous Rural Development*. Assen: Van Gorcum.

Veak, T. J. (2006). *Democratizing Technology: Andrew Feenberg's Critical Theory of Technology*. New York: State University of New York Press.

Verbeek, P. P. (2000). *De Daadkracht der Dingen: Over Techniek Filosofie en Vormgeving* [The acts of artefacts]. Amsterdam: Uitgeverij Boom.

Vimala Devi, P. S. and Rao, M. L. N. (2005). 'Tailoring production technology: Bacillus thuringiensis (Bt) for localized production', *Tailoring Biotechnologies*, 1(2): 107–120.

Vroom, W. (2008). 'Redesigning biotechnology: experiences of a public-private partnership in the development of pro-poor transgenic cabbages in India', *European Journal of Development Research*, 20(3): 399–415.

Vroom, W. (2009). *Reflexive Biotechnology Development: Studying Plant Breeding Technologies and Genomics for Agriculture in the Developing World*. Wageningen: Wageningen Academic Publishers.

Chapter 11

Peer-commonist produced livelihoods

Stefan Meretz

Introduction

The class struggle fails because it only addresses the question of how wealth is distributed and fundamentally fails to consider how it is produced. Essentially, production is treated as neutral, and commodities are more or less understood as objects, material or immaterial, that circulate through an economy; capitalism thus becomes an external system of power vis-à-vis the individual, visited only for the sale of our labour power or to buy commodities for our reproduction. Crucially, according to this rendition of socioeconomic and thus political meta-structure, we – the masses, the multitude – and capital – the hegemonic, power – are ontologically distinguished, quite separate entities. This basic analysis and the consequent call to solidarity demands a radical review.

As humans, we increasingly determine the conditions under which we live. Fundamental to this are the requirements of human existence, the production of what people need for their livelihoods, broadly understood (so including, as well as food and shelter and other physical and also intangible goods, things like symbolic order and social relations). The idea of our livelihoods themselves as being produced helps to avoid too narrow a view on current issues as simply questions about the distribution of resources, exploitation of privilege and the like. Such reductions only give the impression of a safe shore, but there is no position 'outside', to which we can aspire and from where we can judge. On the contrary, we are doing capitalism every day; it is not an external system of power, but an internalised and objectified system of how we produce our daily livelihood. It is an important part of who we are and what we do. Since we need something to eat tomorrow, we cannot simply 'stop making capitalism' today (Holloway, 2010). The task at hand is much more difficult than that.

First, we need to start from basics, by deconstructing and reconstructing the notion of a commodity. A commodity is not only the stuff of surplus value, something to sell and make money from. Rather, it is an objectified social form of how we produce our livelihoods in capitalism. This is what Marx ([1887] 2010) meant by his notion of fetishism: social relationships between people are expressed as objectified relations between things. People do not communicate about their needs and efforts in order to satisfy them; rather, distinct products 'communicate' on the market through exchange, resulting in an objective measure of their relation, called 'value'. With the value financially quantified through price, these relationships determine what people have to do in order to make a living.

The commodity form that products take when privately produced and then exchanged was one of the central discoveries of Karl Marx. Indeed, this was so essential for him that it determined the analytical starting point of *Capital*. Subsequent notions, like value, money, capital, labour and class, are thus based on an understanding of the elementary social form in capitalism: the commodity.[1] Aiming to avoid the mistakes of traditional approaches in trying to find ways out of capitalism using its own categories – to produce, that is, our livelihood in a way that does not fall back into the practices of commodity production – an alternative approach would be to start by asking, 'What can be an elementary social form of a new society analogous to the commodity for capitalism?' This then becomes an inquiry into a new mode of production, the search for a new elementary social form of livelihood – and the solution is surprisingly simple: it is the *commons* that is evolving right in front of our eyes.[2] This demands an analysis of the commons, specifically in respect of how it may characterise an embryonic form of a new society.

Like the commodity, I argue, the commons is not simply a thing, and it is not only or primarily even a managed resource (Ostrom, 1990) – rather, or beyond these, it is a social form producing livelihood. Unlike the commodity, however, which is privately produced by distinct entities, commons are created through association and maintained beyond the logics of market and state. This leads to completely different dynamics of mediation between needs and the means to satisfy them, as is highlighted by a listing of problems with the material assumptions and operation of the commodities system and comparison of this with those of a commons-based system.

First, a commodity is produced in the hope that it will meet a stable demand, because otherwise it will not be sold, in which case the resources used to produce the commodity are wasted. Second, even if goods are potentially available to satisfy needs, they cannot be given away for free, because scarcity is a precondition for the existence of commodities.[3] Third, as implied by the second issue, goods are destroyed, not, unusually, as an exception, but as a major feature of the structure through which scarcity is maintained.[4] Thus, the commodities system of capitalism and its requirement of scarcity cannot satisfy the needs and desires of all and yet also leads to waste and destruction. Capitalism is only able to meet demands in a way that is clearly disproportional (with uneven distribution to the extent of meeting and failing to meet people's needs at almost unimaginably disparate rates) and arguably unsustainable (for internal economic and ultimately ecological reasons). Market mediation is not able to allocate resources proportionally, since the only measure expressing the value of commodities is that of money; if a need does not come with money (is not solvent), it does not count in terms of market mediation. The results of this include global hunger, mental degradation, environmental destruction and climate change, among other things.

In the case of commons, on the other hand, production takes place on the basis of the clear needs and desires of people. Clarifying these needs and desires is not an easy task because they are seldom uniform and sometimes contradictory; ways in which they can be fulfilled first have to be discussed and decided on. Commons production is not a blind (inefficient, indirectly wasteful) or manipulative (intentionally wasteful, through market distortion and built-in obsolescence) form, but a conscious, directly needs-driven process. Instead of artificial scarcity through property-based exclusion and intended or systemic waste, inclusion, abundance and diversity become key drivers. Finally, commons production does not rest upon environmental degradation or iniquitous socioeconomic inequalities (these are not implied by the logic of its operation, i.e. among peers associated by common needs).

At the present level of development, in which networking across different commons is rarely realised, we cannot compare the commodity and the commons as elementary forms of different modes of production at the same level of unfolding. Nevertheless, some conclusions can be drawn by analysing their core logics.

Firstly, commodities are produced first and mediated on the market afterwards.[5] This subsequent (*ex post*) mediation *separates* different needs from each other, with every need transformed into a solvent demand that is met only if and insofar as the product exchange for money is realised. At its most basic, a single act of sale/purchase comprises the meeting of a specific need, which thus excludes all other needs (thus, economists dub other needs that are met 'externalities'). This separation and externalisation of needs tends to have bad consequences. For example, if we buy a shirt, then our clothing need is satisfied, but since the shirt is produced in a sweatshop in Bangladesh by women under horrible working conditions, the needs of these women are harmed. Or, insofar as we want streets for our cars but not the traffic in front of our doors, we want to consume goods but not the pollution that goes with them.[6] No specific conflicts of needs or contradictory desires are impelled by the logic of commodities, but the general tendency is clearly a major negative feature of the system.

In the structure and operation of commons, on the other hand, mediation comes first and production follows. Such prior (*ex ante*) mediation is regularly observed in the institution and operation of commons. In the 'classic' case of local, material commons, for example, the work of the Ostroms and the Indiana workshop[7] shows how negotiation between members actually avoids 'tragedy'; in the case of immaterial (virtual), unbound commons, like free software, developers and users first come together and discuss the product features and behaviour they desire (tellingly, perhaps, economists do not employ the term 'internality' for forms of *ex ante* mediations).[8] Since, manifestly, people cannot synchronise their differing needs in ways that avoid externalities, an investigation of the potential of the commons in this respect becomes crucial.

Secondly, commodities are mediated by an abstract means – money. Due to the need to exchange privately produced goods, the commodity disintegrates into two opposing aspects. While it is the concrete properties of the product that are relevant during production and then usage, during the exchange, only the aspect of value representation is important (because the goal is to make money from selling the commodity). Economics praises money for its ability to give price signals, but these signals are purely quantitative expressions of supply and demand. It is impossible to signal needs directly, which must thus be first transformed into a demand. If we want a clean environment then we have to put a price tag on pollution (e.g. for carbon emissions) – which then creates new markets, quickly decoupling from the original aim and transforming into the development of new opportunities for profit.

Commons mediation is mediation via commons. Since the commons is both a common resource and, as commoning, the social process producing and maintaining that resource, the mediation is not separated from itself. Doing commons – commoning – is an all-in-one. There is no third means like money in the case of the commodity, but only the qualitative meanings people combine with the commons. These people are defined as peers, people on an essentially equal footing, with different meanings expressing the different needs of peers mediated by a process called stigmergy (see below; briefly, 'stigmergy' here refers to a form of task distribution).

Thirdly, the commodity needs an outside sphere in order to exist; it cannot reproduce solely on its own ground. Marx ([1887]

2010) analysed the so-called 'primitive' accumulation as a violent process of separating the people from their means of subsistence (*enclosure of the commons*). Rosa Luxemburg (1913) showed that this was not only an initial process followed by an expansion of capitalism in its own logic, but rather that capitalism can only evolve by including non-commodified areas into its own commodity logic. During Luxemburg's time, this was achieved by *land acquisition* through colonisation. Capitalism always needs an 'outside', which is incorporated through enclosure and commodification and divested by the release of unprofitable parts. Crucially, while non-commodified areas – maintained or otherwise, so including (although not limited to) commons[9] – are required for capitalism to exist, commons can do very well without commodities; they reproduce on their own ground. This implies the hypothesis that commons can be the elementary social form of a whole new society beyond capitalism.

Commons as an elementary social form

Although the commodity form seems to be so dominant, even now, in advanced, (post)industrial countries, less than a half of societal reproduction in a broad sense is realised through paid work. This only appears not to be the case because most of the activities necessary for the continuation of society are made invisible by capital and the system of commodification (e.g. see the time budget studies of the statistical offices in Germany and Austria), especially those traditionally called 'reproduction' work done by women (Federici, 2004). Thus, the material establishment of commons as an elementary social form is clearly not something that needs to begin *ex nihilo*; on the contrary, it would rather seem to involve the reclamation and extension of a certain social organisation for livelihood production that remains quantitatively dominant. Commons are, nevertheless, hegemonically marginalised by power and the operation of capital, so a new society does have to be created (even though this involves a materially less revolutionary adjustment than appearances may suggest). In order to set about this, to escape the traps of oppositional approaches that fail to go beyond the normatively defined counter-narrative, it is necessary to apply a categorical reframing. In the following, therefore, I want firstly to develop a new framework of categories, and then, secondly, to outline a transformation scheme describing how it is possible to move from the old, given framework to a new one.[10]

Categorical reframing

From the perspective of capitalism as a way of producing livelihood, the main categories are those that are directly linked to the social forms of production and reproduction, the *commodity* for capitalism and the *commons* as a potential alternative. The commodity represents the elementary social form of the capitalist mode of production and enables analysis to be driven forward to nearly every aspect of the whole system, including incorporation of the commons. This is not the case with commons, which are at an embryonic stage within the ocean of commodities and as yet unmeshed and integrated up to the scale of a fully fledged society. Thus, for a categorical reframing, we need to develop a scenario of an integrated network of commons reproduced from commons, where all required circuits (systems) are closed and do not depend on outside sources of input, as is the case today for the commons within capitalism.

Closing all the loops of inputs and outputs of the commons at the level of an entire society refers to the question of societal mediation. How can the goods that are the output of one entity in one place be related to the required input in another, and how can this be achieved on a societal level for all entities in a proportional way (fairly distributed) without resources being wasted (e.g. due to local overproduction) so that all needs are satisfied? The development of a systemic integration of the commons as an elementary social form assumes the commons as a fundamental alternative and embryonic form of a new society beyond the capitalist categories of exchange, value, money, capital, state and others. This huge task can be approached by taking a closer look at the key aspects of individual and collective motivation and social organisational principles in commodity and commons production and reproduction. First, we need to understand the differences between commodities and commons in more depth.

Exclusion logics vs. inclusion logics

Capitalism is based on personal freedom, which is essentially a freedom of contract of isolated ('free') individuals.[11] This ideology of freedom separates two genuine aspects of human existence from each other. On one hand, there is freedom of choice, the freedom to realise one's personal goals; on the other hand, there is individual accountability for humanity, since everyone is a social being, depending on others.[12] This personal responsibility only operates (or is assumed to operate) with respect to immediate (or direct) reciprocal relations to trusted persons (family, friends etc.). Mediated (or indirect) relationships are delegated to alien structures, like the market. Commodity production creates not only externalities but also commodity consumption, since an individual consumptive choice is indirectly linked to the conditions under which the commodity is produced elsewhere (environmental pollution, resource depletion, slave work, etc.). Thus, in capitalism, individual behaviour is structurally irresponsible (Meretz, 2012a). Irresponsibility does not occur due to personal defect, but by the ways mediation works, in what I call the *logics of exclusion*, which can be condensed to the phrase 'One only gains at the expense of others'. This principle does not mean that there is no cooperation – on the contrary, cooperation is one way to increase one's strength in order to out-compete others – so, more precisely, the logics of exclusion are a permanently changing relation of inclusions and exclusions that are fundamentally based on exclusion. The consequence of exclusion cannot be overcome: the only consideration is that of the details of who will be on whose side at what level and in which field.[13]

The commons, by contrast, represent *logics of inclusion*, at least in its embryonic form. Individual goals can only be reached if the needs of others are not harmed. Karl Marx and Friedrich Engels ([1848] 1969) described a society based on the logics of inclusion as an 'association, in which the free development of each is the condition for the free development of all'. This description of the basic dynamics of a free society can be misunderstood in two ways. Either, it is assumed, there must be an external force (the state) that guarantees a framework, where positive reciprocal relationships between people can unfold; or else 'association' is understood as local, as a small-scale, intimate type of organisation driven by personal goodwill and faith. In fact, both of these have proved to be unhelpful, insofar as (i) the state, as a historical development out of and thus categorical production of capital, does not, in fact, act as guarantor of positive reciprocal relations – on the contrary, it institutionalises capital, e.g. authorising the use of force and providing judicial systems to maintain the iniquities that the capitalist system (re)produce; and (ii) association cannot properly operate at the local level within a system of exclusions, which is the material reality today – the assumption of locality is, in fact, a marginalisation of the embryonic within (by) the existing framework. Instead, the idea of association in which the free development of each is the condition for the free development of all can be understood as a concise definition of the elementary social form of a peer-commonist society, where the commons is the required basic element of a new form of societal mediation.[14] This has to be shown; first, we have to distinguish between three types of commons we face today.

Commons and peer-commonist society

Division of commons

The common may be divided into *traditional commons* – the survivors of the ongoing process of enclosure, understood as the separation of the people from their resources and transformation of these and also human activities into commodities, as outlined (see also Holloway, 2010) – and new or *emerging commons* – often related but not limited to digital or cultural resources, where these resources are the results of peer production as defined by three aspects: contribution (as opposed to exchange), free cooperation (instead of command and control) and possession (rather than property) (see Siefkes, 2007). While traditional commons discourse and action focus on the preservation of existing resources, emerging commons create new ones. Therefore, emerging commons may create (new) cycles of production in which the results of one commons become a resource for (subsequent) others. The distinction between traditional and emerging commons does not mean that traditional commons are unable to relate to other commons, but due to the preservation focus their capacity in this regard tends to be very limited. The rapid propagation of new commons, however, does allow for traditional commons to become part of larger networks. All commons need other commons in order to survive and flourish.

This leads to another, third type of commons, which is often made invisible. *Care commons* has to do with caring for people, especially children, as well as the elderly, ill and handicapped. Care commons are very old, since most care work was traditionally done within families, whereas in capitalism the roots of care work are in the patriarchal societal decomposition of spheres (Federici, 2004). Roswitha Scholz (2000) calls the phenomenon expressed in the invisibility of care work 'value-separation', where there is a sphere dominated by valuation (making money from commodity production) and a separated, opposing sphere containing all activities that are not subject to valuation but have to be performed (usually called 'reproduction'). While the first value sphere is male structured, the latter, 'residual' sphere is female (attributed to women, who provide most of its human labour input).

It is important to be clear that this division of commons into different fields and dynamics is not due to its own specifics, but reflects rather the deformations, separations and unequal developments of capitalism. Thus defined, therefore, these commons all have their limitations constructed from and as specific views and confrontations with capitalist logics. Together, however, they represent all that is needed to build a new society. Before discussing transitional paths, we have to further develop the new categorical framework of a peer-commonist society.

Societal mediation

A society is an intangible entity, but one that can be conceptually reconstructed. More than the sum of individual or collective actions, a society is a system of its own logic reproducing itself. This does not mean that the imperatives of a society immediately determine individual or collective actions, since societal living conditions are only *possibilities* to act. People are genuinely free in the sense that we have 'good reasons' (Dray, 1994) to do what we do. These good reasons relate to our daily living conditions as we perceive them and which are the premises of our actions, and these conditions and premises relate to the societal matrix representing the historical, specific way to produce daily livelihood. The relationship between individuals and society is that of *mediation*, which has to be understood from two perspectives, the psychological, which focuses on the societal mediation of individual existence, and the sociological, which focuses on the societal mediation of the society itself. Both are part of a single process.

Now, we can reconsider the proposal of an elementary social form of creating our daily livelihood, since the double perspective is clearly also valid for this in addressing both the individual production and reproduction of individual daily life as well as representing the basic logic reproducing society as a whole. Thus, saying 'We are doing capitalism every day' is not simply a smart slogan to bridge the gap between the individual and society. On the contrary, it is meant quite literally: we are producing our livelihood by reproducing capitalism and vice versa, and we have good reasons to do it this way, because it is the way that society functions for us. It follows, therefore, that we need good reasons to do commons as the elementary social form of a new society.[15] And thus it is necessary to show that the commons are potentially able to constitute a new form of societal mediation. As explained, this can only be done categorically.

Polycentric self-organisation

Commons are mainly perceived as a local phenomenon. Although this is not applicable in the virtual realm of Wikipedia and the like, commons do not reach the level of societal integration achieved by the commodity, which raises the question of whether they are able to develop, integrate and scale-up to the level of a full societal mediation and thus enable the replacement of the old commodity-based forms. One approach to this is structural: capitalism involves a range of entities, like money, markets, state and law, that perform/facilitate the societal mediation. We may, therefore, set about identifying how these can be replaced, in principle – here, through a sketch of a new society based on peer commons.

In this new society, commons are the basic elements and social entities of societal production and reproduction. However, they are not only horizontally hugely diverse, they are also vertically structured according to the material requirements of societal necessities. The combination of both dimensions leads to a structured network with polycentric self-organisation and governance (Ostrom, 2010). This network does not consist of uniform nodes, but has clusters of commons in order to better organise any given societal task. Let us assume the following commons types: project commons, meta-commons, infrastructure commons and commons institutions.[16] All commons are responsible for the planning of efforts and resources, providing information on their activities, implementing them and networking with other commons as necessary.

- The mission of project commons is *doing*: implementing the self-determined tasks of production and reproduction. These include the production of goods (food, shelter, transport infrastructure, etc.), resource reproduction (atmosphere, land, raw materials, etc.), social services (health, education, culture, etc.), science and research, and so on. The analogy for the current situation is obviously the private enterprise and public service sectors.
- The mission of meta-commons is *coordination*. These create the preconditions for project commons and coordinate their activities, but are only required for fields where the number of commons is too large for them to coordinate themselves. Meta-commons are a kind of outsourced commons for special tasks of coordination, much as we have today in management or planning units in companies or public administrations. This type of organisation can be useful for distinct productive societal sectors (energy, water/sewage, food, etc.) or global commons (atmosphere, oceans, raw materials, etc.).
- The mission of infrastructure commons is *networking*. These provide network services for project and meta-commons. They are infrastructures for data as well as for material flows. Today's analogy is network management (utilities, the Internet, frequency spectrum, etc.). This might also include distribution pools for some common goods that are no longer sold but simply provided.

- Commons institutions focus on the *durability* of services. They provide ongoing social services mainly, but not only for local communities (like local governments today). Following a proposal by Christian Siefkes (2007), this type of 'association' can scale up from the local to the global.

Obviously, these commons are highly meshed, according to their specific requirements. Project commons of a societal area may need coordination by meta-commons; meta-commons and project commons may be highly based on the availability of infrastructures; infrastructure commons themselves may need coordination on a higher level; while commons institutions need all of the above. This sketch of a polycentric arrangement of commons, it should be emphasised, is only illustrative of the contention that commons can very well be developed as the elementary form of a society beyond capitalism. Nevertheless, there are some hidden preconditions that are required for a peer-commons society to function. These can be condensed to *voluntariness* and *openness*.

Voluntariness is a matter of freedom and motivation. Only those people who can voluntarily choose what and how they want to contribute are truly motivated. Despite its ideology, capitalism does not engender a society that is free or allow people to choose how they operate with respect to it; contributions only count societally if they lead to a commodity that can be successfully sold. Thus all activities are subordinated to the dominant and alien logic of valuation,[17] which people have to accept in order to make their living. In contrast, the free development of one's potentials requires unrestricted voluntary decisions about contributing, including whether to. Voluntariness can only unfold within the logics of inclusion, which generate positive reciprocal relations between people, the precondition for responsible actions. This type of reciprocal free development of the personality of each is also called 'Selbstentfaltung' (Meretz, 2012b) – in contrast to the individual development at the expense of others that we have in capitalism.

Openness means complete transparency of all information, in order to gain insights into the processes required to perform a given task. In contrast to the commodity logic, where information and data are keep secret in order to allow only limited and licensed access after payment of an amount of money (a restricted and controlled 'push mode'), in a free society information concerning the production of livelihood is generally available to all (an open, 'pull-mode').[18] This is not only essential for the organisation of social task sharing, but also for the progress of humanity: any discovery at any place on the planet can immediately improve the performance of any commons. This is the reason why, today, open-sourcing is such a powerful and future-oriented strategy – even if embedded in the narrow mind-sets of 'business models'.

Focus-shift of actions

Assuming a free society based on commons with voluntariness and openness already enables the drawing of some conclusions. In capitalism, societal goals are predetermined by the alien logic of the endless valuation cycle. Marx ([1887] 2010) wrote about value and capital as being an 'automatic subject' (*automatisches Subjekt*),[19] indicating that the people are only 'objects' of the logic of capital, which is the true subject in this process – thus the paradoxical consequence of producing livelihood in the commodity form, that the overall process determines the imperatives that people have to follow while (re)creating exactly this process. Under these premises, the purposes of societal (re) production are rarely questionable, because everything must pay off. The focus becomes limited to the *means* (technical and organisational) to profit. This is entirely reversed in a free society, where the main focus is on the *purposes* of (re)production, and the means to do so only play a serving role to the satisfaction of needs. Since needs are hugely diverse, purposes are continuously under debate. Additionally, externalisation is not an option to solve conflicts; internalisation means mediating needs differences prior to production.

Following Ute H.-Osterkamp (1976), needs can be grouped into two spheres, *productive needs, which* refer to participation in the societal process of the provisional production of livelihood, and *sensual-vital* needs, referring to human subsistence and sexuality (food, shelter, health, etc.). These need types depend on each other. Satisfying productive needs is a precondition for the satisfaction of sensual-vital needs, as in the case of hunger, where people not only suffer from not having enough to eat, but also from the fact that they do not have the productive means at their disposal to prevent a situation of hunger. It is important to note that the concrete realisation of productive and sensual-vital needs depend on historical-specific developments. Thus, 'the quality of satisfaction', as Charles W. Tolman (1992: 99) writes, is also a historical product, because it relates to the 'socially produced satisfaction possibilities', which include the fact that satisfaction can 'no longer be measured against the bare fulfilment of basic biological needs'. Concrete needs and their forms of satisfaction are not particularly predictable.[20]

The challenge for any society, then, is to bring productive and sensual-vital needs into a dynamic relationship. Capitalism solves this by attributing the need circles to separated societal spheres, with productive needs linked to 'male attributed public' commodity production and sensual-vital needs linked to reproduction within 'female attributed private' households (to the patriarchal decomposition of societal spheres – see above). Moreover, due to the alien imperative of valuation, productive needs cannot really be satisfied, which is obvious for unqualified or precarious work. Even in creative, highly qualified work, the free development of individual potential is always under the supervision of market requirements and competition. Production is not the place to fulfil one's productive needs, but only to earn the money for the satisfaction of consumerist wishes hoping they will satisfy sensual-vital needs. However, this relegation to consumption as the main way to reach a fulfilled life always leaves a bad taste, since we do not have our living conditions at our full disposal.

A free society based on commons, voluntariness and openness will end the separation between production and reproduction. Actually, this trend is already clearly visible, but in a negative way, since everything is to be subsumed under the commodity logic dominating production. Without societal separation of spheres, everything is production and reproduction at the same time. Then, fulfilling productive needs is not a painful means for another purpose (consumption) but an end in itself. And it can be an end in itself if and only if productive activities are voluntary, which means only choosing to do them if we really want to do them. Realisation of sensual-vital needs, meanwhile, is more satisfying if, at the same time, we collectively control the satisfaction possibilities. All aspects together result in a higher motivation, since all activities lead to a more secure and fulfilled life. Under provisionally secured living conditions, it is far easier to deal with limitations of resources in the broadest sense and with conflicts between people. Thus, a free society is not a society without limits and conflicts but one in which dealing with limitations or conflicts does not occur under the threat of personal well-being. Conflicts can be solved far better if no one can use power or domination in order to enforce individual views and goals at the expense of others.

More pointedly, the main focus of a free society is the reflection on purposes instead of optimisation of the means to fulfil alien purposes (as an end in itself). This leads us to the final and most important brick of the new categorical framework. How does internalisation work, how will different needs be mediated, how can voluntary actions lead to a coherent society? Here, stigmergy comes into play.

Stigmergy

Stigmergy is a type of self-coordination in large, decentralised systems through local information:

> Stigmergy is a mechanism of indirect coordination between agents or actions. The principle is that the trace left in the environment by an action stimulates the performance of a next action, by the same or a different agent. In that way, subsequent actions tend to reinforce and build on each other, leading to the spontaneous emergence of coherent, apparently systematic activity. Stigmergy is a form of self-organisation. It produces complex, seemingly intelligent structures, without need for any planning, control, or even direct communication between the agents.[21]

A combination of the Greek words 'stigma' (sign) and 'ergon' (action), the term 'stigmergy' was originally introduced by Pierre-Paul Grassé (1959) in his behavioural studies of termites (where pheromones are the signs). The applications of this concept of complex self-organisation are limitless, and it has already found its way from biology to, for example, computing.[22] It has obvious potentials too for conscious humans and for commons. Francis Heylighen (2006) applied stigmergy to peer-production, and Christian Siefkes (2013) coined the phrase 'hint-based task distribution'. Heather Marsh (2012) describes stigmergy as being 'neither competitive nor traditionally collaborative'.

The goal of stigmergic task coordination is to transform micro-actions into a coherent macro-dynamics, which is equivalent to capitalist market mediation or central planning. Usually, direct and indirect stigmergy are distinguished. Direct stigmergy involves an action creating a sign that indicates another action. For example, when a Wikipedia contributor creates a hyperlink to another article that does not yet exist, then this link is highlighted in red, inviting other contributors to write the missing article. The process directly generates a sign that others can continue the work. Indirect stigmergy occurs if a sign is separately noted referring to the process (e.g. the Wikipedia list of requested articles),[23] or if a procedural sign is marked with additional information (e.g. the Wikipedia rank list of most wanted articles automatically generated from the red links).[24]

From the perspective of the individual, stigmergy means voluntarily self-selecting a task and self-assigning to work with people already working on it. This mode is clearly different not only from hierarchical command and control systems, but also from flat consensus approaches, which tend to be assumed as the cooperative alternative to competitive hierarchical structures. Consensus, of course, has its own drawbacks: it does not scale up very well, tends towards expanded (sometimes jamming) discussions and is vulnerable to provocateurs. Consensus does not necessarily mean that all participants have to agree to a decision, but rather that there should at least be no reasons left to object and finally veto it; this may result in ambiguous individual motivations to follow the decision, depending on the personal agreement with the group consensus. Self-selection, on the other hand, means that decision and implementation of that decision[25] are not separated from each other, as in hierarchical and even in consensus-based systems.

Stigmergy assumes very high levels of efficacy (successfully reaching the goal) and efficiency (reaching the goal with minimum effort), first, due to the needs-driven basis of action, and second, due to the minimised transaction overheads, since stigmergy does not need (additional) mediation via money. A huge amount of societal effort today is money-related (i.e. accounting, taxing, auditing and other operations on finances) without any immediate useful outcome. These useless efforts bind people's energy, which can be better employed in the creation of useful results through satisfying 'productive' needs. From this perspective, the view that a free society without individual coercion cannot secure the performance of necessary societal tasks appears rather groundless.

Compared to hierarchical or consensus-based task coordination, the motivational position in stigmergy is obvious: I only choose tasks I really want to do. The power of the group I work with is limited to the acceptance or rejection of my contributions. Stigmergical task selection does not mean that all activities are immediately and directly emotionally rewarding; on the contrary, since we desire to reach self-selected goals, we are highly motivated to apply effort and overcome difficulties – which, in fact, is the main reason that stigmergy is a perfect way of satisfying productive needs. Therefore, although motivation should not be confused with immediate reward, motivated actions are far more fulfilling (satisfying, enjoyable) than personally or structurally enforced alien jobs.[26] Voluntary and thus motivated tasks are usually performed with responsibility. This generates trust among the commons and strengthens the logics of inclusion.

Stigmergy follows the network effect. The more people or commons are attracted to a task, the greater the resources and opportunities to reach the goal. This positive feedback loop reinforces itself, as can be observed in the exponential growth of many open source projects. The flipside to this is that the network effect requires a critical mass to take off; a huge number of open source projects do not attract a critical mass. However, this may only be a problem if attaining the critical mass is combined with economic success and personal existence. In an 'anti-economic' (Kurz, 1997) logic, a huge number of experiments constitutes the innovative humus from which successful projects emerge.[27]

Finally, stigmergy scales up very well for large systems. Stigmergy requires diversity to scale successfully, and both the tasks and the people in a society are as diverse as one can imagine. In Free Software, there is a phrase coined by Eric Raymond (1999): 'Given enough eyeballs, all bugs are shallow' (referring to 'Linus' Law', which honours the first Linux kernel developer, Linus Torvalds). Modelled thus, the 'Stigmergic Law' could be phrased as 'Given enough people, you will find a nerd for every task which has to be done'.[28] The term 'nerd' (or 'geek') refers to an individual who does not only bind himself to a task, but enthusiastically digs into the challenge until the task is finished in the best way possible. This type of motivation is not surpassed.

Some doubts considered

Various concerns may be raised questioning whether stigmergy is really capable of replacing capitalist categories of mediation (money etc.) as outlined. One is that some societal needs might not be covered and thus go unaddressed. Here, by way of analogy, we can use the Smithian 'invisible hand' of the market, in which micro-activities are synthesised to a macro-coherence by means of exchange, value, money and suchlike. With stigmergy, these objectified means are replaced by needs-driven voluntariness and openness. While in capitalism we have to subordinate under an alien mediation we do not control, in a free society we *are* the mediation, which we fully control. There is no third 'mechanism'. It may be thought that being the mediation ourselves implies an automatism that acts beyond our free will, but this is not the case. Every society can only continue given a minimum level of coherence. The idea of controlling the coherence of society as whole is absurd. Thus, the question is how the coherence is generated – by religious dogma, by an invisible hand, or by ourselves? Insofar as the commons constitute the elementary form of social life, the answer is us, we are doing it. It may also be thought that society requires planning, directed by government and/or the invisible hand of markets. Of course, planning is necessary, but not in the sense of a top-down, central planning. On the contrary, because needs are hugely diverse and dynamic, planning should mainly be a task of the commons itself.

Assuming a local-to-global distribution of production and reproduction according to needs, then self-planning is the perfect means to satisfy nearly every need (including the self-planning of those commons self-designed as responsible for infrastructure). This simply results from the fact of a huge diversity of people. With high probability, there will be a good match between the results of the realisation of productive needs on one side, and the satisfaction of sensual-vital needs on the other. It may be argued that planning an infrastructure is an alien planning from the perspective of the other commons, so the idea of self-planning collapses at this point. Of course, an infrastructure commons is planning the infrastructure for others, but that is not really any different from other tasks, since most of those are done for others also; production is mainly production for others. Importantly, here, the fact of the planning and maintaining of an infrastructure does not imply that people need permission to use it. It is there and can be freely used; the only issue is a matter of capacity, which may be adjusted by the responsible commons.

Another concern involves the global division of labour. In respect to this, first, if we do not want to say that everything is 'labour', then there will no longer be 'labour' in the sense of a special activity in a separate sphere of life ('economy'). There will no separation between production and reproduction, because all activities are recognised as worthwhile. Second, stigmergy does not mean that a global division of activities will vanish. Rather, some absurd divisions will be re-localised (probably the production of food), while others will remain, due to geographical dependencies (extraction of raw materials) and yet others will decrease (e.g. through avoiding parallel developments due to the sharing of ideas). If a global system of production led by valuation and money is transformed into a system led by needs, voluntariness and openness, then it can be assumed that the whole society will rearrange all activities according to the new paradigms.

Other issues to be raised include injustice and democracy. Regarding the former, we certainly cannot assume that all injustices and divisions along diverse lines (gender, ethnicity, age, etc.) will automatically vanish. However, in contrast to capitalism with its logics of exclusion, in a peer-commons society they may become superfluous, since exclusionist behaviour loses its function; we will have that opportunity. Regarding the latter, a peer-commonist society based on stigmergic polycentric self-organisation is simply beyond what we know as formal democracy in the sense of, for example, representative politics. It is a do-ocracy, in which dealing with our affairs is performed – or, if we wish to stick with the term, a truly inclusive democracy.

Transformation

After developing a categorical skeleton of a peer-commonist society, the logical next step is to discuss how to get there. Manifestly, this is not a trivial question. It concerns how a new mode of production can establish itself while the current mode is dominant and powerful individuals and institutions in particular are interested in keeping the situation as it is. In order to understand the challenges of the coming historical transition we can use the five-step model (Holzkamp, 1983; Meretz, 2012b), often also referred to as the germ form model.

Generally, this is a model employed to understand the concurrent existence and development of phenomena with different qualities. The challenge is to think of the peer-commons production as being a modernisation of capitalist production methods and the embryonic form of a new mode of production beyond capitalism at the same time. The five-step model avoids an either–or thinking and accomplishes this by viewing the emergence and development of peer-commons production as a process of its own contradictory unfolding in time. Normally, applying the five-step-model is a retrospective procedure where the result of the analysed development is well known. By assuming (imagining) the result of a transition towards a free peer-commons society, the emergence of this result can be reconstructed using the model. Here is a rough sketch of the five steps, first listed and then applied to the case of peer-commons production.

1. *Embryonic form.* A new function appears. In this phase the new function must not be understood as a rich seed encapsulating all the properties of the final entity and which only has to grow. Rather, in this phase, the embryonic form shows only principles of the new, but it is not the new itself. Thus, commons-based peer production is not the new itself, but the qualitatively new aspect it shows is the needs-oriented mediation between peers based on voluntariness and openness. During the initial phase, this is visible only at a local level and a few fields at the global level.
2. *Crisis.* This occurs only if the old system falls into a crisis as a whole and is no longer able to maintain the system functions; only then can the embryonic form leave its niche. The capitalist way of societal production and mediation via commodities, markets, capital and state has brought mankind into a deep crisis. It has entered a phase of successive degradation and exhaustion of historically accumulated system resources. The

recurring financial crises and developing ecological danger make this apparent.

3. *Function shift.* The new function grows, leaves its niche, and gains relevance for the reproduction of the old system. The former embryonic form is now double-faced: on the one hand, it can be used for the sake of the old system, while on the other its own logic remains incompatible with the logic of the dominant old system. Peer-commons production may be utilised for the purposes of cost savings and the creation of new environments for commercial activities, but it rests upon non-commodity development within its own activities. Co-optation and absorption into normal commodity-producing cycles become possible (De Angelis, 2007), therefore; so only if peer production is able to defend its own commons-based principles and abilities to create networks on this ground will the next step be reached. Free Software is one example of peer-commons production that is quite clearly at this stage; Open Hardware is currently at the point where it is just about to leave its niches.

4. *Dominance shift.* The new function becomes prevalent. The old function does not disappear immediately, but steps back as the previously dominant function to marginal domains. Peer-commons production reaches a network density on a global level, so that input–output links are closed to self-contained loops. Separated private production with subsequent market mediation using money is no longer required. Needs-based stigmergic mediation organises production and distribution. The entire system has now qualitatively changed its character.

5. *Restructuring.* The direction of development, the backbone structures and the basic functional logics have changed. This

process embraces more and more societal fields, which refocus towards the new needs-based mode of societal mediation. The state is stripped down and new institutions emerge that no longer have the uniform state character, but are means of collective *Selbstentfaltung*. New contradictions may emerge, and a new cycle of development may begin.

This is only an epistemological model, a dialectical conceptualisation of historical transition, not a scheme for immediate action. The main advantage is the possibility it offers to escape from unfruitful either–or debates. It allows for thinking of the emergence of a new mode of production as useful for the old system while maintaining its transcending function towards a free society as a concurrent phenomenon. This double-faced development can be observed when analysing peer-commons projects today.

Practical application

Having developed a categorical framework of a free peer-commons society, a peer-commons modelling (stigmergy) and now the five-step analysis of a transitional path, we need to conclude with concrete examples of peer-commons production today. We ought to look not only at peer-commons projects in a narrow sense, but also at the influence of a global trend towards these new practices more generally. Insofar as the theory of a functional shift of the embryonic form of a new mode of production is valid, then this shift must be observed in its double-faced character in conventional business practices as well as in new emerging practices outside of normal capitalist logics. Therefore, two examples are considered here, the first an open hardware project and the second a conventional stock corporation.

Open Source Ecology (OSE)[29]

Founded by Marcin Jakubowski in 2003, OSE is legally defined as a 'non-profit corporation'. The mission is 'to create an open source economy – an economy that optimises both production and distribution, while providing environmental regeneration and social justice'.[30] The goal of the project is to develop the fifty most important machines – called the Global Village Construction Set (GVCS) – providing a village with the necessary means of production for modern comfort. These machines range from tractors, brick presses, computer numerical controlled (CNC) machines, bakery ovens and dairy milkers to automobiles and trucks. OSE is a distributed project. The Factor e Farm in Missouri (USA) owned by Jakubowski functions as its 'headquarters', where machines are prototyped and tested. Permanent contributors at Factor e Farm are paid for their work. Finance comes from donations and institutional grants.

Key design features are the following:

- *Open source* means that plans, designs, descriptions and educational materials of/for the constructed and prototyped machines are released online under a Free Copyleft License;[31]
- *Modularity* and *flexibility* allow for interchanging and recombining of generalised parts (like motors, power units, electronics etc.) from machine to machine;
- *User accessibility* enables users to create or maintain the machines themselves;
- *Cradle-to-cradle* manufacturing cycles reduce environmental impact;
- *High performance* of the products and *industrial efficiency* of the production at *low costs* is the guiding line;

- A '*distributive economics*' is encouraged by OSE, whereby other enterprises replicate the open technology as well as the business models.

In a broad sense, OSE is a reaction to the crisis of the capitalist civilisation model. Jakubowski was 'frustrated with the lack of relevance to pressing world issues',[32] and creating a distributed and re-localised 'open source economy' was assumed to be a way out of multiple crises. Local communities would not destroy their own environment, and externalisation as in traditional industrial production could be avoided. This, however, was a quite unrealistic assumption. As shown (above), externalities do not occur due to the remoteness of production, but due to its form and purpose: commodity production occurs in order to make money. In OSE, 'economy' seems to be a neutral apparatus of production to satisfy needs, but satisfying needs is only a side effect in commodity production. In fact, economy is the self-feeding system of the endless growth of abstract wealth controlling people's behaviour, since it is the way to make a living. In that sense, the OSE approach is far too short-sighted and inherently contradictory – in a way, that is, which well represents the issues and ambiguous nature of the embryonic form of the five-stage model outlined.

This contradictory character becomes visible in the licence issue. On the one hand, OSE is fully convinced of and obliged to the paradigm of openness and, albeit less emphasised, also to voluntariness. It is definitely a peer-commons project. On the other hand, OSE wants to finance the project by selling its machines. This creates a contrast between beating scarcity by freely sharing all production knowledge and the necessity of offering a unique commodity on the market that depends on a tendency towards scarcity. Thus, a competitor can use the free knowledge and produce the same machines for the same or less money. OSE tries to solve this problem pragmatically by combining the Copyleft License with an appeal to serve the distributive economics: 'We publish our business models openly so that others can replicate any enterprise. Everything we know, you know.' This is intended to generate truly free enterprise and life-giving competition, as opposed to monopoly capitalism or militarism. In a word, distributive economics are called 'sharing'. In the political sense, this phenomenon may be described as 'decentralisation engineering'.[33]

According to this logic, the problem of capitalism seems to be the creation of monopolies, but not the fact that it dictates how we make a living. Thus, selling its machines seems to be the 'natural' way for OSE to keep its project running, although this has not, in fact, played an important role until now.[34] However, the project begins to subordinate its practices to rather question-able goals, like 'single-day-builds' (build one machine a day) as a step to large-scale production. This makes sense if it wants to sell machines on the market, but it detracts a lot of energy away from the original goal of developing the GVCS, and in the long run it may lead to a market dependency.[35]

Open Source Ecology is a remarkable peer-commons project. It shows that openness and voluntariness can successfully be transferred from the digital into the physical realm. The possi-bility of realising one's own productive needs combined with an inspiring vision – providing the world with a set of machines to produce locally on the given level of productive forces – drives the project forward. The project leader has organised a very successful communication campaign, which leads to a respectable amount of donations by 'true friends' or institutions guaranteeing their budget for the next few years. However, the most remarkable result is the machines itself. They are not simply copies of their proprietary counterparts, but rather realisations of a completely different set of design and creation criteria. Modularity is not a marketing slogan but reality.[36] The machines are designed to be user accessible and not to hide nifty features from users and competitors as is usually the case with commodities. They are designed to be easily built and repaired using simple and low-cost methods, while at the same time not waiving performance and efficiency. The machines physically represent a new mode of production, at least in an embryonic form. They give an idea of what is possible in a free society when the means of production are not produced to make money but to serve needs. This project, however, appears to be neither aware of its enormous potential nor of its inherent contradictions, which could yet be its downfall – although not before it will have contributed not only, one hopes, materially, to needs in a direct sense (through its machines), but also indirectly, through its role in the positioning and development of peer-commons more generally (as, at least, an instantiation of the currently contradictory process of peer-commons production).

Open Source Ecology, I would argue, is doing the right thing while having some rather short-sighted ideas about business. Inevitably, contradictions will surface challenging the peer-commons character of the project. Historically, many projects (mostly on a low-tech basis) have started out ambitiously, but then either disappeared or transformed into ordinary companies. To be clear, the contradictions do not occur solely or even primarily due to any individual (human or organisational) shortcomings, but rather because of objective constraints in a society that is dominated by monetary logic and the commodity form. This can be clearly understood using the five-step model. A peer-commons project cannot be anything other than a double-faced entity navigating through the shoals of openness and voluntariness as key motivators on one hand and alien requirements from markets and logics of valuation on the other.

Synaxon AG

A mid-sized stock corporation in the IT sector in Germany, Synaxon AG[37] follows a concept of radical self-organisation. The CEO is Frank Roebers, co-author of a book on the use of Web 2.0 techniques in companies (Roebers & Leisenberg, 2010). In Synaxon, he internally launched a Wiki in 2006 and the communication tool Liquid Feedback in 2012. All company information (operational data, job descriptions, projects, quarter-end accounts, etc.) is published in the Wiki, and every employee can access it. Everyone sees what others are working on, and everyone can change anything, including their own job description – without moderation. To begin with, employees were somewhat reticent about this transparency, since not everyone wanted to share their knowledge and some were anxious that posting the wrong words might cost them their jobs. The first to dare to make changes was a young worker still in his probation period: he deleted the company's mission statement, because he did not like it! After digesting the shock, the management decided to let it go and not use its veto power. 'It was like someone has released the handbrake', Roebers said.[38] Since then, more than 400,000 changes have been made, and Roebers has never felt it necessary to use his veto power. There have been many proposals that saved a lot of money for the company.

Since all employees contribute to the Wiki using their real names, however, truly fundamental changes did not occur. Thus, Roebers decided to additionally implement Liquid Feedback, a communication and voting tool previously developed and used in the German Pirate Party. Every employee uses a pseudonym and can anonymously post proposals. If a proposal gains 10% of staff votes, it enters the discussion phase. After the debate, the topic is frozen for a time-out period of reflection. If, during the final voting, the proposal obtains 50% voter turnout and the majority of the votes, then the proposal is implemented. Rather small but also crucial decisions (related to things like salary payments and career opportunities) have been made in this way, all of which have been realised, even if the management was not in favour.

Wikis and Liquid Feedback can be a problem for weak managers, since openness challenges their monopoly on knowledge and low performing positions may become visible. On the positive side, they can facilitate utilisation of the collective wisdom of the employees, and the success of this strategy is measurable. In fact, Synaxon doubled its revenue while increasing the number of employees by (only) 10%; efficiency and innovation capacity both grew enormously. This was enabled by providing ways for employees to unfold their individual potentials, bring in their ideas and creativity and satisfy their productive needs – even though within the framework of creating products to be sold on markets according to the motto: 'Do what you want, but be profitable'.

Openness and voluntariness are exploited under the imperative of being competitive on the market. It is no longer necessary for 'evil bosses' to dictate what 'good workers' have to do. Instead, the logic of valuation does the job. However, the limitations are obvious. Openness is only allowed within the confines of the company: outside of the company, internal information is treated as business secrets. Voluntariness means voluntarily subordinating under the market imperative. It is not the management's veto power that produces good behaviour, but rather the internalisation of the logic of valuation that leads to an identification with the company's goals. Inclusion of the employees and 'radical self-organisation' is a means to compete with others on (for) the market. This, of course, is exactly what the logics of exclusion are all about: freedom is the freedom to cooperate with your peer group in order to facilitate the exclusion of others and externalise all consequences that are not part of the commodity sold.

The example of Synaxon indicates how peer production is growing everywhere in society. Indeed, the new mode of production emerges within the old framework, just as aspects of the new and the old are engaged with struggles within each individual. It is better to decide freely what job to do than to work under command, even though, of course, it is repellent that the ultimate goals are still alien ones. Manifestly, if we have to use personal freedom in alien ways, it is not freedom. The freedom of self-exploitation is self-exploitation and not freedom. Nevertheless, and even under the premise of valuation, people who have learned to follow their personal abilities are able to do peer-commons. We already know how to self-organise tasks. Next, we need to imagine what could be possible if free stigmergic self-selection of societal tasks were the foundation of society and not caught up in endless cycles of making more money from money.

Comparing Open Source Ecology and Synaxon, we see that they are not as different as they might appear at first glance. The most important difference is the openness of OSE. Open-sourcing all results provides an enormous potential for other commons to copy products and processes. However, this is precisely the main problem of openness within the context of a capitalist environment: the competitor in the market can use them as well. Unilaterally open-sourcing one's own knowledge and being successful on the market is contradictory. Synaxon handles this contradiction by keeping the openness internal. Other companies, however, show that opening up to other producers and customers can generate competitive advantages, due to reduction of transaction costs. There is a clear, if presently limited, trend towards openness.

With respect to voluntariness, Synaxon seems to be more flexible. The management trusts that its employees under the conditions of market demands will choose to do the right thing. In OSE, the founder wants to control the project and people. OSE members have chosen to work in the project, but they are less free to shape the project since the founder wants to have the final say. While the dependency of Synaxon employees is impersonal and indirect (fulfilling market requirements), the dependency of OSE co-workers is rather the opposite (coherence with the founder's ideas). Although the overall goals of OSE are highly motivating, the concrete organisational forms are too restrictive when compared to the overall aim of the project (as well-being for all). This reduces motivation and causes conflicts. At first glance, these problems seem to be rooted just in personal disagreements, but underneath the surface lurk the same alien requirements of profitability, as with Synaxon. Although OSE is a peer-commons project rather than an ordinary enterprise like Synaxon, the latter is more successful in releasing the productive power of voluntariness – within the limits of alien market requirements. Both the project and the company indicate the broad direction in which future developments will go. Capitalism cannot be out-competed on the field of valuation, it can only be out-cooperated beyond that field. The challenge is to deal with the emerging contradictions.

Conclusions

In this chapter, I have tried to argue for a categorical shift away from an emancipatory approach within the framework of the categories of a commodity-producing society and towards an approach that transcends these categories by creating a new mode of producing our livelihood. This new mode of production is not just an idea, since embryonic forms are appearing right in front of our eyes. A key question is whether the elementary social form of the peer-commons is able to constitute an overall societal mediation. It has been shown that polycentric self-organisation combined with stigmergic societal mediation *can* constitute a coherent society. Openness and voluntariness are the preconditions for a new mode of production – which is no longer separated from reproduction – to emerge. In combination with the five-step model of historical transition, these may be used as analytical criteria when looking at our current situation.

It is, perhaps, not disheartening to appreciate that a new mode of production can only emerge through contradictions. Compromise with capital should not be assumed as collaboration with the enemy, since it is inevitable, indeed necessary, at this stage of development of peer-commons production. Certainly, there is no cure-all and no one right thing to do. This has been indicated here through the two concrete examples, one peer-commonist project and one stock company. From these, we can see that highly worthwhile project goals do not guarantee successful developments, while capitalist firms are able to adapt aspects of peer production within their predefined purpose of being competitive market players. So, peer-commons is not an idealistic utopia, but an objective trend in society as a whole. Capitalism is beginning to produce its own gravediggers. But the digging has to be done; it does not evolve independently of people's actions.

Acknowledgements

Special thanks to Pauline Schwarze and Andy Hilton for their valuable editing support.

Notes

1   The notion 'elementary form' is a term used by Marx ([1887] 2010) in the very first sentence of Capital, Vol. 1. There, the commodity is a 'unit' or an 'elementary form' (German, 'Elementarform', see Dragstedt, 1976) of the capitalist mode of production. In the original (1867) publication of Capital, Marx emphasised this word.

2   Cf. Dyer-Witheford's (2007) rather similar approach proposing the 'common' as the 'cellular form of a society beyond capital', with 'the movement' as the social force behind it.

3   The usual ideological scheme, where economic activity is treated as transaction given scarcity, is inverted. (There, scarcity is naturalised and mistaken for limitation; limitations are socially managed by artificially excluding people from access to goods as private property; thus, in capitalism, scarcity is always artificial.)

4   This may occur indirectly, through systemic inefficiencies – e.g. up to 50% of the world's food is wasted (Mechanical Engineers, 2013) – or quite intentionally, as a direct function of the profit motive (through market distortion and planned obsolescence, notoriously originating with the Phoebus cartel in the 1920s and 1930s).

5   Of course, businesses may 'create' markets (just as does capital in general, through the 'production' of scarcity); this does not materially affect the current argument, however.

6   From the perspective of the individual, critical psychologists describe this situation as structural self-hostility (Holzkamp, 1983).

7   See https://ostromworkshop.indiana.edu/research/

8   A negative notion of internality is used in behavioural economics, this being, roughly, the externality of harming oneself (cf. 'self-hostility' above).

9   Commons are only those resources which people make to be commons, through commoning.

10   Methodologically, this can be expressed as rejecting Adorno's (1966) abolition-of-images dogma at the meta-level of categories while accepting the impossibility of giving concrete descriptions of how these categories can be filled.

11   While the level of the individual is assumed, the ideas expressed here generally apply similarly to population groups, institutions and organisations, countries, etc.

12   Usually, limitation of personal freedom is only presumed where the freedom of others is touched. In this individualistic approach people are not conceptualised as societal humans but rather isolated 'commodity monads'.

13   Obviously, the logics of exclusion are performed along a huge diversity of sections and intersectional combinations of sex/gender, ethnicity, religion, age, health, qualification, etc., in forms of division and discrimination that are, actually, central to capitalist (re)production.

14   Alternative terms for peer-commonist society include 'commonism' (Dyer-Witheford, 2007), 'ecommony' (Habermann, 2011) and, more or less, 'peercommony' (Siefkes, 2013).

15   The question of whether, at present, the commons only helps to absorb the heaviest damages or even offer a renovation of capitalism must be left open here.

16   It is not important to predict the types of commons that may emerge, although it is highly plausible to assume that they will be structured but not uniform.

17   In liberal theories, alienation is played down as an 'invisible hand', while Marx called it 'fetishism'.

18   Personal information may be kept secret according to personal preferences.

19   The German version (Marx, 1867) is more pointed than the English translation; whereas in the English version the value in its endless cycle 'assumes an automatically active character', in the German original the value is 'transformed into an automatic subject processing in itself' (author's translation).

20   This also includes the idea that 'wrong needs' (and wrong routes for their satisfaction) do not exist, since over-historical 'true needs' cannot be assumed.

21   https://en.wikipedia.org/wiki/Stigmergy

22   http://www.evolutionofcomputing.org/Multicellular/Stigmergy.html

23   http://www.en.wikipedia.org/wiki/Wikipedia:Requested_articles

24   http://www.en.wikipedia.org/wiki/Wikipedia:Most-wanted_articles

25   Karl Marx ([1875] 1970) criticised this 'antithesis between mental and physical labor' as 'enslaving subordination of the individual to the division of labor'.

26   In capitalism, immediate reward, mostly through commercial events (the entertainment industry), generally has to 'compensate' for missing collective possibilities to dispose of the means of securing livelihoods.

27   In capitalism, there are different forms of the relationship between 'anti-economic' commons and the exploitation of their

outcomes, including some constructive ones (e.g. feeding the commons humus to build business models on).

28   In technical terminology, this is the 'Law of Large Numbers' from probability theory.

29   See http://www.opensourceecology.org/

30   http://www.opensourceecology.org/wiki/Open_Source_Ecology_Paradigm

31   OSE uses the Create Commons Attribution-ShareAlike License, according to which anyone can access and use the material on the proviso that any redistribution is covered by the same licence.

32   http://www.opensourceecology.org/wiki/Marcin_Bio/CV

33   http://www.opensourceecology.org/wiki/OSE_Specifications

34   The position 'GVCS Preorders', last listed under '2012 – Income & Expenditures', shows zero (http://www.opensourceecology.org/wiki/OSE_Financial_Transparency). Two machines were sold, which directly provokes differences on the usage of that income; the following years did not show any sales.

35   There has been an intense debate on whether OSE should be regarded as capitalist. See http://www.forum.opensourceecology.org/discussion/876/is-ose-a-capitalistic-system

36   One example is the 'power cube'. See http://www.opensourceecology.org/wiki/Power_Cube

37   http://www.synaxon.de/

38   Interview with Frank Roebers, *Berliner Zeitung*, 21 September 2012 (author's translation); at http://www.berliner-zeitung.de/wirtschaft/unternehmen-im-wandel-kreative-koepfe-fuehrt-man-nicht-wie-eine-spargelstecherkolonne-5176782

References

Adorno, T. W. (1966). *Negative Dialectics*. New York: Seabury Press.

De Angelis, M. (2007). *The Beginning of History: Value Struggles and Global Capital*. London: Pluto Press.

Dragstedt, A. (1976). Value: Studies by Karl Marx. London: New Park Publications. At http://www.marxists.org/archive/marx/works/1867-c1/commodity.htm

Dray, W. (1994). 'The rationale of actions', in M. Martin and L. C. McIntyre (Eds.), *Readings in the Philosophy of Social Science.* Cambridge, MA: MIT Press.

Dyer-Witheford, N. (2007). *Commonism. Turbulence*, no. 1. At http://www.turbulence.org.uk/turbulence-1/commonism/

Federici, S. (2004). *Caliban and the Witch: Women, the Body and Primitive Accumulation.* Brooklyn, NY: Autonomedia.

Grassé, P.-P. (1959). 'La reconstruction du nid et les coordinations inter-individuelles chez Bellicositermes natalensis et Cubitermes sp. La théorie de la stigmergie: Essai d'interprétation du comportement des Termites constructeurs' [Nest reconstruction and inter-individual coordination in Belicositermes natalensis and Cubitermes sp. The stigmergy theory: an attempt at interpreting the behavior of termite constructors], *Insectes Sociaux*, 6: 48–81.

Habermann, F. (2011). 'Gutes Leben mit Ecommony' [The good life with economy], *Streifzüge*, 51. At http://www.streifzuege.org/2011/gutes-leben-mit-ecommony

Heylighen, F. (2006). 'Why is open access development so successful? Stigmergic organization and the economics of information', in B. Lutterbeck, M. Bärwolff and R. A. Gehring (Eds.), *Open Source Jahrbuch 2007* [Open source yearbook 2007]. Berlin: Lehmanns. At https://arxiv.org/pdf/cs/0612071.pdf

Holloway, J. (2010). *Crack Capitalism.* London/New York: Pluto Press.

Holzkamp, K. (1983). *Grundlegung der Psychologie* [Foundation of psychology]. Frankfurt/New York: Campus.

H.-Osterkamp, U. (1976). *Grundlagen der Psychologischen Motivationsforschung 2* [Principles of psychological motivation research 2]. Frankfurt/New York: Campus. At http://www.kritische-psychologie.de/1976/grundlagen-der-psychologischen-motivationsforschung-2

Kurz, R. (1997). 'Antiökonomie und Antipolitik. Zur Reformulierung der sozialen Emanzipation nach dem Ende des "Marxismus"' [Anti-economics and anti-politics: on the reformulation of social emancipation after the end of 'Marxism'], *Krisis*, 19. In English at http://www.keimform.de/2013/anti-economics-and-anti-politics/

Luxemburg, R. (1913). *The Accumulation of Capital*. At http://www. marxists.org/archive/luxemburg/1913/accumulation-capital/

Marsh, H. (2012). *Stigmergy*. At http://www.georgiebc.wordpress. com/2012/12/24/stigmergy-2/

Marx, K. (1867). *Das Kapital. Kritik der Politischen Oekonomie. Erster Band* [Capital. A critique of political economy, vol. I]. At http:// www.deutschestextarchiv.de/book/show/marx_kapital01_1867

Marx, K. ([1875] 1970). *Critique of the Gotha Programme*. At http:// www.marxists.org/archive/marx/works/1875/gotha/

Marx, K. ([1887] 2010). *Capital. A Critique of Political Economy, Vol. 1*. At http://www.marxists.org/archive/marx/works/1867-c1/

Marx, K. and Engels, F. ([1848] 1969). *Manifesto of the Communist Party*. At http://www.marxists.org/archive/marx/works/1848/ communist-manifesto/

Mechanical Engineers (2013). *Global Food. Waste Not. Want Not*. At http://www.imeche.org/policy-and-press/reports/detail/global- food-waste-not-want-not

Meretz, S. (2012a). 'The structural communality of the commons', in D. Bollier and S. Helfrich (Eds.), *The Wealth of the Commons: A World beyond Market and State*. Amherst, MA: Levellers Press. At http://www.keimform.de/2013/the-structural-communality-of- the-commons/

Meretz, S. (2012b). 'Peer production and societal transformation: ten patterns developed by the Oekonux Project', *Journal of Peer-Production*, 1. At http://www.peerproduction.net/issues/issue-1/ debate-societal-transformation/ten-patterns-developed-by-the- oekonux-project/

Ostrom, E. (1990). *Governing the Commons: The Evolution of Institutions for Collective Action*. Cambridge: Cambridge University Press.

Ostrom, E. (2010). 'Beyond markets and states: polycentric governance of complex economic systems', *American Economic Review*, 100(3): 641–672.

Raymond, E. (1999). *The Cathedral and the Bazaar*. Sebastopol: O'Reilly. At http://www.catb.org/~esr/writings/cathedral-bazaar/ cathedral-bazaar/

Roebers, F. and Leisenberg, M. (2010). *WEB 2.0 im Unternehmen: Theorie & Praxis – Ein Kursbuch für Führungskräfte* [WEB 2.0 in enterprises: theory & practice – course book for managers]. Hamburg: tredition-Verlag.

Scholz, R. (2000). *Das Geschlecht des Kapitalismus. Feministische Theorien und die postmoderne Metamorphose des Patriarchats* [The gender of capitalism. Feminist theories and the postmodern metamorphosis of patriarchy]. Bad Honnef: Horlemann.

Siefkes, C. (2007). *From Exchange to Contributions. Generalizing Peer-Production into the Physical World.* Berlin: Edition C. Siefkes. At http://www.peerconomy.org

Siefkes, C. (2013). *Peercommony Reconsidered.* At http://www.keimform.de/2013/peercommony-reconsidered/

Index